TRANSITIONS AND TRANSFORMATIONS
IN THE HISTORY OF RELIGIONS

STUDIES

IN THE HISTORY OF RELIGIONS

(SUPPLEMENTS TO *NUMEN*)

EDITED BY

M. HEERMA VAN VOSS • E. J. SHARPE • R. J. Z. WERBLOWSKY

XXXIX

TRANSITIONS AND TRANSFORMATIONS
IN THE HISTORY OF RELIGIONS

LEIDEN
E. J. BRILL
1980

fm

TRANSITIONS
AND TRANSFORMATIONS IN THE
HISTORY OF RELIGIONS)

ESSAYS IN HONOR OF JOSEPH M. KITAGAWA

EDITED BY

FRANK E. REYNOLDS AND THEODORE M. LUDWIG

LEIDEN
E. J. BRILL
1980

ISBN 90 04 06112 6

TABLE OF CONTENTS

IV. TRANSITIONS AND TRANSFORMATIONS IN JAPANESE RELIGION

Photo by Dan Davis

JOSEPH MITSUO KITAGAWA

JOSEPH MITSUO KITAGAWA

Biographical Sketch

Joseph Kitagawa was born in Osaka, Japan, in 1915. His youth was spent in his native country, and in 1937 he received his Bungaku-shi (BA) degree from Rikkyo University. In 1941 he came to the United States to pursue his theological education at the Church Divinity School of the Pacific. His theological studies were, however, interrupted by the outbreak of World War II, and he was forced to spend the next four years in a "relocation" camp for Japanese Americans. In this context he carried on an active ministry under extremely difficult conditions. Following the war he married Evelyn Mae Rose of Hanford, California, and proceeded to Seabury Western Theological Seminary from which he received his Bachelor of Divinity degree in 1947. In that same year he entered the Divinity School of the University of Chicago to work in the field of history of religions under the guidance of Prof. Joachim Wach. In 1951 he received his Doctor of Philosophy degree on the basis of his dissertation, "Kō-bō-Daishi and Shingon Buddhism."

In 1951 Joseph Kitagawa was appointed to the Faculty of the Divinity School of the University of Chicago where he has since served with distinction as Instructor, Assistant Professor, Associate Professor, full Professor, and finally as Dean (1970-   ). In addition he has held a joint appointment in the Department of Far Eastern Languages and Civilizations and has been a regular member of the Committee on Southern Asian Studies. In 1955 he was sworn in as a naturalized citizen of the United States. His wife, Evelyn Kitagawa, has become a professor in the University's Department of Sociology, serving as its Chairman from 1972-78, and as Director of the University's Center for Population Research (1978-   ). Their daughter, Anne Rose Kitagawa, was born in 1965.

In addition to his scholarly and administrative work at the University of Chicago, Joseph Kitagawa has carried on research sponsored by the Rockefeller Foundation on eastern religions (1958-59) and by the Social Science Research Council on Chinese Buddhism (1961-62). He has delivered a variety of major lectures including the Joachim Wach Memorial Lecture at the University of Marburg (1959), the American

Council of Learned Societies Lectures in the History of Religions (1962-63), the Charles Wesley Brashares Lectures on the History of Religions at Northwestern University (1968), and the Charles Strong Memorial Lecture in Comparative Religions in various Australian Universities (1975). He has acted as Program Director of the Paul Carus Memorial Symposium on Modern Trends in World Religions (Summer, 1957) and as Director of the Faculty Seminar on Buddhism jointly sponsored by the Associated Colleges of the Midwest and the Great Lakes College Association (Summer, 1968). He has also served as a Visiting Professor at the University of California at Santa Barbara (Winter, 1966), at Koyosan Buddhist University (Summer, 1968), and the University of Tokyo (Summer, 1977).

In recognition of his contribution to religious and theological studies Joseph Kitagawa has received honorary degrees from Virginia Theological Seminary (D.D., 1963), Seabury Western Theological Seminary (D.D., 1970), Meadville Theological Seminary (L.H.D., 1976), and Rikkyo University (D. Hum., 1977). In addition he has recently (1977) been installed as Honorary Canon of the Cathedral Church of St. John the Divine in New York.

Professional Activities

Founding Co-Editor, *History of Religions*: *An International Journal for Comparative Historical Studies*, 1961-   .

Editorial Advisor, History of Religions, *Encyclopaedia Britannica*, 1959-   .

Member, History of Religions Committee, American Council of Learned Societies, 1964-   .

President, American Society for the Study of Religions, 1969-72.

Member, Committee on Buddhist Studies, The Association for Asian Studies, 1968-69.

Member, The Society for the Scientific Study of Religion.

Member, American Academy of Religion.

Member, Association of Religious Studies in Japan.

Member, Board of Directors, International Institute for the Study of Religion, Tokyo, 1969-   .

Member, Board of Editors, *NVMEN*: *International Review for the History of Religions*, 1970-   .

Member, Board of Directors, The Fund for Theological Education, Inc., 1970-   .

Member, Program Committee, American Association of Theological Schools, 1970-   .

Vice President, International Association for the History of Religions, 1975-   .

Chairman, American Council of Learned Societies, Committee on the History of Religions, 1976.

Vice President, Conseil International de Philosophie et des Sciences Humaines, 1977-   .

Bibliography

(A) Author

Religions of the East, Philadelphia, Westminster Press, 1960.
——, Revised and Enlarged Edition, 1968.
*Translations: *Religions Orientales*, Paris, 1961.
        Tōyō no Shūkyō, Tokyo, 1963.
        Tung fang tsung chiao, Taipei, 1965.
        Doyang Chongkyo, Seoul, 1967.
Contemporary World Religions, Syllabus for the Home Study Department, The University of Chicago, 1962.
Gibt es ein Verstehen fremder Religionen?, Leiden, E. J. Brill, 1963.
Religion in Japanese History, New York, Columbia University Press, 1966.

(B) Editor

The Comparative Study of Religions (Posthumous Publication of Joachim Wach), New York, Columbia University Press, 1958.
*Translation: *Vergleichende Religionsforschung*, Stuttgart, 1962.
(With Mircea Eliade), *The History of Religions: Essays in Methodology*, Chicago, The University of Chicago Press, 1959.
*Translations: *Shūkyōgaku Nyūmon*, Tokyo, 1962.
        Grundfragen der Religionswissenschaft, Salzburg, 1963.
Modern Trends in World Religions, La Salle, Illinois, Open Court, 1959.
(With Hajime Nakamura and Fumio Masutani), *Kindai Bukkyō Meicho Zenshū* (Modern Buddhist Classics), 8 vols., Tokyo, Ryubun-kan, 1961.
The History of Religions: Essays on the Problem of Understanding (Vol. 1, Essays in Divinity, Jerald C. Brauer, general editor), Chicago, The University of Chicago Press, 1967.
Understanding and Believing (A collection of essays by Joachim Wach), New York, Harper and Bros, 1968.
(With Alan L. Miller), *Folk Religion in Japan* (1965 Haskell Lectures by Ichiro Hori), Chicago, The University of Chicago Press, 1968.
(With Charles H. Long), *Myths and Symbols: Studies in Honor of Mircea Eliade*, Chicago, The University of Chicago Press, 1969.
Understanding Modern China, Chicago, Quadrangle Books, 1969.

(C) Translator

(With Wing-tsit Chan, Ismaᶜil al-Faruqi and P. T. Raju), *The Great Asian Religions: An Anthology*, New York, Macmillan, 1969.

(D) Contributor to Books and Monographs

"The Scope of Science of Religion," *Theologica Oecumenica*, Tokyo, 1958.

"The Life and Thought of Joachim Wach," *The Comparative Study of Religions*, by J. Wach, ed. J. M. Kitagawa, New York, 1958, pp. xiii-xlviii.

"The History of Religions in America," *The History of Religions: Essays on Methodology*, ed. M. Eliade and J. M. Kitagawa, Chicago, 1959, pp. 1-30.

"The Samgha and the Ecclesia," *Proceedings of the IXth International Congress for the History of Religions*, Tokyo, 1960, pp. 550-56.

"Emperor and Shaman," *X. Internationaler Kongress für Religionsgeschichte*, Marburg, 1961, pp. 124-25.

"Other Religions," *New Frontiers of Christianity*, ed. Ralph C. Raughley, New York, 1962, pp. 154-73.

"Some Reflections on Religionswissenschaft," *Essays in Philosophy Presented to Dr. T. M. P. Mahadevan*, Madras, 1962, pp. 139-54.

"Sociology of Religion," *The Westminster Dictionary of Christian Education*, ed. Kendig B. Cully, Philadelphia, 1963.

"Buddhism," in the 1963-1977 editions of *Britannica Book of the Year*.

"Japanese Religions," *A Reader's Guide to the Great Religions*, ed. Charles Adams, New York, 1965, pp. 161-90; second edition, 1977, pp. 247-82.

"Master and Saviour," *Studies in Esoteric Buddhism and Tantrism*, Koyasan, 1965, pp. 1-26.

"Überlegungen zur Theologie in Japan," *Das Problem einer "Einheimischen" Theologie*, ed. Hans-Werner Gensichen, München, 1965, pp. 32-35.

"The Asian's 'World of Meaning,'" *Glaube, Geist Geschichte: Festschrift für Ernst Benz*, ed. G. Müller and W. Zeller, Leiden, 1967, pp. 469-76.

"Three Types of Pilgrimage," *Studies in Mysticism and Religion: Presented to Gershom G. Scholem*, ed. E. E. Urbach, R. J. Zwi Werblowsky, Ch. Wirszubski, Jerusalem, 1967, pp. 155-64.

"Primitive, Classical, and Modern Religions: A Perspective on Understanding the History of Religions," *The History of Religions: Essays on the Problem of Understanding*, ed. J. M. Kitagawa, Chicago, 1967, pp. 36-65.

"Shinto," "Buddhism," "Hinduism," and "Lao Tse," *Junior Britannica*, 1967.

"Asian Religions," 1968-75 editions of *Britannica Book of the Year*.

"Japan: Religion," "Shinto," "Worship," "Japanese Philosophy," "D. T. Suzuki," and "Zen," *Encyclopaedia Britannica*, 1968 ed.

"Gohei Hasami: a Rite of Purification of Time at Mt. Koya," *Proceedings of the XIth International Congress of the International Association for the History of Religions*, Vol. II, *Guilt or Pollution and Rites of Purification*, Leiden, 1968.

"Some Reflections on Foreign Scholars' Understanding of Japanese Culture and Shinto," *Proceedings, The Second International Conference for Shinto Studies*, Tokyo, 1968, pp. 122-34.

"In Memoriam: Joachim Wach—Teacher and Colleague," in J. Wach, *Under-*

standing and Believing, ed. by J. M. Kitagawa, New York, 1968, pp. 197-201.

"Chaos, Order and Freedom in World Religions," *The Concept of Order*, ed. by Paul G. Kuntz, Seattle, 1968, pp. 268-89.

"Ainu Myth," *Myths and Symbols: Studies in Honor of Mircea Eliade*, ed. by J. M. Kitagawa and C. H. Long, Chicago, 1969, pp. 309-23.

"Western Understanding of the East," and "China in Asia," *Understanding Modern China*, ed. by J. M. Kitagawa, Chicago, 1969, pp. 21-41, 214-28.

"Lo Scintoismo," *Storia delle Religioni*, Vol. V., ed. by Giuseppe Castellani, Torino, 1970, pp. 801-52.

(With Frank E. Reynolds), "Theravada-Buddhismus im 20. Jahrhundert," *Buddhismus der Gegenwart*, ed. by Heinrich Dumoulin, Freiburg im Breisgau, 1970, revised English edition: "Theravada Buddhism in the 20th Century," *Buddhism and the Modern World*, New York, 1976, pp. 43-64.

"New Religions in Japan: A Historical Perspective," *Religion and Change in Contemporary Asia*, ed. by Robert F. Spencer, Minneapolis, 1971, pp. 27-43.

"Religious and Cultural Ethos of Modern Japan," *Selected Readings on Modern Japanese Society*, ed. by G. K. Yamamoto and T. Ishida, Berkeley, 1971, pp. 186-98.

"The Eightfold Path to Nirvana," *Great Religions of the World* (National Geographic Society), Washington, D.C., 1971.

"History of Religions," *Contemporary Christian Trends*, ed. by W. M. Pinson, Jr. and C. E. Fant, Jr., Waco, Texas, 1972, pp. 205-17.

"Shinto," and "Mahayana Buddhism (Japan)," *Historical Atlas of the Religions of the Worlds*, ed. by I. R. al Faruqi and David E. Sopher, New York, 1974, pp. 127-32, 195-99.

"Priesthood in the History of Religions," *To Be A Priest*, ed. by R. E. Terwilliger and U. T. Holmes, III, New York, 1975.

"Kūkai as Master and Savior," *The Biographical Process*, ed. by F. E. Reynolds and D. Capps, The Hague & Paris, 1976, 319-41.

"Japanese Medical Ethics: History," *Encyclopedia of Bioethics*, ed. by W. T. Reich, New York, 1978, vol. III, pp. 922-24.

"Early Shintō: A Case Study," *Science of Religion: Studies in Methodology, Proceedings of the Study Conference of the International Association for the History of Religions*, ed. by Lauri Honko, The Hague, 1979, pp. 87-98.

"Religion as a Principle of Integration and Cooperation for a Global Community," *Proceedings of the First International Conference of Scientists and Religious Leaders on Shaping the Future of Mankind*, ed. by Masatoshi Doi, Yoshiaki Iisaka, and Isamu Nagami, Tokyo, 1979, pp. 77-85.

"Some Remarks on the Study of Sacred Texts," *The Critical Study of Sacred Texts*, ed. by Wendy Doniger O'Flaherty, Berkeley Religious Studies Series, Berkeley, 1979, pp. 231-41.

"Monarch and Government—Traditions and Ideologies in Pre-Modern

Japan," *Proceedings of the 30th International Congress of Human Sciences in Asia and North Africa*, 1979.
(With Theodore Ludwig), "Shintō," "Shintō-Priester," *Japan-Handbuch*, ed. by H. Hammitzsch, Wiesbaden, 1980.

(E) Journal Articles (Selective)

"It Cannot Happen Again" (Report on the Mass Evacuation of Japanese-Americans, 1942-45), *The Living Church* (November 4, 1945).
"Christianity in Japan," *The Scene Magazine* (Spring, 1949).
"Korea: Its History and Culture," *Ibid.* (Summer, 1950).
"The Church in Relation to Non-Christian Cultures," *The Divinity School News*, XX, No. 2 (May, 1953).
"The Case of the Younger Churches," *Pastoral Psychology*, V, No. 45 (June, 1954).
"Evanston—West meets West," *Missionary Research Library Occasional Bulletin*, V, No. 8 (July, 1954).
"Breakdown of Communication in the World Community," *Annual Report of the Association of Professors in Practical Fields* (Autumn, 1954).
"Christianity, Communism and the Asian Revolution," *Missionary Research Library Occasional Bulletin*, VI, No. 2 (March, 1955).
"The Asian Revolution," *World Dominion*, XXXIII, No. 4 (July-August, 1955, London).
"Mary H. Cornwall Legh—'Mother' of Lepers," *The Holy Cross Magazine*, LXVI, No. 9 (September, 1955).
"Human Situations and Religious Experience," *Faith and Freedom*, IX, No. 25 (Autumn, 1955, Liverpool).
"Joachim Wach: Teacher and Colleague," *The Divinity School News*, XXII, No. 4 (November, 1955).
"A Glimpse of Professor Wach," *CTS Register*, XLV, No. 4 (November, 1955).
"Apologetic Theology: An Urgent Need for the Christian World Mission," *The Hartford Theological Foundation Bulletin*, No. 21 (Winter, 1955-56).
"Christianity and Non-Christian Religions in the Contemporary World," *The Cresset*, XIX, No. 6 (April, 1956), 12-28.
"Kyōkai to Shingaku," (The Church and Theology), *Shingaku Nempō* (Annual Bulletin of Theology) (May, 1956, Tokyo).
"Christianity and Buddhism in the Far East," *Proceedings of the Third Biennial Meeting*, Association of Professors of Missions (June, 1956).
"Joachim Wach et la Sociologie de la Religion," *Archives de Sociologie des Religions*, I, No. 1 (Janvier-Juin, 1956, Paris), 25-40.
"Christianity and the Asian Revolution," *World Communique*, LXVII, No. 6 (Nov./Dec., 1956, Geneva).
"Theology and the Science of Religion," *Anglican Theological Review*, XXXIX, No. 1 (January, 1957), 33-52.
"Unitive and Divisive Factors in Contemporary Buddhism," *Civilizations*, VII, No. 4 (1957, Brussel), 29-42.

"The Overseas Mission in the Bandung Era," *The Overseas Mission Review*, II, No. 3 (Whitsunday, 1957).

"Joachim Wach and Sociology of Religion," *The Journal of Religion*, XXXVII, No. 3, (July, 1957), 174-184.

"Bibliography of Joachim Wach," *Ibid.*, 185-188.

"The Nature and Program of the History of Religions Field," *The Divinity School News*, XXIV, No. 4 (November, 1957).

"Religiones Christianas y no Christianas," *El Centinela*, XXX, No. 2, (February, 1958).

"Shūkyō to Kyōiku" (Religion and Education), *Rikkyō*, No. 9 (June, 1958, Tokyo).

"Kokoku no Kyōkai ga chokumen-suru Mondai" (The Task of the Church in Japan), *Vision*, No. 26, (June, 1958).

"Divided We Stand," *Religion in Life*, XXVII, No. 3 (Summer, 1958), 335-351.

"Kyōkai, Shakai, Shingaku" (The Church, Society, and Theology), *Vision*, No. 28 (September, 1958).

"Sanka Gaijin Gakusha no Yokogao" (European and North American Scholars in the Field of General Science of Religion), *Gakujutsu Nempō* (Japanese Scientific Monthly), XI, No. 7 (October, 1958).

"Beikoku ni okeru Shūkyō no Gaku" (Religious Studies in America), *Zaike Bukkyō* (Lay Buddhism), No. 58 (January, 1959, Tokyo).

"Kirisutokyō to Nihon Bunka" (Christianity and Japanese Culture), *Vision*, Nos. 32-39 (Jan.-Oct., 1959).

"Doctrinal Developmental in Buddhism," *Quarterly of the Study Center on Chinese Religions* (March, 1959, Hong Kong).

"Beikoku Shūkyōgaku no Tembō" (The Science of Religion in North America), I, *Shūkyō Kenkyū* (Journal of Religious Studies), XXXI, No. 158 (Spring, 1959, Tokyo).

"Beikoku Shūkyōgaku no Tembō," II, *Ibid.*, XXXII, No. 159 (Summer, 1959).

"Nihon no Bunka to Shūkyō," (Culture and Religion in Japan), *Nihon-bunka Kenkyūsho Kiyō* (Transactions of the Institute for Japanese Culture and Classics), No. 5 (1959, Tokyo), 1-96.

"Nichibei no Shūkyōgaku" (Religio-Scientific Study in Japan and North America), *Tetsugaku Kenkyū* (Journal of Philosophical Studies) XL, No. 5 (1959, Kyoto).

"Appraisal of the Church Related University in Japan," *Kirisutokyō Kenkyū* (Journal of Christian Studies), XXXI, Nos. 2-3 (October, 1959, Kyoto).

"Search for Self-Identity," *The Divinity School News*, XXVI, No. 4 (Nov., 1959).

"Orientals Among Us," *General Division of Research and Field Study Bulletin* (National Council of the Episcopal Church, 1960).

"Glimpses of the Christian Church in Asia," *The Overseas Mission Review* V, No. 2 (Epiphany, 1960).

"Buddhist Ethics and International Relations," *Indogaku Bukkyōgaku Kenkyū* (Journal of Indian and Buddhist Studies), VIII, No. 2, (March 1960).

"Search for Self-Identity" (abridged version), *The Ecumenical Review*, XII, No. 3, (April, 1960), 332-46.

"Beholding His Glory," *Virginia Seminary Journal* (July, 1960).

"East and West—A Dialogue," *Perspectives* (Notre Dame), VI, No. 1 (January-February, 1961).

"Imperialism, Racism and the Christian World Mission," *The Overseas Mission Review*, VI, No. 2 (Epiphany, 1961).

"A Theology of Mission," *The Living Church* (February, 1961).

"The Unity of Mankind in Our Divided World," *The IARF News Digest* (Amsterdam), No. 45 (March, 1961).

"Kaiser und Shamane in Japan," *Antaios*, II, No. 6 (March, 1961, Stuttgart), 552-66.

"The Contemporary Religious Situation in Japan," *Japanese Religions*, II, Nos. 2-3 (May, 1961, Kyoto), 24-42.

"Ainu Bear Festival (Iyomante)," *History of Religions*, I, No. 1 (Summer, 1961), 95-151.

"Nuevas Interpretaciones de la Filosofia Budista," *Philosophia*, No. 24 (1961, Mendoza, Argentina) 1-14.

"Some Reflections on Theology in Japan," *Anglican Theological Review*, XLIII, No. 4 (October, 1961), 375-97.

"Sekai Bummei to Nihon" (World Culture and Japan), *Tōkyō Mainichi* (Dec., 1961).

"The Church and Japanese-Americans—A Diagnosis," *General Division of Research and Field Study Bulletin* (National Council of the Episcopal Church, 1961).

"Koteki Hakase" (In Memory of the late Dr. Hu Shih), *Tōkyō Mainichi* (March, 1962).

"Gendai Chūgoku no Shūkyō" (Religious Situation in Contemporary China), *Tōkyō Mainichi* (March, 1962).

"Uruwashi no Shima ..." (Religious Situation in Taiwan), *Rikkyō*, VII, No. 1 (1962, Tokyo).

"Asia Revisited," *Criterion*, I, No. 2 (Summer, 1962), Chicago.

"Buddhism and Asian Politics," *Asian Survey* (University of California, Berkeley), II, No. 5 (July, 1962), 1-11.

"Buddhism in Taiwan Today," *France-Asie* (Tokyo), XVIII, No. 174 (Juillet-Août, 1962), 439-444.

"Prehistoric Background of Japanese Religion," *History of Religions*, II, No. 2 (Winter, 1963), 292-328.

"Buddhist Translation in Japan," *Babel* (Revue Internationale de la Traduction) IX, No. 1-2 (1963), 53-59.

"Religious and Cultural Ethos of Modern Japan," *Asian Studies*, II, No. 3 (December, 1964, Philippines), 334-52.

"The Buddhist Transformation in Japan," *History of Religions*, IV, No. 2 (Winter, 1965), 319-36.

"Gohei-hasami, Ein Ritus der 'Läuterung der Zeit' auf dem Berg Koya," *Kairos*, VIII, Heft 2, Jahrgang 1966, 114-17.

"Convergence and Prejudice in the United States," *The Graduate Journal*, VII, 1966, Supplement, The University of Texas, 131-55 .

"Nihon no Bukkyō" (Buddhism in Japan, a series of 12 articles in Japanese), *Zaike Bukkyō*, Tokyo, October, 1966—September, 1967.

"Daisetz Teitaro Suzuki" (1870-1966), *History of Religions*, VI, no. 3, (February, 1967), 265-69.

"Appreciation of Daisetz Suzuki," *Journal of Indian and Buddhist Studies*, XV, No. 2, (March, 1967), 986-93.

"Buddhism in America," *Japanese Religions* (Kyoto), V, No. 1, (July, 1967), 32-57.

"Theos, Mythos and Logos," *The Barat Review*, III, No. 2 (June/September, 1968), 85-92.

"The Making of a Historian of Religions," *Journal of the American Academy of Religion*, XXXVI, No. 3 (September, 1968), 191-202.

"Verstehen and Erlösung: Some Remarks on Joachim Wach's Work," *History of Religions*, XI, No. 1 (August, 1971), 31-53.

"The Asian Mind Today: Worlds of Meaning, East and West," *The Worldview*, XVI, No. 1 (January, 1973), 8-11.

"The Japanese *Kokutai* (National Community): History and Myth," *History of Religions*, XIII, No. 3 (February, 1974), 209-26.

"Experience, Knowledge and Understanding," *Religious Studies*, XI, no. 2 (June, 1975), 201-13.

"Matsuri and Matsuri-goto: Religion and State in Early Japan," *Religious Traditions* 2 (1979), 30-37.

"Reality and Illusion," *Journal of the Oriental Society of Australia* (ed. by A. R. Davis), 1979.

(F) Book Reviews, in the following journals

Journal of Religion
Anglican Theological Review
The Christian Century
Church History
The American Journal of Sociology
CTS Register
The American Historical Review
Religious Education
The Living Church
American Anthropologist
Journal of Asian Studies
Asian Students
Journal of the American Academy of Religion
 etc.

INTRODUCTION

A Methodology Appropriate for the History of Religions

In 1947, when Joseph Kitagawa came to study with Joachim Wach at the Divinity School of the University of Chicago, the discipline of history of religions was virtually unknown in American academic circles. Now, just a little more than three decades later, its methodological and substantive contributions are widely recognized in the fields of religious and area studies, and historians of religions are at work in most of the major universities and colleges both in Canada and the United States. There have, of course, been powerful cultural forces that have contributed to the rise of religio-historical studies in the North American context. But there have also been a number of outstanding individuals who have made important contributions. Among these individuals Joseph Kitagawa has played, through his scholarly writing, his lecturing, his practical wisdom, and his teaching, a most prominent and distinctive role.

This volume is intended to honor Joseph Kitagawa upon his completion of two terms (ten years) of dedicated and effective service as Dean of the Divinity School of the University of Chicago. But from the very outset the editors—taking into account what they perceived to be Dean Kitagawa's own commitments and priorities—decided not to compile the traditional kind of Festschrift that would bestow honor primarily through the diversity and venerable status of the contributors. Appreciation from such sources has been, and will continue to be, forthcoming without solicitation or planning. Rather, the editors decided that this Festschrift should honor Dean Kitagawa by exemplifying and extending the particular style of religio-historical scholarship he has fostered through his own career as a writer, teacher and administrator. In order to do this most effectively the editors have turned to a very limited number of outstanding younger scholars who have studied under Dean Kitagawa's direction. (As a matter of fact both editors and all of the contributors have worked on or completed their doctoral studies with him during the 1970s.) Moreover, the editors have quite self-consciously selected contributors whose areas of specialization reflect something of the range of Dean Kitagawa's interests—interests that extend from Israel to Japan, from the pre-

Christian era to the present, and from the symbolic and aesthetic modes
of expression to cultic practices and patterns of religious community.

As editors we have made no attempt to impose methodological
strictures on the contributors. However everyone who has been involved
in the project has a strong commitment to Dean Kitagawa's approach
to the practice of Religionswissenschaft. Following Kitagawa, the
various contributors have recognized the difference between simply
viewing religious data scientifically and viewing the same data religio-
scientifically or religio-historically; they have focused their attention
on the interpretation of specific religious traditions in terms of the
interplay between the universal and the particularistic dimensions of
those traditions; and they have given serious attention to the interaction between religion and other types of human experience and expression. In doing so they have sought to make their own
distinctive contributions to what Kitagawa has called an "integral
understanding" of "the nature and structure of the religious experience
of the human race and its diverse manifestations in history." [1]

The particular kind of history of religions approach which this
volume exemplifies and extends operates with the assumption that
there is a specifically religious dimension to human existence, and that
the scholarly elucidation of this fact requires a specifically religio-
scientific or religio-historical methodology. This is not to say that the
history of religions should be considered the only valid method for
studying religion. On the contrary, there are a variety of methods that
are crucial for the presentation and interpretation of religious data,
disciplines on which the history of religions depends and to which it
contributes. Nor is it to say that the history of religions should be
considered some kind of "queen" discipline whose special status enables
it to suspend the usual rigors of scientific inquiry. Rather, the practice
of the history of religions requires the most rigorous use and testing
of hypotheses, interpretive concepts, and empirical sources. However,
it is to say that the proper task of the history of religions is to interpret
and understand religious experience *qua* religious, to penetrate into
the *meaning* of religious phenomena. And it is to say, further, that
this task requires the use of distinctive kinds of hypotheses, the use of
distinctive categories of interpretation, and the identification of distinctive constellations of relevant sources.

---

[1] Joseph M. Kitagawa, "The Making of an Historian of Religions," *Criterion* 7
(1968), 26-27.

When the task of religio-historical interpretation is seen in this way, the need for a creative resolution of the rigid dichotomy between objective and subjective knowledge is apparent. On the one hand the contributors to this volume recognize the validity and usefulness of the various descriptive, functionalist and structuralist methods which propose to offer thoroughly "scientific" and objective interpretations of religious phenomena. Such ways of organizing and interpreting religious data are often extremely helpful in exposing important aspects of religious belief and behavior; and, as a result, they can make very significant contributions to the religio-historical goal of "integral understanding." On the other hand, we also recognize the validity and usefulness of theological interpretations that give direct and normative expression to the basic principles and inner dynamics of particular religious viewpoints. In fact, as historians of religions we would be among the first to emphasize the role which such theological interpretations must play if religion is to receive responsible expression in the modern world. However, the distinctive goal of the history of religions itself—the understanding and interpretation of the *meaning* of religious phenomena *qua* religious—cannot be reached either through the exercise of scientific imperialism, or through the normative reflections of confessional theologians (whether they be the theologians of the established religions or those of the contemporary counter-culture). Rather, the pursuit of an "integral understanding" of religious experience and expression requires the utilization of a method that involves a continuing oscillation between objective, scientific distance and disciplined, interpretive empathy. As Dean Kitagawa has noted, this self-conscious incorporation of disciplined but necessarily subjective sensibilities into the interpretive process of scientific interpretation is "the most controversial aspect of our discipline." [2] But in many ways it is also the most crucial.

A second, more explicit characteristic of the religio-historical approach which this volume exemplifies and extends is to be found in the fact that it takes, as its empirical starting point, the historical givenness of specific religious traditions. In contrast to W. C. Smith, Robert Baird and others, those associated with this collection of essays work on the assumption that the various religions of the world, both past and present, both preliterate and literate, are the primary subjects of religio-historical investigation. It is further presumed that each of

---

[2] *Ibid.*, 27.

these religions has its own distinctive kind of "wholeness" and "internal consistency" which it is the responsibility of the historian of religions to identify and describe. It is his task, in other words, to understand each religion from its own distinctive center of meaning, that is to say from those essential experiences and expressions which leave their imprint on all other experiences and expressions which that religion generates or appropriates in the course of its history. Thus it is necessary for the interpreter to take seriously into account various levels of expression within the religion including the theoretical, the practical and the sociological; and it is also necessary to follow the unfolding of the tradition through the course of time.

At the same time, the history of each religious tradition must always be considered within the broader context provided by the general history of religions. "No religion," Kitagawa has argued, "however regional and ethnocentric, can be interpreted without reference to universal human themes... Just as in intellectual history, the religio-scientific inquiry has to proceed in the manner of oscillation between the universal religious themes and particular religious systems, communities and histories." [3] This kind of religio-historical approach is closely related to the phenomenology or morphology of religion in that it both draws from and aims to increase our understanding of religion as a basic and universal dimension of human existence. And it also has close affinities with the more philological and historical approaches of Sinologists, Buddhologists, Islamicists, Biblical scholars and the like in that it focuses on the distinctive orientations of particular religions. However the contributors to this volume see their role neither as primarily phenomenologists nor only as area specialists. Rather, we understand ourselves as historians of religions who pursue the goal of religio-historical understanding in a distinctively religio-historical way—that is to say, by directly confronting and interpreting the interplay between the more universal and the more particularistic dimensions of religion as these appear in the on-going life of particular religious communities.

A third characteristic of the religio-historical approach which Dean Kitagawa has developed in his own scholarship and transmitted to the contributors to this volume is the concern to interpret religion in terms of its relationship to other aspects of human life. Kitagawa

---

[3] Joseph M. Kitagawa, "The History of Religions in America," *The History of Religions: Essays in Methodology*, ed. Mircea Eliade and Joseph Kitagawa, Chicago, 1959, 28-29.

has described his own procedure in his major book, *Religion in Japanese History*, in the following way: "Emphasis," he wrote in his introduction, "has been placed on the delineation of the intricate relationships that have existed between the various religious systems of Japan *and the coeval social, political and cultural developments*" (italics added). [4] Following this procedure, Kitagawa has given serious attention to universal themes and structures of religion (for example, kingship and shamanism), to the dialectic between the universal themes and the particularities of Japanese religion (for example, in his discussions of the Imperial system and the *yamabushi* tradition of mountain ascetics), to the impact of historical realities (for example, the incursions from China and the rise of the warrior class) and to the role of various kinds of cultural sensibilities (for example, the distinctively Japanese modes of aesthetic experience and expression). Similarly, in his more broadly conceived *Religions of the East* Kitagawa has also focused attention on the universal, the particularistic *and the contextual* dimensions of his subject—in this case the "holy communities" of Islam, Hinduism, Buddhism, Chinese Religions and Japanese Religions. Thus he emphasized that all of these "holy communities" were firmly and self-consciously rooted in a conception of divine or cosmic order (the Dharma, the Tao, etc.), that this sense of cosmic-social order was differently conceived and embodied in each of the five traditions (in the supra-societal Sangha of the Buddhists, the family system of the Chinese, etc.), and that these conceptions and embodiments were profoundly and often ironically affected by the historical and cultural forces which they encountered in the course of their history (including "modernity," whose impact upon each of the communities was examined with special care).

This emphasis on the interlacing of religion with other basic dimensions of human experience and expression has its obvious corollary in the recognition that the historian of religions must maintain a close relationship with other social scientific and humanistic disciplines. Thus, just as the historian of religions should ideally have a reasonably comprehensive knowledge of at least one religious tradition outside his own area of specialization, so too he should have a reasonably adequate background in the practice of at least one correlate discipline— for example, anthropology, sociology, psychology, history, literary criticism, art history, or the like. In addition, it is essential that he be

---

[4] Joseph M. Kitagawa, *Religion in Japanese History*, New York, 1966, viii.

attentive to the results of relevant work done by scholars in a variety
of other areas where he makes no claim to professional competence.
However, it should be made clear—as it has been in the work of
Kitagawa—that the usefulness for the historian of religions of the
information and insights which these correlate disciplines generate
must be determined in each instance by their contribution to the *norma
normans* of the history of religions itself—the understanding of the
meaning of mankind's religious experiences and expressions *qua*
religious.

Finally, in addition to these emphases on the interpretation of
religious meaning, the dialectic of universalization and particularization,
and the embeddedness of religion in the complexities of history and
culture, there is a fourth very important aspect to Kitagawa's approach
which must be mentioned. Though it is much more difficult to articulate
than the first three, it remains a *sine qua non* for carrying forward
the kind of scholarship which he has consistently practiced and
encouraged. Kitagawa himself expressed it most succinctly when, at
the conclusion of a major address on "The Making of an Historian of
Religions," he called for the appearance of "more historians of religions
who could honestly and courageously say (paraphrasing the artist
Diego Rivera):

> I write what I write. I write what I see.
>   I write what I think.
> And the thing that is dearest in life to me
>   is scholarly integrity." [5]

In this most basic matter of scholarly integrity Dean Kitagawa has
provided us with a model; in this volume (as elsewhere) we and the
other contributors have tried our best to follow it.

In the collection of essays which follows, attention is focused on
one topic in particular: transitions and transformations in the history
of religions. The editors, in consultation with the contributors, decided
that transitions and transformations would be an especially appropriate
and fruitful topic for this volume, not least because they have long
been a key concern in Dean Kitagawa's own work. Moreover, the
general interest in understanding the dynamics of religious change has
quickened dramatically in recent years as the pace of religious developments in east and west has accelerated. The more sophisticated pro-

---

[5] *Op. cit.*, 28.

ponents of various religions and denominations have come to realize that a greater sensitivity to the dynamics of the generation and assimilation of change is crucial to their own confessional orientations. At the same time, scholars in the various areas of religious studies have become interested in investigating major historical transformations, in analyzing the emergence of new movements, and in dealing with problems of modernization and secularization. Up to this point, however, the study of religious change has been left mainly to the historians of particular religions traditions and to social scientists involved in the study of the role of religion in society.

Historians of particular religious traditions have certainly contributed much by identifying and clarifying factors of change, and by tracing the emergence of new configurations of religious teaching and practice in particular traditions. However, their work has generally not been focused on the meaning of religious change as an important dimension of religious experience. Social scientists, on the other hand, have produced a variety of comparative studies on the topic that have been brilliant and useful; yet the primary purpose of such investigation has been the interpretation of *social* change or *cultural* change rather than the meaning of religious transformation itself. Moreover, these comparative and cross-cultural investigations have often been conducted within the framework of the social scientific preoccupation with the important problematics of "modernity" (note, for example, Weber's emphasis on the role of "rationalization" and Bellah's focus on "differentiation"); thus the methods and concepts developed in these studies naturally have had a somewhat limited usefulness in studying religious change in pre-modern societies.

In this situation, it is important for historians of religions to continue the task of developing a specifically religio-historical approach which will combine the analysis of adaptations and new formations in different religious traditions with the study of cross-cultural patterns and interpretations. The recognition of the need to explore this kind of topic is based on the awareness, made acute in today's rapidly moving religious world, that an understanding of religious transformation is central for any adequate conception of what religion *is* and how it interacts with other dimensions of culture and society. What we as historians seek to investigate and understand is really a *living process* of transmission; and such a living process is in itself a continual and dynamic "trans-formation." In Neusner's words, "Tradition involves both the giver and the taker... Tradition, as a process of handing on and passing forward, thus is dynamic and not static. Its interest is not in what was originally said alone but in how what was said in the past endows with meaning, imposes sense upon, the issues of the new age. Tradition is killed when handed on unchanged." [6]

Understanding the meaning of religious experience and expression, then, involves one in the task of interpreting the meaning of religious *traditio*, or trans-formation. As the essays in this volume demonstrate, the religious process of *traditio* must be studied from a variety of viewpoints and in a variety of contexts and stages. Moreover, the variants of the *traditio* process must be envisioned on a continuum ranging from stable religions in which the *traditum* is appropriated over and over again with very little change, all the way to religions involved in violent upheavals in which alienation, disjunction and re-formation are sharply experienced. The variations are legion: primitive beliefs and practices being swallowed up by "high" religions, popularizing trends, liberalizing or restricting reform movements, changes wrought by the simple pressure of external events or internal forces, adaptations towards modernity, and many more. In the titling of this volume we have chosen to encompass all of these (and other) patterns under the general rubrics of "transitions and transformations."

The various essays that have been selected for the volume focus on specific transitions and transformations that have occurred in five major religious traditions (the Jewish, Theravada Buddhist, Islamic, Chinese and Japanese) during various periods from the seventh century B.C.E. to the present. That chronological range is presented in the essays in the first section of the volume, in which Theodore Ludwig (Valparaiso University) analyzes the prophetic transformation in Israel during the drastic disjunction in national life at the time of the Babylonian exile; and Frank Reynolds and Regina Clifford (University of Chicago) focus on the very recent transformation of the Theravada Buddhist social order in Burma and Thailand. The pair of essays on Islam likewise present the classical-modern scope, as Frederick Denny (University of Colorado at Boulder) traces the development of the two modes of scripture piety (exegesis and recitation) in classical Islam; while the modern, very different environment in Canada is the setting in which Earle Waugh (University of Alberta) describes various trans-

---

6 Jacob Neusner, "The Study of Religion as the Study of Tradition: Judaism," *History of Religions* 14 (1975), 194; see also Joseph M. Kitagawa, "The Buddhist Transformation in Japan," *HR* 4 (1965), 319.

formations in the role of the Imam (the community leader responsible for maintenance of Qurʾānic piety).

The tremendous range of Chinese religious tradition—in both its chronological and elite-popular dimensions—is presented by Daniel Overmyer (University of British Columbia) in his study of the popular interpretations which transformed Chinese cosmology into a dualistic perspective; and by Paul Martinson's (Luther Theological Seminary) account of the modern transformation from the Confucian concern with the harmonization of cosmological and social dualities to the Maoist emphasis on the necessity of contradiction and struggle for the creation of the ultimate soteriological community. Finally, ancient, medieval and modern dimensions of Japanese religion are well re-presented as Manabu Waida (University of Alberta) deals with the interaction between Buddhism and Japanese kingship ideology during the formative period (fifth to tenth centuries); William LaFleur (University of California at Los Angeles) provides an interpretation of the interaction between Buddhism and Japanese shamanic traditions expressed in a series of visionaries extending from Gyōgi through Saigyō to Bashō (seventh to seventeenth centuries); and Winston Davis (Kwansei Gakuin University) considers the character and the extent of the so-called secularization of religion in the modern period in Japan.

Viewed from a more cross-cultural perspective, these various essays highlight four different patterns of religious change. The discussions by Ludwig and Martinson each focus on a major transformation in basic soteriology and communal order. In the case of the prophetic transformation in ancient Israel, these changes resulted in radical disjunction and subsequent reorientation within an on-going tradition. It is not yet certain what the full results of the Communist transformation in China will be; nevertheless, a definite disjunction with the past and a significant transformation of the accepted sacred paradigms are clearly in evidence. In both cases there was a definite break with previously accepted soteric realities and a self-conscious attempt to establish new modes of thinking and action—with, however, the sacred paradigm serving as a sort of "grammar" for the interpretation and shaping of new realities.

The studies by Denny and Overmyer take a different tack and single out transformations that have occurred in particular traditions over a rather extended period of time. Thus Denny traces a dialectic of transformations and continuity within the development of Qurʾānic exegesis and recitation—the transformative nature of exegesis in tension with the hardening piety of the ritual-recitational dimension, both together symbolic of the dialectic of continuity and transformation in the Islamic sense of the divine-human encounter. The transformation pointed to in Overmyer's study is that between the monistic cosmology of elite Chinese religion and the dualistic cosmological themes advocated and practiced in the popular movements, a dualistic transformation which, Overmyer suggests, can help in understanding the Maoist sense of a struggle with demonic forces that has played such an important role in modern Chinese political life.

The self-conscious interaction between inherited models and new needs and experiences receives special emphasis in the studies by Waugh and LaFleur. Thus Waugh considers the way in which Imams in North America have related to the normative image of Islamic leadership provided by Muhammed, showing the creation of new forms of classical models. LaFleur elicits an understanding of Japanese religio-aesthetic experience by focusing likewise on classical models, showing how Bashō quite self-consciously utilized communal memories concerning earlier seers in order to express his own quite original poetic vision—and demonstrating at the same time the stadiality or multi-leveledness of Japanese culture.

The studies contributed by Reynolds and Clifford, Waida, and Davis consider three very different changes which raise questions concerning the attenuation of religious traditions. Reynolds and Clifford consider the impact of powerful new conceptions of nationhood on traditional Theravada Buddhist patterns of religio-social order, differentiating between the way in which the process of adaptation and attenuation has worked itself out in two different situations: in Burma where actual political power was in the hands of foreigners who operated on the basis of the new conceptions, and in Thailand where political power was held by indigenous leaders who were sensitive to the traditional paradigms as well as the need for change. Waida studies the "domestication" of Buddhism in its early history in Japan, investigating in this way some of the dynamics involved in the fusing of a foreign dominant religion onto a pervasive indigenous one. In his concluding essay Davis enters into the contemporary debate about secularization, showing that any thesis about the decline of religion in Japan must be tested by investigating all the different aspects of religion and suggesting that, in fact, certain popular religious *tradita* have reappeared in new configurations precisely in the most modernized segments of Japanese society.

These studies in religious transitions and transformations can, of course, be approached from a variety of perspectives. The essays are intended to provide material and interpretation for the non-specialist [7] as well as those with a professional interest in religious studies, be they phenomenologists, philologists, area historians, or social scientists. However, the primary concern of the editors and the contributors has been to honor Dean Kitagawa by contributing a set of studies of mankind's religious experience which will provide ideas, materials, methods and interpretations which our fellow historians of religions can debate, reflect upon and utilize. In this way we hope to contribute to the further development of religio-historical studies in North America—and beyond.

The editors and contributors would like to extend their heartfelt thanks to four colleagues who have given invaluable assistance to this project: Martin E. Marty, Anthony C. Yu, and Wendy Doniger O'Flaherty of the Divinity School, The University of Chicago; and especially R. J. Zwi Werblowsky of The Hebrew University of Jerusalem, whose enthusiasm for the project was responsible for its inclusion in the *Supplements to Numen Series*.

We would also like to express the hope of everyone connected with the project that in honoring Joseph Kitagawa, this volume will be a source of joy and satisfaction to Evelyn Kitagawa and to Anne Rose Kitagawa as well.

FRANK E. REYNOLDS and THEODORE M. LUDWIG

---

[7] It should be noted that the editors have insisted that all contributors severely limit their use of scholarly apparatus. Specialists who seek further documentation of specific points are encouraged to contact the individual authors.

I

RELIGION AND THE TRANSFORMATION OF NATIONAL TRADITIONS

"REMEMBER NOT THE FORMER THINGS"

Disjunction and Transformation in Ancient Israel

THEODORE M. LUDWIG

Valparaiso University

One who reads the recorded proclamation of the Israelite prophets cannot fail to note the overriding theme of radical change and transformation in their interpretation of Israel's existence as the covenant people of their God Yahweh. Deutero-Isaiah, for example, presented the people with this startling oracle from Yahweh: "Remember not the former things and do not keep considering the things of old. Here and now I am doing a new thing! This moment it breaks from the bud; do you not know it?" (Is. 43:18-19). A complete break with past religious tradition seems to be called for, in favor of reliance on some new religious experience.

For the historian of religions, this radical theme in the transmitted message of the Israelite prophets poses sharply the problem of continuity and transition in religious traditions. It is clear that an understanding of religious change is crucial in any adequate conception of the nature of religion. [1] For all religious traditions display some form of change, that is, transition from an accepted authoritative tradition with its mythic basis and social forms to new configurations of religious authority and experience—from the "old" to the "new" in Deutero-Isaiah's terms. This study will seek to contribute to the task of understanding religious transition and transformation by focusing on the neo-Babylonian and early Persian periods in Israelite cultural history, when both heterogenetic and orthogenetic forces brought about a sharp disjunction in the continuity of Israelite religion, and when a far-reaching transformation of religious belief and practice was promoted by leading prophetic spokesmen, especially Jeremiah, Ezekiel, and the prophet among the Babylonian exiles known today as Deutero-Isaiah.

In this case study in the dynamics of religious transformation, we shall explore the thesis that religious change is precipitated when the

---

[1] See, most recently, Peter Slater, *The Dynamics of Religion: Meaning and Change in Religious Tradition*, New York, 1978.

soteric value (the power of *Erlösung*, in Joachim Wach's terms) [2] of the transmitted religious reality (the *traditum*) [3] is experienced as deficient under new circumstances. In such a situation, the meaning and security of the accepted traditum are called into question. Questioning the tradition means distancing oneself from it, becoming conscious of the gulf between the "old" structures of salvation and the realities of the new situation.

We shall see that responses to such experiences of disjunction can take a number of directions, such as alienation, reversion to the old traditum, or transformation of the traditum. Alienation from the traditum can take the form of a kind of "secularization" process, that is, the discounting in practice of the demands and promises of the tradition. Or alienation from the traditum may move in the direction of the uncritical acceptance of alternative soteric means ("foreign gods," new religions). [4] The overriding need for religious meaning and security in a period of disjunction may lead to nostalgic reversion to the old traditum in a "backlash" movement. But in all these responses, the gulf between the new experiential situation and the traditional religious forms is not bridged, with the result that a sense of counterfeit soteriology develops, showing itself especially in a separation between the "social" and the "religious" areas of life.

Another response to religious disjunction we shall call *transformation*: the trans-formation of the accepted religious traditum in the context of new realities of social and cultural experience. Transformation is an important process in religious transmission. It is in fact precisely the living traditio process by which each new generation appropriates the complex traditum of its religious heritage, reinterpreting the central symbols and paradigmatic myths to provide ultimate meaning in the context of the new situation, shaping new configurations of self and society in the light of the tradition. [5] In periods of drastic disjunction, the living traditio process is outrun, as it were,

---

2 *Der Erlösungsgedanke und seine Deutung*, Leipzig, 1922; see Joseph M. Kitagawa, "Verstehung und Erlösung: Some Remarks on Joachim Wach's Work," *HR* 11 (1971), 31-53.

3 See Douglas Knight, *Rediscovering the Traditions of Israel*, SBL Dissertation Series, Missoula, Montana, 1973, 5-20.

4 Cf. David Aberle, "A Note on Relative Deprivation Theory as Applied to Millenarian and Other Cult Movements," in William Lessa and Evon Vogt, eds., *Reader in Comparative Religion: An Anthropological Approach*, New York, 1965 (2nd ed.), 537-41.

5 See Jacob Neusner, "The Study of Religion as the Study of Tradition: Judaism," *HR* 14 (1975), 191-206.

by the press of events, the questioning, and the resultant secularization. In such times, if alienation or nostalgic reversion are not to win out, there must be a creative dialogue between the accepted paradigmatic traditum and the new realities. In other words, there must be individuals or groups committed to the religious tradition, yet open to the demands of the new situation, willing to undergo conflict and isolation in their search for the transforming power of the traditum in the changed situation. In ancient Israel, our study will show, these were the prophets.

In a time of severe disjunction, it seems that the "old" is discarded as a dead traditum which has lost its original soteric value, in favor of "new" redemptive experiences. The historian of religions knows, however, that there is never anything totally "new" in religious experience and that in fact the "old" motivates and shapes the "new." Certain elements in the religious tradition attain a recognized classical or paradigmatic value and so, in the complex traditio process, serve as sources in the creation of the new structures and configurations of religious understanding and experience. [6] These paradigmatic elements function both critically and creatively in times of transition. That is, new forms, experiences and motivations are measured by them. And they supply a model or pattern, a sort of "grammar" [7] for the creation of new structures and experiences. The paradigm thus guides history in the process of religious transformation.

Consequently, a dialectic of "demything" and "remything" is involved in religious transformation. The old bases of salvation are called into question, at least in terms of their redemptive value for the present. Yet the paradigm itself provides the vision for an extension or remything of the old traditum that can incorporate present experience. In a sense, present history is thus mythologized, but under the pattern of the religious paradigm. The theologoumenon of the traditum gives rise to mythologoumena relating directly to present experience. [8] The remythed paradigmatic traditum carries a new authority, as authenticated in the personal experience of the transformers of the tradition; as such, it serves as the basis for new communal soteric experience. When this point has been reached, the religious transition has become a religious transformation.

---

[6] See Slater, *op. cit.*, 28-95.

[7] Cf. Joseph M. Kitagawa, "The Japanese *Kokutai* (National Community): History and Myth," *HR* 13 (1974), 224.

[8] See Hans Küng, *On Being a Christian*, Edward Quinn, trans., New York, 1976, 456.

REMEMBER NOT THE FORMER THINGS

The Loss of Soteric Power: Disjunction

Our discussion of the specific problem of disjunction and transformation in Israelite religion at the time of the Babylonian exile can
commence with Deutero-Isaiah's startling pronouncement (Is. 43:
18-19):

> Remember not the former things
> and do not keep considering the things of old.
> Here and now I am doing a new thing!
> This moment it breaks from the bud.
> Do you not know it?

This pronouncement is of course not an isolated one in Deutero-
Isaiah; rather, it belongs to a series of passages which juxtapose the
"former things" (ראשנות) with the "new things" (חדשות) or the "things
to come" (באות, אתיות).[9]

What are these "former things" that are to be "remembered" no
longer, and the "new things" that are now to be "known" or "experienced"? Scholars generally agree in relating the "new things" in some
way with the startling events the prophet saw about to take place in
the wake of Cyrus' victories: the overthrow of Babylon, the return
of the exiles, and the restoration of Zion—an expectation amply
documented in other sections of Deutero-Isaiah's writings. The meaning
of the "former things," which had been foretold and had already
come to pass, is more disputed. North, for example, favors an interpretation of at least some of the passages (41:21ff.; 43:8ff.; 48:3ff.)
as referring to victories of Cyrus before the fall of Sardin in 547 B.C.—
former victories which will be surpassed by new conquests. [10]

This interpretation, however, softens the sharpness of the disjunction which the prophet felt with the past sacred traditum; it takes the
prophet's words out of the sacral-cultic sphere and interprets them
as a reading of the political and military history of the day. However,
the theological context of Deutero-Isaiah's argument suggests that

---

[9] Note esp. Is. 41:21-29; 42:6-9; 43:8-13; 44:6-8; 45:20-21; 46:8-11; 48:3-8; 48:
14-16. Cf. Aage Bentzen, "On the Ideas of 'the Old' and 'the New' in Deutero-Isaiah,"
Studia Theologica 1 (1948), 183-87; E. Rohland, "Die Bedeutung der Erwählungs-
traditionen Israels für die Eschatologie der alttestamentlichen Propheten," Diss. Heidel-
berg, 1956, 99ff.

[10] C. R. North, "The 'Former Things' and the 'New Things' in Deutero-Isaiah,"
Studies in Old Testament Prophecy, H. H. Rowley, ed., Edinburgh, 1950, 111-26.

these passages do in fact have to do with the problem of the continuity of the sacred tradition. The prophet argues that, in contrast to the "gods" of the nations, products of men's hands and thus bound to time and change, Yahweh has a sovereign purpose with respect to the life of his people. He declared the "former things" and brought them to pass; thus he is trustworthy as both the "first" and the "last." [11]

This theological argument makes it clear that the "former things" must be understood not as secular political events but as the sacred history itself. [12] Indeed, this oracle (43:14-21) explicitly associates the "former things" with the activity of Yahweh "who makes a way in the sea, a path in the mighty waters," the events of the exodus from Egypt in which Yahweh became "the creator of Israel, your king." Here Deutero-Isaiah appeals directly to the ancient cultic tradition expressed, for example, in the hymn in Ex. 15.

However, while appealing to this sacred tradition, Deutero-Isaiah at the same time gave sharp expression to the disjunction between the traditum and the present realities. One cannot overlook the cultic connotations of the words "remember" (זכר), "know" (ידע), and "recite" (ספר-43:21); the sacred history was traditionally "remembered" in the cultus, there the people "knew" or experienced Yahweh's soteric activity and "recited" his praise in hymns. In this light, the injunction to "remember not the former things" throws up a big question mark as to the continuing soteric significance of the accepted sacred history.

This sense of disjunction with the sacred traditum was also expressed by Deutero-Isaiah's earlier contemporaries: Jeremiah in the last days of the existence of Judah, and Ezekiel at the beginning of the exile. At a time when nostalgic reversionists were thinking of making a new ark to symbolize the lost old one, Jeremiah sharply rejected this tie to the past sacred history: "In those days, says Yahweh, they shall no more say, 'The ark of Yahweh's covenant'; it shall not come to mind, or be remembered, or missed; it shall not be made again" (Jer. 3:16). Again, Jeremiah looked to a time when the people would no longer use the old sacred confession, "As Yahweh lives who brought up the people of Israel out of the land of Egypt" (Jer. 23:7); and his vision of the "new" covenant emphasizes the gulf with the "old" (Jer. 31:32). Within Ezekiel's priestly perspective, there could be no more powerful expression of the sense of a radical break with

---

[11] Cf. Bernhard Anderson, "Exodus Typology in Second Isaiah," *Israel's Prophetic Heritage*, Bernhard Anderson and Walter Harrelson, eds., New York, 1962, 186-87.
[12] Gerhard von Rad, *Theologie des alten Testaments*, München, 1965, II, 256-57.

the past cultic and soteric tradition than his vision of the departure of Yahweh's glory from the temple and from Zion, with the sacred city thus abandoned to the executioners (Ez. 9-11). [13] Thus the prophets reflected the experience of religious disjunction which the people sensed even in their continuation of the traditional practices.

To understand the dynamics of this religious crisis, it is important to consider the factors which precipitated it. Certainly many of these factors were heterogenetic forces, that is, pressures arising from outside Israel's religious tradition but causing change within it. The Israelite tradition was of course subjected to many outside pressures through the centuries. We see for example the drastic transformation in religious outlook associated with the transition from pastoralist to agrarian culture, from looseknit tribal league to kingship. The Assyrian period saw the destruction of northern Israel and the reduction of Judah to a vassal state, with corresponding reinterpretations of the sacred tradition offered by prophets like Amos and Isaiah, Amos announcing for the first time in Israel's history a total disjunction in the sacred traditum: "The end has come upon my people Israel; I will never again pass by them" (Amos 8:2). Isaiah saw Yahweh destroying his own people but held fast to the sacred paradigm of Yahweh's continuity of presence in Jerusalem—albeit as a raging fire (Is. 31:4-9).

Thus heterogenetic factors causing changes in religious understanding were not new in Israel's history—but their force and extent in the neo-Babylonian period forced the people into a new situation. Quite simply, what was experienced was the destruction of Israel as a people, together with all her social, political and cultural institutions. The break with the structures which had sustained the life of the community in the past seemed complete and irreversible, precipitated by the cruel movement of historical forces.

One should not discount other heterogenetic forces of change apart from the configurations of political and military power. Cultural changes played a significant part, especially a spirit of questioning and skepticism which was being spread through the international wisdom movement. Israelites became more aware of other peoples' religions and mythologies, judging from Ezekiel's broad knowledge of international culture and religious traditions. Correspondingly, many were adopting a more critical attitude toward their own tradition.

It is also important, however, to recognize orthogenetic factors of

---

[13] Walther Zimmerli, *Ezechiel* (*BKAT*), Neukirchen, 1955ff., 234ff.

change, that is, forces within the Israelite sacred tradition which contributed to change and transformation. Clearly, a central reality in the Israelite religious tradition was the sense of a covenant relationship with their God Yahweh. This covenant relationship was kept alive in cultic reactualization both on the local and on the national scale, so that the Israelite's sense of the sacred traditum was tightly bound up with his experience of living in a dynamic political relationship with Yahweh. There was always potential tension between adherence to developing social institutions and loyalty to the covenant God; the emergence of the prophetic movement itself is an expression of this transformative covenant relationship.

The sense of sacred history was a related force of continuing transformation in Israel. The notion that soteric divine activity is experienced in a series of historical events awakened a sense of divine plan and purpose in historical existence. New situations were understood in the light of the divine purpose and, further, projections of the divine purpose into the future could supply new motivations and transform present social structures.

Further, the tradition of a personal relationship with a God who is known in historical experience fostered a spirit of dialogue and questioning in Israel. Individual and community laments became punctuated with questions about Yahweh's will and purpose. The Deuteronomic picture of Moses set him in continual dialogue with Yahweh; and the prophets increasingly took the role of questioning Yahweh even as they questioned Israel. Thus the covenant itself, the sense of divine involvement in history, and the attitude of dialogue and questioning represent orthogenetic elements in the Israelite sacred tradition which provided fertile ground for change and transformation.

To these orthogenetic forces of change in Israel we can perhaps add the Israelite cultus itself, as the main locale for the ongoing transmission of the sacred traditum. Notions of the cultus as timeless repetition of mythic realities have led some scholars to downgrade its importance in transition and transformation. The cultus is seen as static and resisting change, preserving the old values and upholding security, while the anti-cultic forces such as the prophets are seen as the instigators of reformation and transformation. [14] However, since the cultus was the locale for the transmission of the central transforma-

---

[14] Cf., e.g., Georg Fohrer, *History of Israelite Religion*, David Green, trans., Nashville, 1972, 276-87.

tory experiences of the covenant relationship and for the recitation of the *magnalia dei*, it represented a potential force toward change and transformation. Ringgren notes, "The cult means a re-experiencing of ancient events, an awareness of their effects here and now, and a corresponding shaping of the future." [15] As a matter of fact, since the studies by Mowinckel and others, it has been recognized that the prophets also stood in continuity with cultic tradition, that they used cultic forms, that many of them were even cultic personnel, and that the prophetic oracle had a definite place within the cultus. [16] Even Deutero-Isaiah's drastic call to "remember not the former things" follows the pattern of the cultic *Heilsorakel*. [17] Perhaps there is no better statement of the contribution of the cultus to transformation than that of the Deuteronomic covenant renewal scenerio: "Not with our fathers did Yahweh make this covenant, but with us, we who are all alive here this day" (Dt. 5:3; cf. Dt. 29:13-14 Heb.).

Alienation from the Traditum

In the neo-Babylonian period, heterogenetic and orthogenetic forces together brought about a spiritual crisis in Judah, the remnant of Israel. The sense of disjunction with past tradition brought with it a strong feeling of pessimism with respect to the soteric validity of the sacred traditum. The recital of Yahweh's ancient deeds, the reactualization of the covenant relationship, and the cultic proclamation of Yahweh's continued bestowal of salvation failed to evoke the sense of Erlösung for the hard-pressed Judeans.

In the so-called Deuteronomic reform movement, a valiant attempt was made under King Josiah to revitalize the sacred traditum as a saving power for the present. Coinciding approximately with the new developments in Mesopotamia as the neo-Babylonians under Nebopolassar made themselves independent in 625 B.C. and thus greatly reduced Assyria's dominance in Palestine, this revitalization movement centered around a comprehensive reinterpretation of covenant theology "directed solely toward making the people of the time believe that the covenant had a meaning for their own day and generation." [18] This

---

[15] Helmer Ringgren, *Israelite Religion*, David Green, trans., Philadelphia, 1966, 260.

[16] S. Mowinckel, *Psalmenstudien III: Kultusprophetie und prophetische Psalmen*, Kristiania, 1923; A. R. Johnson, *The Cultic Prophet in Ancient Israel*, Cardiff, 1944; A. Haldar, *Associations of Cult Prophets among the Ancient Semites*, Uppsala, 1945.

[17] J. Begrich, *Studien zu Deuterojesaja*, München, 1963, 14ff., 88.

[18] Gerhard von Rad, *The Message of the Prophets*, D. M. G. Stalker, trans., New York, 233.

movement reveals a lively religious debate going on, at least in some quarters, and a religious renewal which for some years apparently satisfied the prophet Jeremiah.

However, for our purposes here we note the drastic measures necessary for the movement to reach to the hearts of the disheartened and skeptical population. The homilies in Deuteronomy insist over and over again that Yahweh's activity is taking place "today" (היום), that his word of judgment and promise is effective "today." Indeed, this very homiletical device shows the depth of the disjunction: "Not with our fathers... but with us" (Dt. 5:3). The widespread sense of the failure of saving power in the cultic tradition of Yahweh's mighty deeds is spelled out by the homilist in Dt. 29:1-3 Heb.:

> You have seen with your own eyes all that Yahweh did in Egypt, to Pharaoh and to all his servants and to all his land, the great trials which your own eyes saw, those great signs and wonders. But up to this day Yahweh has not given you a heart to understand, or eyes to see, or ears to hear.

The great signs and wonders of Yahweh's acts of salvation were still being "seen" and "heard" in the cultus (cf. Ps. 48:5-9 Heb.). But the "heart" to understand and to appropriate the seeing and hearing as soteric power for the present had failed. [19]

A spirit of skepticism resulting from this distancing from the past bases of salvation can be seen both in the people of Judah and in the prophets themselves. This was "a time when men had become even more detached than before from the ties of religion." [20] Jeremiah's contemporary Habakkuk reproached Yahweh's failure to intervene to uphold the justice proclaimed in the sacred tradition: why is Yahweh, who cannot endure evil or wrong, apparently completely silent in the face of the Babylonian atrocities (Hab. 1)? Although the cultic answer, "But Yahweh is in his holy temple, let all the earth keep silence before him" (Hab. 2:20), amplified by the traditional theophanic depiction of Yahweh as warrior (Hab. 3:1-15), was supposed to call forth a spirit of waiting on Yahweh to reactualize his salvation (Hab. 3:16), the extent to which the people were experiencing the "silence" of Yahweh and consequently questioning the sacred traditum was quite unprecedented in Israel's history.

---

[19] Cf. Is. 42:18-20: the deaf and blind servant sees many things but does not observe them, and his ears are open but he does not hear.

[20] von Rad, *The Message of the Prophets*, 230.

Jeremiah typically quoted real or hypothetical confessions, laments and questions of the people, mixing them together with his own in giving expression to doubt and confusion:

> Is not Yahweh in Zion? Is her king not within her?...
> Harvest is past, summer is over—but we are not saved! (Jer. 8:19-20).

> O hope of Israel, its saviour in time of trouble,
> Why should you be like a stranger in the land,
>   like a traveller pitching his tent for a night?
> Why should you be like a man overwhelmed,
>   like a mighty man who is not able to save? (Jer. 14:8-9).

Jeremiah's own "confessions" of course must be seen in the light of his own conflict and struggle, but the overall sense of doubt and questioning certainly reflected the experience of many: Yahweh was "like a deceitful brook, whose waters fail" (Jer. 15:18). The sacred traditum no longer delivered its saving, renewing power.

Ezekiel quoted the proverb, "The days run on, but every vision comes to naught" (Ez. 12:22), as a common saying of his time, reflecting the general sense of religious failure. And a dominant complaint among Ezekiel's contemporaries was that "The way of Yahweh is not just" (Ez. 18:25; 33:17)—what they were experiencing was in conflict with the soteric renewal promised in the tradition. Throughout the message of Deutero-Isaiah it is clear that his main task was to encourage and motivate an audience that was "weary," "blind and deaf," "shamed," and "bereaved"—doubters who questioned the continuing efficacy of Yahweh's saving power. The very depth of Deutero-Isaiah's arguments shows a tremendous amount of questioning and reflection on his own part, for the religious situation was desperate.

Another side of the new skepticism should be noted. Not only did the people question the continuing efficacy of Yahweh's saving power, but there were widespread doubts about the continuing existence of the covenant community which could be faithful to Yahweh. Given the social realities of Judah, the idea of Yahweh as the holy one in the midst of his holy people seemed ironic and even terrifying: "Who is there among us that can dwell with the devouring fire? who among us can dwell with the everlasting burning?" (Is. 33:14). [21] The old "people of Yahweh" who fought with Yahweh in the holy wars, who formed Yahweh's covenant partner in the Davidic kingdom, was

---

[21] von Rad, *Theologie*, II, 277.

no more than a shell if not completely dead with the rapid fading and extinction of this last remnant of David's kingdom. The short-lived Deuteronomic reform sparked some hope that Judah could renew her side of the covenant, but the death of Josiah brought back cynical political leadership and further alienation from the covenant ideal.

Further evidence of the alienation from the traditum of a covenant community was the new growth of individualism. While one's identity as a member of the "people of Yahweh" formerly had provided security and meaning in the context of the sacred traditum, now the people complained that Yahweh was not just in lumping the generations together in wholesale acts of judgment: "The fathers have eaten sour grapes, but the children's teeth are set on edge" (Jer. 31:29; Ez. 18:2). The questioning and distancing from the old tradition now led to the individual's alienation from the corporate religious base. Not only was the divine soteric reality questioned, but the ideal of the "soteriological community" [22] likewise seemed an inauthentic and cruel bit of dead traditum.

One recognizable effect of this distancing from the sacred traditum was the secularity or "practical atheism" displayed by many of the people, according to some indications in the prophetic message. Zephaniah, a contemporary of Jeremiah, spoke out in the days of king Josiah against "those who do not seek Yahweh or inquire of him, ... who sit in stupor over the dregs of their wine, saying to themselves, 'Yahweh will do nothing good, nor will he do evil' " (Zeph. 1:6, 12). Jeremiah and Ezekiel likewise complained of people who act wickedly, saying confidently, "God will not see what we are doing" (Jer. 12:4); "Yahweh does not see us, Yahweh has abandoned the land" (Ez. 8:12). People mocked and scoffed at Jeremiah and Ezekiel because nothing came of their visions and words (Jer. 20:7-8; Ez. 12:22). The divine reality did not seem to be engaged in doing either good or evil—which was precisely Deutero-Isaiah's stinging mockery of man-made gods (Is. 41:23). Thus a degree of secularity was reached in the lives of some of the people; they were no longer motivated by the religious traditum.

Another tendency among some of the people was the attraction to alternate sacred traditions which seemed to deliver soteric power. In the syncretistic climate of Israel's existence, the desire to supplement or supplant the Yahweh covenant tradition with alternate religious practices ("foreign gods") was always strong; in fact, the very shape

---

22 Kitagawa, "The Japanese *Kokutai*," 221-24.

of Israel's own religious tradition was much affected by conflict and transformation in dialogue with alternate religious traditions. While these struggles in the earlier periods centered around the problem of fertility powers (Yahweh versus Ba°al), in the period of the great Mesopotamian powers the attraction of the religious traditions of the victorious powers was strong.

It is telling, for example, that Jeremiah's last words were spoken in Egypt to some Judean women who claimed that this disaster would not have befallen them if they had not terminated their sacrifices to the "queen of heaven" (Jer. 44:17-19; 7:18), probably the Assyrian-Babylonian Ishtar, the *šarrat šāmē* ("queen of heaven"). [23] Ezekiel's visionary experience of transportation to Jerusalem and viewing of the "abominations" being practiced in the temple probably reflects both his own memory of the temple from the time of Josiah's successor Jehoiakim and subsequent reports which reached him among the exiles in Babylon (Ez. 8). A great flourishing of Mesopotamian and Egyptian cults in Jerusalem was taking place: there was a clandestine Egyptian Osirian cult supported by the patrician families of Judah, including the son of Shaphan, Joshiah's chief assistant who inacted the Deutero-nomic reform (Ez. 8:7-13). The Sumero-Accadian god Dumuzi was especially popular among "women weeping for Tammuz" (Ez. 8:14-15); and the sun god was worshipped by people before the holy place in the temple, who turned their backs to the throne of Yahweh in order to face the rising of the Sun (Ez. 8:16). [24]

Ezekiel indicates that among the exiles in Babylon there was a strong tendency to identify with Babylonian cultic practices, including setting up images of Babylonian gods in their houses (Ez. 14:1-11) and using Babylonian incantations and magical practices (Ez. 13:17-18). Apparently they even wanted to continue Yahweh worship in Babylon by setting up an image of "wood and stone," probably copying Baby-lonian prototypes (Ez. 20:32). [25] In the message of Deutero-Isaiah can be see the religious situation of the exiles a generation later, when

---

[23] Wilhelm Rudolph, *Jeremiah* (*HAT*), Tübingen, 1968, 55; John Bright, *Jeremiah* (*Anchor Bible*), New York, 1965, 56; but M. J. Dahood, *Revista Biblica* 8 (1960), 166-68, holds that the goddess is Shapash; and G. Widengren, *Sakrales Königtum im Alten Testament und im Judentum*, Stuttgart, 1955, 12, argues for the goddess °Anat.

[24] For the debate about the interpretation of these scenes, see W. F. Albright, *Archaeology and the Religion of Israel*, Baltimore, 1956 (4th ed.), 165-68; Zimmerli, 210-24; Georg Fohrer, *Ezechiel* (*HAT*), Tübingen, 1955, 50-52; Walther Eichrodt, *Ezekiel: A Commentary*, Philadelphia, 1970, 119-29.

[25] *Ibid.*, 179-80, 169; Fohrer, *History of Israelite Religion*, 311.

the influence of Babylonian religious practices had gained strength and later when anticipation of the triumph of Cyrus and the Persian gods escalated. While specific foreign religious practices taken over by the Jewish exiles are not mentioned, the fact that Deutero-Isaiah again and again inveighs against the power and authority of the "other gods" shows that the exiles had acquiesced to the superiority of the Babylonian and Persian sacred traditions. [26]

Another response to the sense of the soteric inadequacy of the traditum in Israel was a blind, desperate reversion to the old tradition in spite of the questions raised by the present. One of the most notable examples of this tendency comes to light in the circumstances surrounding the so-called "temple sermon" of Jeremiah (Jer. 7 and 26). "In the beginning of the reign of Jehoiakim the son of Josiah" the reform measures taken by Josiah were undone and a great reversion set in. The spiritual mentality of the now dominant party was characterized by backlash against the Deuteronomic revitalization and a throwback to the doctrine of the inviolability of Zion. The old traditions of the promises to David and the Zion traditions of perpetual protection by Yahweh were dogmatically reasserted, in spite of the real and present danger of invasion and total destruction by the neo-Babylonians (which became a reality within the next two decades). In the face of such a threatening situation, the dominant leaders were singlemindedly repeating the slogan, "This is the temple of Yahweh, the temple of Yahweh, the temple of Yahweh" (Jer. 7:4). They were going through the motions of standing before Yahweh, making the offerings, and hearing the liturgical promise of Erlösung: "We are saved!" (Jer. 7:10). So desperate was this reversion that those who questioned this doctrine, like Jeremiah and the unfortunate Uriah (Jer. 26:20-24), were subjected to mob action and capital punishment.

Another aspect of the nostalgic reversion to the security of the old traditions was the apparent proliferation of priests and prophets who repeated the sacral traditum and on that basis promised peace and security for Judah. Admittedly, the problem of "false prophets" is colored by theological and polemical considerations in the message of Jeremiah and Ezekiel. And it must be recognized that the individualization of prophecy in this period made clashes unavoidable between prophets who saw the same situation with different eyes, each speaking with his own sense of authority on the basis of the sacred tradition. [27]

---

26 Cf. Is. 40:18ff.; 43:9-10; 44:6-8; 44:9-20; 45:1-7; 45:20-21; 46:1-7.
27 von Rad, *Theologie*, II, 273.

Yet there is no reason to doubt Jeremiah and Ezekiel's assertions about the existence of many prophets who attempted to assuage the people's anxiety about the worsening situation with the balm of the sacred traditum. A political motivation was of course involved: a policy of resistence to Babylon could be handily supported by religious justification, while a realistic prophet like Jeremiah was truly "weakening the hands" of the resistance (Jer. 38:4). At the same time, the sacral traditum did offer much to draw from in terms of hope of rescue, refusal to submit to foreign powers, and anticipation of Yahweh's intervention (cf. the prophet Isaiah a century earlier!); and prophets steeped in these traditions would be speaking of hope, saying, "It shall be well with you," "No evil will come upon you," "You will not serve the king of Babylon" (Jer. 23:16-17; 27:14; cf. 28:2-4; Ez. 13:10).

We see, in summary, a religious crisis taking shape in Judah in the neo-Babylonian and early Persian periods, involving a deeply-felt alienation from the soteric experience of the accepted tradition. It gave rise to a widespread skepticism in that people questioned Yahweh's continuing saving activity and also questioned the existence of a soteriological community. Many people lived in a kind of secularity, while other grasped at new religious options; still others reverted desperately to the seeming security of the old traditum. Yet the soteric meaning sought after in these ways was found to be counterfeit, for it did not bridge the disjunction between the accepted traditum which defined the covenant community and its God, on the one hand, and the new realities of political and cultural experience, on the other.

HERE AND NOW I AM DOING A NEW THING

Old Traditum and New Realities in Tension: The Prophets

There were individuals and groups among the Judeans who felt the inadequacy of these alternative responses to the spiritual crisis and who inspired a fundamental transformation of the accepted religious tradition. They stood squarely in the tension between the sacral traditum which had sustained the community in the past and the new reality of life in the neo-Babylonian period. They shared to a large extent in the new tendencies of their age: a spirit of questioning, both of Yahweh's power and of the existence of an authentic covenant community; and a highly individualistic self-concept, both over against Yahweh and over against the community. In themselves the spiritual crisis was most deeply experienced, for they lived in a constant dialogue between their own experiences and reflections, on the one hand, and their total commitment to the sacred tradition, on the other. It is from this dialogue, which finds expression especially in the recorded message of Jeremiah, Ezekiel, and Deutero-Isaiah, that a far-reaching transformation of Israelite religion was effected.

It should be noted that the relation of the prophets to the authority of the traditum is a matter of some disagreement among scholars. Views range from the extreme thesis that the prophetic message represents standard cultic pronouncements based in the old traditions, [28] on the one hand, to the view that the prophets rejected all cultic tradition and gave expression to a new existential experience of Yahweh's will, on the other. [29] Certainly these prophets did not merely revitalize the ancient traditions once again; nor were they simply "reformers," calling the people back to the old traditions. On the other hand, they did not merely move to the other end of the traditum/experience polarity, dissociating themselves from the cultus and the accepted traditum. Rather, the prophetic "transformation" of Israel's sacred tradition was possible precisely because they lived in the tension between the authoritative traditum and the new experience, taking both seriously in a radical way.

The prophets' continuity with the sacral traditum has been well demonstrated in recent studies: [30] they were closely connected with cultic forms of speech, specific traditions and formulae, cultic festivals and roles. Thus, on the one side, the prophets participated in the authority which tradition bestowed on their particular activity as prophets in Israel. Yet, in their acceptance of new experience of Yahweh's reality, in their questioning of the traditum and in their reinterpretations, they demonstrated a sharp discontinuity with the traditional role of prophet and thus invited a crisis of prophetic authority. This is seen of course in the sharply increased number of conflicts with prophets of different views ("false prophets") and in the burning interest these prophets displayed in the nature of the "word of Yahweh" which they felt compelled to speak. [31] This creative tension gave them a unique authority among their people; their authority was clearly recognized in principle, yet their message was

---

[28] Cf. Mowinckel, op. cit.; Johnson, op. cit.
[29] Cf. Fohrer, History of Israelite Religion, 276-87.
[30] See J. Lindblom, Prophecy in Ancient Israel, Philadelphia, 1962, 78-83; 202-10.
[31] von Rad, Theologie, II, 273-74.

often bitterly contested and rejected. A striking illustration of the ambiguity of their authority was the episode of Baruch's scroll containing Jeremiah's message, which king Jehoiakim dutifully listened to but which he subsequently cut up with a penknife and threw into the fire (Jer. 36:1-23).

In these prophets of the neo-Babylonian period, the sense of individuality and the spirit of questioning brought about an experience of conflict and isolation. The "confessions" of Jeremiah are unique in Israelite literature in the depth of questioning, the radical expression of doubt and suffering, and the sense of total compulsion to proclaim the word of Yahweh come what may. The memoirs of Baruch record the conflict and failure of Jeremiah in his role as prophet in this age of transition (Jer. 37-45). And Ezekiel became a man of conflict among the Judean exiles, symbolically representing in himself the judgment and destruction of the covenant people. While it is beyond the scope of this paper to examine the revelatory experiences of these prophets, it is clear that they considered their own experiences of conflict, questioning and suffering to be concrete data through which they came to understand the present actuality of Yahweh's soteric activity. In Heschel's words, these prophets experienced a kind of "sympathy with the divine pathos." [32]

Form-critical studies have clearly demonstrated that the prophets' sense of inspiration by Yahweh's word did not destroy their individuality or their rational capacities. Their proclamation of "the word of Yahweh" always carried with it their own interpretation and application based on their own experience. [33] We do find in the prophets of the neo-Babylonian and early Persian periods a drastic increase in the freedom which they demonstrated in the reception, interpretation and proclamation of the word of Yahweh. Of central importance to our study is the recognition that the new experiential situation of these prophets placed them in a dialectical relationship with the sacred traditum, so that not only their application of Yahweh's word but their very "revelatory state of mind" [34] showed the effects of their spirit of questioning and reflection. That is, their own experiences of the new realities of their day made them sensitive to aspects of the divine pathos, and in this light they radicalized the soteric paradigm received from the tradition and transformed it for the present.

---

[32] Abraham Heschel, *The Prophets*, New York, 1962, 221ff.

[33] See von Rad, *Theologie*, II, 79-88.

[34] Lindblom, *op. cit.*, 173-82.

The prophets in this period of religious and cultural disjunction continued to take the old traditum with complete seriousness; they never abandoned the need to "ask for the ancient paths" (Jer. 6:16). They differed from their nostalgic reversionist contemporaries, however, in their radicalization of the soteric paradigm and in their critical use of this paradigm to develop a new understanding of present experience. To a certain extent they "demythed" the traditum by brushing aside the *tradita*, popular notions and practices accumulated over the centuries. They applied this radicalized paradigm rigorously to criticize and root out present conceptions and practices. But they also "remythed" the traditum by using the sacred paradigm as a kind of grammar for a far-reaching reinterpretation of the sacred history incorporating present and future realities.

Most central perhaps to the prophetic radicalization of the soteric traditum was their emphasis on Yahweh's activity toward his own covenant people, not only in saving them, but also in judging and destroying them. The tradition of election and covenant was of course central to the sacred traditum from ancient times, founded in the Mosaic inheritance expressed in the historical traditions, the cult, and legal usage. The prophets understood the root reality of the election in the bilateral participation by Yahweh in his soteric activity, on the one hand, and the covenant people in their faithful response, on the other. According to the ancient tradition, Yahweh saved his people by destroying their enemies (cf. Ex. 15; Judg. 5). The prophets radicalized this tradition by connecting it with Israel's response in the covenant relationship. In that they did not live up to the demands of the covenant relationship, Yahweh's judging and destroying activity was directed precisely at them; yet this was at the same time a soteric reality for the covenant community, for it pressed the people to return to the covenant God and opened the way for tranformation and renewal.

Amos had heralded this prophetic radicalization of the soteric paradigm with his statement of Yahweh's oracle: "You only have I known of all the families of the earth; therefore will I punish you for all your iniquities" (Amos 3:2; cf. 8:2). This startling theme of Yahweh's destroying presence within the covenant relationship was continued and elaborated by other prophets of the Assyrian period, always in combination with the saving dimension of his presence. As Lindblom points out, the prophets proclaimed a dynamic soteriology, with judgment juxtaposed to the "perhaps" of salvation (Amos 5:14-15), his resolve to destroy swallowed up by his compulsion to heal

(Hos. 11:8-9), his destroying activity seen as part of a "plan" for the revitalization of his covenant people (Isaiah and Micah). [35]

The prophets of the neo-Babylonian and early Persian periods laid hold on this radicalized soteric paradigm and applied it intensively to their own day. The Deuteronomic reform movement attempted to revitalize the sense of being in a covenant relationship with the God who says, "I kill and I make alive, I wound and I heal" (Deut. 32:39). Jeremiah spent most of his time pointing to the coming destruction of Judah in Yahweh's wrath; yet he combined with this a tenacious insistence that Yahweh was active for good, not for ill (e.g., Jer. 24:4-7; 29:10-14; etc.). Ezekiel's vision of Jerusalem abandoned by Yahweh's glory and left to the destroyers is a radical statement of judgment against the covenant people; yet Ezekiel too saw the rebirth of Israel as the covenant community through Yahweh's soteric activity (Ez. 36; 40ff.). For Deutero-Isaiah, the destroying activity was past, the saving activity was breaking forth (cf. Is. 40); still, the same basic soteric paradigm of Yahweh's judging and saving activity within the covenant relationship is the root theologoumenon for all that he says.

Involved in this radicalization of the soteric paradigm was a certain "demything" or stripping away of popular conceptions of the soteric efficacy of the sacred traditum. Most of these popular conceptions had to do with the understanding of the covenant relationship as a perpetual guarantee of divine protection and blessing. Amos was probably repeating such a popular belief when he quoted the words, "You only have I known of all the families of the earth...," to be followed by a "therefore" promising continued covenantal blessing and protection—twisted to judgment, however, in Amos' radicalization of the soteric paradigm (Amos 3:2). In the neo-Babylonian period, it was the traditum of the perpetual protection of Zion, together with the promise of the endless reign of the house of David, which Jeremiah and Ezekiel felt had to be stripped away. These tradita had been forged in past critical situations in Israel and built upon the basic soteric tradition (cf. e.g. Pss. 89; 132). But when people in his day laid claim to the soteric efficacy of the traditum—"This is the temple of Yahweh, the temple of Yahweh, the temple of Yahweh" (Jer. 7:4)— Jeremiah castigated this belief as "deceptive tradita" (דברי השקר) which provided a false sense of religious security. For those who clung to the "temple" as their guarantee of life and meaning did not reflect faith-

---

[35] *Ibid.*, 323-41.

fulness to the covenant relationship in their lives (Jer. 7:4-10). Because of this misuse of the traditum, Jeremiah proclaimed that the covenant God was going to destroy this temple just as he had destroyed his temple at Shiloh during the period of the amphictyony (Jer. 7:12-15). In fact, Jeremiah stripped down the sacred history to the extent of denying that Yahweh had even commanded his people to offer burnt offerings and sacrifices (7:22); rather there was only the root covenant stipulation: "Obey my voice, and I will be your God and you will be my people, and you shall walk in the entire way which I will command you, in order that you may prosper" (Jer. 7:23). In Jeremiah's view, this fundamental covenant stipulation had never been realized by the people; they had apostasized from the start, substituting comfortable tradita for the transforming discipline of the covenant (Jer. 7:24-29).

Ezekiel also spoke from the viewpoint of a radicalized soteric paradigm in criticizing the accepted notions of Yahweh's dealings with his people. Ezekiel's own roots were in the sacred tradition of the priesthood, and this sacral understanding of the covenant relationship shaped his view of the current religious situation. Of special interest to us are the three reviews of Israel's history (ch. 16, 20, 23), in which Ezekiel totally rewrote the saving history from the perspective of his radicalized soteric paradigm. In ch. 20, Ezekiel's recapitulation follows the traditional schema of the saving history; yet he made the sacral tradition into a record of Israel's failure. Already at the beginning in Egypt the people refused to obey, continuing to practice the old cults, and Yahweh all but rejected them already at this point. In the wilderness Yahweh revealed the commandments, but the people refused to obey; so finally Yahweh gave commandments "that were not good," in particular the command to offer up their firstborn sons, so that Israel was inevitably defiled (Ez. 20:18-26). In ch. 16 and 23, Ezekiel reviews the history of the monarchical period. Judah-Jerusalem was an abhorred foundling, exposed at birth. Yahweh kept her alive and married her; but by her continual unfaithfulness the covenant relationship was irretrievably broken, and now her "lovers" were summoned to execute ghastly judgment upon her.

Ezekiel's point in this unprecedented revision of the sacred history was to place Israel's whole existence, past and present, under judgment as a total failure. Thus did he demyth the sacred traditum, ruthlessly stripping the beloved tradita away from his contemporaries so that they could no longer find uncritical refuge and security there. Even Deutero-

3

Isaiah, speaking after the great catastrophe, pruned the sacred history mercilessly: "Even your first father transgressed, and your mediators rebelled against me"—Deutero-Isaiah speaks the oracle of Yahweh to those who argue that the assurances of the sacred history have failed— "Therefore I have given Jacob over to utter destruction and left Israel to reviling" (Is. 43:27-28).

What colors this new prophetic perspective on the saving history in a way that distinguishes it from that of earlier prophets is the strong sense of skepticism and questioning—not so much questioning the reality of Yahweh's power and faithfulness, but questioning whether it is possible for Israel, the people of the covenant, to maintain the covenant relationship at all. The Deuteronomic movement had raised this question (cf. Josh. 24:19), and Jeremiah reflected often on the problem of Israel's disposition toward disobedience. Yahweh appointed Jeremiah an "assayer" (Jer. 6:27), and in his searchings he discovered that the people's heart was "deceitful" and "incurable" (Jer. 17:9). "Can the Nubian change his skin or the leopard its spots? then also you can do good, who are trained to do evil" (Jer. 13:23). Ezekiel also demonstrated the total dominion of the spirit of dis-obedience, the deep-seated inability to obey, which had characterized Israel from the beginning. How could "this rebellious house," these "men of a hard forehead and a stubborn heart" (Ez. 2:3-5) change themselves and become faithful people of the covenant?

Thus perhaps the most fundamental area of demything of the sacred traditum was in the area of anthropology: Israel was (and always had been) simply unable to respond faithfully in the covenant relationship. That is why the old soteric traditum was inadequate, why it was no longer possible simply to revert to it. The only hope lay in a new soteric event which would radically change the covenant relationship itself.

Remything: the Present and Future Soteric Realities

Having applied the radicalized sacred paradigm to criticize and pass judgment on present conceptions and practices, these prophets remythed the traditum by using this paradigm as a kind of grammar for a far-reaching reinterpretation of the sacred history in terms of present and future realities. They extended the sacred history to include the present historical process; the motif of passing through Yahweh's judgment to reach new life became the schema for an understanding of a new and greater act of salvation taking place in their present experience.

Further, the sacred history was cosmocized in that the cosmogonic myth now provided a new and broader basis for the sacred paradigm. In this way the prophets provided the possibility of new religious experience and transformation in the crisis of their day.

The sacred history of the acts of judgment and deliverance by which Yahweh created the covenant community was extended by the prophets to included significant aspects of the contemporary historical process. Following the theological understanding of Amos, Hosea and Isaiah with respect to the significance of the Assyrian expansion within Yahweh's "plan" (cf. Is. 14:24-27), Jeremiah insisted that the climactic events of his day were still part of the sacred history. Divine soteric activity in the covenant relationship was not limited to cultic remembering and reactualization. The sacred history was reopened, and the radicalized soteric paradigm was the grammar for understanding and interpreting the activity of the covenant God in the events of the present.

There were apparently no lack of prophets in Jeremiah's day who agreed that the divine soteric activity was still present, who applied the traditum of Yahweh's perpetual deliverence and salvation also to the threat of the neo-Babylonians: "The prophets are saying to them, 'You shall not see the sword nor shall you suffer famine, but I will give you lasting prosperity in this very place' " (Jer. 14:13; cf. 23:16-17; 27:16; 28:2-4). To Jeremiah, however, this message was a "lying vision, worthless divination, and their own deluding fancies" (14:14), for it did not correspond to his understanding of the soteric paradigm. This "lying vision" in fact expressed the old sacral traditum which pitted Yahweh as Israel's tribal God against all their enemies, holding that Yahweh would again, as in the exodus and conquest, pass judgment on all their enemies and their gods (cf. Ex. 12:12); that he would still, as he promised David, shatter the enemies at the right hand of the king (cf. Ps. 110:5); that his presence was still a perpetual guarantee of the defeat of all who came against Zion (cf. Pss. 46 and 48). Jeremiah's vision of the soteric paradigm, however, incorporated precisely the presence of those enemies as an element of the divine soteric activity. Again and again he uttered very blunt oracles from Yahweh: "I will make Jerusalem a heap of ruins, a haunt of jackals" (Jer. 9:10 Heb.); "I will deliver this city into the hands of the king of Babylon" (32:3).

The leitmotiv of Jeremiah's understanding of the soteric paradigm was expressed in his call audition, calling him to share in Yahweh's activity, "to pull down and to uproot, to destroy and to demolish, to build up and to plant" (Jer. 1:9-10; cf. 12:2-3, 15-17; 18:7ff.; 24:6-7; 31:28, 40; 32:41; 42:10; 45:4). The seeming contradictory activities of destruction and deliverance are united in the soteric paradigm—not, it should be noted, in a mere chronological succession, but in an experiential simultaneity. [36] Through this extension of the divine soteric activity to include also the destruction of Judah in the vicissitudes of history, Jeremiah established the precondition for a renewed experience of salvation: precisely in the present crisis they were confronting the power of the God of the covenant.

In spite of Jeremiah's interpretation of the neo-Babylonian destruction of Judah as Yahweh's soteric activity, his voice apparently had little immediate effect, and Ezekiel and Deutero-Isaiah had to keep insisting on this broadened view of the saving history. Corresponding to his revision of Israel's sacred history (chs. 16; 20; 23), Ezekiel spared no words in insisting that the Babylonian havoc was Yahweh's long-delayed destruction of his own people: "It is I who am bringing the sword upon you ... with the slain falling in your midst, you shall *know* that I am Yahweh" (Ez. 6:3-7 *et passim*). It is, says Ezekiel, precisely *in* his destroying activity that the apostate covenant people will experience a renewed "knowledge" of Yahweh and thus be given the possibility of transformation and renewal.

As in Jeremiah's day, so also Ezekiel dealt with fellow-prophets whose view of the soteric traditum led them to see "visions of peace for Jerusalem" (Ez. 13:16). To Ezekiel these were "false visions and lying divinations" which misled the people. This was daubing a wall with whitewash in a vain attempt to hold it up, papering over the deficiency of the old traditum and ignoring the invalidity of its soteric delivery. Thus it hindered the confrontation with Yahweh in his present activity. "Therefore the lord Yahweh says, 'In my rage I am unleashing a stormy wind ... and I will collapse the wall which you daubed with whitewash and level it to the ground, with its foundations laid bare... thus you will know that I am Yahweh'" (Ez. 13:13-14). [37] The disaster taking place around them was senseless and inexplicable from the viewpoint of the old traditum—unless it could be experienced as the saving activity of the covenant God.

---

[36] Cf. Artur Weiser, *Das Buch des Propheten Jeremia: Kapitel 1-25:14 (ATD)*, Göttingen, 1960 (4th ed.), 8; Volkmar Herntrich, *Jeremia der Prophet und sein Volk*, Gütersloh, 1938, 19; Paul Volz, *Der Prophet Jeremiah*, Tübingen, 1930 (3rd ed.), 46.

[37] Cf. Eichrodt, *op. cit.*, 167-68.

Deutero-Isaiah's concern was with disheartened exiles who apparently experienced the catastrophe as evidence of the superiority of the gods of Babylon and the inadequacy of Israel's own divine support. Thus he formulated persuasive arguments about Yahweh's broad historical designs "from the beginning," designs which had not been thwarted but which had come to pass even in the destruction and exile of Judah. "Who was it who gave Jacob away for plunder and Israel for spoil? was it not Yahweh?" (Is. 42:24; cf. 43:28; 51:17-20). In his interest of establishing a new soteriological experience for the exiles, Deutero-Isaiah articulated a theological conception of history centered in the belief that Yahweh and none other had both created the soteric design for his people and was in the process of carrying it out. This design involved also Yahweh's activity in judgment against his own people. It was important for the exiles not to have the notion that the catastrophe which they had experienced had been the work of other divine powers or even that it had been a mere quirk of fate. Thus Deutero-Isaiah quotes Yahweh's words, "I have tried you in the furnace of affliction; for my own sake, for my own sake, I have done it" (Is. 48:10-11). With Deutero-Isaiah, the horizon of the saving history was expanded drastically; there was no longer any area of Israel's experience which fell under the control of any alternate power or meaning. The exiles were now provided with a broad basis for a new experience of soteric power; by "knowing Yahweh" precisely in the catastrophe they could "prepare the way of Yahweh" in a new experience of Erlösung.

Having broadened the basis of the saving traditum by including the present events of destruction, the prophets further extended its reality into the future and in fact made the future events decisive for a revitalization of the covenant people. The whole problem of this "eschatological" dimension in the prophets' message has of course been the subject of an enormous amount of research, without fully agreed conclusions. [38] Of course the prophets had no dogmatic doctrine about the last things, yet their message can be considered eschatological in the sense that they point to events to come that are decisive and final, when the break with the present "goes so deep that the new state beyond it cannot be understood as the continuation of what went

---

[38] Cf., e.g., H. Gressmann, *Der Ursprung der israelitisch-jüdischen Eschatologie,* Göttingen, 1905; J. Lindblom, "Gibt es eine Eschatologie bei den alttestamentlichen Propheten?," *Studia Theologica* 6 (1952), 79ff.; T. C. Vriezen, "Prophecy and Eschatology," *Supplements to Vetus Testament* 1, Leiden, 1953, 199-229.

before." [39] For the prophets, Yahweh's work of destruction (his "alien" work, Is. 28:21) was one aspect of his eschatological activity; in fact, without his destructive work, there would be no new creation. For Israel with her whole religious traditum had to be thrown back to a *Nullpunktsituation*, before the reality of the "new thing" could be known. [40]

In the message of Jeremiah, Ezekiel and Deutero-Isaiah, the sense of the death of Israel as a soteriological community was very strong and vivid; perhaps for that very reason the vision of the renewal of the covenant people was likewise much more clearly articulated than in the previous prophets. As mentioned earlier, these prophets saw a great gulf between the "old" and the "new" realities, "a gulf in whose depths God's people lay dead (Ezek. 37)... In this state, nothing remained for them but to cast their whole being on the future saving act which was already imminent." [41] The shape of the new soteric reality was discerned by the prophets, guided by the radicalized soteric paradigm, along the lines of the old saving history: new covenant, new exodus, new Zion, new David, etc. It is of course not possible here to thoroughly analyze the "new" reality proclaimed by these three prophets; we will note only some representative models which show that the pattern of the sacred tradition shaped the new vision.

In his early years, especially in sympathy with the Deuteronomic revitalization movement, Jeremiah looked for new soteric events which would bring the northern exiles back and reunify the tribes of Israel as David's kingdom at Zion (Jer. 3:11-25; 31:1-22). [42] He saw the coming salvation as an expression of Yahweh's "everlasting love" which compels him to continue his covenant faithfulness, in spite of the continued faithlessness of his people (31:3, 10).

In his disillusionment following the death of Josiah and the resurgence of the antireform party, however, Jeremiah turned increasingly to his vision of the total destruction of Judah and Jerusalem in Yahweh's judgment—yet he continued his earlier theme of Yahweh's design for Israel's salvation in the midst of judgment. His letter to the Jewish exiles in Babylon (Jer. 29) specified that Yahweh still had his design of salvation for those who had already passed through judgment:

---

[39] von Rad, *The Message of the Prophets*, 91.
[40] von Rad, *Theologie*, II, 125.
[41] von Rad, *The Message of the Prophets*, 238.
[42] Theodore M. Ludwig, "The Shape of Hope: Jeremiah's Book of Consolation," *Concordia Theological Monthly* 39 (1968), 527-32.

"I alone know the thoughts I have for you, says Yahweh, thoughts of prosperity and not evil, to give you a future and a hope" (29:11). His symbolic act in buying a field at the time when the Babylonians were throwing up earthworks against the city was a visible promise that Yahweh would see to it that "houses and fields and vineyards shall again be bought in this land" (32:15). Yahweh has promised a new exodus for the exiles and a new planting in their own land never to be uprooted again (24:6). They will be ruled by a new son of David who will fulfill the ancient ideal of executing justice and righteousness as Yahweh's representative, "and Judah will be saved and Israel will dwell in security" (23:5-6; 30:21). The decisive new soteric act was that Yahweh would give his people a "new covenant" relationship with himself, based on a new spirit of knowing Yahweh (31:31-34; 24:7). In all of Jeremiah's prophecy of restoration, however, the discontinuity with the old was never mitigated: life comes through death in new experience of the soteric reality.

Ezekiel, like Jeremiah, made his vision of the death of the covenant people the precondition for renewal of soteric experience. It may be said that no other prophet posited such a deep gulf between past traditum and new experience; the presence of Yahweh's glory departed from the temple and the city, leaving the covenant community to the executioners (Ez. 11:22ff.); all that was left of past glories were dead bones (Ez. 37). But Ezekiel looked for the revival of those dead bones, the house of Israel which had said, "Our bones are dried up, and our hope is lost; we are totally cut off" (37:11). They would be revived in a new soteric experience: "I will put my spirit into you and you shall live, and I will settle you in your own land; then you will know that I, Yahweh, have spoken and will do it" (37:14).

Ezekiel drew from various traditions to flesh out his vision of the new saving event. Like Jeremiah he envisioned a new exodus involving the long lost northern tribes, to be made again into one nation in the land, upon the mountains of Israel. This new kingdom of David would be ruled by one king and shepherd, Yahweh's servant David (Ez. 37:15-25; cf. 34:23-24). But Ezekiel also saw the new salvation especially in the context of the Sinai covenant tradition: "I will be their God, and they shall be my people" (37:27; 34:30). And Ezekiel harked back to the old tradition that Yahweh was the true shepherd and king of his people (34:7-16). The "covenant of peace" with his people involved also blessings of nature and fertility (34:25-29); it was to be an "everlasting covenant" in which Yahweh would "bless and multiply" them—after the pattern of the covenant God made with Noah (37:26). Echoing Jeremiah's pericope on the new covenant, Ezekiel promised that Yahweh would cleanse them from their uncleanness, take out their heart of stone and give them a new heart of flesh, a new spirit which would "cause" them to walk in his statutes (36:24-28). Ezekiel made much use of priestly traditions in describing the ideal new Zion and temple, filled again with the glory of Yahweh (ch. 40-48, esp. 43:2-5). Yahweh would place his sanctuary in their midst for evermore; "then the nations will know that I Yahweh keep Israel sacred to myself" (37:28). Significantly, the name of the city was henceforth to be יהוה שמה, "Yahweh is there" (48:35).

As we have seen earlier, Deutero-Isaiah very sharply marked off the "old" saving history from the "new" soteric realities which were breaking from the bud at the present moment (Is. 43:18-19). The old saving history had come full circle with the destruction and exile, and now the new saving event was on the point of beginning, signalled by the rise of Cyrus and the impending overthrow of the Babylonians. With forceful rhetoric this prophet proclaimed one basic theme to the exiles: the new turn in world history means that Yahweh's advent is imminent, when he will reveal his glory to all the world by delivering his people from Babylon and bringing them back to Jerusalem. Cyrus is his servant, his anointed one, to fulfill Yahweh's will that the exiles return home and that Jerusalem and the temple be rebuilt (cf. esp. Is. 40:1-11; 44:24-28; 45:1-13; 52:7-12).

Of primary interest to us is the relationship between the "old" traditum of Israel and the new saving event, for Deutero-Isaiah makes it very clear that, for all the disjunction in the sacred history, the soteric traditum from the past shapes the vision of the new saving event. Of primary eschatological significance to Deutero-Isaiah was the *Heilsgeschichte* centering on the exodus from Egypt, the journey through the wilderness, and the entry into the promised land; these old saving events provided the pattern for his description of the crucial events of the new age just now breaking forth. [43] Of the many examples of Deutero-Isaiah's use of the exodus tradition as the pattern for the coming saving event, the oracle in Is. 43:14-21 paints the most complete picture:

---

[43] See esp. Is. 40:3-5; 41:17-20; 43:1-3; 48:20-21; 49:8-12; 51:9-11; 52:11-12; 55: 12-13; also Anderson, *op. cit.*, 181-88.

Thus says Yahweh, your redeemer,
    the Holy One of Israel:
I have sent to Babylon for your sake;
    I will lay those fleeing prostrate,
    the Chaldaeans, their triumph shout turned to lament.
I am Yahweh, your Holy One,
    your creator, O Israel, your king.
Thus says Yahweh,
    who opened a way in the sea,
    a path through the mighty waters,
who drew out to destruction chariot and horse,
    a whole army, men of valour;
they lay there, no more to rise,
    they were extinguished, snuffed like a wick.
Remember not the former things
    and do not keep considering the things of old.
Here and now I am doing a new thing!
    This moment it breaks from the bud.
    Do you not know it?
Even in the wilderness I will make a way,
    rivers in the barren desert.
The wild beasts will honor me,
    the jackals and the ostriches;
for I will provide water in the wilderness
    and rivers in the barren desert,
to provide drink for my chosen people,
    the people whom I created for myself,
    so that they will proclaim my praises.

Although the past events should not be "remembered" cultically because of their loss of soteric power for the present, they set the pattern for the new events. Not that there is to be a simple return to the time of the beginning, as if the *Endzeit* were to be a full return to the *Urzeit*; the new event involves a heightening (*Steigerung*) which fills it with fresh soteric meaning.

The most significant aspects of the heightened meaning of the new saving event have to do with the universalizing and cosmicizing of the new exodus. Though the new divine activity was specifically directed toward the new creation of Israel as the covenant community, Deutero-Isaiah saw that it would have an effect for all peoples: "Yahweh has bared his holy arm before the eyes of all the nations, and all the earth from end to end will see our God's salvation" (Is. 52:10; cf. 40:5; 45:22-23). Not only is the exodus event universalized in its paradigmatic saving benefit, but also the patriarchal covenant tradition (42:6-7; cf. Gen. 12:2-3), the royal David tradition (55:3-5), and the Zion tradition (52:7-10).

Like no one before him Deutero-Isaiah cosmicized the divine saving activity; that is, he fused the old cultic creation tradition with the exodus tradition and made this cosmogonic-soteric paradigm the basis of his proclamation of a new cosmic salvation. The creation tradition was certainly well-known in ancient Israel, and it seems clear that cultic representations of creation did in fact associate it with the saving history, as evidenced, for example, in the ancient cultic song in Ex. 15, which associates cosmogonic motifs with the deliverance at the Reed Sea, the conquest of Canaan, and the establishment of Zion. But it is above all in Deutero-Isaiah's words that the cosmogonic basis of the soteric activity is stressed, not as "ancillary" to the exodus tradition or as an "afterthought" but as a heightened mythological structure of religious understanding to provide new strength for the new experience of saving activity. [44] In Is. 51:9-16, for example, the cultic tradition of conflict with chaos and resultant cosmic ordering is connected both with the old exodus and with the new saving event of the return of the exiles to Zion. And in 44:24-28 the cosmogonic work of Yahweh forms the foundation for the new saving activity: the drying of the "deep," the mission of Cyrus, the rebuilding and reinhabiting of Judah and Jerusalem, and the rebuilding of the temple (see also 40:12-31; 42:5-9; 45:9-13, 18-19) .

Thus the remything of the traditum in Deutero-Isaiah reached a high point in the transformation of Israelite religion. He saw the whole earth as the arena of Yahweh's concern, to be reestablished from its current chaos by Yahweh, with the new exodus of Israel and the cosmogonic refounding of Zion and the temple as the center of the new creation. With this vision he set before the disheartened exiles the possibility of a revitalization of their covenant relationship with

---

[44] Gerhard von Rad, "The Theological Problem of the Old Testament Doctrine of Creation," *The Problem of the Hexateuch and Other Essays*, New York, 1966, 134, says the doctrine of creation has only an "ancillary function" in Deutero-Isaiah; Christopher North, *The Second Isaiah*, Oxford, 1964, 13, says the doctrine of creation was "an afterthought" for the Hebrews. But see P. B. Harner, "Creation Faith in Deutero-Isaiah," *VT* 17 (1967), 298-306; Theodore M. Ludwig, "The Traditions of the Establishing of the Earth in Deutero-Isaiah," *JBL* 92 (1973), 345-57; and Dieter Baltzer, *Ezechiel und Deuterojesaja: Berührungen in der Heilserwartung der beiden grossen Exilspropheten*, Berlin, 1971, 181-82, who says, "Statt von der soteriologischen Funktion des alttestamentlichen Schöpfungsglaubens zu reden (G. v. Rad), scheint hier umgekehrt die Soteriologie eine Funktion des Schöpfungsglauben geworden zu sein."

Yahweh and a renewal of their experience of the soteric power of the tradition.

The remythed paradigmatic reality was authenticated in the personal experience of Jeremiah, Ezekiel and Deutero-Isaiah. Thus in a sense they themselves, together with the disciples and the community gathered around them, represented the renewed soteriological community. Just as they symbolically personified the community under judgment and destruction (cf. Jer. 16:1-9; Ez. 24:15-27), so also in their visions and in their actions they represented the new community about to be created. [45]

The exiles lamented, "How can we sing Yahweh's song in a foreign land?", expressing the bewildered sense of loss of identity as a soteriological community. Jeremiah envisioned the restoration of the Davidic community, under the just leadership of a righteous branch from the house of David (Jer. 33:14-16; 23:5-6). But in this new community the flaws of the old covenant would be rooted out; specifically, Yahweh himself would put his torah within the people, writing it on their hearts, so that all the people, from the greatest to the least, would "know" Yahweh (31:31-34). The faithless heart which had doomed the old covenant relationship, the "spirit of adultery" which kept the people from fulfilling their side of the relationship, would finally be healed by new soteric experience (3:22).

Ezekiel's vision of the restored cultic community and the renewed historical and political existence of Israel within their ancestral land was predicated upon prior divine saving action. This divine action would both vindicate the holiness of Yahweh's own name and would cure Israel from her uncleanness:

> I will give you a new heart and put a new spirit within you; I will take out of your body the heart of stone and give you a heart of flesh. And I will put my spirit within you and make you to walk in my statutes and live in observation of my laws. You will live in the land which I gave to your fathers; and you will become my people, and I will become your God (Ez. 36:26-28).

Thus, like Jeremiah, Ezekiel sees the soteriological significance of the new saving events particularly in the new motivation and the new sense of identity as the covenant people which will make the people able finally to live according to the will of Yahweh.

---

[45] See Jer. 32:6-44; Ez. 37; Is. 49:1-6; cf. Lindblom, *Prophecy in Ancient Israel*, 191; Herntrich, *op. cit.*, 35-40; von Rad, *The Message of the Prophets*, 240-44.

Deutero-Isaiah further supplied a new sense of purpose and mission for the people of Yahweh, closely related to his theological view of the universal significance of Yahweh's saving activity. They, the covenant community of Yahweh, were to be witnesses of Yahweh's salvation and glory, created to show forth his praises among the nations (43:7, 10-13, 21; 44:8). Deutero-Isaiah likened the new covenant to the everlasting covenant which Yahweh made with David; however, now all the royal promises and royal mission were transferred to the people themselves:

> I will make with you a covenant, forever,
>   like my steadfast, sure love for David.
> For I made him a witness to all peoples,
>   a prince and a commander for peoples.
> Thus you shall summon nations that you do not know,
>   and nations that knew you not will come running to you,
> because of Yahweh your God, because of the Holy One of Israel,
>   for he has made you glorious (55:3-5). [46]

The renewed community will participate in the glory of Yahweh and thus share in the goal of bringing this glory to all the peoples.

This new sense of mission for the covenant community was of course most completely expressed in the so-called servant songs of Deutero-Isaiah. Without entering into the extensive scholarly debate over the precise interpretation of these songs, it can be assumed here that these songs stem from Deutero-Isaiah himself and that the "servant" is representative of the true people of the covenant. [47] Woven into these songs is an interpretation of Israel's suffering as a participation in Yahweh's concern for his creation, a vicarious suffering which issues in soteric possibility for "the many" (50:6; 53:1-12). The servant is to bear Yahweh's spirit and bring forth truth in the nations (42:1). Not only will the whole people of Israel be restored through this faithful servant, but "I will make you a light to the nations, to be my salvation to the farthest bounds of the earth" (49:5-6).

With this presentation of a vision of the new soteriological com-

---

[46] Cf. Otto Eissfeldt, "The Promises of Grace to David in Isaiah 55:1-5," *Israel's Prophetic Heritage, op. cit.,* 196-207.

[47] See C. R. North, *The Suffering Servant in Deutero-Isaiah,* London, 1948; H. H. Rowley, *The Servant of the Lord and Other Essays,* London, 1952, 3-57; S. Mowinckel, *He That Cometh,* Oxford, 1956, 187-257; W. Zimmerli and J. Jeremias, *The Servant of God,* London, 1957; Otto Kaiser, *Der königliche Knecht,* Göttingen, 1959; Ivan Engnell, "The Ebed-Yahweh Songs and the Suffering Messiah in 'Deutero-Isaiah.' " *BJRL* 31 (1948), 54-93.

munity which as the servant of Yahweh would bring soteric experience to the bounds of the earth, the prophetic transformation of Israelite religion in the neo-Babylonian and early Persian periods reaches a completion of sorts. The prophets have exposed the soteric deficiency of the old traditum under the new social and cultural circumstances, and they rooted out all counterfeit soteriologies. However, on the basis of the radicalized soteric paradigm, the prophets supplied the people with an interpretation of their destruction and with a vision of a new soteriological community created by their covenant God. That the people heeded the call of the prophets and found new soteric experience in their message is evidenced by the fact that the words of these prophets became holy scripture, a part of the sacred traditum itself.

SANGHA, SOCIETY AND THE STRUGGLE FOR NATIONAL INTEGRATION

Burma and Thailand

FRANK E. REYNOLDS AND REGINA T. CLIFFORD

University of Chicago

Theravada Buddhism has generally—and justly—been regarded as one of the most conservative of the great historical religions. But when the Theravada tradition is viewed from the perspective of the history of religions, it immediately becomes evident that Theravada teachings, practices and institutions have been involved in a continuing series of transitions and transformations. The Theravada form of Buddhism first appeared as one of several schools generated by divergences and controversies within the early Buddhist tradition (ca. 5th-3rd centuries B.C.). As Buddhism began to spread beyond the confines of its Indian homeland, the Theravada tradition became the established religion and the dominant civilization force in Sri Lanka, and later assumed a similar role in southeast Asia. During the early and middle centuries of the first millennium A.D. the Theravadins developed new and distinctive patterns of religious and social organizations in Sri Lanka and in various areas of Burma, Thailand, Laos, and Cambodia. More recently (19th and 20th centuries) these various Theravada traditions have become deeply involved in a wrenching struggle to accommodate and adapt new conceptions and institutional patterns emanating from the West.

In the present essay we will focus our attention on the distinctive kind of religio-social ideal that was embedded in the classical forms of Theravada religion. We will then examine the way in which this ideal has traditionally been implemented at the royal and village levels of society in Burma and Thailand. Finally, we will consider some of the ways in which these established Theravada patterns have both affected and been affected by the recent (and still continuing) Burmese and Thai struggles to achieve a modern style of national integration. [1]

---

[1] Since several of the ideas that are basic to this paper were originally formulated in a lengthy discussion between Dean Kitagawa and the authors, it is especially appropriate that the article appear in a volume dedicated to him.

The Buddhist Theory of Action and Ideal Order (Dhamma)

The Theravada religio-social ideal differs significantly from those of many other religious traditions in that it is not a divinely given or pre-existing reality. Rather, this ideal is constituted entirely by human action and is characterized by continual becoming. Thus the empirical and the ideal merge, for social action must be structured according to the ideal if the social order is to embody it. It is by conforming to the cosmic *Dhamma* (Norm or Law) which the Buddha discovered and taught that action makes of the social order an ideal religious order, and specifically an ideal soteriological order. [2]

The Theravadins have expressed their very distinctive religio-social ideal in and through doctrinal, mythic, communal, and ritual modes, all of which participate and interrelate in the greater cosmological framework structured by the law of *kamma* (deeds and their effects). According to the first and normative mode of expression, the doctrinal, the cosmos, including the human world, is characterized by *dukkha* (suffering), *anatta* (the absence of any kind of self), and *anicca* (impermanence). Suffering describes the condition of *samsaric* (this-worldly) existence that arises from actions generated by ignorance of *anatta* and *anicca*. The doctrines of no-self and impermanence are thus the keystones of *dhammic* order.

While within the Buddhist perspective the same entity cannot be said to exist from one moment to the next, the process of flux is by no means random, but is characterized by continuity. The action, the flux that comprises *dhammic* order, is regulated by the cosmic law of moral causation, commonly known as the law of *kamma*. Every action bears *kammic* fruits that are the just retribution for that action, hence there is continuity in flux, there is becoming. Since the law of *kamma* serves both to regulate and generate order based on the nature of the actions constituting it, perfect actions bear *kammic* consequences that perpetuate the *dhammic* order. *Dhammic* order, then, means a dynamic equilibrium that embodies change while it maintains balance and order.

Within the Buddhist orientation, action refers not only to physical acts, but to mental and verbal "acts" as well. Therefore, ignorance of the *dhamma* constitutes action that conflicts with the natural process of becoming and causes the *dhammic* order to degenerate. The cycles

---

[2] For a somewhat different, but complimentary discussion of these issues see Frank E. Reynolds, "Four Modes of Theravada Action," *Journal of Religious Ethics* 7 (1979), 12-27.

of transmigration, known as *samsara*, are fraught with suffering because
they are constituted by actions that embody ignorance of selflessness
and impermanence and, consequently, attachment to the fruits of one's
actions. Knowledge of the *dhamma*, on the other hand, constitutes
action that concurs with the natural process of things causing world
order to regenerate. The prototype of action that embodies selflessness
and impermanence is selfless giving. Its centrality to the generation
of *dhammic* order within society, that is, its generation of a *dhamma-*
realm, accounts for the emphasis it receives both within Buddhism
itself and within this study.

An important implication of the law of *kamma* is that, as a cosmic
law that includes the regulation of human action within its jurisdiction,
it links *causally* in the Buddhist universe what are kept distinct in the
rational, scientific universe, namely morality and physics, or the social
and natural orders. Social action and reaction, therefore, are not played
out strictly within the realm of humans. On the contrary, they rebound
along moral lines throughout the various realms of the cosmos, including the realm of nature. The key formula expressing this relationship and taking a central place in this investigation is as follows:
pure, selfless action generates resplendent order. Given the nature of
kammic law, resplendent order includes both the social and natural
realms within its perfectly balanced, continually regenerating moral
order. It is indicated as much through social categories such as material
wealth and status as through natural, or environmental categories such
as fertile land and timely rain. Resplendent order, then, refers to
humanity and nature *kammically* linked and thriving in response to
moral action that resonates order throughout the universe.

Implicit in this formula for world order is an important difference
between Theravada Buddhist and western notions of efficacious action.
Action that accords with the pure *dhamma* of the Buddha is powerless
in and of itself because it is fully supra-worldly and without regard
for its results. This is not to say, of course, that it bears no results.
On the contrary, action that is selfless has the effect of releasing
resplendent, moral order in the world. The relative purity of an action
brings about a corresponding degree of moral order in the world.
The moral order released is more resplendent the more the action
performed is selfless. This apparent conceptual disjunction in *dhammic*
action between its intention and its effect is pivotal for the social order,
and contrasts strikingly with pragmatic action.

The mythic mode through which the Theravada religio-social ideal has been expressed is clearly represented in the well-known "genesis" story of the Agganna *sutta*. According to this myth, *dhammic* order prevailed at the beginning of time when all action was pure and selfless and therefore *dhammic*. Its results likewise were *dhammic* because all action receives its just result depending upon the degree to which it embodies the *dhamma*. The *dhammic* order implies perfect balance, it is process at its perfect dynamic equilibrium. Humanity and nature, linked by the law of moral causation, participate in this same order, embodying *dhamma*. Hence, when the primordial beings gathered rice, the reason for gathering rice, as well as the physical activity, participated in the natural process of things. Only as much rice was taken as was necessary to satisfy present needs. Because the beings gathered and ate rice in harmony with the natural process of things, the rice grew back spontaneously and the *dhammic* order was maintained.

But, as the *sutta* goes on to relate, the degeneration of the cosmos proceeded, and the *dhamma* of pure and resplendent order was lost when the primordial beings failed to embody the *dhamma*. Rather than pick only that amount of rice necessary to satisfy their present needs, greedy ones began to hoard rice for themselves. They began to act not out of the knowledge of themselves as embodiments of *dhamma* without self and impermanent, but out of the ignorant idea of themselves as particular entities. And they began to be attached to the fruits of their actions, acting pragmatically and selfishly, rather than *dhammically* and altruistically.

Because these primordial beings failed to understand themselves as embodiments of *dhammic* order, and so failed to act according, their world, in *kammic* response, failed to embody *dhamma*. Further, because their actions embodied ignorance, suffering arose in the world. Since they no longer embodied knowledge and the acceptance of becoming, *dhammic* order degenerated. Once it had been set in motion, the process of degeneration further reduced the level of *dhamma* embodied in the world, causing actions to be less efficacious. The conceptualization of the phenomenal world (*samsara*) as cycles of transmigration is reflected in the circular or spiraling relation between the purity of action and the efficacy of subsequent action that is possible as a result.

The communal expression of the Theravada ideal is epitomized in the distinctive relationship that is maintained between the laity and the *sangha* (monastic order). The this-worldly/supra-worldly distinction between laity and *sangha* not only makes possible, but indeed institutionalizes selfless action as an effective, practical mode of action that is

4

capable of achieving world order. Again the ideal merges with the real and pragmatic. Realizing the ideal of the "genesis" myth in society, the monks through their actions embody a high degree of selflessness and goodness. As in the myth the natural order responds with splendid and spontaneous regeneration, so the laity respond with material support and honor. Indeed, selfless action is *practical* action for the monks because unless they direct all their actions toward a supra-worldly, altruistic embodiment of the pure *dhamma*, they will not be worthy of lay support and deference. Furthermore, if their actions are not pure, they will not effect resplendent world order. *Kammically*, if their actions do not embody *dhamma*, the results of their actions will not embody *dhamma*. Hence, a lax *sangha* threatens social degeneracy.

The relation between the monks and the laity is crucial to the Theravada social order. Within the Theravada system, the ideal order consists in the fundamental division into two interrelated yet distinct aspects. In the Theravada idiom these are identified as two wheels of *dhamma* that are cosmologically linked by *kammic* law, and sociologically linked by selfless giving. The two wheels are embodied in the social order in the monastic and lay paths of action, and designate respectively the *dhamma* of pure action and the *dhamma* of resplendent world order. They are as two gears, both of which are necessary to the soteriological machinery of cosmos and society. Selfless giving sets these wheels in motion and, to varying *kammic* degrees that are evidenced in the hierarchical order of society, constitutes the commonality of all Buddhists whether monastic or lay. The key context for selfless giving and for the engagement of the two wheels is the merit-making ritual. [3]

The last of the four modes of expression, the ritual, not only articulates the social structure but, indeed, constitutes and legitimates it. Specifically, it is the rituals of merit-making that express the soteriological structure of the social order and make the social order into a *dhamma*-realm. Because they create the context in which action can achieve *dhammic* purity, these rituals actualize the pure *dhammic* order of original times and effect regeneration of the social order. The key dynamic resides in the perfect act of selfless giving. The significance of the gift calls for further elaboration because it activates the Buddhist social/soteriological order.

---

[3] For a study of the early development of the "two wheel" pattern see Reynolds' lead essay in *Two Wheels of Dhamma*, ed. B. Smith, AAR Monograph Series No. 3, Chambersburg, Penna., 1972.

The significance of a gift pivots on an underlying dynamic of exchange that is simple though paradoxical: one must give in order to have. What one receives depends upon to whom or to what one gives. For instance, if one gives to someone who has less than oneself, one establishes and indicates unequal socio-economic statuses, namely one's superior position. Similarly, if one gives to an equal, the return gift will reflect equality. Within the Buddhist cosmological system, society is one realm, and as such is regulated in all of its constitutive actions by the law of *kammic* retribution. All the strictly social trans-actions necessary to keep society going fall into the category of action with attachment to the fruits of that action. Therefore, as with these secular exchanges, to expect material returns on gifts implicates one in worldly *samsaric* concerns; but to give without thought of material returns breaks one's bond to worldly attachments. By emphasizing giving without material exchange, Buddhism transcends the social/ *samsaric* exchange system and creates a social/soteriological exchange system. Only when action embodies some degree of supra-worldliness, some degree of selflessness that is commensurate with one's place in the moral and social hierarchy, does it result in merit and world order.

According to the social/soteriological structure of Theravada society, the monk pursues the morally higher path of the Buddha and clearly in Burma and Thailand holds the position of preeminent status, higher than any lay person including the king. Selfless giving by the laity to the *sangha* launches the laity on their upwardly mobile social/soterio-logical path. As a result of selfless giving, the laity earn merit which manifests itself in the world as greater power such as greater wealth and status. Giving to the *sangha* is necessarily part of the social/ soteriological, as opposed to social/*samsaric*, exchange because the monks, being temporally powerless, have no material goods to ex-change. Instead, they give to the laity the opportunity to make merit by accepting lay offerings on either an individual or community scale, and by giving edifying sermons expounding the teachings of the Buddha. The laity, therefore, engage the monks in an assymetrical exchange: material goods for spiritual rewards.

In the context of their exchange relationship, the monk and layperson can be seen to stand on a continuum based on selfless giving. For the householder to observe the five Buddhist precepts brings about less merit than for the householder to give a son, or robes, to the *sangha*. The most meritorious action for the typical householder is not the practice of the five precepts, because that activity alone only makes one a poor monk; rather, the most meritorious action for the typical householder is the giving of material wealth. As a householder one must give materially in order to embody the *dhamma* of world order and to perfect selfless giving in accordance with the lay path. The monk, on the other hand, has offered the ultimate gift: he has offered himself to the pure *dhamma* embodied in the *sangha*. Hence, he no longer embodies the *dhamma* of resplendent order, but the *dhamma* of pure action which has as a by-product the generation of world order.

The monastic path leads to *nibbana* (salvation or release) while the lay path leads only to better rebirth within *samsara*. The paradox is, however, that *samsara* is at once the basis and antithesis of *nibbana*. In order to attain *nibbana* or release from the *kammically* conditioned existence that is *samsara*, one must realize the nature of *samsara* as *dukkha, anatta, and anicca,* and then perfect that realization by embodying it in all one's actions. Hence, as *samsara* is both the basis and antithesis of *nibbana*, so the lay path is both the basis and antithesis of the monastic path. The quantitative difference in selfless giving between monk and layperson becomes qualitative when one encounters the world as it really is and gives oneself totally to the *dhamma* by entering the monastic path. Yet, as *samsara* is necessary to *nibbana*, so the lay path and the world order that the laity generate through their *kammic* actions are necessary to the monastic path and the pure action that the monks embody. The ritual of merit-making is the dynamic that establishes, affirms, and maintains their paradoxical relation. Thus it assumes paramount importance in authenticating the social order as a *dhamma*-realm.

As related in the Aggaññña *sutta*, the monks constitute the perfect primordial humans, while the laity constitute the resplendent power of the natural world order. As a result of the monk's pure and selfless action, the laity prosper, they bear children, they enjoy successful and abundant harvests, they own healthy livestock, and so on. The monks for their part, offer themselves selflessly to the pure *dhamma* and, as a result, the *dhamma* of world order flourishes thereby enabling the laity to continue to support the monks in their ascetic and renunciative endeavor. Thus the soteriological universe or *dhamma*-realm that is created in this exchange contains the paradox of *samsara* and *nibbana* which is also the paradox of the lay and monastic paths.

However, there is still another dimension to the gift which plays in counter-point to the monks' morally superior status. It is that as the givers, the laity are superior to the monks who are powerless without them, who depend on the laity to support them, and who, without the laity, could not even be monks at all. So while according to the system, it is true that the laity depend on the monks for their prosperity, it is also true that the monks depend on the laity for their support. As the necessary providers of spiritual well-being, the monks are superior; however, as the necessary providers of material well-being, the lay householders are superior.

This tension lies at the very heart of the Theravada tradition in the two wheel structure of its social/soteriological order. The tension is creative toward establishing and authenticating a legitimate social order in so far as it finds expression and periodic resolution in the merit-making rituals. However, merit-making rituals have not always sufficed to maintain the two wheels in balanced tension, and the history of Theravada societies bears witness to the destruction of established order by the actualization of certain other "orders" that exist as possibilities within the tradition itself. 4 Indeed, this structural tension is crucial to a historical understanding of the Theravada tradition generally, and of the societies of Burma and Thailand in particular. While it is curious that the same structure facilitates both stability and disruption of the established order, it is all the more interesting that stability and instability tend largely to characterize the village and capital, respectively. The following sections will examine three major units of social order, namely the capital, the state, and the village, for clues that might shed light on this particularity.

The Capital as Dhamma *Realm*

As virtually all other social units within Theravada society, the capital embodies the two wheel structure of *dhammic* order. In contrast to other units such as the village, however, the capital operates at a high level of *dhammic* expression, not only during merit-making ceremonies, but all the time. In fact, that is the nature of a capital and the basis of its position as the center and ordinating principle of the kingdom.

---

4 In contrast to the traditional two wheel structure, there occur temporary millenarian *dhamma*-realms that are created and characterized by incorporation and hence collapse the two wheels into a single person identified structurally and/or functionally with Buddhahood. Ideally, the presence of a Buddha, such as the future Buddha Metteya, would bring about the centralization of the moral and socio-political hierarchy because all beings, monastic and lay alike, would submit to the Buddha's unparalleled purity and power, the Buddha's superior order. However, the actual historical results of attempts to establish such *dhamma*-realms have been quite disruptive and short-lived.

Culminating the lay path is the king, the most meritorious of all laity. On the basis of incalculably greater merit than all other house-holders accumulated through selfless action over many life-times, the king takes his rebirth at the apex of the lay order. While *kammic* law as the governing force behind rebirth provides the initial legitimacy with which he begins his reign, the king nevertheless must continue to embody the ideal, to act according to the *dhamma* of world order if he is to hold his position legitimately. Two key models of action that a king must embody to evidence continued legitimacy are those of the king of the gods, Indra, and of the lay Buddhist ideal, the *bodhisatta* (future Buddha). While Indra protects and oversees the *dhammic* order from his throne atop the cosmic Mount Meru, the king, as the human embodiment of Indra, protects and oversees the *dhammic* order of the kingdom from his throne atop the socio-political hierarchy. As the embodiment of the *bodhisatta* ideal, the king seeks to facilitate the soteriological quest of all beings within his *dhamma*-realm.

Culminating the monastic path are the most meritorious monks in the kingdom. On the basis of incalculably greater merit than all others, accumulated through the perfection of selfless action in accordance with the *vinaya*, the monastic rule, these monks take up residence in the capital, the most pure and resplendent of *dhamma*-realms. Again, while *kammic* law provides the initial facility with which these monks practice the *vinaya*, they are nevertheless expected to continue to em-body the *dhamma* of pure, selfless action. Thus they maintain their position and effect resplendent order within the community as a whole.

The capital embodies, then, the two wheel structure of *dhammic* order common to virtually all Theravada social units, but more speci-fically it hosts the highest status adherents of both paths. In both Burma and Thailand, royalty is the symbol of and idiom for describing high status, regardless of whether one's status derives from the lay or monastic path. [5] Hence not only is the king, the householder of highest status, referred to as the *dhammaraja*, lord of the *dhamma*, but the monk of highest status similarly is referred to as the *sangharaja*, the lord of the *sangha*. Royal terms, therefore, do not designate secular status only, but high status generally. The distinction between the this-worldly and supra-worldly orientations that characterizes the lay and monastic paths becomes all the more important to maintain in

---

[5] For a fascinating discussion of this ambivalence of royal categories see Steven Kemper, "The Social Order of the Sinhalese Buddhist Sangha," unpub. Ph.D. diss., The University of Chicago, 1973, 202ff.

light of the use of royal terms to describe high status. The ambivalence in the monk-householder relation with regard to superiority is heightened by their similar royal designations. By maintaining the clarity of their respective orientations, a relationship of complementarity can be achieved by the monk and the householder. Nevertheless, the possibility of competition and even incorporation always exists.

The prestige and legitimacy of the capital stems from its cosmologically-based conjunction of the most exalted embodiments of the two wheels of *dhamma*. Because of the degree of *dhamma* actualized in the capital, it provides a domain of action that replicates the *dhammic order* of primordial times and is particularly efficacious in furthering the quest for salvation pursued by all Buddhists within the kingdom. Merit-making rituals effecting the exchange of selfless action and resplendent world order affirm and engage the two wheels, and so create and legitimate the capital as the *dhamma*-realm *par excellence*. Also, because high status levels exacerbate the already tensive relation between the two paths—a problem that will become clearer a little later in the discussion of inclusive hierarchy—merit-making rituals are important in maintaining the discreteness of the two paths and their respective this-worldly and supra-worldly orientations.

In both Burma and Thailand the royal *kathin*, or robe offering ceremony, is one of the most important of the Buddhist merit-making rituals that serves to establish the capital as a preeminent *dhamma*-realm. It takes place at the end of the Vassa, or Buddhist Lent. While there seem to be slight variations between the traditional *kathin* ceremonies of Burma and Thailand, their more essential similarities allow generalizations to be posited for both.

According to H. G. Q. Wales, the Thai royal *kathin* was the most important Buddhist ceremony in which the king traditionally played a predominant role. [6] As the embodiment of the *dhamma* of world order, the king personally or by proxy offers gifts to the monks of the royal monasteries. Royal monasteries are those which are supported by the king and are generally cooperative with the political order. By accepting material support, the monks of the prestigeous royal monasteries extend necessary legitimation to the king as patron and protector of the *sasana*, the Buddhist religion. Because there are royal monasteries located both within the capital and throughout the kingdom, the *dhamma*-realm created in the ritual interaction of monks and

---

[6] H. G. Q. Wales, *Siamese State Ceremonies*, London, 1931, 199-212.

king extends beyond the capital and incorporates the entire kingdom.

According to the logic of *dhammic* action, action by the king for the good of his subjects finds its highest expression and efficacy not in direct support of them, but in support of the pure *dhamma*. Indeed, the king legitimates his position by displaying his merit and power, and by deploying it selflessly for the soteriological good of his subjects. It is interesting in this regard that when the royal procession proceeded through the canals of Bangkok to the various royal monasteries, the barge which in other ceremonies typically served to convey the king himself, was loaded with the royal gifts. The king and royal family followed in another barge. The substitution was significant in indicating the heightened selflessness of the king's giving as well as the identity between the king and his gifts.

Upon reaching the royal monastery the king first pays homage to the Buddha. He then offers the gifts to those monks who have attained "fruitfulness in holy living" and who practice the rules of monastic etiquette. These stipulations ensure that these are not ordinary monks but monks sufficiently accomplished in the practice of selfless action according to the monastic rule. Furthermore, by maintaining high standards in the royal monasteries, the king ensures that greater merit and moral order will be released in the world by the veneration of such pure monastic embodiments of the *dhamma*.

After receiving the offers of the king, the monks reciprocate with a blessing: [7]

> May you live over one hundred years in the fullness of vigour, free from disease and happy; may all your wishes be fulfilled, all your works accomplished, all advantages accrue to you; may you always triumph and succeed, O Paramindra (the king's name), august Sovereign. May it be so forever! We beg to tender (to you) this blessing.

This blessing provides an excellent description of the ideal conditions that obtain in a *dhamma*-realm. It is a domain of action that is created by the merit-making exchange between the highest status of laity and monks. Actions within this domain are extremely efficacious, unobstructed by obstacles such as disease and mental anguish, because they embody such an abundance of *dhamma*.

After receiving the monks' blessing and again paying homage to the Buddha, the king departs. Having visited all the royal monasteries

---

[7] *Ibid.*, 205.

where he planned to personally offer gifts and robes, the king holds a great feast for all who participated in the *kathin* as well as the general public. The feast also serves to evidence the success and legitimacy of the king as the fullest embodiment of resplendent world order and further, to draw all subjects in the land into the beneficence of the king's order. Through his selfless action in honor of the monks, the king creates a *dhamma*-realm, and at this stage of the ceremony his crucial role in the establishment of *dhammic* order is recognized.

Throughout the kingdom similar ceremonies take place, many under the sponsorship of the king who obviously cannot personally attend all, and many, though of much smaller scale, under the independent sponsorship of nobles, wealthy patrons, and village communities. The entire kingdom expresses the purity and righteous power of a *dhamma*-realm; however, the capital expresses its encompassment of all others by virtue of the king's superlative embodiment of the *dhamma* of world order and the monks' superlative embodiment of the *dhamma* of pure action. Only the capital conjoins such high levels of selfless action and moral order and so, by extension, only the capital provides such a context of efficacious action.

The process of creating a *dhamma*-realm that includes all lesser ones within it expresses the particular Buddhist logic of incorporative or inclusive hierarchy. It is with this logic that the capital asserts its preeminence as the center and ordinating principle of the kingdom, seeking thereby to mediate world order and salvation to all other *dhamma*-realms. The logic of inclusive hierarchy also, of course, serves to subordinate all others to the superior efficacy of the capital. The way the moral hierarchy operates is closely related to the way spiritual progress is understood within the tradition. Advancement means that with the perfection of each of the Buddhist virtues one improves the performance of all previously practiced virtues as well. For example, at a relatively early stage of spiritual development, physical, verbal, and mental action remains very much within the concrete, external, and instrumental realm. This is illustrated by the lay path's emphasis on meritorious deeds in order to gain better rebirth. As action accrues more and more merit and becomes purer and purer, it becomes more and more internalized and effective. The advancement may be characterized as inclusive or incorporative. In terms of the eightfold noble path, action proceeds from the practice of morality, to the practice of meditation, to the practice of insight or wisdom. With each successive state action becomes less and less conscious practice, and more and more internalized discipline. Spiritual advancement, in other words, signifies a progression that does not leaves the previous stage behind, but rather incorporates it into the next stage. Such is the dynamic of *kamma* and rebirth such that previous action informs the present situation. Hence, the king occupying the apex of the lay social/soteriological hierarchy includes all beneath him in the merit and order of his rebirth status. Recalling the discussion above on the gift, the moral hierarchy based on selfless action crosses the boundary between this-worldly and supra-worldly, between laity and monks. So monks of high status, of high purity and spiritual power, likewise, include all beneath them in their status. The capital, therefore, embodying the two wheel structure of *dhamma* in the fullest expression of each, includes all other *dhamma*-realms within its order.

Perhaps the most significant repercussion of the logic of inclusive hierarchy is that which is felt in the political arena. The logic of inclusive hierarchy provides the important ideological underpinning for the centralization of the Theravada kingdom under the capital. A high degree of centralization depends upon the legitimacy of the capital as *dhamma*-realm. If the two wheel structure, tensive though it may be, is not maintained but is collapsed in the claims of a king for monastic achievements, or of a monk for royal jurisdiction, the capital ceases to be a legitimate paradigm of order and fails to effectively centralize the kingdom. The two wheel structure becomes unstable at the capital because of the potential for conflict that exists in the delicate but volatile relationship between the principle of inclusive hierarchy and the qualitative difference between the two paths. When the two wheel structure collapses the typical reason is that one path has sought to incorporate the other rather than uphold its qualitative difference.

However, if the two wheel structure is maintained, the ideological basis upon which the capital's legitimacy rests is secure and typically convincing. Then the soteriological order of the capital extends throughout the kingdom overriding lesser lights such as provincial capitals and villages by incorporating them in the superior merit and power of its domain of action. The religious and socio-political orders become identified and, as a result, such merit-making rituals as the royal *kathin* serve to affirm the political and religious legitimacy of the king's order. Such merit-making ceremonies centralize the kingdom by effectively doubling as ceremonies of Buddhist soteriology and political allegiance.

The State as Oscillating Order

In marked contrast to the picture of the Theravada kingdom as a centralized and hierarchical order linked in its various constitutive parts to the ideal soteriological cosmos through the mediation of the capital is another view that must be considered. This is the view of the kingdom as a congeries of autonomous peoples ranging from vassal states to small scale villages both in the valleys and in the hill country. Seen in this perspective, each unit maintains the integrity of its own internal power structure and cosmology regardless of the status of its relation to the capital.

The importance of the capital's cosmological and soteriological position in maintaining order throughout the rest of the kingdom pivots on an ideological rather than an historical assessment of the situation. Because, for all the cosmological and soteriological order reflected in its architecture, ritual cycle, and socio-political structure, the capital has traditionally suffered considerable political instability and frequent physical looting and destruction. If the people of the surrounding areas believed that the order of cosmos, nature, and society depended on the capital, why did these units not undergo serious crisis when the life of the capital was disrupted?

The answer nags at the neat schema that posits the religious and political centrality of the capital: the surrounding satellites did not necessarily accept the capital as their symbolic center. The autonomous groups, being quite capable of taking care of the cosmological and soteriological order themselves, were in fact little affected by the turmoil and vicissitudes of the capital. While the court chronicles and state rituals present the king both as Indra and a *bodhisatta*, his military campaigns, corvees, and taxes still tended to identify him as one of the five evils that befall the surrounding peoples. From its own ideological viewpoint, the capital constituted the normative embodiment of a soteriologically ordered cosmos, but from the perspectives of the various autonomous groups within the capital's sphere of influence, it was a provisional or secondary embodiment to which only formal assent was given, frequently in acknowledgement of the capital's superior military strength. The primary embodiment, however, continued to be the particular autonomous entity itself.

Theravada kingdoms of Southeast Asia knew very little political and territorial stability. Depending on the fluctuations of the capital's fortunes, the kingdom expanded to include surrounding villages, provinces and vassal states or contracted to little more than the villages in the immediate vicinity of the capital. There were no set boundaries. Indeed, prior to Western colonialism and specifically the arrival of the British and French who divided Southeast Asia between them thereby imposing set boundaries, the modern states of Burma and Thailand did not exist as such. Rather, the better known Burmese and Thai capitals were only several, albeit historically the suzerains, among the wide variety of political and religious centers. The traditional Southeast Asian kingdom therefore, comprised an order that oscillated between moments of strength and centralization and moments of weakness and decentralization. The process of oscillation may be fruitfully approached through the relationship between the religious order and rituals on the one hand, and political centralization and decentralization on the other. [8]

The proper relation between the king and the *sasana* (religion) and hence the legitimacy of the capital as a *dhamma*-realm is closely related to the political centralization of the kingdom. If the king ensures high standards of monastic discipline, that is if he maintains the supra-worldly orientation of the monks, and maintains his own position as the embodiment of world order and as patron of the *sasana*, he furnishes some of the key pre-conditions for political centralization. The *sangha* provides the king with the legitimacy necessary for effective rule. Under a strong and effective king factionalism within the *sangha* will tend to be minimal and generally supportive. The reasons for this include a genuine belief in the legitimacy of a strong and just king, the capabilities of the leaders of the *sangha* hierarchy whom he appoints and, if necessary, the availability of the force needed to coerce any monks who may refuse to conform. Since the existence or character of *sangha* factionalism makes an important statement concerning the legitimacy and efficacy of a king's reign, he must do his best to control or direct it.

Factions arise within the Theravada *sangha* not so much on the basis of doctrinal differences but rather on the basis of differences concerning the monastic discipline. [9] The factions legitimize their formation by claiming their action to be a return to orthodoxy through strict

---

[8] Stanley Tambiah has used the colorful term "pulsating galactic polity" to characterize the pre-modern political situation in southeast Asia. For an excellent discussion see his *World Conqueror, World Renouncer*, Cambridge, 1976.

[9] For an excellent study of this kind of factionalism see E. M. Mendelson, *Sangha and State in Burma*, ed. John Ferguson, Ithaca, 1975; for the Thai situation, see Christine Gray, "The Politics of the Middle Way: A Study of King Mongut's Monastic Career," unpub. M.A. diss., The University of Chicago, 1977.

adherence to the *vinaya*. They contend that they are not creating schism within the *sangha*, which is traditionally considered a grievous offense, but rather that they are reforming and purifying the *sangha* in order to strengthen it. How stringently a faction observes the *vinaya* and how effectively its elders trace their lineage indicates the faction's degree of purity in the renunciation of worldly concerns, and hence its spiritual power and prestige.

If a faction arises that refuses cooperation with the main body of the *sangha* on the basis of sangha laxity, it effectively brings into question the legitimacy not only of the rest of the sangha, but of the king and the kingdom as well. While the reform faction may choose to remain unaffiliated with the political order, as many Burmese factions have, the possibility nevertheless exists that a political group aspiring to take over the government may affiliate with the reform faction through merit-making exchange. Such an affiliation would constitute a *dhamma*-realm capable of competing with the *dhamma*-realm of the king and the unreformed *sangha*. Needless to say, the process of centralization is inhibited by such factionalizing, and it behooves the king to attempt to unify the *sangha* or at least to prevent the alienation of the factions which do exist.

In order to centralize the kingdom a strong king demonstrates and guarantees the legitimacy of the capital as *dhamma*-realm not only by maintaining unity in the *sangha*, but also by establishing an encompassing hierarchy through rituals such as the ceremony of drinking the waters of allegiance. The oath of allegiance required of all officials including royal family, governors, and vassal princes, provides an excellent example of the importance of Buddhist notions of hierarchy in the establishment and maintenance of political centralization.

Prior to the 1932 *coup d'etat*, the ceremony of drinking the waters of allegiance took place two times a year in Thailand, and prior to the British occupation, the ceremony took place three times a year in Burma. This difference in frequency may reflect a chronically more turbulent political situation in Burma which the oath of allegiance was designed to allay. In any event, at these times all subjects of the king, especially royalty and nobles, were obliged to take the oath of allegiance, and then to drink specially consecrated water. It was reportedly not uncommon for some participants to contract cholera after having drunk the water which, of course, was interpreted to mean that that person had committed rebellious acts of thought, word, or deed.

The three jewels of Buddhism as well as a variety of deities witness the ceremony and serve as potential sources of enforcement. Should any disloyal acts occur, the participants vowed: [10]

> We pray to the deities of lands and forests; the guardian deities; the atmospheric deities; the goddesses who care for the earth, especially the powerful deities who are located where is the great white Umbrella, emblem of royalty, may plague us with evil, destroy our lives... when we shall have departed this life from earth, cause us to be sent and all to be born in the great hell, where we shall burn with quenchless fire for... limitless transmigrating; and when we have expiated our penalty there... Let us not meet the Buddha, the sacred teachings, the sacred priests... should we meet them let them grant us no assistance.

From this graphic passage emerges the picture of the kingdom as the cosmos, and the king as the legitimate culmination of cosmic order and hierarchy. The entire cosmos attests to the legitimacy of the king and to the power and purity centralized in him. The soteriological dimension is implicit in this moral hierarchy, and is further heightened by the possibilities for action that will effect one's rebirth and one's ultimate hopes for the attainment of *nibbana*. The hierarchy of the kingdom implies the spirit realms as well as the political realms. It is an all-encompassing hierarchical order whose legitimacy derives from its structure as a *dhamma*-realm.

The oath of allegiance demands loyalty under pain of cosmic and soteriological consequences, and an affirmation of subordinance within the inclusive hierarchy of the capital and kingdom. It establishes the *dhammic* cosmology to which all must submit because of the superior power of the *dhamma*; it leaves intact, however, the internal organization of the vassal states and provinces. Quite a bit of leeway is granted to the various groups within the kingdom and in most matters local custom is allowed to prevail. The basic demands upon subject groups are that their leaders take the oath of allegiance, that they provide tribute and taxes, and that they contribute the manpower necessary for military campaigns and royal corvees. Thus despite the high degree of ostensible centralization a strong king can effect, the various groups within the kingdom never relinquish their latent potential for autonomy.

The *stupa* cult provides another key mode whereby soteriological ritual doubles as a political activity that serves to locate the culmination of hierarchy and centralization in the capital. *Stupas* (memorial monuments which, ideally at least, contain a relic of the Buddha) are

---

[10] Wales, *op. cit.*, 194.

particularly significant because as symbols and embodiments of world order, either constructed or repaired by a strong king, they tacitly identify the king with the Buddha as the universal sovereign who generates world order through selfless action. This tacit identification between the king and the Buddha lends considerable weight to the king's bid for legitimacy. It is a delicate issue, however, because should the identification cease to be tacit and indeed protested by the king, he can be accused of violating the boundary line between the path of the monk and the path of the layperson. The veneration of the *stupa* by local peoples and pilgrims links their soteriological action to socio-political action, thereby constituting and maintaining the state as an all encompassing *dhamma*-realm. For example, Dhammaceti, a king of the Mon kingdom in lower Burma whose name literally means *dhammic stupa*, either built or repaired *stupas* in each of the thirty-two provinces that comprised his kingdom on sites that were historically centers of local spirit authority. By either building or refurbishing the *stupas* on these sites, he sought to override the local powers by incorporating them into the *dhamma*-realm of the capital.

Yet no matter what degree of centralization a strong king managed to achieve, it would quickly disintegrate under a weak successor. At the first sign of a decline in merit as evidenced by inadequate displays of wealth, a loss of military strength, or the emergence of factionalism in the *sangha*, the always latent autonomy of local groups would reassert itself. The king would soon lose his ability to bring provincial governors and vassal princes to the capital to take the oath of allegiance, and would find it impossible to keep the *stupas* in repair and the cult effective. Whatever tacit identification might have existed between the king and the Buddha would quickly dissipate with an ineffective leader on the throne. The kingdom would once again become a congeries of autonomous socio-political units and, in the case of Buddhist socio-political units, autonomous *dhamma*-realms. The next section examines the village as just such an autonomous *dhamma*-realm.

The Village as Dhamma Realm

Every village must have its temple, no matter how modest, no matter how few monks it houses. That is, the village, like the capital, must embody the two wheels of *dhamma* if it is to authenticate itself within traditional Theravada society. The ideological autonomy of the village derives from its structure as a *dhamma*-realm. Because the village embodies the soteriological ideal, because it is a *dhamma*-realm, it is perfectly capable of taking care of the cosmological and soteriological order itself quite apart from the king, the capital, and the kingdom. In contrast to the undependable order of the capital and the oscillating character of the state, the village demonstrates significant autonomy and stability. A number of important differences between the village and the capital contribute to this.

To begin, the tension between the two wheels finds sufficient acknowledgement and hence periodic resolution in both individual and community-wide merit-making rituals so that as a rule neither lay purification nor monastic reform are needed. Related to this difference, the hierarchical ordering of society intrinsic to the capital and state is largely absent from the more egalitarian ordering of village society. Hence, the tendency implicit in the principle of hierarchy to try to incorporate one path into the other is likewise diminished. Furthermore the village is not particularly concerned to establish an empire subordinating other villages to itself. In most cases the village seeks to enhance its status as a *dhamma*-realm so as to enhance its effectiveness on a more strictly soteriological level.

Village life is replete with a variety of ceremonies centered on lay/ *sangha* exchanges through which the village's identity as a *dhamma*-realm is continually established and reestablished. While clearly the least elaborate of these merit-making ceremonies, the daily offering of food to the monks is nevertheless the most universal and the most fundamental. In addition annual ceremonies such as the village *kathin* perform the same function on a grander and more extensive scale. But the village ceremony that is perhaps the most interesting in this connection is the initiation of a boy or young man into the *sangha*.

Initiation into the *sangha* is the most meritorious and elaborate of the merit-making ceremonies that are likely to occur in the village. Only sponsoring the building of a temple brings more merit and prestige to the sponsor and to the participating community, but with its cost so phenomenal, such a project is an extraordinary event far beyond the means of any ordinary villager. The initiation ceremony, on the other hand, holds a very prominent place within the range of social responsibilities that a husband and wife have to their son and to their community. In Burma the ceremony seems to have even more social significance than in Thailand. While an important rite of passage in both countries, a more elaborate ceremony and a more opulent material display are mandatory dimensions of the Burmese initiation. Indeed, in Burma, it is better not to sponsor an initiation at all than to sponsor a modest affair. And it is not at all uncommon for a wealthy layperson to sponsor an initiation for the son of a villager who lacks the necessary funds.

Within the context of the ritual, the initiate assumes the status of a prince. The manifest purpose of this is to invoke the image of Gotama Buddha as the prince Siddattha prior to his renunciation of temporal power and wealth for the life of the mendicant monk. But this interpretation is further compounded with the general descriptive significance that the royal idiom holds for high status whether monastic or lay. To enter the *sangha* evidences a great deal of merit and power that is best described in royal terms. Moreover the merit-making ritual itself establishes a context of concentrated *dhammic* order such as that portrayed in the Agganna *sutta* or in the capital.

The royal theme does not stop there. Indeed, the young prince is carried on a palanquin in a royal procession comprised of village elders, relatives, and friends all dressed in their finest, bearing offerings and royal insignia. The prince and his entourage proceed to the site of an imitation palace that has been constructed specially for the occasion. It is truly a gala affair in which all who participate in the royal procession evince the merit and power that characterizes royalty and abounds in a truly *dhammic* world. The spirit of royal abundance and *dhammic* resplendence is signified by a plentitude of food, at this point typically cakes and tea. An orchestra provides music; and in some cases there is the recitation of a traditional version of the history of the area.

A prominent ethnographer captures many of the important themes in a segment of his narrative description of a particular initiation he observed in Upper Burma: [11]

> Next a conch shell and water are used to play the tune of Asoka, the manifest meaning being blessing and fertility. The village and the people attending are compared to the mythical past times of better mortals, greater prosperity, and sounder morality.

In this account three particular striking elements are recorded. First, attention is called to the paradoxical presence of symbols of fertility and blessing in the midst of a ritual which has, as its primary purpose, the initiation of a young boy into the ascetic life of the *sangha*. Second, it is the "village and the people attending [that] are compared to the mythical past times of better mortals, greater prosperity, and sounder

[11] Manning Nash, "Ritual and Ceremonial Cycle in Upper Burma," *Anthropological Studies in Theravada Buddhism*, ed. M. Nash, New Haven, 1966, 109.

morality," not simply the monks. And third, the reference to King Asoka highlights the fact that the *dhamma*-realm that is portrayed in the village ceremony is permeated with royal themes. An examination of these three points will provide a deeper insight into the ceremony and its social implications.

The association between material well-being and monastic renunciation can be understood in terms of the paradoxical merit-making exchange between this-worldly order and supra-worldly action. With the gift of a son to the *sangha*, the lay householders offer the utmost of their fertility and prosperity. In accordance with the logic of exchange implicit in the gift, the householders, the embodiments of the *dhamma* of world order, give of their fertility and prosperity, their merit and power, in order that through the presence of a revitalized *sangha* their fertility and prosperity may be still further enhanced.

In the central Thai context the fact that the initiate is not (as in Burma) a boy who becomes a novice, but rather a sexually maturing young man who becomes a fully ordained monk, gives added significance to the gift. By renouncing his sexuality at this crucial stage of his development, the initiate sublimates potentially chaotic power into the moral power of world order. Emphasizing the ambivalent power inherent in nature and sexuality, the initiate is called *naga*, or serpent. According to tradition, this practice began in the time of the Buddha when [12]

> A *naga* assumed human shape and was ordained a Buddhist monk in order to obtain more quickly a human nature. But his true nature having been disclosed in his sleep, he was expelled from the monastery by Buddha. (Mahavagga I, 63, 1-4). But in leaving he asked that he might make of his name an offering to Buddha and this was granted, hence candidates now bear the name *naga*.

The *naga* as monk thus signifies nature and sexuality that in being sacrificed or offered through monastic discipline engendered moral order. [13]

Similarly, the spirits or *nats* of Burma and to a lesser extent the

---

[12] K. E. Wells, *Thai Buddhism: Its Rites and Activities*, Bangkok, 1960, 135.

[13] This conception of the *naga* as monk is reflected in other contexts such as the Bun Phaawes ritual in northeastern Thailand. In this ritual a series of conflicts are depicted in which the great *naga* monk named Uppakrut (Skt. Upagupta) who personifies the moral power in nature and sexuality prevails over Mara, the Buddha's classic antagonist and the personification of nature out of control and threatening destruction and chaos. For a full discussion see Stanley Tambiah, *Buddhism and Spirit Cults in Northeastern Thailand*, London, 1970, 300-04.

spirits or *phi* of Thailand also embody nature potentially out of control and destructive of the proper ordering of the world. Thus in the initiation ceremony, as in all Buddhist ceremonies, they are subordinated by the power of righteousness.

Indeed, in the course of the initiation ceremony, the entire cosmos assembles to acclaim the purity and power of the *dhamma*. [14]

> The Buddha is called to be a witness. The master of ceremonies sprinkles water over the boys.... Then the company and the upper *nats*, the village guardian *nat*, the tract *nat*, and the inherited *mizaing* and *hpasaing* are invited to eat. The monks eat, seated on a dais, with the laity eating below them.

The village as *dhamma*-realm comprises the entire soteriological cosmos. The power of *dhammic* order is asserted over the powers of chaos, and the spirits are warned to abide by it. In final renunciation of his sexuality and lay existence, the young initiate has his head shaved. Exemplifying the paradoxical dynamic of exchange, the shaving of the initiate's head is followed by the water-blessing ceremony which signifies the release of moral order and splendid regeneration. As Nash records the event, [15]

> The monks then shave the heads of the *koying*, and there is the water-blessing ceremony. Next a verse is read by the monks to drive away evil spirits and to call upper and lower *nats* to take heed.

Within the Burmese and Thai traditions the theme that power constitutes an ambivalent force that must always be offered in ethical sublimation, notably as selfless giving, so that its chaotic, destructive potential is precluded and its orderly, regenerative potential enhanced is also enacted by the sponsors. Not only do the lay householders give selflessly of their material wealth by sponsoring an elaborate and costly merit-making ceremony, but also of themselves and their fertility by offering their son. And thus they and not strictly the monks are compared to the primordial beings. With their gift of a son to the *sangha*, the lay householders generate world order, they generate a *dhamma*-realm. A variety of ethnographic accounts provide examples of this emphasis. Spiro, for example, records a short sermon delivered by a monk in which the sponsor of the initiation ceremony is compared to the Buddha himself. [16]

---

[14] Nash, *op. cit.*, 109.
[15] *Ibid.*
[16] Melford Spiro, *Buddhism and Society*, New York, 1970, 246.

The great importance of the initiation among the merit-making ceremonies of the village clearly derives from the direct way in which it supports the pure *dhamma* of the Buddha. Clearly, the Buddha stands as the model of and for the monk striving to embody the pure *dhamma*, yet in this merit-making ceremony he also stands as the model of and for the lay householder striving to embody the *dhamma* of world order. Both wheels are necessary to engage the soteriological order, and both are necessary for the village to realize its ideal as *dhamma*-realm. By alternating the focus between monks and laity, the tension between the two wheels remains in balance while the stability of the village as *dhamma*-realm is greatly enhanced.

The ambivalence of royal power has much to do with village autonomy as well. Like nature and sexuality, royalty also embodies ambivalent power. The king may earn his place among the five traditional evils, or he may earn his title as *dhammaraja*. But village royalty, the royalty of the merit-making ceremonies, is moral power. Its reference is to soteriology. As the above description suggests, the village and the people recreate the resplendent, moral order of primordial times. Both nature and society embody *dhamma* in its fullest expression. Within the ritual context and the *dhamma*-realm thus established, all beings enjoy high status and its attendant riches because all embody *dhamma*.

Thus the village's ritual structure and the soteriological cosmos it generates closely parallel the ritual structure and soteriological cosmos of the capital. The legitimacy of the capital derives from its embodiment of the soteriological ideal, and its centrality to the kingdom derives from Buddhist principles of inclusive hierarchy. However, given that the Buddhist ideal is realized in a replicable pattern of human action, the capital is by no means the only embodiment of the ideal. Rather, the village has access to legitimacy within Theravada society by actualizing the two wheel structure of the *dhamma*-realm within its own social order. In this way, the village itself stands as the primary embodiment of the soteriological cosmos and need not acknowledge the capital as the all-encompassing and normative center. Only when actually confronted with the reality of the capital's superior wealth and strength must the village acknowledge the hierarchy of the state. Otherwise, in matters more strictly related to soteriological and cosmological order such as socio-religious and agricultural life, the village remains quite autonomous and far more stable than the capital. The modern problem of national integration stems precisely from this decentralized structure of the traditional kingdom. And what is equally significant, some of the modern efforts to solve this problem stem precisely from the ideology and tactics of the traditional monarchies. The next section explores this situation in greater detail.

The Traditional Order and National Integration

The arrival of the colonial powers in the 19th century brought some significant new ideas and forces related to social order and nationhood which were to change the face of the traditional kingdoms of Burma and Thailand. While the rubric of these changes is modernization, only a theory of modernization that gives the momentum of tradition its due can prove fruitful. The challenge posed by the west affected the structure of the *dhamma*-realm both in terms of the relation of its two wheels, and also in terms of its national organization and territorial extension. Nevertheless, the centrality of the *dhamma*-realm in this process marks it not only as the paradigm of traditional order, but also as the arena within which changes have taken place.

As we have seen, the traditional Theravada order was a complex totality composed of relatively autonomous parts related to one another through the medium of ritual activity. Thus, within the strictly Buddhist context of the *dhamma*-realm, the traditional order was comprised of monks whose primary governance issued from the *vinaya* laws, and of laity whose primary governance issued from basic morality and local customs. Circumscribed in their respective domains of action by these different laws, they related to one another on the basis of merit-making rituals. Similarly, in the case of a Buddhist capital and a non-Buddhist or ethnically different vassal-state, or a Buddhist capital and its surrounding villages, each adhered to its respective customs and yet related to the other on the basis of rituals that established hierarchy and allegiance. Moreover, in their traditional context both the whole and its parts were simultaneously religious, social and political units.

In the face of the pressures that impinged from the west some very significant changes occurred in the relations between *sangha* and laity, particularly at the level of the state. Whereas traditionally monks and laity existed together as complementary opposites circumscribed in their respective domains, developments around the turn of the century placed monks in closer contact with the domain of the laity. The 1903 charter for the *sangha* in Burma and the 1902 Sangha Act in Thailand both required the monks to recognize the common law of the land. Following in the wake of these developments, the *sangha* in both countries became organized into national hierarchies that achieved a kind and degree of centralization that had never previously been known. Yet for all the similarities between the Burmese and Thai situations, the contrasts are at least equally significant.

The crucial backdrop to the changes in the Burmese context is, of course, Burma's direct experience of British colonial rule. While the loss of Burmese kingship was clearly disruptive, it, in and of itself, was certainly not unprecedented, nor was it necessarily intolerable. However it ultimately proved intolerable when the British, despite initial promises to the contrary, failed to behave as the Burmese kings. Central in this respect was their initial failure to appoint a monk to the office of *sangharaja* and their subsequent issuance of the charter of 1903. The divergent presuppositions underlying the misunderstanding are telling.

To the *sangha,* the appointment of a *sangharaja* by the political authority, traditionally the king, signified a ritual relation between the internally autonomous groups of monks and political laity, the two wheels of *dhamma.* As the merit-making rituals demonstrate, order arises in and from the ritual exchange of the two wheels, that is from the structural relationship between them. The exchange is crucial. While each path embodies different action content, through ritual exchange they create the paradoxical whole which is *dhammic* order.

In contrast, the appointment of the *sangharaja* by the political authority signified to the British the violation of the separation of church and state so crucial to a secular nation. The church was the sacred domain of belief, it was an interior world based on faith and it was not one entered by the state. The state, on the other hand, was the secular domain of action, it was the exterior world common to all persons and based on the civil law which kept order in the world so that each could hold religious beliefs of a personal choosing. Hence, according to British reckoning, order arises not from the structural relationship between two autonomous, action-based groups, but from the acceptance of a common content of citizenship that was delimited by civil law. The distinction between belief and action was crucial to British goverance and conception of nationhood.

The furor over the charter of 1903 begins to come into clearer focus now. Issued by the British Lt. Governor, this charter ratified the *sangharaja's* appointment and delineated his jurisdiction. Far from recognizing and upholding the sanctity of the monastic domain, the charter both failed to grant the *sangharaja* any real political support and also limited his authority to affairs that in no way transgressed what the British considered civil jurisdiction. In other words, the *sangharaja* had no authority over any monk's actions, only over his beliefs! Furthermore, any monk who transgressed civil law was required to appear before a civil court. The monks were outraged that the British Lt. Governor, after initially failing in his ritual duty, then had the audacity to *ratify* an appointment. The autonomy of the monastic and lay paths was a cosmological and soteriological given, and no monk worth his robes would allow a layperson legislative authority over the morally superior monastic domain. That the British assumed such authority by their action of ratification was a rude awakening to the realities of colonial rule. Yet ironically, the separation of church and state had initially been attractive to many members of the *sangha* who were weary of the encroachments of powerful kings on their domain.

The significance to the king of the office of *sangharaja* lay in its provision of an access route to monastic discipline and hence, to some measure of control over the *sangha*. The king's use of the office, clothed in the appropriate rhetoric of his traditional concern for monastic purity, also benefited the *sangha*. They, after all, needed royal support as well as purification if they were to pursue their supra-worldly quest. Existing as a point of ritual exchange, the office expressed the proper relation between the two paths maintaining them as complementary opposites, rather than as competitors. It also expressed the limits to which either path could approach the other. In the hands of skillful kings, it was an effective means of control because the *sangharaja* could act upon monastic affairs without violating his supra-worldly status and domain, while the king could support the decisions of his *sangharaja* without violating his worldly status and domain. And indeed, this is the way it happened in Thailand. In this symbiotic relation, the autonomy and integrity of each domain was respected, and order was established and expressed through the proper ritual actions of both monk and king. The structure of traditional Burma, based on the relation between the two wheels, now, however, was threatened. From the *sangha's* perspective, the British sought to place soteriological action in the realm of *samsara*.

Without the symbolic and ritual language of purification, the British were unable to adequately respond to and control the monks. As a result, their attempt to universally impose civil law created a situation which, in fact, fulfilled their worst fears and certainly precluded any hope of their tolerance of a separate *vinaya law*. Many monks, rather than withdraw from the political arena, militantly entered it. Under their banner of nationalism, the monks and their peasant supporters demonstrated the extent to which the well-being of Buddhism and Burma's independence were considered to be synonomous.

From the British perspective authority to act in any way that was at variance with civil law could neither be acknowledged nor tolerated. The British assumed that to be subject to *vinaya* law and not civil law meant to be lawless. They could not understand order based on the *relation between* two relatively autonomous groups, but only one based on the common observance of civil law. Rather than seeing the complementarity, the British saw only the opposition: civil law plus *vinaya* law meant law versus lawlessness.

Hence, the charter of 1903 stated that while the British reluctantly agreed to ratify a monk in the office of *sangharaja*, they could recognize his authority in matters of doctrine and belief only. Further, any action by a monk that violated civil law must be treated as a civil offense and tried in a civil court. This was received by the monks as a patent disregard for the sanctity of *vinaya* law as the primary law to which a monk is responsible. Any violation committed by a monk must be recognized first as a violation of monastic law. If the *sangha* found the monk's action to warrant his defrocking, then as a layman he could be tried in a civil court.

At virtually the same time that Burma's monks were served notice of their accountability to civil law, King Culalongkorn and his *sangharaja* did the same to Thailand's monks. The Sangha Act of 1902 established quite clearly that in addition to the *vinaya*, monks were also expected to observe the law of the land as well as local custom. The Thai, like the British, recognized the importance of a law common to all persons within the territorial limits that define a modern nation. However, the Thai were also aware of, indeed bound by, their own cultural parameters such that they were able to go about accomplishing this by transforming, rather than violating, the traditional structure of the *dhamma*-realm.

Certainly a key factor in Thailand's greater success story is its unbroken sovereignty. While Thailand clearly experienced many of the dimensions of western imperialism, direct political subjugation was not one of them. Furthermore, Thailand's Chakri dynasty has not only provided an unbroken tradition, but also one in which innovation was implicit from the start. Here again the Thai situation differs significantly from the Burmese where any changes wrought by one king were dissolved by the next. However, with a tradition of innovation already implicit in their dynasty, and the further possibilities of innovation enhanced by an emergent sense of history, the Chakri kings, particularly Rama IV (reigned 1851-1868) and Rama V (reigned 1868-1910), ushered in many reforms that were helpful in meeting the demands of a changing world. Through their intelligence, sensitivity, and political acumen, these kings introduced many new elements without violating the key dynamics of meaning and order that had traditionally structured the local polity.

The sustained relationship between the king and his *sangharaja* was crucial toward effecting the transformation and reflected the already close articulation of lay and monastic domains. Yet the close articulation did not violate the autonomy and integrity of the two wheels. While the monks now became subject to the law of the land, any disputes or violations in this regard were to be handled within the monastic order itself. Of course, the political laity constituted an attentive audience in such situations. But by recognizing the office of the *sangharaja*, both laity and monks affirmed the structural relation that preserved the *dhamma*-realm. And furthermore, by recognizing the *sangha's* right to manage its own affairs, rather than subjecting it to a civil court, the primacy of action and its integral relation to one's status and domain of action were also recognized and affirmed.

In both Burma and Thailand, the altered relation between the monks and laity at the state level resulted in an increasingly hierarchical *sangha*. Yet the ends to which the respective hierarchies were put differed drastically. While the actions of the British impelled many Burmese monks into the thick of nationalist political activity, they drove many others more vehemently into the domain of monastic action and strict observance of the *vinaya*. As early as King Mindon and the British occupation of Lower Burma, sectarian activity had accelerated. With the loss of Upper Burma and the subsequent colonial policy, the sects were convinced of the necessity of withdrawal from any political affairs and the revival of *vinaya* purity. These reform groups made no overtures to protest or reformulate the 1903 charter on the grounds that even that much acknowledgement compromised their autonomy. Laity, and particularly non-royal laity, simply had no authority to legislate in monastic affairs.

Registering their dissent with all who could decode the meaning of their actions, the reform sects withdrew from the political arena and organized themselves into tight, well-disciplined hierarchies.

Furthermore, reform sects of Upper and Lower Burma allied themselves to create a formidable resistance on a national scale. The hierarchical organization of the sects facilitated their resistance to political control in a way far more effective than ever before, and in a way that has continued even after independence, much to the chagrin of zealous lay politicians. While in virtually every other instance throughout Burmese history hierarchy crumbled in the preservation of autonomy, the sects now hierarchized themselves in the name of this same autonomy.

Reflective of the traditionally more compatible relation between hierarchy and autonomy, the Thai *sangha* likewise assumed a national hierarchical organization, but in cooperation with the government rather than in opposition to it. Monks and laity were of a common mind with regard to the general direction of modernization, and their cooperation reflected as much. Indeed, it was the sectarian activity of the reform-minded Thammayut monks which, far from thwarting the efforts of the government, spearheaded them. A shared understanding of the process of modernization as both religious and socio-political finds its explicit expression in the preamble to the Sangha Act of 1902: [17]

> Whereas the amendment of the law and the reformation of the administrative system of the State have brought about manifold developments and outstanding progress to the country, it is obvious that the religious affairs of the Buddhist Church are also of no less importance to the development both of Buddhism and of the country in that systematically administered, they will serve to attract more people to the study and practice of Buddhism under the guidance of *bhikkhus*, thereby leading them to the right mode of living in accordance with the Buddha's instructions.

Yet modernization is not the most accurate statement of purpose at this point. In 1902 King Chulalongkorn (Rama V) was primarily concerned to consolidate his kingdom and hence his strength in order to better resist the encroachments of the colonial powers. National integration was a matter of survival, of continued sovereignty or of colonial subjugation. Hence, one of the most significant effects of the Sangha Act and the national *sangha* hierarchy was its incorporation of a variant of central Thai Buddhism known as Yuan Buddhism. Yuan Buddhism was practiced in the northern province and hence

---

[17] Tambiah, *World Conqueror*, 238.

was articulated with the local power structure of the province. In other words, as in the village situation discussed above, Yuan Buddhism expressed the autonomy of the religious, social and political entity that was the northern province. By enforcing the Sangha Act in the northern province and by superimposing the national *sangha* hierarchy on the Yuan Buddhist monks, the central Thai government sought, through the mediation of the *sangha*, to draw the northern province more tightly into its sphere of sovereignty. The dynamic is very traditional and follows the same logic as the royal *kathin* ceremony, but now it is expressed through the modern *sangha* hierarchy. Buddhist ritual and the participation of the Yuan monks in the national *sangha* now served to express the place of the northern province in the hierarchy of the king and the national government. With this development the importance of the *sangha* and the symbolic efficacy of the *dhamma*-realm toward national integration finds its first expression in a modern idiom. [18]

The importance of national integration did not emerge in Burma until independence was won in 1948, although it is certainly presaged in the actions of the reform sects. Nevertheless, with the end of colonialism *per se*, both Burma and Thailand were confronted with the realities of the territorially defined state rather than the traditional suzerainty, and hence of citizenship based on birth within certain territorial limits rather than on the traditional ritual of allegiance. The territorial definition of nationhood and its implications for citizenship introduced an emphasis on being rather than on action. These new territorial states now included among their citizenry autonomous groups which may have avoided vassalage, such as hill tribes, or perhaps accepted it only insofar as their internal order was permitted to remain. So the problem of hierarchy versus autonomy reared its ugly head again. But the rituals of allegiance which had negotiated such relationships before no longer obtained because these were now territorially defined states, not suzerainties.

Burma, in particular, was being torn apart by civil war and communist insurgency. Each of the various non-Burmese ethnic groups took advantage of Burma's weakened state by revolting against the predominance of ethnic Burmese in a way that was quite consonant with medieval patterns. Thailand experienced similar difficulties especially in the north and northeast, but not nearly to the same extent.

---

[18] For a full account see Charles Keyes, "Buddhism and National Integration in Thailand," *JAS* 30 (1971), 551-68.

Yet history having given them no other choice, Burma and Thailand have been forced to hitch modern realities to the wagon of traditional patterns of order and meaning. The modern notion of citizenship must come to terms with the traditional model of action, status, and domain, which, of course, continue to be understood as simultaneously religious and socio-political. Hence, the post-colonial problems of both countries, though more intensely so in Burma, were considered to have a very significant religious and moral dimension. The importance of the revival of traditional values that occurred in the 1950's and 1960's and specifically of the *sangha's* role in the attendant missionary and social development projects achieve greater clarity in this light.

The revival of traditional values in Burma occurred overwhelmingly in terms of Buddhism, and culminated in the 6th Buddhist Council. This revival was strongly promoted by the Anti-Fascist People's Freedom League (AFPFL) under U Nu who, as a lay politician, behaved in striking accordance with the royalist tradition. U Nu rallied popular support through his appeal to Buddhist moral principles as the key emphasis in the regeneration of Burma. Through the Buddhist revival, Nu sought to symbolize and thereby effect sufficient unity and prosperity to counteract the internal strife rampant in the country.

An important part of the Buddhist revival consisted of a series of missionary movements to the hill country in an effort to "bring about unity and cooperation between peoples of the plains and the people of the hills." These missionary projects were initiated by certain groups of monks who were more or less cooperative with the government when the possibilities of the projects for national integration became apparent.

The parallel revival of traditional values in Thailand occurred both in terms of Buddhism and kingship. During the 50's and 60's in addition to a number of rituals and ceremonial days that were either initiated or reemphasized, a number of missionary and social development projects were conducted by the *sangha* with government support. Like those in Burma, these projects aimed at integrating non-Buddhist groups into the national fold by converting them or, in cases where the groups were already Buddhist, at precluding political disaffection among the economically disadvantaged by organizing social development projects.

Clearly, both the *sangha* and the state had strong reasons to support these development projects. On the monastic side, the secularization of education that came with the influence of the west posed a serious threat to the monkhood. In large part, this development began pushing the *sangha* from the center of Burmese and Thai life. It threatened to minimize the extent to which the *sangha* provided both a national rite of passage into manhood and an important avenue of social and political mobility. As the *sangha* ceased to be as crucial in these respects, it lost much of its relevance to modern life which signalled a decline in the numbers of young men who would enter the *sangha*. In reaction to this, and spurred by the social gospel preached by the Christian missionaries, the *sangha* moved more enthusiastically into missionary and social development projects.

On the more strictly political side the stimulus for this kind of activity derived from the fact that variant religious practices constituted a source of resistance to the unity of the state. However, if the religious practices that express local customs and autonomy could be used to encourage identification with the central government, then local customs and autonomy could be subsumed within the hierarchy of the central government. Hence the government sought to sponsor Buddhist monks in their religious and social projects. In non-Buddhist areas this meant missionary programs aimed at articulating the soteriological path with the local order. In areas that were already Buddhist, this frequently meant bringing local Buddhist practice into conformity with the practice of the national *sangha* and developing the area through social services so that dissatisfaction would not lead to subversion. The important thing was to strengthen the links of villages as well as other outlying areas to the central government through the agency of Buddhist action.

The results of these projects are not yet fully known. In Burma, the projects have been handicapped by the same dynamics that have handicapped the relation between *sangha* and state. In Thailand, where the tension between hierarchy and autonomy has achieved a more adequate resolution, and where the relation between *sangha* and state has both expressed and facilitated this resolution, the projects have met with greater success. Traditionally autonomous villages as well as whole regions have begun to include a sense of nationality within their identities. Through the mediation of Buddhist action, hierarchy and autonomy have begun their process of accommodation.

The importance of Buddhism in forging these emergent nations clearly reflects the continued predominance of the *dhamma*-realm as the structure informing social order among the Burmese and Thai. It has not been without its backlash, however. The modern realities of religious and political pluralism cannot be ignored. The emphasis, more or less explicit, in the governments of Nu in Burma and Sarit in Thailand on the *dhamma*, and specifically on the practice of Buddhist morality as the solution to problems in the country has proved alienating to minorities who are either not Buddhist or not ethnically Burmese or Thai. It reflects the royal model of the suzerainty that is no longer compatible with the democratic ideals of a religiously and ethnically pluralistic citizenry. In Burma, U Nu's declaration of Buddhism as the state religion created perhaps the last straw of dissatisfaction that brought about his overthrow. In the military regime of Ne Win that replaced him, Buddhism plays a quieter part, though there are frequent reports of continued intolerance of ethnic and religious pluralism. In Thailand, polarization of political parties has developed, with both extremes claiming legitimacy through appeals to the traditional Buddhist paradigm. But similar claims made by such divergent groups can only harm the credibility and efficacy of the Buddhist model.

The studies that have been done on Thai civic religion may prove particularly fruitful toward understanding future developments. [19] For it may prove that whatever gains have accrued toward national integration on the basis of the traditional Buddhist paradigm of action and ideal order, particularly with regard to the legitimation of political power, can only continue if a more inclusive model is developed. [20]

---

[19] Mendelson, *op. cit.*, 267.

[20] See, for example, Reynolds' discussion of "Civic Religion and National Community in Thailand," *JAS* 36 (1977), 267-82.

II

TRANSITIONS AND TRANSFORMATIONS
IN ISLAM

EXEGESIS AND RECITATION
Their Development as Classical Forms of Qurʾānic Piety

FREDERICK M. DENNY

University of Colorado at Boulder

From the beginning of Muhammad's prophetic career there were two important aspects of the reception and application of the Qurʾānic revelation. The first was the concern for its correct recitation for the purposes of proclaiming, pondering and remembering the Message in worship and the devotional life. The second was the desire to obey it through understanding and applying its contents in the practical concerns of the community's life and order. These requirements led to the development of two dominant modes of Qurʾānic piety, which came to be embodied in the sciences of recitation and exegesis. They were practices before they were sciences, but their gradual development into formal disciplines did not lift them out of the realm of practical religion; on the contrary, their ultimate evolution into orthodox sciences served to undergird and regulate the ways in which the community was to conserve and apply the Qurʾānic message.

In a way my distinction of the two modes is more analytical than descriptive, for in reality they contributed to the formation of a system of symbols, beliefs, practices and common life in which they were incorporated as essential, integral, mutually supportive elements of a single piety. But it is worth emphasizing in a work such as this that Western studies of the Qurʾān have generally concentrated on the kinds of issues which call for an exegetical-expository approach, while the ritual-recitational dimensions of the Qurʾān in its own setting have been relatively neglected. To emphasize the one mode without due concern for the other as a normal approach to Qurʾānic studies leads to serious distortions in our understanding and appreciation of the place and function of the Book in the life of the Muslims.

For example, the Muslim exegete and the non-Muslim one share a considerable terrain of common scholarly assumptions and techniques, such as Arabic grammar, philology and rhetoric, and a sensitive regard for authentic documentation. But unlike the detached, outside Qurʾān expert, the Muslim exegete also stands *under* the Message which he is at pains to interpret and its imagery and cadences are as much a part

6

of him as his blood and skin. Before the Muslim exegete reaches the position where he may make bold to interpret the Qurʾān for others, he must first have proven himself obedient to it on the ritual-recitational level, where he stands alongside his co-religionists. Muslim exegesis of the Qurʾān is a very high calling, reserved for only a few trustworthy, qualified individuals in any particular time and place.

Recitation is also an exalted vocation, but its practice and benefits are shared by the many in an immediate manner in the cultivation of the religious life. The charge to recite the Qurʾān was the first task given to Muhammad and recitation has ever since been the main means by which the Message has been preserved and transmitted in the Islamic community. It has been a tremendous conserving and uniting force due to its central position not only in individual and common worship and devotion but also in the elementary school curriculum of countless believers who have taken quite literally the words of the earliest Sūra, "Who taught by the pen, taught man what he did not know" (96:4, 5).

This study is an attempt to understand Qurʾānic piety in the two modes of exegesis and recitation by means of a survey of some dominant trends and conventions, beginning with the text of the Qurʾān itself and proceeding through the period of the classical development of the two sciences. We shall see that the custody, the interpretation, and even the text of the Scripture underwent important changes and developments in the formative centuries of Islam and that these paralleled to a remarkable extent the evolution of the orthodox Sunnī legal systems and were in some respects definitively shaped by them. This is a story of "transitions and transformations," to be sure; but it is also one of *continuities*, without which Qurʾānic piety is unintelligible.

I. THE QURʾĀN ON ITS OWN INTERPRETATION AND RECITATION

The Qurʾān itself contains pronouncements, commands and terms pertaining to interpretation and recitation as well as to other dimensions of its proper employment in the community of faith. While such materials are neither comprehensive nor systematically arranged, they are nevertheless prominent and clear enough to provide a basis for a number of specific observations, and they comprise the fundamental elements which were later elaborated in the sciences of recitation and exegesis.

Interpretation

The very name of the Book, Al-Qurʾān, means "the Recitation," and recitation terms are prominent throughout. On balance, there is more emphasis in the text on its ritual-recitational uses than on exegesis or exposition. This is not because the Qurʾān's view of itself subordinates content to form, or meaning to mediation; rather, the Qurʾān repeatedly presents itself as a Message which is already quite clear and comprehensible, due to the many similes and illustrations which help to drive home the meaning. Moreover, the Arabs, who had not had a prophetic book of their own, were during Muhammad's career receiving God's Message of old in a language which they could understand for the first time.

> Indeed We have struck for the people in this Koran every manner of similitude; haply they will remember; an Arabic Koran, wherein there is no crookedness; haply they will be godfearing. [1] (39:27,28)

In many places the Qurʾān speaks of God making things plain for the people. The Arabic root *b-y-n* is frequently employed, as in 5:15, "There has come to you from God a light, and a Book Manifest... [*kitāb mubīn*]." In another place we read,

> Move not thy tongue with it to hasten it; Ours it is to gather it. So, when We recite it, follow thou its recitation. Then Ours it is to *explain* it. (75:16-19 emphasis mine)

Some sort of elucidation apparently accompanied the initial revelation to Muhammad, suggesting that God was the original exegete of the Message. There is throughout the Qurʾān the sense, borrowing Cowper's memorable line, that "God is His own interpreter, and He will make it plain."

The usual word for exegesis in Arabic-Islamic usage is *tafsīr*, from the root *fassara*, meaning "to interpret, explain, comment," and so forth. However, another term, *taʾwīl*, is also encountered often, and, while in its later, more developed sense it meant "spiritual" or "allegorical" interpretation, it was in early Islamic times synonomous with *tafsīr* and used more commonly, perhaps because it occurs more frequently in the Qurʾān itself. *Tafsīr* is an *hapax legomenon*, and no other combination of its radicals appears whatsoever in the Qurʾān. In the one passage where it appears we find it linked with recitation.

---

[1] Unless otherwise noted, the translation of the Qurʾān used in this study is that of A. J. Arberry, *The Koran Interpreted*, New York, 1955.

The unbelievers say, "Why has the Koran not been sent down upon
him all at once?" Even so, that We may strengthen thy heart thereby,
and We have chanted it very distinctly. They bring not to thee any
similitude but that We bring thee the truth, and better in exposition
[wa aḥsana tafsīran]. (25:32,33)

Taʾwīl occurs some seventeen times, of which eight refer to Joseph's
interpretation of dreams and events. Five occurrences refer to a scripture
or the Qurʾān itself. Let us take, for example, the fateful passage

It is He who sent down upon thee the Book, wherein are verses clear
that are the Essence of the Book, and others ambiguous. As for those
in whose hearts is swerving, they follow the ambiguous part, desiring
dissension, and desiring its interpretation [taʾwīl]; and none knows its
interpretation [taʾwīl], save only God. And those firmly rooted in
knowledge say, "We believe in it; all is from our Lord"; yet none
remembers, but men possessed of minds. (3:7ff.)

This passage deals with one of the most vexed issues in the history
of the Qurʾānic sciences, that of the so-called "ambiguous" verses
(al-mutashābihāt). On the simplest level, the Qurʾān is saying that
all is not clear, except to God, thus introducing an element of suspense
and tension, particularly when one contrasts this kind of statement
with the many expressions of the Qurʾān's self-proclaimed clarity.
Here, also, is a clear indication that the highest knowledge is belief,
which takes precedence over endless attempts at interpretation. The
"ambiguous" verses deal with religious mysteries which are best "understood" when accepted uncritically and without insisting on explicit
definitions.

We need to remember the original place of the Qurʾān in its own
context as an Arabic document directed, in its initial phase of revelation,
to native Arabic speakers. As Ibn Khaldūn wrote, "All Arabs understood it and knew the meaning of the individual words and composite
statements." [2] There is a certain amount of truth to this statement,
but it perhaps overestimates the capacities of the first hearers to
comprehend the new teaching unaided. It is necessary also to remember
that the materials which we know collectively as "the Qurʾān" were
not, when the Prophet was being inspired to deliver them, gathered
into a canon-codex such as the later Muslims possessed. Nevertheless,
there was even in the primitive period of its existence in the Muslim
community a clear sense of how the revelations were to be properly

---

2 Ibn Khaldūn, The Muqaddimah, tr. F. Rosenthal, Princeton, 1967, II, 443.

regarded and employed, in the ritual sense. It must also be remembered that the early community had access to Muhammad himself, who was the best interpreter at hand.

Something like scholarly study of scripture is touched upon in the Qurʾān, but infrequently:

> It belongs not to any mortal that God should give him the Book, the Judgement, the Prophethood, then he should say to men, "Be you servants to me apart from God." Rather, "Be you masters in that you know the Book, and in that you study." (3:79)

Proper mastery includes recitation and prayerful meditation as well as academic study. In using the Scripture in worship and devotion, the Muslims come to understand it in ways which transcend plain exegetical activity. The Qurʾān clearly states that it is not to be treated like other writings, whether by scholars or anyone. The one who would attempt to explain it must do so as one who stands under it in obedient faith.

> No indeed; it is a Reminder (and whoso wills, shall remember it) upon pages high-honoured, uplifted, purified, by the hands of scribes noble, pious. (80:11-16)

Recitation

With respect to the performance of recitation, the Qurʾān contains both specific and laconic instructions. As with interpretation, the question of proper attitude and approach is important and inseparable from recitation proper. Recitation is *heard* as well as uttered, moreover, and each activity has its requirements. One prominent physical act indicating correct attitude is prostration at certain places in the text. Another is weeping. Still another indication is respectful and expectant silence (37:205; 19:58; 7:203).

There are several terms which mean recitation, the most prominent of which of course is *qurʾān*, whose root can also mean "read." Following the standard chronology which regards Surah 96:1 as the earliest revelation, we find God commanding Muhammad to "Recite: In the name of thy Lord who created, created Man of a blood-clot." Most of the occurrences of this root are in the verbal noun *qurʾān*, which generally refers to the scripture given to Muhammad, sometimes in the collective sense (e.g., 2:185; 55:2), and at other times in the sense of a particular unit of revelation (e.g., 12:2; cf. 13:31).

So, the very name of the Scripture is a verbal noun, denoting not a static collection of written-down words in a gathered canon, but rather a living assembly of revealed verses which were transmitted by the Prophet to his community and kept alive in memory and frequent rehearsal, as well as in written form.

The actual technique of recitation is treated only sketchily and centers in the rare Qur'ānic word *tartīl*, "slow and very distinct chanting." The locus classicus of Qur'ānic instruction on correct chanting is 73:4—"And chant the Koran very distinctly" (Arberry). Bell has "And *arrange* the Qur'ān distinctly" [3] (emphasis mine), a translation which, while correct in one sense, is liable to be misunderstood as composition on Muhammad's part. In 25:32 it is God who speaks— "And We chanted it very distinctly" (Arberry)—if that is the correct way to render the phrase. Bell's "arrange" is quite likely correct here, for preceding the utterance is the question, "Why has the Koran not been sent down upon him all at once?" (Arberry). Two Muslim translations, Mohammed Marmaduke Pickthall's [4] and Muhammad Zafrullah Khan's [5] translate 25:32, respectively, "and We have arranged it in right order" and "and We have arranged it in the best form." These two translations render the previous passage (73:4), respectively, "and chant the Qur'ān in measure" and "and recite the Qur'ān in a slow and distinct manner."

It is evident, then, that *tartīl* means more than simple reading aloud. Notice that both Arberry and Pickthall translate the imperative form (*rattil*) in 73:4 as "chant." I prefer this rendering, also, but feel that it must be used advisedly. It does not mean musical chanting, or singing, although the line between the two is sometimes very difficult to draw. The term "chanting" is often used indiscriminately with reference to recitation of the Qur'ān. There are technical terms in Arabic which were developed to distinguish the different types of Qur'ān recitation; applying the word "chanting" to them all does not take the varieties into account.

The same could be said of the word *tajwīd*, "euphonious recitation." That is, it, like "chanting," is used loosely at times. If we employ the English word "chanting," then we should do so with the understanding that it is only an approximation of *tajwīd* and that in most cases we need further to specify what kind of chanting (slow and

---

[3] Richard Bell, *The Qur'ān Translated*, Edinburgh, 1937.

[4] Mohammed Marmaduke Pickthall, tr., *The Meaning of the Glorious Koran*, New York, 1930.

[5] Muhammad Zafrullah Khan, tr., *The Koran*, New York, 1970.

deliberate, monotonous, "musical," rapid, and so forth). It is never incorrect to use the word "recitation," but that term is so general that it fails to indicate precisely what is meant in a given instance.

On balance, then, what is meant by *tartīl* is the precise, deliberate, rhythmic recitation/chanting of the words and phrases of the Qurʾān, measuring them out properly in relation to each other, in correct sequence and without haste.

> Move not thy tongue with it to hasten it; Ours it is to gather it, and to recite it [*qurʾānahu*]. So, when We recite it [*qaraʾnāhu*], follow thou its recitation. Then Ours it is to explain it. (75:16-19)

Tartīl, then, is the most important technical term contained in the Qurʾān for actual recitation performance. In addition, we find admonishment neither to recite too loudly nor too softly, but in a moderate manner (17:110; cf. 7:204,205). Moreover, the Qurʾān is not to be altered in any way whatsoever (10:16-18) and this applies to interpretation, implicitly, fully as much as it does to recitation.

Another Qurʾānic recitation term is the fairly frequent *talā/yutlā*, "to follow, rehearse, read, declare, meditate," from which is derived the verbal noun *tilāwa*, "recitation, reading," which occurs only once (2:121).

> Those to whom We have given the Book and who recite it [*yatlūnahu*] with true recitation [*ḥaqqa tilāwatihi*].

An added dimension of meaning of *tilāwa* is the sense of "following" or "conforming to" the Qurʾān's message, and not simply the reading or reciting of it. As Lane has aptly remarked, "Every *tilāwah* is *qirāʾah* ["recitation" in the plain sense], but the reverse is not the case." [6] One may recite in a technically proficient manner, in the sense of uttering the words and phrases correctly, but that is not the same as conforming oneself to their meaning.

This double meaning of *tilāwa* can be illustrated by a personal experience I had while I was engaged in field work on recitation in Cairo. One day I came upon a lovely old Ottoman building near the great mosque of Sayyida Zaynab and spotted a small sign which read (in translation), "The Society of the *Tilāwa* of the Noble Qurʾān for Religious Betterment and Community Service." I entered and inquired whether the members gathered periodically to recite the Qurʾān

---

[6] Edward William Lane, *An Arabic-English Lexicon*, I, 1, 13.

together, hoping that I might be fortunate enough to be invited to listen. A kindly old gentleman in the office informed me that the group, which was founded some forty years ago, meets for recitation and prayer two evenings a week. It is significant that these sessions are directed toward increased spiritual and ethical motivation and strengthening for the doing of good works in that poor neighborhood, such as distributing food and clothing and helping the unemployed. I was told that *tilāwa*, while it does indeed mean recitation, also means *following* the teaching of the Qurʾān in one's life. I was reminded of the passage in the Sūra of the Cow, which teaches the meaning of true piety, especially the lines "to give of one's substance, however cherished, to kinsmen, and orphans, the needy, the traveller, beggars, and to ransom the slave, to perform the prayer, to pay the alms" (2:177).

A final Qurʾānic term which should be mentioned, at least, is *dhikr*, "remembering, reminding, mentioning." The root-group occurs variously and frequently and, as is well known, became a central dimension of Ṣūfī practice, which so prominently features the constant remembering and repeating of Qurʾānic words and phrases.

> We shall cause thee to recite without forgetting.... And We shall make it very easy for thee. So remind, if the Reminder [*al-dhikrā*] profits. (87:6,8,9—Bell)

II. The Two Forms of Qurʾānic Piety in their Classical Development

A remarkable story is told by the great conservative jurist, Aḥmad Ibn Ḥanbal: "I saw the Almighty in a dream and asked, 'O Lord, what is the best way to manage to be near you?' He replied: 'My Word, O Aḥmad.' I enquired, 'With understanding or without understanding?' He said, 'With or without understanding.' " [7] This section of the study seeks to understand the kinds of piety which would traverse the two poles of Aḥmad's question. *Tafsīr*, exegesis, seeks understanding, but even where that is absent the Qurʾān still plays a vital role in the beliefs and practices of the Muslims through recitation in numerous contexts, the most important being the ritual prayer (Ṣalāt). I do not mean to suggest that the latter type of piety is not interested in understanding the very message which it sedulously preserves and transmits, for it certainly is. The highest kinds of standards for preserving the text clearly and correctly and passing it on in

---

[7] Anwar Chejne, *The Arabic Language: Its Role in History*, Minneapolis, 1969, 12.

authentic form are absolutely necessary in the pursuit of understanding. But the Qurʾān is a presence and a blessing as well as a source of doctrine and information. There is a pattern of grateful acceptance of the recited Qurʾān among Muslims which is more celebratory than rationally reflective. Yet even in its sometimes lulling cadences, the recitation provides an occasion for meditation on God's great acts and His assurance of felicity to those who submit and obey. When the Book is recited the "Tranquility" (sakīna, cf. Hebrew shechina) descends, we are told in a well-attested tradition (al-Bukkārī).

The Main Outlines of Classical Exegesis

During the Prophet's lifetime, and even more afterward, there were problems in understanding the Qurʾān, so that interpretation of at least a simple sort was needed. In addition to the Book's own claims to being clear and understandable, there are also the statements of the Prophet and his Companions. These latter, collected in traditions, are the main sources for classical tafsīr. Actually, while we possess many Prophetic traditions on the Qurʾān, not very many of these deal with exegesis, as ʿĀʾisha, the Prophet's wife and a prime source of traditions, herself admitted in a famous statement. [8]

While Muhammad was still alive people could turn to him directly for clarification and exposition; thus in the traditions of his Companions we find the kinds of information which are of primary value for exegesis. These deal with such topics as chronology of events in relation to the revelation of specific passages, the meaning of words in certain contexts, the practice of the Prophet with respect to many everyday issues of life, prayer, morality, leadership, traditional lore and custom, much of which information is helpful in interpretation. The exegetical traditions which are traceable to the Companions and others of the early generations comprise the sources for what is known as tafsīr maʾthūr, "interpretation handed down." This type of exegesis dominated the field for some three centuries and continues to hold the place of highest esteem among Muslims.

Muhammad's cousin, ʿAbdallāh ibn ʿAbbās (d. 688) is considered to be the founder of traditional exegesis (tafsīr maʾthūr) and there is attributed to him a commentary, although it is doubtful that he actually composed it himself. Ibn ʿAbbās was only in his teens when

---

[8] Rashid Ahmad (Jullandri), "Qurʾānic Exegesis and Classical Tafsīr," IQ 12 (1968), 83.

Muhammad died, but he had set out at an early age gathering information on the Prophet as well as on many other things. There are a
bewildering number and variety of traditions traced back to this famous
scholar, who was called from earliest times "the Commentator of the
Qurʾān" and "the Ocean," because of his great learning. According
to one tradition, the Prophet prayed for the younger man: "O God.
Bestow on Ibn ᶜAbbās wisdom and teach him interpretation (taʾwīl)." [9]

This remarkable person does indeed appear to have been highly
knowledgeable about the Qurʾān and the Prophet's life, but so were
others, like Abū Bakr, ᶜUmar, Ibn Masᶜūd and ᶜAlī, who had been
close to Muhammad since the beginnings of the venture back in
Mecca. The descendants of Ibn ᶜAbbās, it must be remembered, seized
power in the Islamic empire in 750 A.D., creating the great ᶜAbbāsid
dynasty which lasted some five-hundred years and witnessed the coming
to maturity of the basic Islamic sciences and the legal, political and
religious institutions. The collection of traditions had begun to pick
up a great deal of momentum by early ᶜAbbāsid times and a ḥadīth-
centered popular piety had formed which was to be the main ingredient
in the solidification of Sunnī Islam. The new leaders in Iraq "began
to exaggerate the piety, the righteousness, and the knowledge of Ibn
ᶜAbbās for their own political ends," according to Rashid Ahmad. [10]
So, Ibn ᶜAbbās appears to have increasingly *become* the brightest star
in the firmament of *tafsīr* over a considerable period of time. It is
difficult to know for certain just what the extent of his real learning
and influence was during his own lifetime, because so many of the
traditions traced back to him are fabrications (and were declared so to
be in ᶜAbbāsid times by such respected orthodox experts as al-Shāfiᶜī,
who held that there were only one-hundred genuine traditions from
Ibn ᶜAbbās). [11] Even so, it seems true that Ibn ᶜAbbās was unusually
industrious and intelligent, as well as deeply pious, even after adjustments are made to the enhanced portrait provided by his descendants.

Ibn ᶜAbbās is known to have consulted with Jewish and Christian
contemporaries on matters of reports and traditions. But the practice
of conferring on and discussing scriptural matters with Jews
and Christians was by no means limited to Ibn ᶜAbbās among
early Muslims. We are told, for example, that Abū Hurayra, although
illiterate, had a wide knowledge of the Torah. [12] The early develop-

---

[9] Ibn Saᶜd, *Al-Ṭabaqāt al-Kubrā*, Leiden, 1325/1912, II, ii, 119.
[10] Ahmad, "Qurʾānic Exegesis," 79.
[11] *Ibid.*, 80; al-Suyūṭī, *Al-Itqān fī ᶜulūm al-qurʾān*, Al-Qāhira, 1370/1951, II, 189.
[12] Al-Dhahabī, *Tadhkirat al-Ḥuffāẓ*, Ḥaidarābād, Deccan, 1968-70, I, 36.

ment of the science of traditions seems to have been part and parcel of the rise of *tafsīr* as well as of jurisprudence. The sources for the knowledge gained by early Muslim scholars were very varied and went well beyond the scriptures of the older Near Eastern religions to the ancient Arabic poetry and language itself. Ibn ᶜAbbās probably was the first to open up this last angle of approach to exegetical problems, [13] which flourished later in the development of the Arabic grammatical schools. These schools were, of course, definitively grounded in the Qurᵓānic language, but sought in the Arabian dialects and indeed in the entire ancient literary and linguistic record the means to understand it fully. The "clear Arabic Qurᵓān" drew forth an enormous expenditure of intellectual energy and genius to be understood, especially by the many peoples over the generations who converted to Islam and were not native Arabic speakers. *Tafsīr* was an absolute necessity for these peoples and they made monumental contributions to it.

Traditional commentary developed in a variety of ways, some finding acceptance and some rejection. It culminated in the great commentary of al-Ṭabarī (d. 932 A.D.), which sums up and reproduces most of what had been accomplished down to his time. In addition to *tafsīr* works proper, we find exegetical traditions in the great canonical collections of *Ḥadīth*, or traditions, although such reports are far outnumbered by sayings pertaining to the merits of the Qurᵓān and its proper ritual uses.

There are ample indications that during the period of development of Islam's basic institutions and sciences *tafsīr* was at times considered in some ways to be suspect. Goldziher argued that opposition to *tafsīr* started very early, [14] during the time of the second Caliph, ᶜUmar, but subsequent research tends toward the view that only certain types of exegesis were criticized and disapproved and that the chief early type to be censured was that which treated the "ambiguous verses" of the Qurᵓān. [15] Later, we find opposition to that which was based upon inadequate chains of transmitters and that which was founded upon rational opinion (*raᵓy*) rather than on accepted traditions. [16]

---

[13] Helmut Gätje, *The Qurᵓān and Its Exegesis*, tr. Alford Welch, London, 1976, 32-33.

[14] Ignaz Goldziher, *Die Richtungen der islamischen Koranauslegung*, Leiden, 1920, 56.

[15] See Harris Birkeland, *Old Muslim Opposition Against Interpretation of the Koran*, Oslo, 1955, 14; cf. Nabia Abbott, *Studies in Arabic Literary Papyri*, II, *Qurᵓānic Commentary and Tradition*, Chicago, 1967, 106-13.

[16] *Ibid.*, 113.

However, criticism of transmission chains arose only after a Sunnī orthodoxy had been fairly well established and in a dominant position among jurists; and the last type, centering in personal opinion, reflects dogmatic disputes arising from the conflict between reason and revelation, Muᶜtazilite theologians versus Sunnī legists.

One very interesting type of opposition to *tafsīr* is that which was based on pious fear. According to H. Birkeland, [17] Aṣmaᶜī (ᶜAbd al-Mālik ibn Qurayb, d. 215 or 217 A.H.), an eminent philologist of high Caliphal times in Baghdad, abstained from interpreting the Qurʾān, or even anything corresponding to it in the *Ḥadīth* or in secular literature. This was because of his great fear of profanation, which he felt could occur when God's words were explained by means of man's. Birkeland's appealing case has been challenged by Nabia Abbott, who, while not denying the pious dimension of Aṣmaᶜī's avoidance of *tafsīr*, argues that it was only one factor, and probably not the crucial one at that. The fact is, says Abbott in review of the evidence, Aṣmaᶜī was basically afraid of being accused by a rival scholar of *tafsīr bi al-raʾy*, exegesis on the basis of rational opinion, which would have placed him within the heterodox Muᶜtazilite orbit. [18]

Some of the opposition against *tafsīr* which arose was not against the practice of exegesis properly pursued, but rather against some of its unreliable practitioners. If a person could not prove mastery of one of the chief religious sciences, such as traditions, or "readings" (*qirāʾāt*), or jurisprudence, then his exegetical labors were regarded as unsound *a priori*. [19] In a similar vein, we are told that a certain Bādam ibn Ṣāliḥ—whose nickname was "He of the Commentary"—was attacked because he was not a *ḥāfiẓ*, that is, he did not have the Qurʾān by heart. [20]

The great *tafsīr* of al-Ṭabarī, "The Collection of Explanations for the Interpretation of the Qurʾān," marks the high point and culmination of traditional commentary. [21] Its great depth and breadth of sources provide an invaluable mine of information on the Qurʾānic sciences down to the author's time, the third Islamic century, as well as a number of related fields, such as poetry, philology, grammar,

---

[17] Birkeland, *op. cit.*, 15.

[18] Abbott, *op. cit.*, 113.

[19] Birkeland, *op. cit.*, 26.

[20] *Ibid.*

[21] Abū Jaᶜfar Muḥammad ibn Jarīr al-Ṭabarī, *Jāmiᶜ al-bayān ᶜan taʾrīkh āy al-qurʾān*.

traditions and history. Ṭabarī's *tafsīr*, which has only relatively recently begun to be utilized extensively by Western scholars, is amazingly detailed and complete, citing and evaluating what had come before in the practice of exegesis to such an extent that our reconstruction of the early history of Qurʾān interpretation is possible largely because of this enormous depository of information, much of which is otherwise lost. For example, Ṭabari cites the content of given traditions more than once in a single section if they have been received through different chains of attestors. This meticulous marshalling of sources is occasionally confusing, not to mention time-consuming to read, because of their sometimes conflicting and contradictory content. But in the author's favor is his frequent rendering of his own well-considered judgement on specific interpretations; nevertheless, good, bad, strong, weak and indifferent sources are all arrayed for the scrutiny of scholars of the future. Ṭabarī was also a great historian—indeed his reputation rests even more definitively on his universal history, in many volumes, than on his commentary—and his historiographical method was very much at work in his *tafsīr*, as well. Yet for all of his massive citation and documentation, he hewed to a fairly severe standard of interpretation eschewing pedantry and preferring the obvious meaning of any given passage, whenever possible.

While Ṭabarī extensively, almost exhaustively, recorded the material which had been circulating in traditional circles, his commentary is not purely traditional. It makes its own judgments and does not shrink from occasionally rejecting the interpretations of those who came before. The immense value of Ṭabarī's labors in Qurʾānic commentary was fully recognized by his contemporaries as well as by posterity. As Abū Ḥamīd al-Isfarāʾinī, "the Jurist," said, "If a man travelled to China in order to acquire the *tafsīr* of Muḥammad ibn Jarīr [i.e., Ṭabarī] that would not be too much trouble..." [22]

While the type of *tafsīr* beginning with Ibn ʿAbbās and developing during the first three centuries or so of Islamic history was predominantly based on traditions attributed to the Prophet, the Companions and Successors during the first century of the Hijra era, in Qurʾānic commentary no less than in jurisprudence the scholars based their arguments and views also on sound opinion or independent reasoning (*raʾy*), as well as on other elements of the cultural and

---

[22] Yāqūt, *Muʿjam al-Udabāʾ*, ed. Margoliouth, London, 1931, VI, 423; cited in Ahmad, "Qurʾānic Exegesis," 85.

intellectual history of the regions which came under Islamic domination. With the rise of jurisprudence, especially the basing of its principles on traditions, there developed gradually an orthodoxy in favor of tradition and increasingly opposed to ra⁾y. This was the rise of Sunnism, which insisted on the authority of the *sunna*, or "practice" of the Prophet and his Companions, as well as the Qur⁾ān in all matters pertaining to the religious life (which in Islam extends to most areas of individual and communal activity.) Goldziher performed for modern Islamic studies the service of demonstrating the close association between the rise and employment of tradition criticism and traditional *tafsīr*. [23] As Birkeland has summarized the situation in his provocative discussion of this development, by about 200 A.H. "a relative ⁾iǧmā͞ᶜ [consensus] had developed within traditionalistic Islam concerning certain exegetical questions in every Surah. At this time *tafsīr* was recognized when it appeared as a subdivision of *ḥadīth* [tradition]. An ⁾iǧmā͞ᶜ, consequently, on an exegetical question must have a foundation recognized by the new criticism." [24]

By Ṭabarī's time Islamic jurisprudence had been firmly established into the major schools which we know now, as well as others which were important for more limited periods (including one which Ṭabarī himself founded.) In Ṭabarī's *tafsīr* are found a great many authenticating chains (*isnāds*) which stop at the name of a certain Ibn Saᶜd (d. 276/888), a younger relative of his greater namesake, the expert on biography and tradition and secretary to the celebrated historian al-Wāqidī, one of the founders of *ḥadīth* criticism. These chains go all the way back to Ibn ᶜAbbās, the "Commentator of the Qur⁾ān" who was introduced above. Now, Ibn Saᶜd was in some ways sympathetic with influential "orthodox" scholars who were opposed to *tafsīr*, so much so that, in Birkeland's words, he "is inclined to make old authorities of *tafsīr* traditionalists, substituting *tafsīr* by *sunna*, or make them lawyers or Readers [i.e., of the Qur⁾ān]." [25] If this were the case, then how do we explain the large number of exegetical traditions which end with Ibn Saᶜd and go all the way back to Ibn ᶜAbbās? Birkeland argues that by Ibn Saᶜd's time it was considered necessary to authenticate every legal *ḥadīth* by tracing it back to the Prophet or a Companion. His chains indicate that he regarded *tafsīr* traditions as requiring the same kind of authentication; so his *isnāds* go all the

---

[23] *Die Richtungen der islamischen Koranauslegung.*
[24] Birkeland, *op. cit.*, 39.
[25] *Ibid.*, 34ff.

way back, too. But many of the chains found in Ṭabarī's commentary do *not* go back all the way to Ibn ᶜAbbās or even to the primitive period of Islam. Birkeland argues that such chains "must originate from a time when a Companion or even a Successor was not required to authenticate an exegetical information." He further suggests that it is probable that such exegetical *isnāds* are older than the ones traced by Ibn Saᶜd all the way back to Ibn ᶜAbbās. [26] Here we have a clear illustration of the fact that a strict Sunnī position in these matters developed only gradually, however strenuously it tried to reinterpret and manage the past once it gained the ascendancy in Islam, after the second century.

By Ibn Saᶜd's time there were a great many exegetical positions, interpretations of specific passages, which could not be authenticated by a *ḥadīth*, and Birkeland rightly says that "the very aversion of many traditionists against *tafsīr* had contributed to this state of things." [27] However, current interpretations of Qurᵓānic passages were often accepted *consensually* (i.e., by *ijmāᶜ*) by groups of prominent Muslim spokesmen who could not be ignored. Ibn Saᶜd himself learned such interpretations from his father, who in turn had received them from his forebears back in a family chain. This so-called "family-*isnād*" then took the place of a public, well-known one, and in any event was better than no chain at all. As Birkeland wryly observes: "As a traditionist [Ibn Saᶜd] was convinced that the current interpretation had its source in the 'Ocean' Ibn ᶜAbbās." Birkeland concludes his penetrating examination of this issue with the suggestion that "truth" in this circle of orthodox Muslim scholars must be regarded as having been anchored in the paradigmatic past of the Prophet and his Companions and Successors. The recognition of the truth was "in itself held to be evidence of that transmission." [28] Muhammad was transformed over the early generations into a figure of unquestioned authority in all matters of significance for the Muslim community. This is epitomized perhaps most dramatically in the fateful *ḥadīth* attributed to him: "Truly, my Community shall never agree together upon an error" (Ibn Māja, *Fitan*, 8).

So we see that *tafsīr* came into its own in close association with the rise of jurisprudence, particularly in the field of tradition criticism, and drew upon the methodology of that field for its acceptance among

---

26 *Ibid.*, 36f.
27 *Ibid.*, 37.
28 *Ibid.*

the emerging orthodox mainstream of Sunnism. Ṭabarī, it is true, exercised personal judgement in exegetical matters. However, this judgement was not *raʾy*, but *ikhtiyār*, "preference," for a certain interpretation which was itself based on a tradition possessing an acceptable chain of attesters. Ṭabarī considered himself to be an independent legist, a *mujtahid*, but he was one of the very last before the "Gate of *Ijtihād*" ("independent judgement") was closed in his own century, a fateful event which sealed the exercise of jurisprudence into a closed system in the belief that all possible issues and developments had been aired and provided for.

The other main type of exegesis is sometimes called *"rational"* *commentary*, or *tafsīr bi al-raʾy*. As has been observed already, the early Muslims exercised personal opinion (*raʾy*) from the beginning and this seems to have been countenanced both by Muhammad and the Qurʾān (e.g., 4:82,83—"Will they not then ponder the Qurʾān....."), at least in a general sense. But *tafsīr bi al-raʾy* is far removed from the kind of common sensical exegesis of the early generations. It is, by and large, a rationalistic, highly sophisticated philosophico-theological enterprise which arose in the second and third centuries along with the development of the Muʿtazilite (sometimes called "rationalist") *kalām*, or systematic theology. It culminated in the brilliant and influential commentary of al-Zamakhsharī (d. 538/1144) and received considerable support from no less an orthodox figure than al-Ghazālī (d. 505/1111).

Ghazālī, while he did not leave us a full *tafsīr*, did write on the methodology of exegesis. [29] He criticized *tafsīr maʾthūr*, "traditional commentary," as being an insufficient approach in and of itself, arguing that since the traditions often disagree among themselves, one should accept only those which can be traced back to the Prophet himself. This does not leave the traditionalist exegete with very much, which seems to have been Ghazālī's point.

Ghazālī reflects that the Prophet prayed that God would grant Ibn ʿAbbās, the founder of *tafsīr*, wisdom and penetration, thus suggesting that there is a source besides tradition for exegesis. [30] Recall that in the Qurʾān itself we read of God's approval of study and

---

[29] For example, in his masterpiece, "The Revival of the Sciences of Religion" (*Ihyāʾ ʿulūm al-dīn*), Al-Qāhira, 1358/1939, esp. I, 296ff.; also al-Ghazālī's *Mishkāt al-Anwār: the Niche for Lights,* tr. W. H. T. Gairdner, London, 1924. See Ahmad, "Qurʾānic Exegesis," 86ff.

[30] *Ihyāʾ*, I, 297.

deduction (e.g., 4:82; cf. 3:79—"Be you masters in that you know the Book, and in that you study.") Ghazālī held that one could interpret the Qurʾān directly provided that he did not follow his biases in ambiguous or contradictory cases, and that he first knew the entire text well. [31] Above all, he held that one must be able to think clearly and logically, in addition to being solidly grounded in the Qurʾānic sciences. Ghazālī wrote that "the obvious traditional Tafsīr is not the highest achievement of intellectual effort." [32]

The great Persian philologist and Muʿtazilite thinker, al-Zamakhsharī, went farther than Ghazālī or anyone else in his embrace of reason as a source of exegesis and turned the enterprise very much into a theological one, emphasizing the main elements of Muʿtazilite doctrine: [33] God's Unity and Justice, de-anthropomorphism, reason's ability to comprehend matters of faith, the Qurʾān's having been created in time, and free will. Zamakhsharī's commentary [34] contains much less of the rich traditional and historical matter which makes Ṭabarī's and other commentaries in the *tafsīr maʾthūr* category such valuable source collections. Instead, in addition to considerable dogmatic content and intricate hermeneutical reasoning, we have in Zamakhsharī's *tafsīr* some of the highest quality philological and grammatical explication ever to appear in Islamic literature. Its repugnant Muʿtazilism (to the orthodox) notwithstanding, this commentary has continued to be studied because of the wealth of valuable guidance which it provides in understanding the actual language of the Qurʾān and its often opaque grammatical constructs. This resulted in Zamakhsharī's *tafsīr* being used and taught even in orthodox Sunnī Islamic circles, with the caution always to avoid the dogmatic content. As Ibn Khaldūn memorably summarized the issue, Zamaksharī

> uses the various methods of rhetoric (*balāghah*), arguing in favor of the pernicious doctrines of the Muʿtazilah, wherever he believed they occurred in the verses of the Qurʾān. Competent orthodox scholars have, therefore, come to disregard his work and to warn everyone against its pitfalls. However, they admit that he is on firm ground in everything related to language and style (*balāghah*). If the student of the work is acquainted with the orthodox dogmas and knows the

---

[31] Ahmad, "Qurʾānic Exegesis," 86.

[32] *Iḥyāʾ*, I, 297.

[33] See *Shorter Encyclopedia of Islam*, 421-27.

[34] *Al-Kashshāf ʿan ḥaqāʾiq ghawāmiḍ al-tanzīl wa ʿuyūn al-ʾaqāwīl fī wujūh al-taʾwīl.*

arguments in their defense, he is no doubt safe from its fallacies. Therefore, he should seize the opportunity to study it, because it contains remarkable and varied linguistic information. [35]

A very familiar and widely used commentary to this day is one which in many respects is based on Zamakhsharī, but laundered of Muᶜtazilite matter and condensed drastically in other ways as well. It is the "Lights of Revelation and the Secrets of Interpretation" of al-Baydāwī (d. ca. 1286, possibly later), [36] a commentary of the orthodox tafsīr maᵓthūr type and considered to be perhaps the most highly valued in Sunni Islām, because it contains tried and trusted interpretations of earlier commentators and provides a ready reference for readers who desire the facts without long scholarly discussions and comparisons.

Another orthodox commentator who was concerned to stem the tide of rational exegesis was the theologian Fakhr al-Dīn al-Rāzī (d. 606/ 1209), who composed an immense, unfinished tafsīr. [37] This very significant work has yet to be fully studied and appreciated in the West. Rāzī was himself strongly influenced by the very Muᶜtazilism which he strove to refute, but he comes down solidly on the orthodox Ashᶜarite side in his positions, which are argued brilliantly and with an awesome erudition. [38] Exegesis for Rāzī was an occasion for theological controversy and apologetic and the old quip that the "Keys to the Hidden" contains "everything except tafsīr" has more than a dash of truth to it. As well as being bold and combative, Rāzī was also quite evidently a devout Muslim, as is seen in various places in his writings as well as in a rather poignant testimony which he penned toward the end of his life, in which he expressed a sense of futility in devoting one's life to systematic theological studies. [39]

These few examples of classical exegesis cover most of the range of Sunni tafsīr. There are many more individuals who could be mentioned, but space prohibits it. Conspicuously absent, unfortunately, are examples of Shīᶜī tafsīr. [40] Suffice it here to say that it varies considerably, depending upon the branch of Shīᶜī Islam and, in addition

---

[35] Ibn Khaldūn, op. cit., II, 447.

[36] Anwār al-tanzīl wa asrār al-taᵓwīl.

[37] Known by two titles, Mafātīḥ al-ghayb and Al-Tafsīr al-kabīr.

[38] See Jane I. Smith, An Historical and Semantic Study of the Term "Islām" as Seen in a Sequence of Qurᵓān Commentaries, Missoula, Montana, 1975, 101-18.

[39] Ibid., 106f.

[40] For two Shīᶜī approaches, see ibid., 76-88.

to the traditional materials used in Sunnī exegesis, draws heavily on the authoritative Imāms, or spiritual leaders, who received, in the Shīʿī view, ʿAlī's copy of the Qurʾān, believed to be the genuine one delivered through the Prophet, and not the ʿUthmānic recension, which will be considered in the following section. [41]

Another broad field of commentary is that of the Ṣūfīs, or mystics, who, while they do not constitute anything like a unified movement, nevertheless have in common a distinction between exoteric and esoteric dimensions of truth. Esoteric exegesis employs a method which takes the name *taʾwīl*, a term which was defined in the first part of this essay in connection with *tafsīr*. In Ṣūfī exegesis it means "allegorical interpretation," poised at an esoteric level above the literal, exoteric meaning. Obviously, traditional commentary does not occupy a prominent place in this kind of scholarship. Ghazālī himself made the distinction between the hidden and the obvious meanings a central part of his hermeneutic, but in a manner which sought to ensure Ṣūfī exegesis a respected place within Sunnī orthodoxy which centered in the Sharīʿa, the Religious Law. His position was that the esoteric level, the *bāṭin*, should never lose sight of the external, obvious meaning, the *ẓāhir*, that there should be in this world a balance between the two. [42]

The Classical Developments in Readings and Recitation

The Arabic word *qirāʾa* can be translated either as "reading" or as "recitation." The former means the actual textual matter, including such elements as voweling, spelling, arrangement, variants and peculiarities. However, a reading is not limited to orthographic matters, because it may exist also in memory. The second sense, recitation, has to do with orthoepy, correct oral performance. The department of Qurʾānic sciences dealing with *qirāʾa* in both senses is called *ʿilm al-qirāʾāt*, the "science of readings." Recitation as performance, as chanting, is called *tajwīd*. This is not an independent field, rather it is a sub-field of "readings/recitation."

Before one may perform recitation, one must first master the matter to be recited, and that matter must be authentic and correctly recorded or remembered in every detail. This section, then, will take *qirāʾa* in both of its meanings, because they are inseparable in the thought and practice of the Muslims and indeed constantly overlap.

---

[41] See Gätje, *op. cit.*, 38f., 239-47.
[42] See *Mishkāt al-Anwār: the Niche for Lights*, 137.

Readings. This section centers in what a historian of religions could call the establishment of the Qurʾānic canon and text. The Prophet himself recited routinely, or had recited by others, portions of the Qurʾān which had already descended, so that after a time there was a rather extensive and still growing accumulation of material which was being actively preserved and rehearsed. It is probable that the need for collecting and writing all of this down was acknowledged during Muhammad's lifetime, but, according to a respected tradition, "the Prophet of Allah was taken before any collection of the Qurʾān had been made." [43] Short of a comprehensive collection, Muhammad, it appears, had ordered certain passages to be written down during his lifetime, particularly of a legal nature as well as those which had to do with formal worship, centering in the Ṣalāt, and doubtless known to a considerable number of people by heart, for the Qurʾān constituted from the very beginning the "prayerbook" of Islam. [44]

Between the time of Muhammad's death (10/632) and the official recension of the third Caliph, ʿUthmān, a period of about twenty years, there was considerable collecting and recording activity, by no means of a unified sort, by various parties. The amanuensis of Muhammad, Zayd ibn Thābit, possibly made a preliminary recension under the first Caliph, Abū Bakr, who had feared that knowledge of the Qurʾān would be lost because of the large number of reciters (*qurrāʾ*) who had perished in the Battle of Yamāma. According to the story, Zayd gathered the revealed materials from such diverse substances as "pieces of papyrus, flat stones, palm-leaves, shoulder blades and ribs of animals, pieces of leather and wooden boards, as well as from the hearts of men." [45] All of this was transferred to sheets and lodged with ʿUmar, and after his death it went to his daughter Ḥafsa. It is held later to have become the basis of the ʿUthmānic recension, which was carried out by a special commission of appointed scholars, including Zayd, during the third Caliph's reign (644-656). After this recension was completed (it is in essentials the one which we possess today) the Caliph reportedly had all other versions in circulation collected and destroyed, to the extent that their contents were not accepted by the commission, which had gone to great lengths to gather, compare and

---

[43] Arthur Jeffery, "The Textual History of the Qurʾān," *The Qurʾān as Scripture*, New York, 1952, 89-103; 91.

[44] *Ibid.*, 92; W. Montgomery Watt, *Bell's Introduction to the Qurʾān*, Edinburgh, 1970, 38; *Shorter Encyclopedia of Islam*, 491-99; S. D. Goitein, *Studies in Islamic History and Institutions*, Leiden, 1968, 88ff.

[45] Watt, *Bell's Introduction*, 40; this famous report has many variants.

evaluate all the Qurᵓānic materials which were in circulation in whatever preserved form.

There were, by the time of ᶜUthmān, however, four other codices in use. These were, by and large, in agreement with what resulted in the official recension, but there were significant differences. One of the most important of these ancient codices was that of Ibn Masᶜūd (d. 653), which continued for some time to be preferred in Kūfa and in Shīᶜī circles and was still being consulted *centuries* later, as we shall see below in connection with a famous incident. [46] One of the things in which the two versions disagreed was the ordering of the chapters, and the total number varies. For example, Ibn Masᶜūd's codex did not include the first Sūra, "al-Fātiḥa," nor the last two (113 and 114), sometimes called the "Two Charms," apparently because they were considered to be spurious. Ibn Masᶜūd had been Muhammad's servant for a time and was close to him for many years, having been an early convert of the Meccan period.

It is not difficult to appreciate ᶜUthmān's concern for bringing together an authoritative edition of the Qurᵓān, because the differing versions had already led to dissension and heated disputes in various parts of the empire and the potential for future schism was very great. When the task of editing the official version was completed, copies were made and sent out to the major provincial capitals: Kūfa and Baṣra in Iraq, Damascus, and possibly also to Mecca. We do not possess any of the original copies and are uncertain as to its form in detail, but it is basically the one which the Muslim world uses now both as to content and arrangement. There was no numbering of verses (although there was a scheme of division), and the Sūras did not receive their traditional names until much later. The *basmala* and so-called "mysterious letters" prefixed to a number of chapters were included. [47]

One would think that once this recension had been promulgated and widely distributed the problems of variation and rival readings would have been solved. [48] They were, to some extent, but there

---

[46] See below, 116.

[47] On this recension see Gätje, *op. cit.*, 25-26. The *Basmala* is the name of the formula *bismillāh al-raḥmān al-raḥīm*, which opens every Sūra except for the ninth.

[48] John Burton, *The Collection of the Qurᵓān*, Cambridge, 1977, has raised serious questions about the traditional accounts of the formation of the ᶜUthmānic canon. His thesis, which cannot be reviewed within the scope of this article, is that the *muṣḥaf* which we regard as ᶜUthmānic is actually the *muṣḥaf* of Muhammad; the other "ancient codices" were generated later as a result of legal developments.

remained serious difficulties owing largely to the unvowelled consonantal text and its inadequate orthography, which were subject to
different readings. Now the work of the Caliphal editors was aimed
not only at collecting the authentic materials, but also at writing them
down in the Prophet's dialect, that of the Quraysh tribe. But as Jeffery
has pointed out, dialectal variations, or the majority of them, would
not have appeared in the written Arabic of those days. However, this
is one of the arguments which ᶜUthmān had set forth to justify the
commission's work in the first place. Jeffery avers that Zayd ibn Thābit
and his colleagues on the ᶜUthmānic commission were regarded even
then as recording a text *de novo*,

> for we read that at times when there was only one witness available
> for a certain passage they would wait till another witness who knew
> that passage had come back from the wars, or wherever he had been,
> and recite it to them; and there were discussions among them as to
> where certain passages belonged in the collection. Finally, the mass of
> variant readings that has survived to us from the Codices of Ubai and
> Ibn Masᶜūd, shows that they were real textual variants and not mere
> dialectal peculiarities. [49]

It is important to observe here that modern Western critical scholarship on the history of the Qurʾān text is not widely accepted by Muslim
scholars. There is much agreement on details, because all scholars must
use the same basic sources, but the relative evaluations and interpretations of these sources vary considerably in some instances. Western
scholars of the present century, like Jeffery, Bergsträsser, Pretzl and
Bell were working toward the establishment of a critical text of the
Qurʾān, [50] and this is still far from being accomplished. But Muslims,
who accept the ᶜUthmānic recension, hold that it is authentic in that it
embodies the correct collective remembrance of the first generation. [51]
But as this brief review has shown, even though there was an official
text, there was still no truly uniform text. That had to develop over
several centuries.

The bare consonantal text, or *scriptio defectiva*, of the early Qurʾān
copies, in whatever version, was a kind of shorthand reminder and
check on the content of the Message and its proper order and arrange-

---

[49] Jeffery, "Textual History," 96-97.

[50] See Arthur Jeffery, "The Present Status of Qurʾānic Studies," *Middle East
Institute* (Washington), *Current Research on the Middle East*, 1957, 1-16.

[51] See Labib as-Said, *The Recited Koran: a History of the First Recorded Version*,
tr. Bernard Weiss *et al.*, Princeton, 1975, 31-41.

ment. From the time of Muhammad the Qurʾān had been memorized, and in the early Caliphal period a class of professional reciters, called *qurrāʾ*, arose. [52] We do not know much about them, but it is certain that their work was considered to be important and that it did much to keep the Qurʾānic text alive and spreading. The Muslim position is that the text has been handed down through the centuries both in written and recited form. Interestingly, in theory, the latter takes precedence over the former. [53] As an old aphorism has it, "It is a grievous mistake to take the written page as your shaikh." [54] The Prophet is believed to have received the revelations orally from Gabriel, and he then passed it on in similar fashion, thus providing the example for posterity. As is well known, it has been considered very meritorious in all times and places for Muslims to memorize as much of the Qurʾān as possible, and early education has long been centered in that task.

Nevertheless, there were variant readings, and the ᶜUthmānic text did not and could not stop them from developing, *even within itself.* As the generations passed, there came into being a tendency among reciters toward *ikhtiyār*, "preference" (the same term was introduced above in connection with *tafsīr*.) This preference was for the way in which the text was recited aloud, made from a field of possibilities which had become more or less conventional. Schools of reading of the same basic ᶜUthmānic text developed and the reading/recitation was passed down from master to student so that there developed chains of transmission in different regions of the Muslim world in a manner exactly parallel to the chains of authorities of the tradition experts and exegetes. There appeared fairly early, in the practice of *ikhtiyār*, three principles to guide the reciter: [55] the first is called *muṣḥaf*, meaning the "written text" of the Qurʾān, and it required that recitation be in accordance with it; the second is *ᶜArabiyya*, which means the "Arabic language," and this meant that recitation had to be in conformity with generally accepted grammatical rules; the third principle was *isnād*, which required that one's recitation or reading had to be derived from a reputable, accepted authority of the past. These three principles

---

[52] See G. H. A. Juynboll, "The Qurrāʾ in Early Islamic History," *JESHO* 16 (1973), 113-29; and his "The Position of Qurʾān Recitation in Early Islam," *JSS* 19 (1974), 240-51, where he argues that *qurrāʾ* sometimes refers to "villagers" and has a political meaning, quite removed from the notion of recitation.

[53] This refers to the preferred way of teaching and learning the text; actually, both written and oral tradition have been considered crucial; cf. Labib as-Said, *op. cit.*, 60.

[54] *Ibid.*, 54.

[55] Jeffery, "Textual History," 98.

exerted a considerable standardizing and restraining influence within an otherwise somewhat free field.

It was not long before the religious leaders realized that the plain, unvowelled ᶜUthmānic text was a source of serious difficulties in establishing uniform reading. By the Caliphate of the Umayyad ᶜAbd al-Mālik (ruled 688-705) work on the script had begun. Not only were indications of vowelling and pointing of letters, Masoretic matters, needed; over the years a problem of incorrect copying had also arisen. [56] Beginning during the last part of the seventh century A.D. and continuing for perhaps two more centuries, there gradually emerged a *scriptio plena*, a fully vocalized and pointed text, which was generally agreed upon. (An interesting and important related field, which cannot be explored here, was the development of a standard exemplar and the approved scribal methods for copying it.)

Of course, during all of this time the Qurʾān was preserved in memory as well as in written form, and the manner of conserving and reciting it, while it varied regionally, was remarkably uniform, owing partly to the high mobility of Muslims and the standardized cult in which recitation was prominently featured. In other words, the fact that there was no standard exemplar or fully finished written text until about 900 A.D. does not mean that there was prevailing confusion and ignorance before that time. The early tenth century A.D. witnessed a culmination, not a beginning, of the process of establishing textual uniformity.

It centered in the work of the great *muqriʾ* ("master of readings") Abū Bakr Ibn Mujāhid (d. 324/936), who took the initiative, once an adequate text had been fixed, in laying down precise regulations about the proper "readings" of it, which he forcefully and in the end triumphantly argued numbered seven, based on a very widespread Prophetic tradition which reads, in one of its variant forms:

> ᶜUmar b. al-Khaṭṭāb said: I heard Hishām b. Ḥakīm b. Ḥizām reciting *sūrat al-Furqān* in a different manner from my way of reciting it, and God's messenger had taught me to recite it. I nearly spoke sharply to him, but I delayed till he had finished, and then catching his cloak at the neck I brought him to God's messenger and said, "Messenger of God, I heard this man reciting *sūrat al-Furqān* in a manner different from that in which you taught me to recite it." He told me to let him go and told him to recite. When he recited it in the manner in which I had heard him recite it God's messenger said, "Thus was it sent

---

56 Watt, *Bell's Introduction*, 47f.

down." He then told me to recite it and when I had done so he said, "Thus was it sent down. The Qurʾān was sent down in seven modes [aḥruf] of reading, so recite according to what comes most easily." [57]

This remarkable ḥadīth is the basis for Ibn Mujāhid's system. Aḥruf (the pl. of ḥarf) is a term which is difficult to understand fully in this connection, because it means "letters," normally. But in this case it meant "readings," all of the same basic text. Seven scholars of the eighth century A.D., that is, the late first and early second Hijra centuries, were selected by Ibn Mujāhid as authentic transmitters of each of the "Seven Readings." The term for "authentic" in this context is mutawātir, which Labīb al-Said explains as "transmitted by indepen- dent 'chains' (asānīd) of authorities on a scale sufficiently wide as to rule out the possibility of error. The principle entailed in this definition is that a large number of readers scattered over a wide area could not possibly concur on an erroneous or fabricated reading." [58] Here we see ijmāʿ, "consensus," being employed as a guarantee of soundness, just as it was in the legal sphere in Sunnī Islam.

The seven readings reflected the schools which prevailed in five different Islamic centers: Medina, Mecca, Damascus, Baṣra and Kūfa. Ibn Mujāhid's system before long prevailed, with official support, and has been accepted to this day. There was great and at times bitter opposition and debate in certain quarters over this muqriʾ's de facto preemption of the entire field of qirāʾāt, for there was a good bit of arbitrariness in his selections which caused resentment among other well-qualified masters. Hence, we find lists of ten and even of fourteen readers, all of whom found acceptance in some region or other. A very influential muqriʾ of a later period, Ibn al-Jazarī (d. 833/1429) favored ten readings; yet even though his treatise on the subject [59] is standard, the tradition of the seven according to Ibn Mujāhid has remained the official way.

The appearance of seven readings and their regularization into systems reflects something of the diversity which existed in the forma- tive Islamic centuries concerning the preservation of the Qurʾānic text. There were many more than seven readings, obviously. It may have been that Ibn Mujāhid's classification was an attempt to make a virtue of necessity, and it is not difficult to appreciate the tremendous practical

---

[57] Al-Baghawī, Mishkāt al-Maṣābīḥ, tr. James Robson, Lahore, 1965-66, II, 466.

[58] Labib as-Said, op. cit., 53f.

[59] Abū al-Khayr Muḥammad ibn Muḥammad al-Dimashqī al-Shahīr bi ibn al-Jazarī, Al-Nashr fī al-qirāʾāt al-ʿashr, 2 vols., Dimashq, 1345/1926.

value which his systematization had in sociological as well as religious terms. The whole phenomenon of seven *aḥruf*, or "readings," is consequently regarded by Muslims as an evidence of God's mercy for mankind.

The work of Ibn Mujāhid led to the end of *ikhtiyār*, "preference," a development comparable to the closing of the "Gate of Ijtihād" (independent judgement) during the same period in the field of jurisprudence. From this time on no one was permitted to deviate from the "seven readings," at least in public recitation. During the time of Ibn Mujāhid it had been the practice of some readers still to include passages in their recitation from the old codices, especially from that of Ibn Masᶜūd, which was still favored by some even after the influential jurist Mālik ibn Anas (d. 795) had declared its use in worship invalid. [60]

One case of a reader who continued to choose his own recitation materials will serve to illustrate the seriousness of the offense and consequently the great prestige of Ibn Mujāhid's regularization efforts. [61] Ibn Shanabūdh (d. 328/939), a contemporary and rival of Ibn Mujāhid, one day in Baghdad while leading the public worship included some "rare and singular" readings in his Qurʾān recitation and created a furor. Called before a special tribunal to hear the charges against him, Ibn Shanabūdh forthrightly defended his right to do as he had done, drawing attention to his wide learning in the readings as well as his extensive travels in search of knowledge in the field (an acknowledged mark of the superior scholar). He reportedly defended himself in an arrogant and insolent manner, which resulted in his being convicted and punished with seven floggings. After an examination of his unauthorized readings, Ibn Shanabūdh recanted and signed a declaration to the effect that he thereafter would use only the ᶜUthmānic text of the Qurʾān according to the system worked out by Ibn Mujāhid, any deviation being punishable by death.

Recitation. This section deals with the actual recitation of the Qurʾān in the sense of performance, especially its development alongside the "readings."

We do not know much for certain about the performance of recitation during the times of the Prophet and early Islam. For one thing, the technical term for chanting, *tajwīd*, seems not to have been

---

[60] Watt, *Bell's Introduction*, 48.

[61] *Ibn Khallikān's Biographical Dictionary*, tr. M. G. de Slane (1868), repr. New York, 1961, III, 16-18.

employed much, perhaps not at all, until later. It does not appear in the Qurʾān in any sense and is rare in the Ḥadīth (and is never reported as having been a term which the Prophet used.) One tradition, attributed to ʿAlī (Muhammad's son-in-law), is frequently encountered in the recitation literature, which has its own preferred sources and chains of attesters. When asked about the meaning of the command found in Sūra 73, v. 4, "And chant [*rattil*] the Qurʾān very distinctly [*tartīlan*]," ʿAlī replied, "It [i.e., *tartīl*] is the excellent rendering [*tajwīd*] of the letters/words and the knowledge of the correct pauses." [62] Ibn Masʿūd is reported to have said: "Render beautifully [*jawwidū* = by means of *tajwīd*] the recitation of the Qurʾān and adorn it with the best of voices and give it Arabic inflection, for indeed it *is* Arabic and God loves it to be inflected in the pure Arabic manner" [63] (emphasis mine). Fully developed definitions of *tajwīd* appear rather late and are so detailed and carefully qualified that they bespeak a highly structured and crystallized conception of the field, as will be seen below.

According to al-Kirmānī, the Prophet learned *tajwīd* from Gabriel and then taught his Companions, some of whom in turn transmitted the correct technique down through succeeding masters. [64] The works on *tajwīd* and readings contain specific information on this, with chains of transmission going often all the way back to Muhammad. [65] All that is necessary after the time of Ibn Mujāhid (and it seems to be the case that only after him [66] did *tajwīd* and *qirāʾāt* handbooks begin to appear, or to be preserved), is to trace one's teachers back to one of the "Seven." Thus while written treatises on recitation appear late (or at least those which are still extant did), it has been a matter of accepted practice and fact that an *oral* tradition of correct recitation practice descended from the formative period of the Prophet. Here, then, we come into the same kind of situation as with the readings, but with the difference that it is the manner and not the matter of recitation which is the central concern. These two dimensions

---

62 Muḥammad al-Ṣādiq Qamḥāwī, *Al-Burhān fī tajwīd al-qurʾān*, Al-Qāhira, 1972, 41.

63 Ibn al-Jazarī, *op. cit.*, II, 210.

64 Shihāb al-Dīn al-Qasṭallanī, *Laṭāʾif al-ʾishārāt li-funūn al-qirāʾāt*, Al-Qāhira, 1392/1972, I, 209.

65 For example, Ibn al-Jazarī, *op. cit.*, II, 206.

66 The first to write on recitation appears to have been not Ibn Mujāhid but the Jewish convert to Islam, Hārūn ibn Mūsā (d. 184/800); *Shorter Encyclopedia of Islam*, 283, no. 18.

are at points so closely related to each other as to be only analytically distinguishable, for we know that the way in which the Qurʾān was recited had much to do with its meaning. And of course the variant readings were for generations orally preserved, because of the limitations of the *scriptio defectiva*.

The *Ḥadīth* do not provide much information on how the Prophet recited except to say that he favored beautiful voices and the embellishment of the recitation with sweet intonations. We read, for example: "He is not one of us who does not chant the Qurʾān." (The word for "chant" here is *yataghannī*, which can also mean "sing.") [67] The great traditionist Muslim relates (from Abū Hurayra) that the Prophet said: "Allah has not heard anything (more pleasing) than listening to the Prophet reciting the Qurʾān in a sweet loud voice." Another widely circulated tradition says that the Prophet was heard reciting Sūrat al-Fatḥ ("Victory") while riding on his camel on the day of the conquest of Mecca, and he recited with repetition of verses, a practice which became standard in *tajwīd*, and adds drama, suspense and rhythm to the performance. Ibn Saʿd reports that the Prophet's ordinary speech was distinct and that he had a high regard for his hearers, speaking in an unhurried manner (*tartīl wa tarsīl*). The same traditionist reports that Muhammad, in his recitation, made clear each letter and lengthened his speech, presumably by drawing out the vowels (*kān yamuddu ṣawtahu maddan*). [68]

Muhammad very much enjoyed listening to the recitation of others, and to no one more than Abū Mūsā al-Ashʿarī, whose performance the Prophet likened to that of David, specifically a "flute of the flutes of those belonging to the family of David." [69] Ibn Khaldūn wrote of this *ḥadīth* that it

> does not refer to cadence and melodious music, but it refers to a beautiful voice, a clear pronunciation in reading the Qurʾān, and a clear distinction in the articulation and enunciation of the letters. [70]

The great cultural historian's glossing of this celebrated tradition reads more like a late *tajwīd* manual than an appreciation of a spontaneous high compliment which a delighted Muhammad bestowed on his favorite reciter.

---

[67] Al-Baghawī, *op. cit.*, II, 462, n. 1.
[68] *Ṭabaqāt*, I, ii, 97-98.
[69] *Ṣaḥīḥ Muslim*.
[70] Ibn Khaldūn, *op. cit.*, II, 401.

There is a goodly amount of material in the collections of tradition by way of admonition and instruction about recitation performance in a general sense, although it is not systematically arranged. Most of the *ḥadīths* on recitation do not address the specific question of performance technique; rather, the occasions, purposes and merits of recitation are more frequently emphasized. The categories of traditions dealing with recitation can be summarized as follows: "readings"; contexts and times (in varied ritual settings); amount (covering such issues as whether rapid recitation of a lot of material reaps greater merit than slow, careful performance); manner and style (dealing with aesthetic dimensions, particularly the "musical" side); problems (e.g., faltering, confusing pauses and starts, and physical impediments of reciters).

As with *tafsīr* and the science of readings generally, so also with *tajwīd*, specifically, we do not find systematic written treatises appearing until the fourth Islamic century (900's A.D.), or the time of Ṭabarī and Ibn Mujāhid. In addition to the long development of the systematization of readings, there was also, before *tajwīd* became a self-conscious sub-field within *qirāʾāt*, a crucial complex of related developments in Arabic grammar, philology and phonetics. The earliest written work on *tajwīd*, then, presupposes the existence of a mature linguistic tradition as well as an established approach to the readings. However, the *practice* of recitation, whether it was called *tajwīd*, or *qirāʾa*, or whatever, had been a central dimension of Islamic piety from the beginning, and it is highly likely that what we find in the manuals is a crystallization of long-accepted techniques and definitions. An oral tradition of teaching had maintained the primitive recitation practice in its essentials, which then later became codified. It is probable that recitation with secular melodies (*qirāʾa biʾl-alḥān*), although it was apparently influential and widespread for a time, was a relatively temporary aberration, at least in its extreme forms. [71] However, it is probable that certain musical modes became associated with *tajwīd* as a consequence of its having been performed in ways akin to art singing.

Our earliest surviving treatise on recitation performance is the ode attributed to Ibn Khāqān (d. 325/937-8), [72] a fascinating, comprehensive work in fifty-one verses ending in "-ri." Interestingly, the word

---

[71] See Muhammad Talbi, "La Qirāʾa bi-l-alḥān," *Arabica* 5 (1958), 183-90; Abū Bakr Muḥammad ibn al-Walīd al-Ṭurṭushī, *Kitāb al-ḥawādith waʾl-bidaᶜ*, Tunis, 1959, 75-86.

[72] See Paulo Boneschi, "*La Qaṣīda fīʾt-tagwīd* atribuée a Mūsā B. ᶜUbayd Allāh B. Ḥāqān," Accademia Nazionale dei Lincei, Rome, Classe di Scienze Morali, Storiche e Filologiche, Rendiconti, ser. 6, 14 (1938), 51-92.

tajwīd nowhere appears in the work; instead, *qirāʾa*, *tilāwa* and *adāʾ* are employed. This work was composed, according to its author, in such a manner as to be memorized easily and thus would help spread the knowledge of correct recitation performance to all Muslim regions. Ibn Khāqān claims to have been transmitting a traditional method of recitation, according to the practice of the earliest masters, who are listed as none less than Ibn Mujāhid's "Seven Reciters."

This ode is a model of terseness and represents a trend toward easily remembered summaries of recitation principles. The work evaluates the merits of slow (*tartīl*) versus rapid (*ḥadr*) chanting, favoring the former because it is more accurate and prolongs meditation and reflection on the message itself. One should recite privately as well as publicly, for practice leads to perfection in *dhikr* (which appears to be a synonym for "prayer"). There follows a detailed yet concise review of the phonetics of *tajwīd*, particularly the means, anatomical and otherwise, of pronouncing the letters, words and phrases; of observing the correct "pauses and starts"; of the fine points of shadings, lengthenings and so forth. Such technical matters make up the major part of manuals on recitation from that time on. They are impossible to understand fully without a living master who can interpret and give demonstrations, once again strongly suggesting that written manuals are but a crystallization of long established practice which had been transmitted orally, "notes" for performance cast in easily remembered form.

The greatest expert on the readings and related fields is generally acknowledged to have been Abū ʿAmr al-Dānī (d. 444/1053), another Maghribī, who spent most of his life in his native Spain. Ibn Khaldūn writes that his reputation as a *muqriʾ* became so great that "people no longer consulted anyone else." [73] In addition to his standard work on the "Seven Readings," al-Dānī also wrote other significant studies, including one on *tajwīd* as well as important treatments of the orthography, copying out and punctuation of the Qurʾānic text.

To this point, *tajwīd* has been defined only in simple terms. But it is a word which came to be carefully defined and qualified and applied in the literature, especially in the writing of Ibn al-Jazarī (d. 823/1429), whose approach is reflected in most treatments of the subject thereafter. Glossing al-Dānī's laconic definition, "between *tajwīd* and its neglect is simply practice for him who tends to it carefully with his jaw," Ibn al-Jazarī writes:

---

[73] Ibn Khaldūn, *op. cit.*, II, 441.

Tajwīd is not slurring of the tongue, nor hollowing of the mouth [so as to make deep tones], nor twisting of the jaw, nor quavering of the voice, nor lengthening of the doubled consonants, nor cutting short the lengthened vowels, nor buzzing the nasals, nor slurring the r's. Recitation [*qirāʾa*] shuns these impressions, and the hearts and ears reject them. On the contrary: gentle, sweet, pleasant, fluent recitation — that we point to and present as of the utmost importance in what we say; with no inaccuracy, nor affectation, nor manneredness, nor extravagance, and no straying from the natural hallmarks of the Arabs, and the speech of the truly eloquent and pure with respect to the "Readings" and accepted performance. [74]

This elaboration is a kind of concluding memorandum of the pitfalls and problems as well as the satisfactions and triumphs which Qurʾān recitation encountered in its long evolution into a mature science. By the time such definitions appeared, there was nothing more of importance to be said about the subject on its practical side.

III. CONCLUSIONS

The careers of Qurʾānic exegesis and recitation were marked by considerable diversity and testing in the formative centuries of classical Islam. The community's conviction of its Scripture's centrally authoritative position was absolute from the time of Muhammad and the Book served as the most important source of inspiration and instruction even after the time when the Prophet's Sunna came to occupy the position of its paradigmatic complement. The means of appropriating, conserving, interpreting and applying the Message had to be mastered through the challenges and experiences of a complex developmental process which has been surveyed and analyzed in this essay. Both modes of Qurʾānic piety were definitively influenced by the emerging sciences of Ḥadīth and jurisprudence, on the one hand, and by grammar, rhetoric and philology on the other. Thus the Qurʾānic sciences did not develop independently or autonomously, although it should be stressed that the religious impulses which motivated people to develop them were of a fundamental character.

The exegetical enterprise, while it culminated in a mature form of traditional commentary, most brilliantly exemplified by Ṭabarī, has always been inherently susceptible of change and unpredictable directions. This phenomenon is by no means unique to Islam; rather, it is in the nature of scripture and its role in religious traditions. Quite the

---

[74] Ibn al-Jazarī, *op. cit.*, II, 213.

opposite tendency is the case with readings/recitation, which came to be increasingly restricted and standardized with the passage of time, in a manner which Muslims would regard as providential in its inevitability. Similar triumphs of sacred writing are known in other religions, although the process is different in every case. It is true that during the early generations readings/recitation exhibited much in the way of variety and parallel developments; but the direction was toward a relative uniformity of approach and what differences remained were carefully provided for in the orthodox framework which centered in the "Seven Readings" of Ibn Mujāhid.

The difference between the exegetical and recitational modes is a product not primarily of circumstances but of the essence of the scripture itself. Like all sacred texts, the Qur³ān is regarded as authoritative partly because it actually does serve as the definitive, enduring source of spiritual guidance, remaining fixed within the flow of change. The wonder is that it also provides new insights into an infinite variety of issues, or can at least be applied to them in deeply satisfying ways. In this sense, it is both a continuity within transformation and an agent of transformation through the expansion of religious sensibility. The wide array of authentically Islamic belief and behavioral patterns which have developed within the Muslim community—ranging from strict Ḥanbalite puritanism to antinomian forms of Ṣūfism— have all centered in the Qur³ān in some way.

Recitation serves to maintain the Qur³ān's integral continuity by rehearsing its changelessness while celebrating its beauties. Exegesis tends toward newness and progressive enrichment of understanding, even while looking backward through layers of tradition and striving to be untainted by the label "bidᶜa," that curious Arabic word for heresy which literally means "innovation." That is, commentary of a responsible sort conscientiously avoids changing or undermining the Qur³ān in any way, whether by reading into it inappropriate meanings or twisting it to fit new circumstances. The Qur³ān itself possesses a dynamic principle of interpretation in its frequent invitations simply to ponder God's many "signs" in nature and history, thus laying the foundation for an expanding, transforming, symbolic awareness.

Recitation and interpretation together provide a dialectic of continuity and transformation within an authentic Islamic vision of the divine-human encounter. They are inseparable and interpenetrating dimensions of a single piety which is poised between the hiddenness and revealedness of God's purposes and life's meaning. Through recitation the believers recapture and inhabit an eternal moment; by means of interpretative effort that moment is arrested in reflection so as to unveil mysteries of time. The continuity of the Qurʾān at the center of faith and action moreover provides the community with the possibility of being itself transformed in each generation from a worldly to a godly people. *Tilāwat al-Qurʾān,* remember means not only recitation of, but more pointedly, *following* the Message.

There never was a time, then, in the earliest phase of Islamic religious development, when the Qurʾān's proper recitation and interpretation were fixed in official or universally accepted ways, although initiatives had been set in motion. The constant throughout the gradual development and crystallization, the unity amidst the diversity which has been traced in this discussion, was of course the Qurʾān itself as accepted norm for belief and gracious agent of faith and guidance. This is a somewhat paradoxical situation: the Book was master of the Muslims before they had achieved proficiency in its interpretation and use. The revelation had in a real sense established and nurtured the fledging community and then progressively engaged it in a mutual relationship through which its true and enduring character was affirmed and articulated in progressively institutionalized ways. The science of interpretation enabled the believers to apply the Message to the world and in the process make sense of both, while the discipline of recitation made accessible to all the treasure of God's Speech, which guided them even as they guarded it.

THE IMAM IN THE NEW WORLD
Models and Modifications

EARLE H. WAUGH

University of Alberta

Readers of the Arabian Nights will be familiar with Imam Abu Yusuf, the scholar and religious lawyer who was called upon to make it instantly possible for Harun al-Rashid to marry a slave girl who had smitten him, even though the law required a period of time for her purification. By dint of legal gymnastics, the Imam complied. He was heaped with gold by the grateful Caliph. Imam Yusuf mused to his friends: "There is no easier nor shorter road to the goods of this world and the next, than that of religious learning: for, see, I have gotten all this money by answering two or three questions." [1]

The story leads one to contemplate more than the lucrative profession the lawyer had pursued; it brings us soon to the thorny question of the ideals of Islam and the responsibilities of leadership in the Muslim community for promoting a society that would embody them. There is an evident gap, sometimes quite massive, between what was supposed to be the case, and what those in authority, like Imam Yusuf, produced.

It is perhaps because Islam had seen only too clearly the vagaries of the human heart that it had theologically and institutionally rejected a sacramental role for man in its system. Still there was (and is) a sizeable group of Muslims, the Shīʿa, who saw the role of inspired leader as essential for the correct guidance of the community and who built a religious interpretation of Islam around that conception. For them, the word *Imam* took on transcendent dimensions that had an impact on the religious world of the believer far beyond that agreed upon by the more numerous Sunnī Muslims. [2] In addition there was the quasi-soteriological role which the saints played in popular Islam

---

[1] *The Book of the Thousand Nights and a Night*, trans. R. Burton, Boston, 1885, IV, 155.

[2] The Shīʿa understanding of Imam is beyond the scope of this article; see *Encyclopedia of Islam*; and Marshall Hodgson, *The Venture of Islam*, Chicago, 1974, I, 256-67, 372-76.

in many countries. [3] It might even be argued that the scholars of the Imam Yusuf mold, insofar as they mediated between the ideal religious community as expressed in the sharīʿa and the individual confronted with the holy law provided some measure of sacramental presence in Muslim society. [4] Hence, despite its lack of institutional priesthood or ministry in any of the usual senses of that word, Islam did foster a leadership that was both infused with and responsible for spiritual norms in the community.

In the light of this revaluation of Muslim leadership, it is instructive to consider the role and position of the Imam in North America, and specifically one who serves in a mosque built by immigrants from Muslim countries. There one can perceive where the steady hand of tradition operates, and where it breaks down, where customary conceptions guide the manner in which the Imam responds, and where old forms are being modified in the direction of professional religious leadership much different than has existed hitherto. It is a creative moment for one who serves as Imam in the new world. Primarily, the material used in this article was drawn from Imams who have served in the Mosque in Edmonton, along with comments and insights provided by other Muslim believers, [5] but it would likely apply, with varying degrees of adjustment, to other North American immigrant mosques, particularly to Sunnī Mosques.

History of the Muslim Community in Edmonton

The Muslim community in Edmonton began in the late 1890's and early 1900's when merchants and workers came through the area. Settlement had begun before 1910 by such pioneers as Alex Hamilton (so named by an immigration officer who found his name too difficult), Sam Jamha and Mike Tarrabain, all of whom came from the village of Lala in Lebanon. Later they were joined by Alex and Ahmed Awid (Amerey), Andy (Mohammad Ali) Hamdon, and other Tarra-

---

[3] E.g., the marabouts in North Africa or the Sūfī shaikhs in Asia; see Ignaz Goldziher, "Veneration of Saints in Islam," *Muslim Studies*, Albany, N.Y., 1971, II, 256-341.

[4] Scholars are reconsidering the nature and role of the ʿulamā on several fronts; see H. A. R. Gibb and Harold Bowen, *Islamic Society and the West*, Oxford, 1962, II, pt. 1, ch. 9; Gabriel Baer, ed., *The ʿUlamāʾ in Modern History*, Jerusalem, 1971; and Nikki Keddie, ed., *Scholars, Saints, and Sufis: Muslim Religious Institutions in the Middle East since 1500*, Los Angeles, 1972.

[5] I am especially indebted to the current Imam, Yussef Chebli, the past Imam, Ahmad Sharkawi, and the president of the Mosque Association Executive, Mr. Saleem Ganam. Naturally my interpretation of their remarks are my own responsibility.

bain relatives from Lala, and a small group from other places in Lebanon. This group was to form the nucleus of the local Muslim community. [6] At the same time others from the Christian and Druze groups migrated to the city, joining with the Muslims in the Canadian Arab Friendship Association, an organization still active.

Contact among Muslims was limited due to the great distances involved (other Muslims settled in Lac La Biche, Alberta, Saskatchewan and Manitoba) [7] but continuous contact was maintained with relatives back in Lebanon, and the others who had immigrated to South America. In effect, then, the resilience and closely-knit family and small village life was carried on in a Canadian environment because that way of life was natural to them, it was continually reinforced, and Canadian society was so alien. [8]

When children began growing up without the rudiments of religious tradition, the small group became increasingly concerned. Some among the group advocated a community hall, where traditions from all the Arab-speaking community could be preserved; but others argued that a mosque was necessary, notably James Ailley who had moved to Edmonton from Winnipeg in the 20's. [9] Since they were so few, the cost seemed prohibitive, but they persevered, and in January, 1938, a group called "Arabian Muslim Association" was formed, and a lot at 101 Street and 108 Avenue was obtained. The building permit was obtained on May 15, 1938, and gifts from Muslims, non-Muslim Arabs and friends allowed them to complete the building by November 2, 1938. The first official use of the mosque was the funeral of one of the pioneers in the area, Ali Tarrabian, held in November with the inauguration on December 12, 1938. The first wedding reception was held there August 8, 1941.

In 1946, the City of Edmonton indicated that it needed the mosque site for an addition to Victoria Composite High School, and negotiations resulted in the City moving the building to its present location at 102 Street and 111 Avenue on November 5, 1946. The Royal Alex

---

[6] I am indebted to Jane Barclay for her help in gathering data in this summary.

[7] See Harold Barclay, "A Lebanese Community in Lac La Biche, Alberta," *Immigrant Groups*, ed. Jean Elliott, Scarborough, Ontario, 1971, 66-83; also Baha Abu-Laban, "The Arab-Canadian Community," *Arab-Americans: Studies in Assimilation*, ed. E. Hagopian and A. Paden, Wilmette, 1969, 18-36.

[8] See Louise Sweet, "Reconstituting a Lebanese Village Society in a Canadian City," *Arabic Speaking Communities in American Cities*, ed. Barbara Aswad, Staten Island, N.Y., 1974, 39-52.

[9] See the pamphlet, *Al-Rashid Mosque, 25th Anniversary Celebration*.

hospital is currently projected to expand and plans are underway to secure another site and build a new mosque. These have not been finalized as of this writing.

Like mosques in Muslim lands, the Al-Rashid mosque has been a social and religious centre. A Ladies Muslim Auxiliary was founded on February 19, 1941, with their primary task being the annual dinner, and the food for feast day celebrations. The group held one bazaar at the mosque, but there was some resistance to this idea and it has never been repeated. The Auxiliary has also spearheaded the drive to organize the "Sunday" school, which has been operating for three years, and Arab language classes, which have only recently been regularly held. A nearby school has been used for these endeavours. More traditionally, the mosque is open for prayer, and groups of men gather there in the evenings to carry on the social interaction that is common to men in the Middle East.

James Ailley acted as Imam after the mosque was first completed in 1938 and he continued to play an active role until his death in 1959. His death was the catalyst that persuaded the Egyptian government and al-Azhar to provide one of its scholars, and in July, 1960, Imam Abd al-Ati arrived to take up full-time duties. Since the community appeared too small to pay an Imam, outside funding has come from various sources, [10] including the Muslim World League, headquartered in Mecca. Through it various Arab governments support Imams abroad.

The community has grown considerably since the 30's, with Muslims from Iraq, Egypt, North Africa, Africa, and Pakistan now living in Edmonton. The Muslim population in the city has been estimated at 5,000, obviously fertile ground for an active Islamic organization.

MODELS OPERATIVE IN THE IMAM'S EXPERIENCE

Traditional Educational and Societal Norms

> "Verily I make you an Imam for mankind."
> "...make us a model to the godfearing."

The word Imam, deriving as it does from *amma* meaning to lead someone, guide, or proceed on the way, carries a cluster of meanings. [11] It is used in the Qurʾān in both the senses of being an example and as

---

[10] Imams have worked at outside jobs to supplement the stipend paid.

[11] See Hans Wehr, *A Dictionary of Modern Written Arabic*, Ithaca, 1960; S. and N. Roman, *Concise Encyclopedia of Arabic Civilization*, Amsterdam, 1959.

leading God's people, and consequently involves norms or ideals, along with the ongoing process of leading. Perhaps harking back to the image of guiding a caravan, the word implies the solidarity of the leader and the group he is leading... there is none of the solitariness of leadership so prevalent in contemporary politics. But the word grew with the expansion of Islam and took on other nuances. First applied to Muhammad, as a political leadership cipher, it became synonomous with the caliph after his death. During his lifetime, Muhammad had been both leader of the forces of the ummah, and the community in prayer, particularly the Friday noon prayer incumbent on all believers. The expansion of the empire required the delegation of authority, and the role of Imam was transferred to the governors of the provinces, who in turn delegated the responsibility of leading in prayer to the rising learned men, the ʿulamā. [12]

But the educated class were never allowed to monopolize the word. It retained some of the intimate flavour attending Muhammad's initial relationship with the community, and the traditions asserted this character: Bukhārī records that slaves and *mawlā* could be Imams, [13] and other collections affirm that women could perform the same role. [14] Consequently, Sunnis especially have stressed the openness of the Imam's position to any individual who is best prepared to do it in the community, and have eschewed the professionalizing tendencies implied in the delegating procedures of the caliphs.

Despite this however, the requirements of being "best" for the role within the ummah has exercised a selection process that implies a religious system. A quick run through the traditions associated with the Imam and prayer indicates that: the Imam is meant to be followed, the oldest should lead, believers should wait for the Imam before beginning the prayer, there are distinctive benefits to praying with the Imam, religious learned men are entitled to precedence in leading prayers, and the Imam has the power to shorten the prayer if need be. [15] Moreover, there are duties incumbent upon an Imam, such as recitation of the Qurʾān, [16] or he should know the Qurʾān better than any other, or he should lead the prayer perfectly lest he commit a sin. [17] Bukhārī also reports that prayer should not be made if the leader is effeminate

---

[12] See *Islamic Society and the West*, I, pt. 2, 95ff.
[13] Bukhārī, *Ṣaḥīḥ*, I, ch. 54.
[14] See Ahmad Ibn Hanbal, *Musnad*, Cairo, 1313, VI, 405.
[15] Bukhārī, I, ch. 61.
[16] *Ibid.*, II, ch. 14.
[17] *Ibid.*, I, ch. 55.

(*mukannaṭ*, i.e. bisexual, effeminate, powerless, impotent, weak) unless there is no alternative. [18] All this indicates that the religious system has definite meanings that embody the community's religious consciousness.

But the impact of the Imam does not rest solely upon these religious prerequisites, since Islam has developed other religious personages with their own values and these have played an important part in the ranking accorded the Imam. For example, the centrality of the Friday prayer and the need for all men in the community to gather in a common group dictated that the place of congregational prayer take on special significance. It followed that the leader who was accorded the duty of leading the Friday prayer before the whole community would be given an honored place in the group, since, by definition, he was the best for the position. Furthermore, only those places which were the locales for the Friday prayers would be given a professional Imam, [19] although, in time, every mosque probably made that claim. Of increasing significance was the role of the preacher or *khattib*, whose task involved the blessing of God upon the congregation and particularly on the sovereign, who was mentioned by name. [20] This added political dimension meant that an authority not resident in the Imam was conferred by the khattib, and he became a functionary of greater importance. [21] Finally a preacher who taught after the Friday prayer, and by virtue of speaking last was held to be more learned and important, the *waᶜiz*, rounded out the professional religious functionaries who had special training. [22] The Imam was part of a group of professional people whose tasks were religious in nature, and his role and expectations were governed by the value given those positions.

Hence the Imam belongs more to an institutional religious continuum than to the temporary allegiance granted a saint or holy man. [23] One way of seeing this difference is to view the latter as presenting ultimate reality in a personal charismatic manner, totally dependent upon the religious aura which his piety generated. When he dies, his piety may be institutionalized by being passed on to his successor, but certainly the

---

[18] *Ibid.*, I, ch. 56.

[19] *Islamic Society and the West*, 95.

[20] See Hodgson, *op. cit.*, I, 210.

[21] The local governor choses him; cf. *Islamic Society and the West*, 95-96.

[22] Additional attendants and functionaries included the *muᵓaḍḍin* who called the faithful to prayer, and the *qurrāᵓ*, the professional Qurᵓān reciters; *ibid*.

[23] See Canon Sell, *The Religious Orders of Islam*, London, 1908 (reprint 1976), 9-12.

dimension he added to Islam was personal rather than institutional in form.

The same could not be said of the Imam. While his role was, in some measure, derived from the manner in which he expressed his Muslim faith and the norms he embodied in his everyday life, they derived from a value system that was rooted in community views rather than something of his inner personal experience. The primary focus of that system was the loosely-grouped scholarly class, based on religious knowledge and understanding, imparted by study and literary learning. In time, these scholars developed their own collection of values, which in turn became the norms for piety within their class:

> He excelled in law, the rules of inheritance, and calculation, and possessed by heart a great deal of verse of a religious, ethical and didactic character. He was pious and upright; a devotee, frequently spending his nights in prayer; concerned with his own inmost soul; sound-hearted knowing nothing of deceit or envy; doing good to those who did him ill; of handsome form and cheerful countenance; full of humility and dispensing with formality; with a strong trust in God, truthful in speech and of a happy disposition; an eager reader of works of learning; avoiding what did not concern him; easy and open-handed in his worldly affairs, but strict in matters of religion; preferring solitude and retreat; with no inclinations for high position and no ambitions reaching out towards it. [24]

Certainly a learned saint who would be respected in any tradition.

Knowing the Qur'ān was regarded as the bottom line for one who would be the Imam but the impact that this "knowing" had escapes one with that hasty statement. The first point to note is that the position of the Qur'ān in Muslim society, while always important, was something that had to be established in the ongoing history of the community; it was not automatically established. For example, the role of the Qur'ān could not be fixed until some decision had been made about the legitimacy and nature of Muhammad's career. Nawbakhti records:

> A group stood aloof from Abū Bakr and said: "We will not pay the alms until we are certain of who is in command and know whom the prophet has nominated as successor. We will divide the alms among the poor and the needy of our numbers." Another group apostatized and abandoned Islam. Banū Ḥanīfah called for the recognition of the prophethood of Musaylimah; the latter had claimed prophecy during the life of Muḥammad. Abū Bakr sent against them his cavalries under the command of Khālid b. al-Walīd al-Makhzūmī. Khālid fought them,

---

[24] Murādī, quoted in *Islamic Society and the West*, 103, n. 9.

Musaylimah was slain, others were killed, and the rest repented and
acknowledged the caliphate of Abū Bakr. They therefore were called
apostates, Ahl al-Raddah. [25]

Apart from the question of what would have happened had Khalīd
lost the battle, it is clear that the leadership value of Muhammad was
the key to the acceptance of the Qurʾān. Had the group not been so
convinced of Muhammad's absolute verity, or the ideology of the group
around Abū Bakr more fractured about continuing the community,
the history of the Qurʾān would have been much different. As it was,
the Qurʾān became the principle symbol and founding stone for
the ummah. [26]

Another point is that the message revealed through the Prophet was
not just a basis for Muslim law and practice because it expressed great
judicial truths, but because it was, in contemporary terms, an existential
imperative questioning every act of the believer, ultimately colouring his
perception of the world:

Allahumma! make the Qurʾān a mercy for me and set it as a model
for me, a light, a guidance, and a mercy.

Allahumma! cause me to recollect what I have forgotten of it, teach
me what I am ignorant of about it, grant me the blessing of reciting
it all day and all night, and make it a thing that pleads for me (on the
Day of Judgment), O Lord of mankind. [27]

This attitude toward the Qurʾān makes it understandable that the
closest we find to a professional religious group in early Islam is the
al-qurrāʾ, the Qurʾān reciters, who were sent out by ʿUmar wherever
Islam had conquered. Their importance is by no means vitiated by the
current scholarly controversy over how numerous they were and their
true nature. [28] Tradition insists that it was because of unusual numbers
of them being killed that prompted the Qurʾān being written down.
At any rate, their commitment to the Qurʾān was an early expression

---

[25] Quoted in E. S. Shoufani, *Al-Riddah and the Muslim Conquest of Arabia*,
Toronto, 1973, 100.

[26] See R. Blachere, *Introduction au Coran*, Paris, 1959; or Richard Bell, *Introduction to the Qurʾān*, Edinburgh, 1953.

[27] Muhammad Ṭāhir al-Kurdī, quoted in *Islam: Muhammad and His Religion*, ed.
A. Jeffery, New York, 1958, 68.

[28] H. A. R. Gibb, "An Interpretation of Islamic History," *Studies on the Civilization
of Islam*, ed. S. J. Shaw and W. R. Polk, Boston, 7f., sees the religious party opposed
to the tribal group, with the Qurraʾ organized into fighting contingents; but M. A.
Shaban, *Islamic History A.D. 600-750 (A.H. 132): A New Interpretation*, Cambridge,
1971, 51, sees them as a group of tribesmen who never apostacized, and not primarily
reciters at all.

of Islamic piety, and representative examples of their diligence is found
over and over in the Muslim community from that day to this. It also
helps us understand the ardent work in memorizing the Qurʾān which
formed the basis of all achievement in traditional Islam:

> Note, also, the account given by the Maghribi scholar, Ibn Naji (d.
> 1435), of his early education. His uncle paid for an instructor to teach
> young Ibn Naji the Qurʾān, and the uncle would drop by the house
> from time to time to hear the youth recite.
>
> "One night", Ibn Naji relates, "(my uncle) gave me a slap because I
> stopped at each word. I don't think he had ever struck me before that
> night. I kept on reciting while crying. My mother, standing outside
> the room by the door cried upon hearing me cry. Hearing her, my uncle
> silenced me and cried out: 'ᶜAisha, it's your fault. You took him to the
> country with you and he has abandoned his surahs for over a month.
> I told you not to, but you refused, claiming that you couldn't be
> separated from him. But for this there would be no need to say anymore
> on this subject.'
>
> "She answered, 'Sir, if I cried for him it is for another reason. It is
> because, small as he is, he recites each night in the dark. So far you
> have not let me light a lamp.'
>
> "Thereafter, he let her light a lamp... Later, my mother told me,
> 'When he left this evening for his prayers, he told me as I followed
> him to close the gate, "Have patience, for he will be long separated
> from you to go to Tunis to study. He will become a qadi in numerous
> places." ' " 29

When we reflect, then, upon the requirement that the Imam "know"
the Qurʾān, we perceive that he must know more than the words or the
phrases that make up the popular sections. He must also reflect in
attitude and concern, the traditional values held to be exemplified in
the words of the Qurʾān. This perception is reinforced by the fact that
the site of most Muslim learning in traditional Islam was the mosque
school, an institution that grew up around the knowledge imparted
by the Qurʾān and the traditions, 30 and by the fact that the Qurʾānic
verses had to be commented upon to explain their significance. Even
the choice of verses for reciting involved an ordering process, thus
implying judgments of importance for the occasion, or the religious
needs the verses met. At any rate, the process suggests a religious

---

29 Quoted in L. Carl Brown, "The Presidential Address," *Middle East Studies
Association Bulletin* 11 (1977), 7.

30 See Nehdi Nakosteen, *History of Islamic Origins of Western Education, A.D.
800-1350*, Boulder, 1964, 46-48; and B. Dodge, *Muslim Education in Medieval Times*,
Washington, 1962, 2.

sensitivity to both the religious power of the Qurʾān, and the needs and conceptions of the people who heard its words, a talent which Islam recognized early, but which it never allowed to hold sacramental authority in an official way. This may be both beneficial and propose difficulties for the present-day Imam in North America, as we shall see later.

The ʿUlamā

One ingredient most characteristic of Muslim society that plays a key role in Imam definition is the ʿulamā. We have already seen that the Imam belongs primarily to this institutional class (above, p. 130), but it is well to note that while Muslims have always respected the role of the ʿulamā, they have not relied upon that group for community definition. Rather, the ʿulamā have served as one abiding element in a series of power centers within Islam that have continuously moved and shifted with the community, so that the stress has been on the voluntariness rather than on hierarchical institutional forms. [31] Hence the ʿulamā have both presented a learned position on Islam and have continuously needed to clarify their role in society in light of popular conceptions.

The prestige of the ʿulamā depends upon the evaluation of the Muslim society, which, in turn, has developed its views out of statements of the Prophet: "It is better to teach one hour in the night than to pray the whole night through." "The ink of the learned is as precious as the blood of the martyrs." "Honoring a learned man is worth honoring seventy Prophets." [32] In the same vein, the purpose of a Muslim education was primarily religious with the basic goal to understand the revelation of God. Since the Imam must first of all be learned in the Qurʾān, he serves as an ever-present visible expression of the status and accomplishments of Muslim learning. Beyond leading the prayers, this meant initially being sufficiently knowledgeable to edify the congregation each Friday. The first one to do this was Tamim ad-Dari who gave the sermon under ʿUmar in Medina, [33] and who received permission to do so twice a week under ʿUthman. Individuals who did this were called qāṣṣ, and their public edifications were held

---

[31] See J. Lapidus, "Hierarchies and Networks: A Comparison of Chinese and Islamic Societies," F. Wakeman and C. Grant, eds., *Conflict and Control in Late Imperial China*, Berkeley, 1975, 26-42.

[32] Commonly said to be quotes from the Prophets; B. Dodge, *op. cit.*, 59.

[33] See Asad Talas, *La Madrasa Nizamiyya et son histoire*, Paris, 1939, 4-5.

in the mosque. The mosque was also the principal locale of the *halqah*
or circle, a group of students who gathered around a scholar and
listened to him teach on some subject relevant to *ahl al-ᶜilm* (tradition
or religious sciences) or *ahl al-adab* (literature). This group is known
as the *majlis*. On the other hand the *kuttab* or *maktab* was the basic
training school for children, since it was concerned to instill basic
knowledge, such as grammar, counting, and Qurᵓān, and may be held in
the mosque, but was more likely held in a private home, shop or
bookstore.

In time distinctive roles developed in these mosque activities; the
qāṣṣ was more popular with the people, and his exhortations were
likely to be based on simple moral truths derived from the Qurᵓān
or hadith. They did not have the authority of learned judgment, the
need of which eventually was to produce a range of educators such as
ᶜalim, ustādh, hakim, and *shaikh.* In addition, the early days of Islam
had *al-qārī,* Qurᵓān reciters who would also interpret the revelation to
listeners, and *al-rāwī,* hadith-relators whose lore could include poems
and proverbs from pre-Islamic times. [34] The *muᶜaddib* also existed in
early Islamic times, perhaps based initially on Jewish masters in Medina
but later on learned slaves and conquered people, who were engaged
by wealthy Muslims to teach their children. [35] What was essential
in all of these roles was the view that the norms of the community
were rooted in the Prophet and the microcosm of the Medinan-Meccan
society; scientific accomplishments based on experimentation, or knowledge from other sources were suspect. [36]

It was from such beginnings that the great institutions of Muslim
education developed... from the translation school of *Bait al-Hikmah,*
to the mosque-colleges and universities such as Nizamiyya and al-
Azhar. [37] The range of subjects taught in them encompass the entire
Muslim field of learning, [38] reflecting the complexity of managing
the affairs of a complicated Muslim empire. While a discussion of
these are outside our interest, it is important to see that they revolved
around religious pursuits and their impetus derived from religious
concerns. This, in turn, brings an order into play that can partly be

---

[34] Dodge, *op. cit.*, 2.

[35] See *Encyclopedia of Islam*, III, 411; and Dodge, *op. cit.*, 2.

[36] *Ibid.*, 28.

[37] George Makdisi, "Muslim Institutions of Learning in Eleventh-Century Baghdad,"
BSOAS 4 (1961), 1-56.

[38] See e.g. A. S. Tritton, *Materials on Muslim Education in the Middle Ages.*
London, 1957, 156.

detected in the standards set by the ᶜulamā themselves, but also partly beyond their control. From within came first of all the discipline imposed by rigorous teachers on their students. Only those who really were committed to this life went past the halqah of the local mosque. Those who succeeded travelled widely to study under the great thinkers, or pursued knowledge wherever they could find it. Much of this required an enforced servitude:

> In return for instruction in Jami's and Jarbardi's commentaries and the Shafiya, his teacher exacted from him "much service," making him and his fellow students collect stones for a house from the neighbouring town. He would not allow them to copy his lecture notes, but they used to purloin them when opportunity arose and transcribe them. "Such was his way of us," says the writer, "yet withal we were well satisfied to serve him, so that we might derive benefit from his holy breaths." [39]

We should not allow our contemporary sensitivity to the student's personal rights blind us to the important fact that however he objected to the cantakerous nature of his teacher, he immediately respected him. This respect permeated the scholarly world and gave it a tone which fit well with an inner discipline that Islam has always had... the learned man may be personally intransigent, but the knowledge he husbands is from above. Hence where the loyalty to a teacher might flag, the honest pursuit of the knowledge enjoined by God would buoy him up. There is little evidence thtn that the students did not accept the discipline of their masters. [40]

From within, too, came the various codes, mainly unwritten, which guided the student. Some of these would solidify into guilds, [41] with internal cohesion and discipline. Others derived from the nature of the material with which they had to deal. Some of it was potentially explosive, requiring that knowledge be circumspectly disseminated. Ghazzālī recognized the problem and advocated that there were two levels of truth, that for the initiate and that for the commoner. This view asserts that there are truths that the ordinary individual cannot bear. [42] The implication for the ᶜulamā is clearly that they could only deal with sensitive issues with those who were truly committed to their livelihood, over whom they had control. Hence the rules were implicitly accepted even at great personal cost.

---

39 E. G. Browne, *Persian Literature in Modern Times*, Cambridge, 1909, 362.

40 Despite such proverbs as "Stupidity is found in tailors, teachers, and weavers," a great affinity developed between students and scholars; see Nakosteen, *op. cit.*, 56.

41 *Ibid.*, 57.

42 See A. J. Wensinck, *La Pensee de Ghazzali*, Paris, 1940.

The greatest impact on the ᶜulamā had to come from the society in which they worked. Scholars could not afford the luxury of disagreeing with the views of the population, especially on an important religious issue. An impressive number of scholars ended up in jail, or worse because they dared to propose something differing from the views of the community in which they lived. One need only to recount the horrendous death of al-Hallāj to be reminded of that fact. [43] Hence, the relationship with the common man was always ambiguous. Saᵓdi once noted that "However men of learning despise the ignorant, the ignorant are many times more scornful of the learned." [44] A scholar who ran afoul of the authorities could not hope to appeal to the mass of the people unless he was himself a holy man, with many pious connections. Then his appeal would be on broad religious grounds, not on the grounds of his perception of the issue that now was about to bring him trouble. In this manner, the scholar was at the mercy of the populace, requiring that he be very careful to ground his work on the great thinkers of the past. The persuasion of tradition rooted his required standards in an earlier time.

But this persuasion is not self-defining, and every society must come to its own awareness of that past. [45] Wide latitude existed in early Islam for diversity of opinion, since the sharīᶜa had not yet been finalized into the four principle schools, and the law still had some local mores incorporated into it. Certainly the days of the Prophet and the Rightly-Guided Caliphs could not be claimed to be the ideal period for the scholars, since much of their work had only been sketched out. What appears to have occurred was a narrowing of the range of methods and themes as the years passed by, under the pressure of maintaining a common, unified approach to Islam and the conviction of a single interpretation of the Qurᵓān's and Sunnah's truths.

The notion of the unitariness of approaches and truths is a complex one, but at bottom it required formulations to appear in the guise of what had gone before, and religious scholarship to be measured in terms of conquering the writings of ancient savants. [46] This, too, is certainly a religious value—what historians of religions in the west call

---

[43] See L. Massignon, *La passion d'al-Hallāj*, Paris, 1922.

[44] Quoted in Nakosteen, *op. cit.*, 122.

[45] Thus the ᶜulamā of al-Azhar could issue a *fatwa* early in the eighteenth century, asserting the ability of saints to work miracles even after their death; see *Islamic Society and the West*, I, pt. 2, 160, n. 1.

[46] The model for this method is surely the *isnad*, where Truth is only acceptable if its source can be established (i.e. the Prophet) and if it has been properly handed on.

a *myth*, since it defined reality for the scholars yet is itself as elusive as the formulation of any other similar cultural metaphor. Muslim commitment to it played a key role in the life and work of scholars, and this continues to our day. [47]

Perhaps only slightly less important was the perception that the learned tradition itself had the responsibility of preserving the true faith. Muslim commoners, despite their antagonism to the ᶜulamā, accepted the guidance of the scholars in many ways, from encouraging their children to become ᶜalim to relying on their opinion of Muslim law in minutae of life. A clear example of this is the final accommodation with Sufism and the eventual winning over of the Islamic masses in India when the mission work had been carried out by the saints and holy men. [48] This perception involved not only the passing on of the archetypal nature of revelation and the Prophet's lifestyle, but the ways of thinking and acting that were hallowed by their long development in the Muslim community. Ghazzālī sums it up:

> ... But, thus says the messenger of God (Whom God may bless with his Grace), more than all other men will be punished at the day of resurrection the learned man whose knowledge has not helped him in the yes of the Almighty... My child, knowledge without action is insanity, but action without knowledge is not action. Know that all knowledge cannot save you from sin and will not make you obedient, and will not free you from the fire of hell, unless you really act according to your knowledge. [49]

While we have been dealing with the dichotomy of exterior and interior pressures upon ᶜulamā, we should also weigh that against their social origins. Despite the hierarchical system in which they moved, and the patronage system that assured their existence, it still was possible for a child from a poor family to climb to great heights through education. [50] If Ottoman ᶜulamā can be taken as representative of the general character of Muslim scholars, they had all the acoutrements of an elite group, buying property, businesses, and investing heavily in trade whenever they had the funds to do so, but were not universal

---

[47] See the analysis of Hava Lazarus-Yafeh, "Contemporary Religious Thought among the ᶜUlamā of Azhar," *Asian and African Studies* 7 (1971), 211-36.

[48] See ᶜAziz Ahmad, *An Intellectual History of Islam in India*, Edinburgh, 1969.

[49] In *Three Thousand Years of Educational Wisdom*, Robert Ulrich, ed., Cambridge, Mass., 1959, 198.

[50] E.g., al-Shāfiᶜī (d. 820) was an orphan from Mecca who became one of the most important conservative theologians in the early period of Muslim history.

in restricting this to a few wealthy families. [51] In Cairo at the same time "there was no hereditary caste of high as against lesser ᶜulamā, but rather the profession presented a case of social mobility. Most of the ᶜulamā were of fellah, peasant origin..." [52] Hence the ᶜulamā were rooted in the views and aspirations of the common Muslim by birth, and his attitudes toward Islam were not likely to take him very far from the context that had provided him with his life and career.

Certainly this connection with the unheralded dimensions of Islamic society gave the ᶜulamā a sense of freedom from the political machinations of government; religious truths were much more important in forming his universe than the practical task of paying salaries and managing an empire. This allowed him to operate in an independent realm, separate from, and, in some cases, antithetical to the government. Even those who were forced into serving as qadis or legal advisors to the state had the possibility available of applying their judgment of the law to the government's activities. Generally, the ᶜulamā eschewed these appointments, even though they could be dismissed for disobedience from any role they played in the Muslim community by the political leader of the ummah. Their concern with the spiritual and theological side of Islam, however, provided them with an authority among the people that the government had to take into consideration. It was a power they seldom brought to bear directly on the rulers. [53]

Muhammad

Joachim Wach, following Max Weber, argued that there were identifiable types of religious authority, and that the scientist of religion would do well to investigate the organization and constitution of the group around each type. [54] Within these, there are figures who are "classic" examples of the religion's essence. Several scholars, including Joseph Kitagawa, have found the classic type as a convenient and illuminating focus around which to build religious leadership studies. [55] The category of prophet, however, is fraught with problems, since,

---

[51] Ottoman Turkey seems to be the exception; Arnold Green, "Political Attitudes and Activities of the ᶜUlamā in the Liberal Age: Tunisia as an Exceptional Case," *Internat. J. of Middle Eastern Studies* 7 (1976), 218.

[52] Afaf Lutfi al-Sayyid Marsot, "The ᶜUlamā of Cairo in the Eighteenth and Nineteenth Centuries," *Scholars, Saints, and Sufis*, 157-58.

[53] See Green, *op. cit.*, 212-17.

[54] Joachim Wach, *Sociology of Religion*, Chicago, 1944, 331.

[55] For an example, see Kitagawa, "Kukai as Master and Savior," *The Biographical Process*, ed. Frank Reynolds and Donald Capps, The Hague, 1976, 319-41.

by nature, the charismatic vision is mediated through the individuality and personhood of the prophet himself. Despite the dramatic manner in which prophets achieve their ends, and beyond the *charisma* that is said to be expressed in them, commonalities are hard to find. The pious Muslim's claim that Muhammad is unique has more truth than our penchant for categories would seem to appreciate. [56]

Nevertheless, it is helpful to view Muhammad as a figure whose classic character continues to impress and mold the community in its history. Thus, in the case of the Imam, we might search for those dimensions of his life and ideals which implicitly call to mind the Prophet. Muhammad is not just the man who lived some twelve centuries ago, and who provided the impetus for a new religious community, but is a living presence, through the ideals and religious conceptions associated with him, in the everyday definition of the Imam of his role.

Some measure of this can be gauged by studying various *Lives of the Prophet*, a genre of which Muslims are quite fond. One of the earliest, and perhaps foundational of these is Ibn Ishaq's *Sirat Rasul Allah*. The following quotes should give the flavour of that author's views:

> The apostle of God grew up, God protecting him and keeping him from the vileness of heathenism because he wished to honour him with apostleship, until he grew up to be the finest of his people in manliness, the best in character, most noble in lineage, the best neighbour, the most kind, truthful, reliable, the furthest removed from filthiness and corrupt morals, through loftiness and nobility so that he was known among his people as "The trustworthy" because of the good qualities which God had implanted in him.
>
> We used to prepare his evening meal and send it to him. When he returned what was left, Umm Ayyūb and I used to touch the spot where his hand had rested and eat from that in the hope of gaining a blessing. [57]

The characteristics and qualities adjudged to be part of Muhammad, according to Ibn Ishaq's *Life*, can be broken into several aspects depending upon their intentionality; thus there are characteristics held to be given to him by God, i.e., protection from doing or thinking evil, his prophethood, and chosenness to give guidance and truth; charac-

---

[56] Wach seems to have recognized this when he placed Muhammad in the founders column, despite his prophetic characteristics, and sees al-Ghazzali as an example of a cultus prophet; *op. cit.*, 347-49. Muslims reject Muhammad as a founder, ultimately, of Islam.

[57] *The Life of Muhammad*, trans. A. Guillaume, Lahore, 1967, 81, 230.

teristics deriving from his role as leader, e.g. an excellent mediator, a caring shepherd for his flock, an evangelist and reprover, a peace-maker, a warner who makes plain his message, a rightly-guided imam, a preacher who is gentle with his people, a sage political leader, a strong and courageous commander, a generous man with prisoners, a righteous judge, an honorable and vigorous spokesman for Allah. In addition, there are personal graces which are part of Muhammad's natural mein, viz., his trustworthiness, generosity, humility, gentleness, love for others, humanness, honesty. All of these contribute to the view that the Prophet is an individual around which the faithful crystalized their ideas of excellence, and a pristine standard by which they could evaluate their own lives. Since the meaning of these values are rooted in a culture and community, they in effect become reinterpreted according to the social and religious forces at work at the time. Hence the figure of the Prophet is open to expressing excellence in whatever social or religious context the believer may find himself, and the Prophet himself becomes a focal point for piety and meditation.

A contemporary example of this dimension is the book in honor of the Prophet by Kausar Niazi, entitled *To The Prophet*. [58] A random sampling reflects how the time and piety have modified the views of the Prophet: "This Man of Perfection was so dignified in character that the moon itself would have spots on it and the dew-drops falling on leaves and petals might be filthy, but there was no room for finding fault with what he said or did" (p. 42). "His presige was so great that a person at first sight of him shuddered with awe and dared not speak; but soon after when he talked to anyone he impressed him so much with his hospitality, mildness and sociability that he felt the intimacy of an old friend with him" (p. 47). "One of his distinctive features is that his life presents an ideal for all human communities and groups. He is a model for kings, generals and judges; and so he is for husbands, fathers and sons. There is a guidance for traders, teachers and saints in his life and he is a perfect example for the rich, the poor and the pious. There is a complete guidance in the sacred life of the Prophet for every man, provided he is a man, whatever his profession or capability" (p. 107) .

The role of Imam draws upon the life of the Prophet from several directions. The first is the character of the Imam; according to the

---

[58] Kausar Niazi, *To the Prophet*, Lahore, 1976. At the time of publishing this booklet, Niazi, a respected religious scholar in Pakistan, was Minister of Religious Affairs.

customs of the community, he who is most worthy should lead the prayers. The notion of worthiness requires social definition, since it might be possible for someone to know the Qur²ān by heart but still not be worthy of leading prayers. A good case in point is found in Ibn Ishaq's *Sira*, where he indicates that ᶜUmar questioned whether Mujammiᶜ, a youth with some connection with a group that were not true Muslims (i.e. hypocrites, *munafiq*) should be allowed to lead prayers even though he was qualified to do so. He was not allowed to do so until he had cleared his name of any connection with those dubious in faith. [59] The conception of worthiness thus depends on religious perception, which itself derives from its association with the religious figures who have represented it before. Ultimately it is rooted in the worthiness of the Prophet as it was seen by the community.

Second, the efficacy of the Imam depends on how well he functions in the tasks assigned to him. Normally this involves the leading of prayers only. But the range of meanings within Muslim leadership indicates that there is an openness to the Imam to function in a larger role, if the need should arise. As we shall see, the Imam in North America has to respond in this tenor, and hence has available for consideration the many functions which the Prophet performed as a model. Such chores as leading discussions, mediating between disputants, encouraging the despairing, evangelism and teaching all have antecedents in the work of the Prophet.

THE NORTH AMERICAN SITUATION AND THE ROLE OF THE IMAM

The North American environment presents a multifaceted challenge to those who serve as Imam. The functions he must perform, the levels of society, both immigrant and North American, that make demands upon him, and the dictates of the traditions he tries to represent place him in many difficult situations. Certainly much of what he faces could hardly be conceived by his brethren who serve as Imams in Middle Eastern countries.

As we might expect, he models his work upon what he knows to be the traditional role of the Imam. He is available for the prayers during the day like his counterpart in the small mosques in the Middle East, he serves as Friday preacher, *mu²ezzin*, general preacher, and mosque supervisor. The requirements of tradition must be met in his character and abilities, such as knowing Arabic, good reciting voice, community

---

[59] *The Life of Muhammad*, 242.

acceptance as representative of piety, directing his concerns toward the religious dimensions of Islam. These norms are universally expected from those who regularly attend the mosque.

As the individual in the community most trained in the sharīᶜa and ḥadīth, he is expected to give educated opinion about the law. As Thais' informant implies, being a specialist puts a responsibility upon the Imam as a member of the ᶜulamā class:

> ... All the people cannot go and be specialized and learn the laws and regulations of Islam as everyone cannot go and become a doctor or an engineer, (for) if they do the order of the universe becomes mixed up..., we cannot understand everything about religion ourselves and so God has to guide people and he cannot do this for everyone so as a result he has chosen a group of people and has ordered them to accept the job of guiding people. [60]

But this authority places the Imam in North America in a peculiar position; on the one hand his authority is rooted in the traditional Muslim order, but he is challenged by the very society within which he is trying to give guidance. For example, the question of having the Friday Prayer on Sunday was raised by a group in Calgary. Imam Sharkawi gave a "fatwa" or guidance against it. He explained his decision this way:

> We have noon prayers on other days (i.e. Sunday) but there is no way for its replacement. Some people asked if it was possible to have the prayer on Sunday noon as the congregational prayer and have the same reward. I can't allow them to have Sunday replacing Friday. Even if you are not able to make the jamaᶜ prayers, you are forgiven if you are busy. But it is not a fundamental release from duty for everyone. We try to keep it alive in the hearts and minds of the people and believe they can do it. ...A special sura in the Qurᵓān indicates it is fundamental psychologically and religiously to bring the people together and I believe it should be strictly held. [61]

Despite this he acknowledgees the difficulty of making this effective in Canadian society, where Sunday is the universal day of leisure. The number of faithful in the prayers on Sunday is usually much larger than on Friday.

There are various degrees of rejection of the Imam's views, both on this and other matters. It is especially noticeable among children of the

---

[60] Gustav Thais, "Religious Symbolism and Social Change: the Drama of Husain," unpub. diss., Washington University, 1973, 114.

[61] Imam Sharkawi interview, July, 1977.

third generation in Edmonton. Accustomed to making personal decision on religious matters, as is the norm in Canadian society, they view the decision as too traditional for the situation. The Imam loses stature with these people and is branded as representing the ideas of the newly arrived immigrant from the Middle East, who, quite naturally, regards the decision as the correct one. Acculturation becomes a challenge that the Imam is not schooled to handle. If he reflects the traditional views, especially on these sensitive issues, he loses a whole generation of young Muslims, who reject the rigid rules. As a sensitive man, he feels this loss very deeply, even though, as a recent immigrant from the Middle East himself, he finds it difficult to comprehend the values that these Canadians express. On the other hand, if he modifies his position on key issues, he loses the respect and authority among those more traditional, because they see him capitulating to the Westernized and materialist system of Canada. He can little afford to do this... newly-arrived, he needs the support the close community life-style that the people from back home provide. Moreover, he feels he must keep his children in touch with their culture. It is a dilemma not easily bridged.

The demands for informed opinion about the law require him to continue his study, and here too he finds himself in a strange position. Canadian culture imposes much greater demands on his time than his colleague in the Middle East. In addition to his tasks at the mosque, he is called upon to deal with the emotional and social problems of his people: recent immigrants who find the adjustment difficult, conflicts within families and friends that need his impartial wisdom, and counselling regarding marital strife. In this latter area, he must represent to the couple the values and ties of traditional marriage in Islam besides serving the role contextually provided by relatives in Muslim countries. It is his responsibility to reinforce the images and the moral system that have tied couples together in that culture. Among a mobile population of the contemporary North American city, demands upon him can be substantial. He has little time left to devote to the traditional study that marked the pious member of the ʿulamā.

This is confounded by the additional roles he must play as Imam in Edmonton. He must represent the Muslim community at cultural and civic affairs, respond to local demands from schools and churches for someone to present the Muslim religion, organize programmes in conjunction with the Mosque committees, and provide the image that will appeal to the variety of wishes in his congregation. He is more and more being called upon to join with clergy of other faiths in expressing concern over social issues, and to take a stand against the continuous secularization of society. In short, he is beginning to exhibit the diversity expected of Christian clergy. [62]

But he has suffered important losses in North America. Elite groups among the Muslims, including many of the professonal class, privately admit that the Imam has little influence upon them. "He's good for the people who have just come to this country," is really damning with faint praise. They are not likely to seek his advice on business matters, or request him to mediate with someone with whom they have a disagreement, or provide any of those mediatorship roles that Imams and ᶜulamā have traditionally had in eastern societies. [63]

The more the Imam senses the system under which Canadians live, and respond to the pressures to adjust to it, the more he moves into the role of a priest or minister. Those roles he is forced to play mentioned above commit him to responding in North American religious specialists' terms, rather than as a modest representative of common obedience to God. Assimilated Muslims find this acceptable, [64] but traditional Muslims resent the movement of power into his hands. Educated Muslims in Edmonton look upon this as a mixed blessing, and are ambiguous about his directions. There may even be some of the nostalgia for the old ways as some resent that he is not sticking to the traditional role, and teaching their children what that is, instead of adjusting and reflecting Canadian mores. [65]

He has also suffered from the conflict between representing a culture (i.e. Middle Eastern) and representing Islam. Clearly the mosque should be a place of universal representation. And yet problems have arisen in the past because many of the Imams who served in Edmonton were from Egypt, while the majority of the people attending the mosque came originally from Lebanon. The current Imam is a Lebanese trained in al-Azhar, and appears to have much greater rapport with the people. It cannot be just a matter of leading the people at prayer;

---

[62] Joseph Fichter, "The Religious Professional, Part II," *Review of Religious Research* 1 (1960), 150-70 and his other works cited there.

[63] See Thais, 107f., 159f. On the structure of mediatorship in one Lebanese village, see Victor Ayoub, "Resolution of Conflict in a Lebanese Village," *Politics in Lebanon*, ed. L. Binder, New York, 1966, 107-26.

[64] See Abdo Elkoly, *Religion and Assimilation in Two Muslim Communities in America*, unpub. diss., Princeton University, 1960, 243.

[65] One Imam told me his response to the demanding members was: "You might like to push a button and give you everything you want in an Imam."

clearly the Imam must serve as a repository of the lore and folk traditions of the majority. [66] Hence the cultural component of the Imam's
role has its effect on the influence and strength he is able to express.

Another dimension of this is noticeable among young Muslims.
Those of second or third generation immigrants have known nothing of
Middle Eastern culture, except the rules kept at home, prayer in the
mosque, and the public dancing and cultural programmes in the city.
They feel acute disjunction with the mosque and the Imam. One
told me:

> I am a Muslim, I honour the Qurʾān, and respect God. But I cannot
> stomach the baggage the local mosque group force upon us. I really
> don't know what to do. I have a young son, and he should be getting
> some religious training, but why should I send him to the mosque
> Sunday school. They spend their time trying to get him to see how
> rules made 1200 years ago should apply to him. They want to force
> him to read Arabic and learn stories about a country my son may never
> even visit. We're Canadian. We have no need of Arabic. We need
> positive programmes to convey the meaning of God, and the essential
> truth of Muhammad's message. Not all this stuff from another culture.
> I really don't know what to do.

The Imam's response to this kind of view is what we might expect:
people like him want a "modernized Imam," so they can enjoy the
"permissive society." They feel discomfort with him because he represents a disciplined way, a simple life in obedience to Islam. Surely there
is more to the conflict than the perceived permissiveness. The religious
world is fundamentally different. [67]

While the world view of the immigrant may be retained for some
time in North America, [68] children raised in industrial metropolitan
society will not find it reinforced, and the whole system eventually
will be called into question. [69] The two Muslims seem to be speaking to
each other across a great chasm.

There are others who see merit in the ways of the Imam, but feel

[66] It is interesting to note that the Shīʿa have established their own mosque in
Detroit, along with a Shīʿa Imam; see Elkoly, *op. cit.*, 120.

[67] Imam Sharkawi felt that education is the problem: "First and second generation
(Muslims) think only of the world to come, immortal paradise, and whatever is around
them in this world is nothing. They are just crossing the bridge toward the world of
peace and happiness. But Muslim kids are created by the system of education and these
children have no time. It's not easy to encourage them to be in contact wtih the Imam
for spiritual things." For some indication of the religious world from which the Imam
comes, see Anne Fuller, *Buarija Portrait of a Lebanese Muslim Village*, Cambridge,
Mass., 1961, 27-29.

[68] As in Detroit; see Elkoly, *op. cit.*, 136-37, 146, 151.

[69] Marriage and dating codes seem first to be challenged; *ibid.*, 107.

some accommodation to North American values should be made. A good example is the question of building a new mosque. The old Edmonton mosque should be replaced, and various plans have been suggested over the years. There is a conflict between two groups on the nature and scope of the building. Some argue that the meaning of Islam has nothing to do with how attractive the building appears. Therefore they are opposed to the expensive plans of building a new mosque with attached educational and recreational facilities. But some, especially those who have been in Canada longer, see the building as a reflection of how people value their religion. There is some evidence here of the influence the church building plays in Christianity. By extension, they see the Imam as part of that respect. The Imam recognizes the validity of both sides, and suggests that the mosque should be able to house both groups... that is, simple architecture, dignified in the Islamic way, sufficient to appeal to the sensitivities of Canadian people, but not so outlandish that the other group feels out of place. Besides, since Muslims have prospered in Canada, they should be allowed to put their money into the building if they want to. Clearly some modification of traditional conceptions are under way. In terms of North American ideas, this adaptation of the Imam and the role of the mosque may be acceptable, but it is a marked change for recent immigrants, and they find it disconcerting. [70]

These pressures contribute to a fragmentation of the Muslim community, and many of them realize something must be done. Imam Sharkawi suggests that Muslims may well form their own schools and colleges in the next few years to combat the inflences upon the ummah from Canadian secular education. Certainly the prerequisite of just surviving as a Muslim has had its effect on immigrant attitudes toward their own particular traditions and the lines between Shīʿa, Sunnī and Ismaʿīlī are not as dramatic as they are in eastern countries. He also indicates that children of Shīʿa and even Druze people attend Arabic and religious classes and maintaining religious identity as Muslims tends to erase the fine lines of difference. This would seem to be born out by studies at the mosque in Iowa. [71]

---

[70] It should be noted that the focus on the mosque is foreign to Shīʿīs; *ibid.*, 27, 118.

[71] H. A. R. Gibb, "Unitive and Divisive Factors in Islam," *Civilizations* 7 (1957), 509, noted that the dominance of political issues has minimized these divisions among Muslims. It is interesting to note that Imam Chebli spoke with pride of the Imam in his home village in Lebanon who arranged for the Christians of the village to use the mosque for worship when their church was destroyed in the recent fighting; it was the first time such a move had ever been made, to his knowledge.

Imams are very conscious that this new situation raises important questions about their own education, and the ideals involved in it. In a culture that rejects Muslim law, it hardly seems legitimate to spend thirty years of ones life preparing to give educated views upon it for Muslims. Yet the best qualified Imams still are required to work 20 years before graduating as a recognized authority. The disconnection between what is required in education, and the actual demands of their positions must put a severe strain on career goals of Imams. [72] The need for specialist counselling techniques for North American Muslims will automatically require some modification of the Imam's training. Moreover, the requirements that the Imam perform marriages, assure that proper dowery and other arrangements have been made, and in general act like a qādi, are duties he has not traditionally, nor presently is trained to do. Yet they are situations every North American Imam must face. So he does need extensive background education in traditional Muslim law. On the other hand, the rejection of Arabic by North American Muslims (a rejection encouraged now by the diversity of languages represented among those who attend the mosque) would appear to cut to the heart of traditional Imam education, with its emphasis on the holy language. Although the international Muslim community has not seen the conflict as deep as this analysis would suggest, it has now realized that education must be geared to the diverse regions in which the Imams serve. Hence at a recent conference on the mosque in Mecca, the following are among the resolutions passed: [73]

> Attention should be given to the formulation of Islamic programs for Daʾwah in accordance with the actual conditions of the Islamic movement in each region. Such programs should also be reviewed between now and then in the light of the experience of the duʾat in their practical life and field work.
>
> Schools and colleges of Daʾwah should coordinate their efforts in the Islamic world so that each one would pay special attention to its specific geographical area.
>
> Regular meetings should be held for the Imams of the mosques in each region for the exchange of ideas and experiences, for the study of difficulties that confront the mission of the mosque and for the adoption of proper solutions to deal with these difficulties with methods that aim at the welfare of the Muslims in the correct Islamic framework.

---

[72] Imam Sharkawi left his position as Imam to study counselling and psychology at the university; it is doubtful he will return to the position of the Imam again.

[73] Muslim World League Publication, Mecca, April, 1976, 7-8.

It is important to train the Imams and their assistants because the
most important part of the message of the mosque depends upon their
ability and qualifications.

What this document recognizes is that the Imam is at the centre of
mosque life, that he must have an independence to exercise leadership
in the community, and that he must be properly equipped to deal with
the problems in his area. While it does not explicitly advocate a modification of his education, the message would seem to indicate that some
rethinking of the present educational system is in order. Moreover,
the declaration goes a long way toward acknowledging the professional
nature of the Imam's position, an understanding that not only roots
the Imam firmly among the ʿulamā group, but affirms a much more
key role for him in Islamic religion than traditionally has been recognized. It agrees that approaches may differ according to regional charac-
terizations, perhaps a tacit acceptance of national "ummahs," presumably
with institutes to equip leaders for that milieu. Finally, it emphasizes
the classical Muslim context of sharʿīa as the mold out of which the
Imam must come, but it sees the mosque as the nexus of the ummah's
life. In that sense, its message is more "traditionist" than "traditionalist."

Muhammad as a Personal Model For Change

Thus far we have concentrated primarily upon the dimensions of the
Imam as a member of an educated minority, the ʿulamā, however lowly
he may be in that structure. It is now essential to turn to the personal
nature of the Imam, his models and goals.

> Muhammad is, as mentioned in the Qurʾān, to be and was for all time
> the beautiful pattern of conduct ... the hassan al-hasāba ... the best
> model. The ʿulamā of the Muslim school, usually the Bahrain, is the
> inheritor of the prophet, so the same rule of the prophet is supposed
> to be done by the Imam. He tries every time to come closer (to him).
> We respect, for example, the hadith that says "I am sent in an era and
> an age where if you only heed 10% of what has been revealed to me,
> you would be destroyed, but it will come a time if you follow 10% of
> what has been revealed to me you will be safe." That is one of the
> least known sayings of the Prophet to his people. We know that
> people here and the Imam here cannot do what they do in a very
> conservative village in upper Egypt or Saudi Arabia, but the model is
> still living and we cannot forget that. It is a fundamental thing for the
> children to know the life of the Prophet and to know his behaviour
> and conduct; and not only him but all prophets, including Jesus Christ.
> But how much of that is 10% for following or neglecting, or how near
> we are to approaching this period is very difficult to say. We struggle
> to see this behaviour as he was acting in relation to neighbours, and

how he dealt with his wife, as a husband, as a father, as a ruler, as a judge. There are confrontations with other things, other discouragements, but still the model is there and Muhammad should be looked at all the time as a pattern of conduct. [74]

In view of the great diversity of roles the Imam in North America appears to fulfill, it is crucial that the image of the Prophet offers some guide for his adaptation. It is instructive in this connection to note the characteristics of the Imam as envisaged by the Mecca conference. [75]

His qualities are ranged according to the roles he must play, i.e. sociospiritual, liturgical, ameliorative, educative, and the ideals of Muslim piety, i.e. contentment, righteous conduct, learned, respected, oriented to paradise, and faithful to his commitments. Yet of these, the meaning of the sociospiritual, ameliorative, and educative roles have changed because of his new situation in North American society. In addition, he faces the multiplicity of roles assigned to him with all religious leadership in religious institutions in this country: competent in administration, civic affairs, business, recreational organization, and an exemplary family man. His piety too will be re-evaluated in North American terms, since contentment may be interpreted as lack of aggressiveness, being learned requires training in techniques and disciplines beyond the traditional, righteous conduct has to be judged according to the dictates of North American values systems, and respect is an element that involves both self-image and social dictates. [76]

In a situation where treasured norms are no longer adequate, the image of the Prophet becomes available for redefining meaning. As hero, leader, legislator, judge, inspired prophet, preacher, administrator, family man and Imam, his personal image is open to the variety of needs into which the Imam must expand. While the Imam who serves the mosque in Edmonton is fully aware of the disparity between what men will do with the Imam's position and would admit that some may even turn it into great individual aggrandizement, just as Imam Yusuf in the *Arabian Nights*, the impact of the Prophet provides both a challenge and a discipline, and has the potentialities needed for a proper realignment of his life. In history of religions terms, we are seeing a fresh, immediate and modified example of the classic figure as he is being interpreted by the community under the pressure of a new situation.

---

[74] Ahmad Sharkawi interview, July, 1977.

[75] Moslem World League Publication, April, 1976, 9-10.

[76] Cf. Fichter, *op. cit.*, 101.

III

TRANSITIONS AND TRANSFORMATIONS
IN CHINESE RELIGION

DUALISM AND CONFLICT IN CHINESE POPULAR RELIGION

Daniel L. Overmyer

University of British Columbia

> The method of releasing and driving away is a ritual form going back to antiquity for expelling pestilence (Wang Ch'ung, 27-c100 A.D., "On Exorcism") [1]

Transformations of religious meaning occur not only through time, but also between different levels of understanding and expression within a cultural system. In the religion and thought of traditional China, one of the key focal points of such transformation was the difference between elite philosophy and popular myth and ritual. Though both of these levels shared a common worldview, their means of expression and forms of ritual action diverged. For philosophy the world was produced by the interaction of abstract modes of energy such as *yin* and *yang* and the Five Phases. The wise man sought to understand and conform with these forces. At the popular level, at least from the Sung dynasty (960-1279 A.D.) on, such forces were person-ified and given dramatic roles. In the process modes of power once considered complementary came to be perceived as potentially or actively hostile toward each other. In such a richly mythological context, one's task was not so much to conform with the natural order of things as to seek allies in a struggle with malevolent forces. Behind the struggle was the assumption that victory was possible because everything hung together in a great hierarchical system to which both gods and demons belonged, with the gods on top. But in the foreground the emphasis was transformed, and a view of life appeared which was quite different from the mainstream of elite philosophy, poetry and painting. This different perspective can be seen most clearly in rituals of exorcism.

Of course, in practice the situation was more complex, in the first place because elite philosophy was not so harmonious and non-dualistic as it has often been portrayed. On closer examination the thought of the most optimistic sounding Confucian or Buddhist can be seen to be concerned with ambiguities and tensions as well, chiefly in the gap between the Tao as incipient and the Tao as realized. Between the two

---

[1] *Lun-heng* (Taipei reprint of SPPY edition, 1968), 25:6a.

there could be many obstacles which might be overcome only after years of study and meditation. In addition, the background of dualistic sounding popular understandings can be traced in orthodox texts and rituals, most obviously in rites of exorcism carried out by court officials and Taoist priests. The difference was really one of relative emphasis, with a sense of overt struggle and fractured polarity more pervasive at the popular level. [2]

In what follows I attempt to describe the popular emphasis on dualism and conflict against the classical background. In every case I am concerned to indicate the transformation of perspective that takes place between these two levels, a transformation in which their relationship is still apparent. After mentioning earlier scholarly discussions of our topic, I proceed to outline the evidence for harmony and conflict in Confucian philosophy and orthodox Buddhism and Taoism. Following a summary of court rites of exorcism in the Han period (206 B.C.-220 A.D.), the article moves to a discussion of struggle with hostile forces in popular religion, under the categories of demonology, exorcism, charms and the role of spirit-mediums.

A concluding section suggests some historical and cultural reasons for the different emphases described above, and discusses the implications of all this for a definition of popular religion in China. The essay ends with questions concerning the relevance of traditional themes of dualism and conflict to similar themes in Maoist thought.

Representative Views

Students of Chinese popular religion have long been aware of the importance of conflict in this tradition. Let us look briefly at the views of three scholars whose work together spans the 20th century, de Groot, Maspero and McCreery.

In his own somewhat hostile and over-stated way, J. J. M. de Groot described the basic attitude of Chinese popular religion as follows:

> All *shen* or gods, being parts of the *Yang*, are the natural enemies of the *kwei*, because these are the constituents of the *Yin*; indeed the *Yang* and the *Yin* are engaged in an eternal struggle... The worship and

---

2 "Dualism" is, according to *Dictionary of Philosophy*, ed. Dagobert Runes, Paterson, N. J., 1961, 84, a "theory which admits in any given domain two independent and mutually irreducible substances." With the exception of sectarian Manichaeism, no Chinese school or sect proposed an ultimate metaphysical dualism. No matter how powerful a moral, psychological or exorcistic dualism might be, it remained penultimate at the philosophical level. Hence, the use of the term "dualism" in this article should be understood to mean a limited "dualism-in-practice."

propitiation of the gods, which is the main part of China's Religion, has no higher purpose than that of inducing the gods to protect man against the world of evil, or, by descending among men, to drive spectres away by their intimidating presence....

The main function of this religion consists in muzzling the *kwei*, also by stimulating the operation of the *shen*. Taoism may then actually be defined as an Exorcising Polytheism... connected with a highly developed system of magic, consisting for a great part in Exorcism. This cult and magic is, of course, principally in the hands of priests. But, besides, the lay world, enslaved to the intense belief in the perilous omnipresence of spectres, is engaged every day in a restless defensive and offensive war against these beings. [3]

The description of Taoism in this passage is of course long out of date, but the fundamental point being made is supported in rich detail by de Groot's voluminous work.

Writing a few decades later, Henri Maspero made a more sober observation which bears on the same issue. In his essay "La religion populaire moderne" he emphasizes that from the Sung dynasty on popular religion was a system in its own right, quite different from the older "three religions," despite its syncretism. In this system Buddhist monks and Taoist priests both had the role of "sorcerers," the Buddhists with more concern for the souls of the dead, the Taoists for delivering the living from evil forces. He continues, "The idea of a solidarity between man and the world, which de Groot called 'universism,' survived, but was supported chiefly by the Confucians.... The Chinese peasant who consulted the calendar or complied with geomancy was not trying to orient himself in time and space, but wanted only to know of good or bad influences in the particular circumstances of time and place." Later in this same essay Maspero stresses that, "evil beings abound," and describes the frequent need for exorcism. [4]

Since I will be discussing the views of modern anthropologists below, let me here just cite a few passages from the very helpful Ph.D. dissertation by John McCreery, "The Symbolism of Popular Taoist Magic," based on field work with a magician and healer in Taiwan. In distinguishing between the two ritual processes of worship and exorcism, McCreery writes as follows:

Unlike worship, which dramatizes a complex interaction—offering, petition, then payment—exorcism dramatizes only the mobilization and

[3] J. J. M. de Groot, *The Religious System of China*, Leiden, 1892-1910, VI, 930-32.
[4] Henri Maspero, *Mélanges posthumes sur les religions et l'histoire de la Chine*, Paris, 1950, 112-15, 126-28.

then the release of concentrated, violent forces. Where one suggests a social dialectic, the other suggests a social manipulation and implacable hostile confrontation, ... [In exorcism] again and again the repetition of charms and incantations culminates in increasingly violent gestures. The message is clear. Overwhelming terrifying power is being mobilized to destroy the agents of evil. [5]

Thus, the perspective of this article relies to some extent on that of earlier studies. What remains is to enlarge upon this beginning and indicate the dialectical relationship between popular dualism and conflict and the elite or classical traditions.

The Philosophical Background

From the Han dynasty on (206 B.C.-220 A.D.) Confucian cosmology was constituted by its emphasis on a balanced harmony of hierarchical relationships. The world was understood to be unified through both its origin and structure. Concepts such as *yin/yang* and the Five Phases were borrowed from other schools and combined with the Confucian ethics of reciprocal obligations. In the resulting system everything had its proper place and function in relationship to everything else. Human beings were an integral part of this world, all of which influenced them, and within which they played an important role.

The first major formulator of this position was Tung Chung-shu (c. 179-104 B.C.), who wrote:

> In all things there must be correlates. Thus there must be such correlates as superior and inferior, left and right, before and behind, external and internal.... The *yin* is the correlate of the *yang*, the wife of the husband, the son of the father, the subject of the ruler. There is nothing that does not have such correlates, and in each such correlation there is the *yin* and the *yang*. [6]

Here the *yin* and *yang* are held together as equally necessary modes of cosmic movement. This is a persistent theme in philosophical writings from the Han on, a theme emphasized by the Sung Neo-Confucians as well. For example, in Chou Tun-i's (1017-1073) *T'ai-chi t'u shuo* (Explanation of the Diagram of the Supreme Ultimate), we read,

---

[5] John McCreery, "The Symbolism of Popular Taoist Magic," unpub. Ph.D. diss., Cornell University, 1973, 86, 112.

[6] Tung Chung-shu, *Ch'un-ch'iu fan-lu*, quoted in Fung Yu-lan, *A History of Chinese Philosophy*, tr. Derk Bodde, Princeton, 1973, II, 42; the Chinese text is in Fung Yu-lan, *Chung-kuo che-hsüeh shih*, Shanghai, 1934, 521.

"...The Supreme Ultimate through movement produces the *yang*. This movement, having reached its limit, is followed by quiescence, and by this quiescence it produces *yin*. When quiescence has reached its limit, there is a return to movement. Thus, movement and quiescence, in alternation, became each the source of the other." [7]

This "dualism in a monistic context" becomes even more explicit in the attempt by another Neo-Confucian, Ch'eng Hao (1032-1085) to explain the necessary role of evil in the cosmic system:

> The goodness and evil of the world are both equally Heavenly Principle. To say that something is evil does not mean that it is inherently so. It is merely because it goes too far or does not go far enough....
>
> Among all things there is none that does not have its opposite. Thus for the *yin* there is *yang* and for goodness there is evil. When the *yang* waxes the *yin* wanes, and when goodness increases, evil diminishes. This is their Principle, and how far, indeed, it can be extended! [8]

As is well known, in the thought of the Chinese elite such "correlative thinking" was applied to every possible realm, from physiology to the role of the emperor, and from music to landscape gardening. This emphasis, described in detail by Granet and Needham, has been attractive to Western scholars in a variety of fields. [9]

But there is another side to the story, even within the realm of philosophy. Along with the major emphasis on harmony between *yin* and *yang* there is a persistent minor theme, which states that *yin* is inferor to *yang* and even evil in relationship to it. This was pointed out long ago by Derk Bodde:

> A common feature of Chinese dualisms... is that one of their two elements should be held in higher regard than the other... so, in the interplay of the *yin* and *yang*, the former is definitely inferior to the latter.... The inferiority of the *yin* to the *yang* is accepted—explicitly or implicitly—by all thinkers who adopt the *yin-yang* ideology. A noteworthy characteristic of the *yin-yang* dualism... is the fact that definite preference is given to the positive element, the *yang*, and not to the negative element, the *yin*. [10]

---

[7] Fung, *History*, II, 434-35; *Che-hsüeh shih*, 820-21.

[8] Fung, *History*, II, 518; *Che-hsüeh shih*, 884.

[9] See Marcel Granet, *La Pensée chinoise*, Paris, 1934; and Joseph Needham, *Science and Civilisation in China*, Cambridge, 1956, II, 216-94, 455-505. Needham stresses (p. 277) that "... undertones of good and evil were in fact *not* present in the Chinese formulations of Yin-Yang."

[10] Derk Bodde, "Harmony and Conflict in Chinese Philosophy," *Studies in Chinese Thought*, ed. Arthur Wright, Chicago, 1953, 54, 61-62.

There is evidence for this imbalance of *yin* and *yang* in the work of Tung Chung-shu, particularly in his discussions of human nature, where *yin* is seen as the source of the emotions, and thus the cause of confusion and evil. In a discussion of the annual cycle of the seasons Tung notes that, "...[*yin*]... holding itself low... pursues its business, [because] Heaven has trust in the *yang* but not in the *yin*; it likes beneficence but not chastisement" (This refers to increasing *yin* influence in autumn, when plants die and prisoners are executed.) Elsewhere Tung makes it clear that *yin* is inferior to *yang* as wife is to husband and subject is to ruler. [11]

When describing the structure of human nature Tung Chung-shu equates *yin* with the feelings (*ch'ing*), and *yang* with the *hsing*, or the rational faculties. His negative valuation of *yin/ch'ing* is revealed by his correlation of them with covetousness (*t'an*), while *yang* is paired with the supreme Confucian virtue, *jen*, humanity. [12]

This negative valuation of the emotions was first clearly stated in the Confucian tradition by Hsün-tzu (f. 298-238 B.C.), and it continued without serious interruption right on through Wang Yang-ming (1472-1529). Tung Chung-shu's correlation of the emotions with *yin* was, I believe, assumed in later psychological discussion, but its metaphysical implications were never emphasized. In consequence the role of *yin* was understood at two different levels, with the relationship between metaphysical good and psychological evil never fully clarified. It is significant that at a penultimate level a certain amount of polarized hostility between *yin* and *yang* was granted, even in philosophy. Here *yin* was equated with death and confusion. At the popular level this rift in the metaphysical web was much expanded.

Another important aspect of the philosophical background of our topic is persistent ambiguity concerning how to realize the potentials of human nature. This ambiguity is well stated by the Neo-Confucian scholar Chang Tsai (1020-1077 A.D.): "Heaven's capacity for goodness is fundamentally our own capacity for goodness. The only thing is that we have destroyed it." [13] Even Mencius (c. 371-289 B.C.), the paragon of optimists, held that it is only our "inner natures" which tend toward goodness; we are born with the beginning points of such

---

[11] Fung, *History*, II, 29; *Che-hsüeh shih*, 512.

[12] Fung, *History*, II, 32-34; *Che-hsüeh shih*, 515. Wang Ch'ung writes that for Tung, "the rational nature arises from *yang*, while the emotions arise from *yin*. The *yin* material-force (*ch'i*) is inferior (*pi*), while the *yang* is humane (*jen*)," *Lun-heng* 3:14b (*Pen-hsing p'ien*).

[13] Fung, *History*, II, 490; *Che-hsüeh shih*, 863.

virtues as compassion and righteousness, but these seeds must be nour-
ished by a supportive social environment if they are to grow. As he
wrote of the human vital spirit, "Nourish it with integrity and place
no obstacle in its path and it will fill the space between Heaven and
Earth.... Deprive it of [righteousness and the proper way] and it
will collapse. It is born of accumulated righteousness and cannot be
appropriated by anyone through a sporadic show of rightness.... You
must work at it, and never let it out of your mind." [14]

In the next century Hsün-tzu also allowed that "the man on the street
can become a Yü (sage)," [15] but stressed more than Mencius the need
for constant effort to restrain selfish desires. From Hsün-tzu on it was
assumed by most Confucians that human beings on their own cannot
generate order and harmony, and thus the state is necessary to provide
both control, and guidance for moral transformation.

Neo-Confucianism developed a deeper psychological awareness within which affirmations concerning human goodness became statements
of faith to be realized only through study and meditation. Thomas
Metzger, following T'ang Chün-i, has recently argued that "the 'inner
life' of moral struggle, not cosmology, is the key to Neo-Confucian
thought.... the tension between 'good' and 'bad' was central to Neo-
Confucianism." This was so because, "...they held to an idea of incomplete or even elusive immanence [of the cosmic way]...." [16]
The Neo-Confucians longed for a state of complete inner peace and
social harmony, but found such a state opposed at every turn by their
own desires and the chaotic, harmful dimensions of experience. At the
level of inner struggle this problem is well expressed by Kao P'an-lung
(d. 1626) who wrote at one point in his autobiography, "I realized
that within myself principle and desire waged battle upon battle
without peaceful resolution." [17]

This profound tension in Neo-Confucian thought, discussed at length
by Metzger, serves to remind us again that dualism and conflict in
Chinese popular religion resonated with similar themes in philosophy
which were expressed at different levels of symbolization. One man's
demon was another's selfish desire.

---

[14] *Mencius* 2A:2, tr. D. C. Lau, *Mencius*, Harmondsworth, 1970, 77-78.

[15] Hsün-tzu, "Hsing o lun," tr. Burton Watson, *Hsün-tzu: Basic Writings*, New
York, 1963, 166.

[16] Thomas Metzger, *Escape from Predicament: Neo-Confucianism and China's
Evolving Political Culture*, New York, 1977, 91, 108, 111.

[17] Quoted in Rodney Taylor, "The Centered Self: Religious Autobiography in the
Neo-Confucian Tradition," *HR* 17 (1978), 278.

There are other aspects of the Confucian philosophical tradition which deserve discussion from the point of view of implicit or moral dualism, but such discussion would take us too far afield. I refer, for example, to the theory of the "Mandate of Heaven" with its assumption that moral evil is punished by cosmic forces, which gave divine justification to conflict and warfare. The conviction of Confucian scholar officials that they represented the forces of cosmic and social order against all that would oppose them also deserves further exploration in this regard. Popular dualism represents a different emphasis, but is not so different from philosophy as it might first appear to be. [18]

Dualistic Aspects of Liturgical Taoism

In liturgical or priestly Taoism there is evidence for limited dualism in rituals and texts which deal with driving away evil influences. The Taoist world-view is similar to that of Han philosophy, with an emphasis on harmonious interrelationships, but with a certain denigration of *yin* as well. Let us look first at some explicitly cosmological material, then at texts discussing methods for expelling evil, and finally at the reports of modern specialists on Taoism and its rituals.

The earliest detailed statements of Taoist cosmogony occur in the *Huai-nan Tzu*, compiled in the second century B.C. In them the appearance of the world is due to impersonal forces which develop in stages. In the beginning there was only "undifferentiated formlessness," out of which emerged the Tao, then material force (*ch'i*), a primordial ether of varying density. Eventually the lighter *ch'i* "drifted up to become heaven, and that which was heavy and turbid solidified to form earth.... The material forces of heaven and earth combined to form *yin* and *yang*. The concentrated forces of *yin* and *yang* became the four seasons, and the scattered forces of the four seasons became the myriad things [that is, the universe]."

W. T. Chan notes that "in its broad outline this cosmogony has remained the orthodox doctrine among Chinese philosophers...," [19] and indeed, similar accounts can be found in the Taoist Canon.

For example, in the *Tao-fa hui-yüan* there is an elaborate five stage cosmogony, complete with a chart, moving from *T'ai-i* (Great Change)

---

[18] The closest traditional Chinese philosophy came to metaphysical dualism was in the thought of Chu Hsi (1130-1200), with its distinction between *li* (principle, pattern of organization) and *ch'i* (material force). See Fung, *History*, II, 533-71; and W. T. Chan, *A Sourcebook in Chinese Philosophy*, Princeton, 1963, 588-653.

[19] *Ibid.*, 306-08; *Huai-nan tzu* (SPPY), 2:1-2, 3:1.

to *T'ai-ch'u* (Great Beginning), to *T'ai-shih* (Great Commencement), to *T'ai-su* (Great Simplicity) and finally to *T'ai-chi* (Great Ultimate). As in the *Huai-nan Tzu,* in the first stage all is formless and empty; *ch'i* appears in the second, and *yin* and *yang* in the third. In the *Tao-fa hui-yüan ch'i* first emerges as the formless "primal ether of the prior heaven" (*hsien-t'ien yüan-ch'i*); form appears together with *yin* and *yang* in the *T'ai-shih* period, and matter (*chih*) with stage four, *T'ai-su.* The world as we know it begins with the *T'ai-chi* stage, which is equated with *hun-tun,* a premordial "chaos" of undifferentiated potentials, shaped like an egg. This splits, and for the first time the pure and turbid are distinguished; the pure to rise as *yang* and form heaven, the turbid to descend as *yin* and become earth.

This passage goes on to describe the origin of the "myriad phenomena," and then plays the whole process in reverse, from the "myriad phenomena" to heaven and earth, to *T'ai-chi* and on back to *T'ai-i,* specifying that return occurs because each stage depends on its predecessor. The moral of the story is:

> Therefore, the "Realized Man" (*chih-jen*) exhausts the origin of creation and transformation, siezes the handles of creative chaos, commands the two [types of] *ch'i* in [the time] before form appeared, and becomes master of the 10,000 spirits in [the time] after form had taken shape.... [20]

Thus, Taoist cosmogony on the one hand affirms the integral role of *yin* in the creative process, but on the other hand equates it with *chuo-ch'i,* material force which is turbid and impure. It is important to note that this cosmogony provides for a Taoist form of transcendence, through psychic return to the formless stages before the world appeared. Here the adept attains supreme power, because he is identified with the source of all things, the period of "prior heaven," which Taoists distinguish from "posterior heaven" (*hou-t'ien*) the time and situation of our present world. Gods, spirits and demons all belong to the world of "posterior heaven," and hence can be controlled by one who has

---

[20] *Tao-fa hui-yüan* 1:9-10. This and all other Taoist texts are cited from the *Cheng-t'ung Tao-tsang* (The Taoist canon of the [Ming] Cheng-t'ung reign period), 1444-47, reprint Taipei, 1962. I shall refer to them by their number in the indices of the *Tao-tsang tzu-mu yin-te,* Harvard-Yenching Institute Sinological Index Series, No. 25, reprint Taipei, 1966 (hereafter, HY). The *Tao-fa hui yuan,* 268 chüan, is HY 1210; the latest dates given in this huge collection of texts are from the Yüan dynasty (1280-1368), acc. to Kristofer Schipper, "The Divine Jester, Some Remarks on the Gods of the Chinese Marionette Theater," *Bull. Inst. Ethnology, Acad. Sinica* 21 (1966), 86.

penetrated to higher levels of reality and power. Thus, cosmogony sets the stage for Taoist "dualism" and exorcism. [21]

There are other intimations of limited dualism in Taoist texts as well. For example, in the *T'ai-p'ing ching* we read:

> Therefore, superiors imitate *yang* while inferiors model themselves on *yin*. Those on the left imitate *yang*, while those on the right follow *yin*. [Those who accord with] *yang* like to nourish and give birth, while the *yin* like to kill; the *yang* carry out the Tao, while the *yin* carry out punishments. The *yang* do good and *yang* spirits aid them; the *yin* do evil and *yin* spirits assist them. When one accumulates goodness without ceasing, blessings of the Tao arise, and cause the people to be daily more fortunate. *Yang* dwells in the head, *yin* dwells in the feet. Therefore the ruler values the way and its power and considers punishments inferior.

This passage is all the more interesting because it occurs in a text which exalts the perfect harmony of *yin* and *yang* as the way to utopia. [22] Here we see a more conventional form of limited dualism by denigration of *yin*, a form closer to the popular understanding.

At another level, there is an emphasis on conflict with evil forces within the body of the meditating adept. In every organ of his body there dwells a deity, but these deities are threatened by three malevolent worms, one in each of the major areas of the body. Since these worms can find release only through the death of the body, they cause illness to hasten the event. To attain immortality the adept must expel the worms, retain the gods and develop a new embryo within himself. This he does through proper diet, circulation of the breath and the development of "interior vision," to observe and direct the whole process. [23]

This struggle with the "three worms" is a kind of "interior exorcism" carried out against forces of decay and death. Since the exorcism of external demons long antidated such techniques, one can only suggest that this emphasis on inner conflict may have served to psychologically reinforce the larger struggle with hostile influences.

---

[21] Michael Saso, *Taoism and the Rite of Cosmic Renewal*, Seattle, 1972, 38, comments that "The Prior Heavens are exempt from the changes of *Yin* and *Yang* and are the sources of life, primordial breath and blessing in the world of the Posterior Heavens."

[22] *T'ai-p'ing ching*, 119 *chüan* (HY 1093), 2:1; this text was begun in the 2nd century A.D., but much of it was compiled later. See Ch'en Kuo-fu, *Tao-tsang yüan-liu k'ao*, Peking, 1963, 1:81-89.

[23] This discussion is based on Henri Maspero, *Le Taoisme et les religions chinoises*, Paris, 1971, 295-302, 358-73.

The most direct expression of conflict and limited dualism in Taoism is found in the large number of *Tao-tsang* texts dealing with exorcism, particularly through written charms. The *Tao-fa hui-yüan* is full of such material, with frequent use of such terms as *fu-mo* or *hsiang-mo*, "subdue demons," *ch'ü-ch'üeh pu-hsiang* "expel the inauspicious" or *ch'u ching*, "get rid of [evil] essences." The basic dichotomy is between that which is correct and orthodox (*cheng*), and that which is evil and heterodox (*hsieh*). Note for example, the text of a typical charm, in four character lines:

> Dissipate, disperse, loosen, release
> Defeat demons, destroy evil essences
> Summon and gather together blessings and good fortune
> Make clear and bright the mirror of Tao

The commentary for this charm elaborates on its efficacy for any situation. [24]

There are a number of *Tao-tsang* texts with exorcistic terms in their titles, one of the more interesting of which is the *T'ai-shang pei-chi fu-mo shen-chou sha-kuei lu* (The demon slaying register, divine invocation which subdues demons, of the great superior northern apex) (HY1205). This is a ritual text of the Cheng-i school of Taoism, which the first page tells us can, "assist Heaven in carrying out its transformations, save the people, cut off and annihilate evil essences (here, *hsieh-ching*), disperse disasters and rescue those in difficulty." Then follow five pages listing fifty celestial generals of the northern apex (region of the north polar star, source of cosmic order and power), with their armies. The armies range in size from 300,000 men to 3,000, and then to 120, each with a leader given an awe-inspiring name such as "Flying Lightning, Mirror of *yin*" (mirrors expose demons); "Resister of Wild Beasts," "Flying Tiger," "Destroyer of Evil (*P'o-hsieh*), "Healer of Illness," etc. The remainder of the book (seventeen folio pages) is taken up with charms, invocations and official name seals, putting all this terrible military power into action. The efficacy of a characteristic charm is described as follows:

> This charm heals every sort of illness. If one wears it, it will preserve his person, protect his life, rescue him from difficulty, lengthen his life, prohibit and cut off all devils (*kuei*), decapitate evil spirits (*hsieh-shen*), get rid of calamities, and annihilate misfortune.

---

[24] *Tao-fa hui-yüan* 5:11b-12a. These charms are written in a very cursive code-like style; fortunately, charm texts usually provide standard characters as well.

In several of the passages commenting on official seals (symbols of authority), specific armies and types of troops are ordered to slay demons. [25]

It is clear from this material that the Taoist canon is part of the background of the popular emphasis on struggle between good and evil forces. This being the case, it should not surprise us to find detailed discussions of exorcism in the writings of two modern specialists in Taoism, Kristopher Schipper and Michael Saso.

Writing of the role of the Taoist priest in *chiao* rituals of community renewal, Schipper says, "But the Taoist priest or *Tou-su* in Taiwan is not just a ritual master. He also acts as an exorcist and healer, expelling and pacifying demons. And it is this aspect of his role that normally is highlighted in literature and art."

After translating a memorial to the gods used in a collective service which prays for increase of blessings and release from calamities and illness, Schipper goes on to describe a private ritual addressed to a particular deity, for the healing of illness. The memorial reads in part:

> Considering that this person is prostrated by an unhealthy body and by much bad luck, we fear that the mighty planets are having a destructive influence and that obnoxious rays are attacking him; we wish to seek peace and security and particularly pray to avert calamity, hoping that the benevolence of the Jade Emperor from Above and the High Saints may bring forth blessings, that the Pole Star may have an auspicious influence, warding off evil luminaries, bringing back auspicious influences, so that the personal fate-controlling star may shine brightly, his lot may improve, calamities be diminished, health be excellent, etc.... [26]

The most explicit statements of exorcistic conflict in liturgical Taoism come from the writings of Michael Saso, also based heavily on field work. In his *Taoism and the Rite of Cosmic Renewal* Saso comments: "The basic theme of the *chiao* is to restore *Yang*, that is, life, light and blessing, to its pristine state of growth, and to expel the forces of *Yin*, darkness, evil and death."

In preparing for this ritual, "...the earth spirits are first removed from the temple to make way for the Heavenly Worthies, the spirits

---

[25] *T'ai-shang—sha kuei lu*, 1-4b, 14b, etc. No date is provided for this text. For other examples of exorcistic texts see HY 52-54, 100-01, 386, 628, 1333, 1346, 1402-03, 1408, etc.

[26] Kristofer Schipper, "The Written Memorial in Taoist Ceremonies," *Religion and Ritual in Chinese Society*, ed. Arthur Wolf, Stanford, 1974, 309-10, 313-15, 322-23.

who dwell in the Prior Heavens, the realm of pure *Yang*. Their presence is necessary in order to effect the renewal of the cosmos... [these spirits] lack any taint or hint of the influences of *Yin*...." Preparation for the ritual involves purification, repentance, special diet and abstention from sexual intercourse.

The priest uses esoteric charts and dances during the ritual, the *Ho-t'u* or "River Chart" to depict the order of the Prior Heavens and the *Lo-shu* for the Posterior Heavens. In discussing these diagrams Saso says, "The Taoist must also know the principles whereby change is caused in the universe, in order to reverse the process from *Yang* to *Yin* and make *Yang* eternally on the pivot of life." [27]

In his Introduction to the *Chuang Lin hsü Tao-tsang* Saso continues in the same vein, pointing out, for example, that:

> Among the distinctive features of orthodox *K'o-i* ritual is that the Taoist High Priest inserts a small flame-shaped pin... into the crown on the top of his head during the rite, showing that he is "alive" as it were with the eternal transcendent Tao of the Prior Heavens.... [This flame represents] the eternal unchanging flame of *Yang*....

In describing the Ho-t'u dance Saso says that in it: "...the spirits, mudras, and mantic conjurations used by the High Priest are directed towards 'sealing off' the village from attacks of evil spirits who might prevent the blessings of the heavens, the new rebirth of *Yang*, from taking effect."

In the Taoist's mind the dance is traced over the Eight Trigrams:

> The trigrams *K'un*... for earth and *Ken*... or "Devils' Door" are considered to be the weakest positions, through which the demonic forces of *Yin* find easiest entrance. It is through the openings in trigrams that the... forces of *Yang* are dissipated.
>
> The Taoist therefore seeks to close all the entrances of *Yin*, to keep the Three Pure Ones (Taoist deities) within the cosmos, and the forces of evil without... the Taoist actually envisions armies of *Yin* demons attacking the community while he performs the dance and repels them by the use of... mudras and mantras. [28]

---

[27] Saso, *Cosmic Renewal*, 34, 57.

[28] Michael Saso, ed., *Chuang Lin hsü Tao-tsang* (The Chuang Lin supplement to the Taoist canon), Taipei, 1974, I, 12-13, 22-24. These fascinating statements are based on the interpretations of Taoist priests "revealed by word of mouth ... rather than written explanation ..." (p. 22), hence there are no texts to check. See also Saso's "Orthodoxy and Heterodoxy in Taoist Ritual," *Religion and Ritual in Chinese Society*, 325-36.

Thus, reports by specialists in Taoist texts and ritual, both of them priests initiated in the tradition, further corroborate the Taoist contribution to themes of dualism and conflict in the history of Chinese religions.

Buddhist Contributions

Mahāyāna Buddhism is at once full of dualities and beyond them all. At the level of "conventional truth" there are such pairs of opposites as nirvana/samsāra, paradise/purgatory, the Buddha/the unenlightened, wisdom/ignorance, attachment/non-attachment, etc. But at the absolute level these distinctions are all "empty," false, artificially created by our desires and concepts. In fact, reality as it is is beyond the grasp of words; it is just there in its "thusness," to be accepted and enjoyed by those who understand.

At the conventional level, however, the distinction between nirvana and samsāra, with all its attendant concepts, is of value for the ignorant and attached, because it teaches them that there is something more. Such distinctions serve to clarify their situation and start them on the path to liberation, but for the enlightened they are all an expression of *upāya*, "skill-in-means." Thus, it is philosophically a contradiction in terms to discuss any form of Buddhist "dualism."

This being granted, it remains the case that at the popular level the various penultimate dualities were taken literally. For most Chinese lay or folk Buddhists life was a struggle to gain paradise and avoid purgatory through attaining merit, merit gained from moral actions and participation in rituals. From its beginnings, Buddhism has adapted itself to the understanding of its listeners, which here means adaptation to pre-Buddhist folk beliefs, or, if you will, the wholesale co-optation of such beliefs for Buddhist purposes. In particular, Buddhism had to meet popular expectations for the healing of illness and the expulsion of evil forces. Hence, Buddhist forms of demonology and exorcism soon developed. Teachings and practices of this sort had a profound effect on the development of Chinese popular religion, and contributed to its conflict-oriented perspective.

Already in pre-Mahāyāna Buddhism there was a whole world of demonic beings called *pisācas, yakkhas* and *rakkhasas*, as well as a type of "fallen angels" named *asuras*. In addition, there was Māra, the chief of demons, symbol of all the forces which impede enlightenment and oppose Buddhism. Māra is a personification of samsāra, the realm of desire, suffering and death. These Buddhist figures of course owed much to their Indian religious background.

In his *Buddhism and the Mythology of Evil*, based on Pāli sources, T. O. Ling tells us of the *yakkhas* that:

a. [They] frequently have a terrifying effect on humans, especially at night, which is the time of their greatest power....
b. They haunt lonely places....
c. They are able to move about freely and assume all kinds of shapes....
d. They often appear to be akin to animals or weird birds....
e. They are connected with [non-Buddhist] sacrificial rites....
f. They are able to enter into and possess human beings....

Māra does all these things as well, though he is more particularly associated with hostility toward the Buddha and his teachings. Māra appears in horrible disguises, accompanied by loud noises, sometimes at the head of an army of demons, "Māra's host." All of these forms of demonic activity will sound familiar to students of Chinese popular religion. [29]

Māra is defeated by mindfulness, right views and right actions, that is, by the Buddhist religion. He is recognized, dismissed or ignored, not really exorcised, though in Pāli texts there are invocations against harm and evil which came to be imbued with magical qualities. [30] Of course, in Theravāda folk-Buddhism a wide range of orthodox texts and symbols were employed in very literal power struggles with demonic forces. [31]

Mahāyāna Buddhism as well provided a variety of means for dealing with inimical forces, though at the orthodox level these remained less dramatic than was the case for Taoism. One senses that Buddhist awareness of *śūnyatā* kept things a bit more relaxed; they did not understand the burden of maintaining cosmic order in the same substantive way as the Taoists. It was enough to see through the unreality of what appears. As a "Perfect Wisdom" *sūtra* says in discussing how to deal with fear, "Furthermore, a Bodhisattva will not be afraid in a district infected by epidemics. But he should consider, reflect and deliberate that 'there is no dharma here which sickness could oppress, nor is that

---

[29] T. O. Ling, *Buddhism and the Mythology of Evil*, London, 1962, *passim*, esp. 45. See also James Boyd, "Symbols of Evil in Buddhism," *JAS* 31 (1971), 63-75.

[30] For one such invocation, see *Chullavagga* V, 6, 1, in F. Max Müller, ed., *The Sacred Books of the East*, Oxford, 1885, XX, 76-77; this passage is intended to ward off poisonous snakes by suffusing them with love and reminding them of the infinite power of the Buddha.

[31] For folk Buddhist exorcism in a Theravāda context, see Melford Spiro, *Burmese Supernaturalism*, Englewood Cliffs, N.J., 1967, 144-94.

which is called "sickness" a dharma.' In that manner he should contemplate emptiness, and he should not be afraid." [32]

All of the symbols of evil developed in earlier Buddhism were assumed and taken over by the Mahāyāna. However, Mahāyāna provided a much richer array of benevolent beings whose aid could be invoked in the struggle, particularly the great bodhisattvas, who were characterized by their wisdom and compassion. The prototype of these saving bodhisattvas was Avalokitésvara, first described in the *Lotus Sutra* as one who will rescue those who call upon him from any sort of injury or danger: fire, drowning, murder, punishment, bandits, etc. Evil beings are also mentioned:

> [If a ship is blown off course and plunged] into the realm of the rākṣasa-ghosts, if there is among [those on the ship] but one man who calls upon the name of the bodhisattva He Who Observes the Sounds of the World [Avalokitésvara], these men shall be delivered from the troubles [caused by] the rākṣasas....
>
> If there should be a thousand-millionfold world of lands filled with yakṣas and rākṣasas who wish to come and do harm to others, if they should but hear the name of the bodhisattva He Who Observes the Sounds of the World, these malignant ghosts would not be able even to look upon those others with an evil eye, how much less to inflict harm on them!

Later in this chapter of the *Lotus* we are told that Avalokitésvara can change his shape at will to the form most likely to convert those whom he meets. All threats and evils can be dispelled, "by virtue of one's constant mindfulness of Sound-Observer, [for he] in the midst of terror, emergency and trouble can confer the gift of fearlessness." [33]

There were other bodhisattvas or manifestations of them who specialized in protection from hostile forces, particularly the Dharma-pāla, defenders of the dharma, best developed in Tibetan tantrism, but present in China as well. These deities are of ferocious appearance, wield weapons, and are sometimes portrayed as leading armies into battle with demon hordes. The role of similar figures in guarding Chinese Buddhist temples is well known. [34]

---

[32] *Astasahasrika Prajñaparamita*, tr. Edward Conze, Rome, 1962, 140 (approx. 1st cent. B.C.).

[33] *Scripture of the Lotus Blossom of the Fine Dharma*, tr. from the Chinese of Kumārajīva by Leon Hurvitz, New York, 1976, 311-12, 317, 315.

[34] See Alice Getty, *The Gods of Northern Buddhism*, Rutland, Vt., 1962, 148-69. Buddhist forms of conflict and dualism were most strongly expressed in Tibet, chiefly symbolized by deities and demons of horrific appearance; see René de Nebesky-Wojkowitz, *Oracles and Demons of Tibet*, The Hague, 1956.

A common Mahāyāna way of warding off evil was through recitation of *dhāraṇīs*, oral invocations, which are presented and described in a variety of short texts in the Buddhist canon. Of the several such texts I have gone through one of the most interesting for our purposes is the *Ch'ing Kuan-shih-yin p'u-sa hsiao-fu tu-hai to-lo-ni chou ching* (The *sūtra* of the *dhāraṇī* which invokes the Bodhisattva Avalokiteśvara to dispel harm), translated in the E. Chin period (317-420).

This *sūtra* tells the story of the people of Vaiśālī (P'i-she-li kuo) who were oppressed by an evil illness with such symptoms as blood-red eyes, pus flowing from their ears, constant nosebleed, dumbness, etc. There were five *yakṣas* as well, with faces black as ink, five eyes, and dog-like teeth, who sucked out people's vital breath.

Some 500 elders of Vaiśālī went to where the Buddha was preaching to seek his aid against these torments, saying to him:

> Our people are suffering from a terrible illness, which our best medical drugs and techniques are unable to cure. We hope only that you, Heaven-honored one, in your compassion for all, will heal this illness and suffering, so that the calamity will cease.

To this plea the Buddha responds by instructing them to seek the aid of the bodhisattvas Avolokiteśvara and Mahāsthāma, who by their mercy are able to bring relief from all suffering. The Buddha, these bodhisattvas and a great assembly of holy followers then go to Vaiśālī, which is illumined by their brilliant golden light. The people offer willow branches and pure water to Avalokiteśvara, who tells them to recite "homage to the Buddha, dharma and sangha," and do homage to Avalokiteśvara, to burn incense and bow to the ground in reverence. They are then taught a *gāthā* affirming that all their sufferings can be healed by the Buddha's mercy.

Next the assembly is given a series of *dhāraṇīs*, with the promise for each that "for those who hear the *dhāraṇī* all sufferings forever cease; they will gain peace and joy, and stay far removed from difficulties of any sort." The *dhāraṇī* follows, in transliterated Sanskrit.

The text continues by affirming that those who recite such invocations will be protected by all the Buddhas and great bodhisattvas, and then be saved from all injury and sickness. At this all the people of Vaiśālī are healed.

Comments about other *dhāraṇīs* given in this text indicate that they stop all "evil devils, tigers, wolves and lions from doing harm," cleanse impurity, destroy bad *karma*, and rescue from every sort of injury:

wild beasts, shipwreck, weapons, bandits, the pain of childbirth, etc.
The lists are long and detailed. At the end of the Buddha's sermon and
instructions the 500 elders attain enlightenment and the whole assembly
is filled with rejoicing, all because of the power of the *dhāraṇīs.*

In the midst of this story there is an account of Buddhist exorcism:

> The Buddha told Ananda that in the city of Rajagrha there was a woman
> who was possessed by a demon named Caṇḍāla. This demon day and
> night came to sport with the woman in the form of her husband, as a
> result of which she gave birth to 500 devils.... In that time [the Buddha
> continued] I taught this woman to call out the name of Avalokitésvara
> Bodhisattva... [and thus] enter a realm of goodness. Ananda, you
> should understand that such is the awe inspiring divine power of the
> Bodhisattva to subdue evil demons.... 35

Other *dhāraṇī* texts give similar assurance that their reverent recitation annihilates all evils and obstacles to Buddhist truth, and protects
from every sort of demon. 36 There is thus a rich textual background
for the Buddhist contribution to popular themes of conflict with
harmful forces.

An important channel for communicating Buddhist ideas to the
people was the *pien-wen* texts of the T'ang and Sung periods, which
were written in a semi-vernacular style. It is significant for our purposes
that among these *pien-wen* are texts with such titles as *P'o-mo pien-
wen* and *Hsiang-mo pien-wen* (the *pien-wen* in which Māra is defeated). The *P'o-mo pien-wen*, dated 944, recounts in dramatic form
Māra's temptation of the Buddha. Māra comes leading a horde of evil
demons millions strong, led by terrifying demon generals, all bearing
weapons. These beings are described in detail: "horse-headed," "disease
bringing" with "lightning," "violent winds," "poisonous dragons," and,
"flying demons with five eyes and six teeth, three bodies and eight
arms, four shoulders and seven ears, nine mouths and ten heads, yellow
hair, red mustaches, pointed heads and wide foreheads." (!) They come,
shaking the earth, with Māra at their head, surrounding the Buddha
on all sides, accompanied by a black rain which covers the sky and blots
out the sun and moon. A fierce wind arises, uprooting trees and blowing
sand until all is dark.

The Buddha, sitting in meditation under the *bodhi* tree, gives rise

---

35 *Taishō shinshū dai-zōkyō*, Tokyo, 1924-32, 20:34-38 (TT 1043); this text was
translated in 420.

36 See the *Fo-shuo an-chai to-lo-ni chou ching, Taishō* 19:744 (TT 1029), for a list
of various types of demons. This text is a good example of the immediate, practical
benefits promised by Mahāyāna Buddhism. There are other *dhāraṇī* texts in *Taishō*
vols. 19 and 20.

to the power of compassion and good karma, and defeats the evil horde with his skill-in-means. The weapons he wields are different: the armor of forbearance, the sword of wisdom, the bow of *samādhi*, the arrows of compassion, the steeds of the ten powers of a Buddha's wisdom. The demons are terrified even before his weapons are raised, and their own are turned against them; those who emit flames and smoke are burned by their own fire, those who carry stones are buried by them; their bows snap in two, their arrows turn to flowers, their spears break, and the blades fall out of their swords. At this Māra leads his defeated army in retreat.

Later, Māra sends his three beautiful daughters to seduce the Buddha, but to no avail. For an educated Buddhist this may all have been an allegory of desire, but for ordinary folk the moral was not far-off; the Buddha can subdue demons, and thus offers hope to me. [37]

Struggle and Conflict in Popular Religion

A.   *The Background in Classical Ritual*

Exorcism rituals, some of great dramatic intensity, emerged in China long before the appearance of Buddhism and religious Taoism. By the Han dynasty ancient popular traditions of this sort had been incorporated into court ceremonial, which has recently been described in detail by Derk Bodde. Though at a later date court exorcisms were discontinued, similar rituals were carried out at the village level until the Ch'ing period.

The most important Han rites for "expelling pestilences" were performed at the La festival in the twelfth lunar month, and at the Mid-summer festival in the fifth month. The "Great Exorcism" or Ta No at the end of the year was led by a demon impersonator or exorcist called a Fang-hsiang-shih of whom we are told that:

> In his official functions he wears [over his head] a bearskin having four eyes of gold, and is clad in a black upper garment and a red lower garment. Grasping his lance and brandishing his shield, he leads the many officials to perform the seasonal Exorcism (no), searching through houses and driving out pestilences. [38]

---

[37] This text is in Wang Ch'ung-min et al., eds., *Tun-huang pien-wen chi* (A collection of *pien-wen* from Tun-huang), Peking, 1957, I, 345-355. Jaroslav Prusek, *Dictionary of Oriental Literatures, East Asia*, New York, 1974, I, 186, defines *pien-wen* as "text of a scene," that is, "popular elaborations of the Buddhist scriptures," starting in the mid-eighth century.

[38] *Chou-li* 31:6b-7a, tr. in Derk Bodde, *Festivals in Classical China*, Princeton, 1975, 78.

In the *History of the Latter Han Dynasty* we are told that this exorcism procession involved 120 young eunuchs, who were led "...to expel demons from the palace." Accompanied by a chant invoking the power of evil-destroying spirits, and carrying torches, the troops went through the whole palace until all the pestilences were driven out. At the end of the ritual, peachwood figurines and rush ropes were set up to prevent the return of unwanted influences. Other accounts of this ceremony mention that the youths, "...with peachwood bows and thornbrush arrows, shoot in all directions. Their flying missiles scatter like rain, bringing certain death to the hard afflicting demons." The language used against the demons is exceedingly violent: "devour," "batter," "chop to pieces," "decapitate," etc. [39]

A Han commentator notes that "[In the twelfth month] the sun moves to the zodiacal positions of the northern quarter, where it is feared that it may be repressed by the great *yin*. Therefore the officials are commanded to perform the Great Exorcism, in order to support the *yang* and repress the *yin*." [40] This of course refers to the annual cycle of *yin* and *yang* in which *yin* reaches its peak at the winter solstice, when the forces of *yang* are reborn as well. It is significant, however, that one looks in vain for a similar ceremony to exorcise demons of *yang*. On the contrary, during the Mid-summer festivals, when *yin* is at its lowest point, steps are taken to suppress *yin* and encourage *yang*, which is hardly an expression of concern for balanced harmony. As the *Hou Han shu says*:

> In the middle month of summer, when all creatures are flourishing, the sun reaches the Summer Solstice, [at which moment] the *yin* ether embryonically begins to function, so that there is fear that creatures will not [continue to] prosper. The ceremony in this connection consists of stringing strong-smelling vegetables together on red cords, so as to ward off destructive insects and poisonous creatures. Peachwood "seals" ... are used to display on gates and doors.

Though this passage goes on to say that at the summer solstice large fires are forbidden and that wells are dredged, thus discouraging *yang* and encouraging *yin*, the main emphasis is on warding off *yin* with *yang* materials, such as red cord and peachwood. [41] Thus, attitudes toward *yin* implied in Han rituals are at best ambivalent.

---

[39] *Hou Han shu* 15:3 and Chang Heng (78-139), *Tung-ching fu*, in Bodde, *Festivals*, 81-85. See pp. 75-136 for the history and symbolism of the Ta No; also, Groot, *op. cit.*, VI, 974-79.

[40] Ts'ai Yung (132-92), *Yüeh-ling chang-chü*, quoted in Bodde, *Festivals*, 81.

[41] *Hou Han shu* 15:2a, quoted in Bodde, *Festivals*, 289-91.

Court exorcism processions were carried out for several hundreds of years after the Han, but were evidently discontinued after the T'ang period. However, they remained a prominent feature of popular cult, often led by spirit-mediums. De Groot quotes a 19th century governor of Hunan who says that the people believe that by such processions, "...the diseases of the season may be successfully expelled... by noise of metal instruments, drums and [fire] crackers; ...this is a survival of the No of the villages, mentioned in the *Chou-li*...."

There was thus an ancient ritual tradition of conflict with hostile forces which preceded the similar concerns of later popular religion, a tradition which for a long time had official support. [42]

B. *Demonology*

There is rich corroborative evidence for the thesis of this essay in emphasis on conflict in vernacular literature after the Yüan dynasty, particularly the great novels. Conflict in this literature is basically between good and evil forces, at both the human level and the level of gods and demons. So we find struggles between good men and bandits, corrupt officials or devils; between righteous rebels and oppressive government; or between orthodox and heterodox groups of Taoist adepts and the spirits at their command. The most important form of conflict was between the forces of decay and rebirth at the end of a dynastic cycle, which was of paramount concern for both gods and man.

Vernacular literature was both influenced by popular religion, and became a source of myths and deities for later religious developments. In both its oral and written forms it was very much a part of the life of the people, and to a large extent an expression of their culture. Though this large body of material cannot be discussed in detail here, it serves to remind us that themes of conflict between hostile forces were not limited to religion alone, but were an important aspect of popular culture as a whole. [43]

One of the literary sources for later vernacular literature was collec-

---

[42] Groot, *op. cit.*, VI, 979-90.

[43] For examples of conflict in vernacular literature see *Shui-hu chuan* (14th cent.), chs. 51-53, in which spirit troops and various magical devices are involved in Sung Chiang's battles with the evil magistrate Kao Lien; *Hsi-yu chi* (16th cent.), chs. 1-2, 8, 13-15, 17-18, etc., for "Monkey's" battles with a variety of demons; and *Feng-shen yen-i* (16th cent.), a fictionalized account of the struggle between the Shang and Chou kingdoms (12th cent. B.C.) when the Shang "mandate" had obviously expired, with cosmic battles raging between gods and demons parallel to struggles between human armies and rival Taoist sects.

tions of strange stories or "tales of marvellous events" by scholars, from the Han dynasty on. Among the literati there were always some who were interested in recording popular customs and legends from areas where they lived or were assigned as officials. It is in these informal writings in classical Chinese that we find some of the earliest accounts of popular demonology; stories of strange beings which could cause harm, illness, and death. While later such beings were mostly the spirits of the dispossessed dead, in the Han period and before some of them were considered to be demonic forms of natural objects, such as mountains or stones.

Demons could be related to a particular earthly locality, usually a tomb, to a variety of subterranean lands or estates, or to purgatory. There was no single demon realm as a unified system of evil influences; purgatory, for all its devils and horrible punishments, was in the last analysis an aspect of karmic salvation. However, though here again in theory we are dealing at most with a limited dualism, in practice the Chinese peasant had to deal with a vast array of terrifying beings, whose power could seem very real. From an empathetic point of view it is quite understandable that such an harrassed and uneducated soul would want to employ all the countervailing exorcism at his command.

The Han sources cited by Derk Bodde list twenty-four types of demons which are expelled by the Ta No ritual, and only two of these appear to be of human origin: the spirits of executed criminals, and "giants." The others are all symbols of abstract categories of evil, natural forces or animals, such as "baneful things," "calamities," virulent poisons, tigers, serpents, demons which are produced by "the uncanny vapor of mountains and forests," or the "essence of mountains and streams," demons of drought, etc. These are all of weird appearance, often with an animal body and a human-like head. [44]

However, other Han accounts make it clear that there was widespread belief in active ghosts of the dead, who on occasion could be harmful. We also read of "flying corpses" and "circulating baneful things" which can cause disease. [45]

In Kan Pao's *Sou-shen chi*, a fourth century text, there are accounts of "fox demons," and a "Mei" monster who successfully defies a Taoist exorcist, as well as of demons in human form. [46]

---

[44] Bodde, *Festivals*, 96-111.

[45] Wang Ch'ung, *Lun-heng*, 20:9 (On Death), 25:5b, 6a (Exorcism).

[46] Kan Pao (f. 345-50), *Sou-shen chi* (A record of investigating spirits), reprint 1929, *chüans* 16-18; see Derk Bodde, "Some Chinese Tales of the Supernatural,"

Such tales continued to develop in more elaborate form, as can be seen for example in Hung Mai's (d. 1202) *I-chien chih*, which contains many stories of ghosts, some of human origin, some not. [47]

The literary tradition Kan Pao began reached its culmination in P'u Sung-ling's (1630-1715) *Liao-chai chih-i*, a large collection of "records of unusual events" first published in 1679. Here we find many stories of fox demons, sometimes whole armies of them, who in various disguises suck the life breath from unsuspecting humans. [48] P'u Sung-ling may have collected these stories in part for his own amusement, but for the people they reflect ancient fears of death and the unknown.

The above indicates just a few examples of the vast literature of Chinese demonology, much of which has been surveyed by de Groot in volume five of his *Religious System of China*. Here he describes twenty-two different types of demons in great detail, with both translation and Chinese text; demons of mountains and forests, water, plants, various forms of animals, etc. These beings, singly or in panic-causing hordes, inflict every sort of terror, illness, injury, drought and death. One who reads this material cannot fail to be impressed with the imaginative power of the Chinese understanding of malevolent forces.

Modern anthropologists stress that devils or *kuei* are the wandering souls of those who have died violently or unjustly, or have not been properly sacrificed to by their families. They are spirits who have not found their rightful place in the multi-dimensional family system, and thus cause trouble by seeking revenge. This is of course true for most *kuei*, but it is important to remember that from ancient times many demons were expressions of inimical forces of nature. The picture painted by anthropology is literally too domesticated; it leaves out a whole, powerful dimension of the Chinese "symbolism of evil." This dimension suggests that for many, their relationship to nature was at least ambivalent, if not fearful, quite different from the oft-cited attitude of Sung landscape paintings. [49]

Harvard Jour. Asiatic Studies 6 (1941), 338-57. Bodde describes the Mei as "... a malevolent creature, either having a bestial form, or with human face and animal body, and born from the supernatural emanations of mountains and forests" (350).

[47] Hung Mai, *I-chien chih* (Preface dated 1166); see *chüans* 18, 40, 47 in *Pi-chi hsiao-shuo ta kuan*, Taipei, 1962, 1:351, 443, 474.

[48] See P'u Sung-Ling, *Liao-chai chih-i* (1679), reprint Taipei, 1968, 1:22, 3:73, 13:404f., for the stories "Hu shih" (Mister Hu) and "Shih pien" (A corpse transforms); see the translation by Herbert Giles, *Strange Stories from a Chinese Studio*, Shanghai, 1916, 47-51, 155-58, 378-80.

[49] See David Jordan, *Gods, Ghosts and Ancestors*, Berkeley, 1972; Arthur Wolf,

C. *Exorcism*

In his chapter on exorcism Wang Ch'ung writes:

> The world trusts in sacrifices, saying that they certainly bring blessings, and trusts in exorcism (*chieh-chu*), saying that it will certainly drive away evil influences. At the beginning of an exorcism ritual sacrifices are offered, similar to the way in which the living treat each other as guest and host. At first a meal is provided, but when it has been eaten, the [ghosts and spirits] are driven away with swords and staves. [50]

This passage is one of the oldest accounts of exorcism in popular custom, a tradition much elaborated and strengthened later by contributions from Taoism and Buddhism, as well as from classical ritual. It has been a pervasive concern ever since. The chief means of popular exorcism were (and still are in Taiwan) a variety of *yang* symbols, such as blood, mirrors and white cocks, used in ritual fashion together with charms and invocations. Its practitioners were either ordinary folk themselves, properly armed, or religious specialists such as Buddhist or Taoist priests, spirit mediums and magicians. Scholars and officials often served as exorcists as well, strengthened by their identification with all that is orthodox and correct. It is exorcism more than anything else which demonstrates the importance of conflict in Chinese popular religion; the people were resigned to fate in matters of social position and death, but in all else they struggled against the forces which beset them, in the best ways they knew.

Since we have already looked at the orthodox backgrounds of popular exorcism, and since here again de Groot has provided a lengthy historical and textual discussion, let us move directly to modern anthropological accounts. [51]

McCreery describes an exorcism ritual performed by a Taiwanese *hoat-su* or magician (Mandarin *fa-shih*) as follows:

> A paper charm is burned and its ashes mixed with a cup of water. Suddenly the rite begins. The orchestra begins a furious caterwauling. The *hoat-su*, holding a bundle of burning incense in each hand, begins to leap and spin about.
>
> First, he makes his obeisance before whatever altars are present. His gestures are a wild parody of the usual gestures of worship. He

---

"Gods, Ghosts and Ancestors," *Religion and Ritual*, 131-82; Philip Baity, *Religion in a Chinese Town*, Taipei, 1975, 238-69; Edwin Harvey, *The Mind of China*, New Haven, 1933.

[50] *Lun-heng* 25:4b.

[51] Groot, *op. cit.*, VI, 929-1185, "The War Against Spectres."

leaps in the air, then falls into a squat, sweeping the bundles of burning incense up to cross them over his bowed head. As he performs these acts before each altar, an assistant takes some of the incense sticks and places them in the altar's incense burners.

Second, he drinks from the cup of water in which the ashes of the paper charm were mixed. Again he leaps up and spins around. He twists his hands into special exorcistic gestures, *ki*. He thrusts them out fiercely before him and spurts the water all around. He does this over and over again, working his way through a series of a half-dozen or more different exorcistic gestures.

Third, he takes up each of the pennants in turn and strikes a dramatic pose, thrusting it out before him. He strikes his pose at corners and then at the center of a square. Thus he thrusts each pennant toward its proper direction, East, South, West, North and Center. At each point assistants come forward to burn spirit money near his feet. These fires are kept fed and flaring as he works his way around the square.

Fourth, he seizes his sword and whip; wildly waving and thrusting with the sword, he works his way around the square for the last time. He lashes out with his whip, scattering the fires of spirit-money. When he has finished, he falls on his knees, exhausted, before the altar in front of the temple at which he began. [52]

McCreery's interpretation of this sort of ritual as an expression of concentrated coercive force has been noted above.

In his study of folk religion in a Taiwanese village, David Jordon discusses "Four enormous trees located near the four corners of the village [which] represent forts... manned by supernatural forces, and a fifth fort... located immediately opposite the temple of another tree." These forts and spirit troops which man them are to protect the village from evil enfluences; the troops are provided with "provisions" (sacrificial food) twice a month. When the village "...is in imminent danger of being invaded by ghosts, the forts may be strengthened by means of an exorcism consisting of purification by fire of the temple and the five forts." Jordon then describes this exorcism, which is centered on producing clouds of flame and smoke by spitting rice liquor into a pot of hot oil.

During Jordon's stay in the village a child was drowned in a pond. Since it was assumed that the child had been pulled in by a ghost, it was necessary to exorcise the pond, in this case by using two small sedan chairs which are possessed by deities. After receiving divine

---

[52] McCreery, *op. cit.*, 29-30; see also 30-35, 84-103. For a similar rite in Hongkong see V. R. Burkhardt, *Chinese Creeds and Customs*, Hongkong, 1953, II, 142f.

instruction through characters traced on a table top by an arm of the chairs the exorcism proceeded:

> Upon arrival at the pond the chairs ran madly about the perimeter of the pond, then hurled themselves and their bearers into the water, where they circled the pond several times more, a swinging up and down into and out of the water to drive out the bad thing [which had killed the child]. At the same time the onlookers shouted high-pitched shouts, hurled burning firecrackers over the pond, and threw handfuls of sesame seeds into the water.

All of this was,

> ...calculated to terrify the ghost.... When the gods climbed out at one bank, they would leap in wildly elsewhere and beat the water with renewed vigor. [53]

One could hardly hope for a better illustration of the struggle against malevolent forces.

In modern popular religion the most important exorcistic process is the use of written charms in the form of commands from superiors (gods) to inferiors (lesser gods, or demons). Such paper charms are ritually activated through gestures, seals or the blood of a possessed medium, all of which impart divine power. After consecration they are usually burned to carry their message to the celestial realm with the ashes mixed with water to make a healing potion. However, in some cases charms are pasted on doorways, etc. to ward off harmful influences. The language of these commands is firm or even violent: "root out," "eject," "subdue," "prohibit," etc. They are channels by which the powers of order are focussed against those of disorder, sometimes at a very specific level.

Henri Doré sums up the structure of charms as follows:

> A charm is an official document, a mandate, an injunction, emanating from the god, and setting to work superhuman powers who carry out the orders of the divinity.... To operate with tremendous effect the charm or spell must denote thunder or lightning... which are intended to smite spectres.... The evil to be destroyed is generally placed at the end, and represented by various characters... all meaning misfortune, calamity or ill-luck.
>
> The charm being an official document... terminates in much the same manner as Chinese Imperial edicts: "let the law be obeyed, let this order be respected and executed forthwith." Taoists sometimes end

---

[53] Jordan, *op. cit.*, 50-59.

their charms by the expressions "quick, quick" or "quick as fire"...,
denoting thereby that destruction of spectres should be brought about
with lightning velocity. [54]

The structure of exorcistic charms reminds us again of the limited
nature of Chinese religious dualism, because the assumption behind
their efficacy is that gods and demons are part of the same system,
the orders of which must be obeyed. Yet the strenuous way in which
charms are employed indicates that destructive spirits have wills of their
own which can be most difficult to subdue.

Perhaps the most direct expression of conflict against hostile forces
can be seen in the actions of possessed spirit-mediums who wield
ferocious weapons and draw their own blood in the struggle. Such
mediums become the deities by whom they are temporarily possessed,
and as such represent concentrated *yang* force in concrete, available
form. The best way to sense the dramatic nature of their role is to see
Gary Seaman's film, "Weapons," taken in Taiwan in the early 1970's.
This film depicts the initiation of a new set of swords, clubs, skewers
and prick-balls by a young medium. This he does by daubing them with
his own blood, and by taking them on a ritual dance through seven
fires representing the north polar stars, centers of cosmic order. [55]

Elliott, in his *Chinese Spirit Medium Cults in Singapore*, writes of
these implements that they are "powerful weapons against evil,"
wielded on behalf of such warlike deities as "Monkey," No-cha and
Kuan-ti. He describes a rite intended to exorcise a haunted house,
involving charm papers daubed with the medium's blood, the use of
swords and whips, a slain white cockerel, etc. Even more interesting
for our purposes are invocations to the gods, imploring them to descend
to the planchette (spirit-writing) altar, there to reveal their wisdom
and power. In a prayer to the "Great Saint Equal to Heaven" (Monkey)
we read, for example,

> ...You hold in your hand a golden bar when you ascend to Heaven.
> Standing upon a coloured cloth you can go anywhere. Sweep away all
> uncleanliness to clean the world. Nothing can resist your golden bar.
> We... beseech you to descend speedily, for we know that when the

---

[54] Henri Doré, *Researches into Chinese Superstitions*, tr. W. Kennelly, Shanghai,
1914-38, III, iii-v; vols. II and III discuss 207 charms from a variety of sources. See
also Groot, *op. cit.*, VI, 1024-61; Majorie Topley, "Paper Charms and Prayer Sheets
as Adjuncts to Chinese Worship," *Royal As. Soc., Jour. Malayan Br.* 26 (1953), 63-
80; McCreery, *op. cit.*, 107-112; also *Ku-chin t'u-shu chi ch'eng*, vol. 476, *chüan* 678.
[55] Film dist. by Far Eastern Audio Visuals, 1010 W. 23rd St., Austin, Tex. 78705.

order is given the Heavenly army will come to our aid as quickly as
we hope.... You can save a myriad of the people. Now we invite jou,
the one who can shake Heaven, to come before this altar. With your
sword you can kill evil spirits... Wake, wake and save us. [56]

This power is then put into effect by the medium.

Concluding Comments

In his *Religion in a Chinese Town* Philip Baity comments as follows:

> Probably the major theme which runs throughout the folk religion is
> the ritual separation of elements which are believed to be pure or
> polluting; between those which are life oriented and those which are
> concerned with death, between *yang* and *yin*.... It is the pervasiveness
> of this dichotimization, cutting across each of the major religions,
> which proves the existence of an underlying stratum of ideology and
> belief in the folk religion....
>
> In theory, at least, both *yin* and *yang* elements are equally necessary
> for the maintenance of balance in the world.... But what appears to
> be a well-ordered universe of mutually balanced forces in theory may
> not be believed so in fact. Although *yin* and *yang* are believed to be
> complementary principles in some instances, in other cases they are
> believed to be mutually destructive, and an attempt is made to banish
> one of them and accentuate the other. In almost all cases, preference
> is put on [sic] the *yang* at the expense of the *yin* principle. [57]

We have seen the validity of such an interpretation, though the
"dichotomization" is not so clear-cut as Professor Baity indicates. In
fact, at many points there are orthodox antecedents for popular practice,
particularly in the denigration of *yin,* Taoist exorcism texts and Buddhist
dhāranīs. In its concern to struggle with hostile forces Chinese religion
is a continuum with different emphases, from the psychological conflict
of the Neo-Confucians to dramatic battles against demons by spirit-
mediums.

In this context popular religion is a structure in its own right at
the level of symbolization and ritual expression, but is permeated with
concepts and terms derived from the classical traditions. Ordinary
folk have reworked what has come to them from their general cultural
background, selected from it, and supplemented it with local customs
and beliefs, but the end result is still a variation of the same under-

---

[56] Alan Elliott, *Chinese Spirit Medium Cults in Singapore,* London, 1955, 52, 74-77,
95f., 170f. See also Groot, *op. cit.,* VI, 1187-1341; Needham, *op. cit.,* II, 132-39;
and Jack Potter, "Cantonese Shamanism," *Religion and Ritual in Chinese Society,*
207-31.

[57] Baity, *op. cit.,* 136-38.

standing of man in the world. This is to say that popular religion is in the same position as vernacular literature and village culture itself.

As Wolfram Eberhard has pointed out, traditional Chinese literature existed at three levels: 1. "Literature written by the educated (scholar/gentry) for the educated;" 2. "Literature written by the educated for the less educated and uneducated middle and lower classes;" and 3. "...works that are written or composed by people with little education." [58] That is to say, literature can be discussed under the categories of elite, popular and folk, which in language is the distinction between literary Chinese, written vernacular and local dialect. In society, each of these forms is related respectively to the scholar official class, a middle level of educated merchants and less successful scholars, and the great mass of illiterate peasants and workers. Examples in literature would be classical philosophy and poetry in the literary language, vernacular novels, dramas and scripture texts, and oral folk tales.

Each of these levels has a distinctive mode of expression, a style, a dramatic range. They deal with different topics and types of people, from cosmologists and mystics speculating about the origins of the world to poor wood cutters who are rewarded by the gods for their hard work and filial devotion. But despite these differences, all forms of Chinese literature are written in variations of the same language, and share common social goals and ethical standards. For all, there is no higher felicity than to become an official, while ethical assumptions throughout affirm such values as filial piety, industriousness, frugality, honesty and loyalty to friends and superiors. [59]

Of the three levels of literature noted above it is the vernacular novels which have the most dramatic intensity and scope. It is here that great battles between good and evil forces are described at length. These novels in turn had a profound influence on orally transmitted folk operas which were an important source of ethical and cultural values in village life. [60] But these values originally came in part from orthodox histories and Buddhist tales, from which the novelists and their predecessors derived characters, situations and principles. [61]

---

[58] Wolfram Eberhard, *Moral and Social Values of the Chinese*, Taipei, 1971, 191-92.

[59] See, e.g., the Peking "pounding song" in praise of Kuan Yü, in Wolfram Eberhard, *Studies in Chinese Folklore and Related Essays*, Bloomington, Ind., 1970, 148.

[60] For texts of orally transmitted operas see Sidney Gamble, *Chinese Village Plays from the Ting Hsien Region*, Amsterdam, 1970.

[61] For the background of two well-known novels see Glen Dudbridge, *The Hsi-yu chi: A Study of the Antecedents of the Sixteenth Century Chinese Novel*, Cambridge, 1970; and Richard Irwin, *The Evolution of a Chinese Novel: Shui-hu chuan*, Cambridge, Mass., 1953.

Chinese popular religion is in a position analogous to vernacular literature, with its own characteristic means of expression, yet profoundly influenced by values shared with the ruling elite. Popular religion, with its vernacular scriptures and semi-educated specialists (healers, spirit-mediums, etc.), reacted in turn with local cults and oral traditions, chiefly through gradual recognition of folk deities believed to be particularly effective. In this way popular religion came to occupy a vast middle ground between elite and folk modes of expression, but overlapping with both.

All of this of course has social ramifications as well, because popular religion was based in the village, and the village in turn was not isolated, but was an integral part of the total cultural system. In China, as elsewhere, peasants, in the words of A. L. Kroeber and Robert Redfield, "constitute part-societies with part-cultures." They are "the rural dimension of old civilizations," defined by "their long-established interdependence with gentry and townspeople." [62] Scholars such as K. C. Hsiao and G. William Skinner have long since demonstrated that the Chinese rural village was not autonomous, but part of a marketing network which connected it with goods, services and customs from a much larger area. Village population was composed of people from a variety of economic and educational levels, often led by local gentry who were representatives of the national literate elite. Though formal government office extended down only to the county level, the court persistently attempted to organise or co-opt informal systems of local control to strengthen its influence and tax base. Such government interventions at the very least were a periodic reminder that the village owed allegiance to a realm beyond its borders. [63]

For popular religion this social context meant that its temples, processions and operas were usually dominated by the more prosperous and literate villagers, including the gentry, who supported established ethical values. The predominance of these values can be seen even in the texts of independently established popular sects. Ecstatic cults which emerged out of oral folk tradition succeeded in the long run only if they attracted support from village leaders, settled down and developed ritual and scriptural traditions, though of course without losing their

---

[62] Robert Redfield, *The Little Community and Peasant Society and Culture*, Chicago, 1960, pt. 2, 20-24.

[63] See Hsiao Kung-ch'üan, *Rural China: Imperial Control in the Nineteenth Century*, Seattle, 1960; and G. William Skinner, *Marketing and Social Structure in Rural China*, Assoc. Asian Studies, n.p., n.d. (reprinted from *JAS* 24 [1964-65]).

promise of immediate benefits for those in need. Such local traditions were enriched as well by touring story tellers and opera troupes in market towns. In addition, there might be a Taoist temple or Buddhist monastery on the outskirts of a village whose clergy could influence popular belief by inviting participation in rituals, sermons and recitation of scripture. In such an evironment the interrelationships and transformations we have been discussing are only to be expected.

The diachronic dimension of elite/popular transformation in China is too complex and little known to be even outlined here. Suffice it to say that one of the central historical factors was the coming of Buddhism and its gradual penetration into Chinese consciousness. Buddhism provided popular religion with vernacular texts and sermons presenting a whole new array of deities, demons and interesting stories. In addition, Buddhist concepts of karma, retribution, purgatory and rebirth came to be assumed by the vast majority of Chinese. All of these factors are integral to popular religion from the Sung on, and seem to have been more eagerly accepted by the common people than by the Confucian elite. Certainly some of the differences in emphasis and expression described above must have been due to this greater Buddhist influence at the popular level, but to demonstrate this would be another project. One of the transmission points, of course, was popular religious sects of predominantly Buddhist origin and orientation. [64]

In sum, themes of dualism and conflict were of fundamental importance in Chinese popular religion, which in turn was intimately related to other dimensions of the cultural system. Of more immediate interest are the implications of these themes for our understanding of Maoism, particularly its expressions among the people. The popular application of Mao Tse-tung's thought seems to be quite dualistic, with sharp antagonism expressed against one set of hostile forces after another: "U.S. imperialism," "Soviet revisionism," "Lin Piao and Confucius," the "Gang of Four," etc. [65] While these vilification campaigns are no doubt to some extent propaganda intended to stir up revolutionary fervor, perhaps they are as well an expression of the old moralistic dualism, a struggle with demonic forces. That the expressed intention

---

[64] See my *Folk Buddhist Religion: Dissenting Sects in Late Traditional China*, Harvard, 1976.

[65] I confine my comments to "popular application" here because Mao's discussion of contradiction indicates that in theory at least it is dialectical; see his "On Contradiction," *Selected Readings from the Works of Mao Tse-tung*, Peking, 1971, 93; and his essay (20 years later), "On the Correct Handling of Contradictions Among the People," *ibid.*, 432-79.

of such language is an attack on political positions does not rule out the presence of deeper psychological implications.

Perhaps it is not a coincidence that articles criticizing the "Gang of Four" apply to them such exorcistic terms as *yao-feng* "evil current," *yao-chuang* "fiendish appearance" and *hsieh-ch'i* "evil and heretical spirit." There is repeated use in such articles of a contrast between evil "black" (*hei* or *yin*) words and actions, and good "red" (*hung* or *yang*) actions. One ditty reads:

> Overthrow the "Gang of Four"
> Seize the fiendish devils (*mo-yao*).

And a headline:

> Utterly drive away the four harmful things
> (*ch'ing-ch'u ssu-hai*).

No doubt many other examples could be given. [66]

Here concepts from old popular religion are used to dramatize conflicts in a modern state. So tradition persists in the midst of radical transformation.

---

[66] I encountered these terms in the *Jen-min jih-pao* (Peoples' Daily), Feb. 6, Feb. 26, and Mar. 2, 1977; I am grateful to Roberto Ong of the University of British Columbia for referring me to these articles.

Note: For a glossary of Chinese terms and names used in this article, contact the author.

FROM RECIPROCITY TO CONTRADICTION
Aspects of the Confucian-Maoist Transformation

PAUL V. MARTINSON

Luther Theological Seminary

It can hardly be doubted that one of the greatest fissures to occur in the history of religions is the transformation which the thought and practice of Mao have brought to China. But strange to say, this contemporary event of potentially massive significance for the history of religions has elicited relatively little intellectual questing by students of religion. That task has been pretty much taken over by students of political and economic affairs. Perhaps that is as it should be, at least initially, but the religious dimension must eventually be addressed.

Perhaps the most heat, if not light, has been generated by the searching minds of "frustrated" missionaries. [1] That is perhaps also as it should be, for the religious implications of the revolution were made immediately obvious to the Christian missionary segment of Western society, at least insofar as the mission enterprise of the church was concerned. To be sure there have been occasional treatments of the religious issue by sociologists and others, but nothing adequate to the dimensions of the problem. No doubt the formidable obstacles presented by an essentially closed society to would-be students has deterred many. Furthermore, the happy pickings for anthropological study in Taiwan and Hong Kong, and the largely unchartered yet beckoning waters of Chinese traditional religion, were quite enough to exhaust the labors of the interested few. Be that as it may, now that Mao is dead and his era begins to recede into the past, an assessment from the perspectives of the history of religions becomes increasingly important.

But where is one to begin? If one is to follow the path traced by Levenson, [2] one might be inclined simply to shrug off the issue and argue that the religious question no longer pertains. Mao made religion an antique, so it is said, and that is the end of the matter. Confucian ideas once current and bearing evident social significance were rendered increasingly senile as the historical context shifted, the questions changed, and the traditionalists gave way to the iconoclasts. The

---

[1] See, for instance, LWF/PMV ed., *Christianity and the New China*, S. Pasadena, 1976.

[2] Esp. his trilogy, *Confucian China and its Modern Fate*, Berkeley, 1958, 1964, 1965.

iconoclasts who were victorious (the Communists) offered an emotionally satisfying and politically enabling construction. Therefore, exit the religious question.

But not so. The dichotomous approach hardly does justice to the complexity of the case. The link between past and present is of greater substance than the emotional tie. Turning temples into museums certainly does make a statement, but there are other statements of religious significance to be made besides this. The perplexing mix of continuities and discontinuities, commitments and counter-commitments, invites our inquiry.

Tradition, transition and transformation: these three terms repeatedly occur in discussions of contemporary China. They are usually used in a chronological historical sense: traditional refers to China before the mid-nineteenth century western impact, particularly Ch'ing China; transitional refers to the uncertain years of passage from the so-called Opium War (1839-42) to the establishment of the People's Republic, including both the dying phases of empire and the abortion of republic; transformation designates post-1949 Communist China. These uses, imprecise though they be, can be assumed in this study.

These terms can also be used in a more processual sense, as three simultaneous processes that reflect different mixes of continuity/discontinuity. The etymology of the words helps. "Tradition" is a "giving over," thus stressing the continuity of the subject in passage; "transition" is a "change of site," and puts emphasis upon the shift of context; "transformation" is a "change of form," indicating a situation in which the subject itself undergoes change. Seen in this perspective the three thematize interlocking processes that relate subject to context in different ways. Thus, even in the People's Republic the process of traditioning remains, for the classics are still studied, however selectively, and a new corpus of classics has arisen as well; transitions continue as the context of events shift requiring continual adjustments; and transformation endures as an inherently incomplete process, despite the seeming finality of the word itself. As these processes intermingle one can expect that the new traditioning and norming process of the revolution will assume increasing importance and once again make traditioning the dominant element. The precise form this new traditioning process will take is still in formation and the issue uncertain. Mao's hope was that the principle of contradiction would become embedded in the traditioning process. It is the will of others that more reciprocal modes of operation will enjoy this prestige. The Great Proletarian Cultural Revolution was a tension between these divergent hopes.

These terms may also be used in a more static structural or synchronic way, lending themselves to a typological approach. Thus, Wach at times uses "transition" in a rather technical sense to mean a mixed or less "classic" type. This usage is most clear in his discussion of "types of religious authority." [3]

In what follows we will be using these terms in all of these meanings. Where the context does not make it clear we will indicate the sense intended. For our purposes, however, the processual sense is the more interesting. One final caveat may need stating—this essay limits itself to the Confucian tradition but does not thereby deny significant congruities with other elements of the Chinese tradition. Indeed, without these further analyses the viewpoint expressed here is incomplete.

MYTHIC CONGRUENCE

The modern Chinese transformation can be described at least in part as a passage from traditional order that gives primacy to reciprocity [4] to a transformed order that gives primacy to contradiction. Reciprocity and contradiction are alike in that in both cases life is experienced and understood in terms of dualities. Reciprocity stresses that which is common or binding between two entities and finds maximal value in exploring and developing the already given relations and mutuality. The Confucian way of seeing society in terms of pairs of relations—e.g., father-son, husband-wife, ruler-ruled—typifies this. *Jen* (humaneness) in the Confucian tradition is one expression of the ideal envisioned. Contradiction stresses that which distinguishes two entities and finds maximal value in moving beyond given relations of mutuality to new and presumably creative possibilities. The Communist ideal of egalitarian classless society, in contrast to hierarchical *jen*, expresses this ideal. Because the Confucian ideal seeks to enhance mutuality, it tends

---

[3] See Joachim Wach, *Sociology of Religion*, Chicago, 1944, ch. 8.

[4] On reciprocity as it pertains to the Chinese tradition see, e.g., Yang Lien-sheng, "The Concept of Pao as a Basis for Social Relations in China," *Chinese Thought and Institutions*, ed. John K. Fairbank, Chicago, 1957, 291-309; Francis Hsu, "Eros, Affect and Pao," *Kinship and Culture*, Chicago, 1971, 439-75; on *kan-ch'ing* as another general reciprocity concept see Morton Fried, *Fabric of Chinese Society*, New York, 1953; and Paul V. Martinson, "Pao Order and Redemption: Perspectives on Chinese Religion and Society Based on a Study of the Chin P'ing Mei," unpub. Ph.D. dissertation, University of Chicago, 1973.

to see history as a series of more or less adequate exemplars of this ideal. The Maoist vision, contrariwise, views history dynamically as a linear process urged onward by lively contradictions. The divergent implications of these views for the ordering of human society are immense.

Nonetheless, there are persistent underlying mythic congruities. It has long been observed that China is unique amongst the great civilizations in its apparent lack of a convincing cosmogonic myth. [5] Somehow, traditional China was overwhelmingly cosmologically concerned. Her question was not, "Why is there something rather than nothing?" but, "Why are things the way they are and not some other way?" [6] Her informing myths, whether it be the story of the Great Yü or other culture heroes, were predominantly myths of order, not origin. Whether it be history, science or politics, this penchant for ordering seemed always to surface most quickly.

Cosmogony

But is China lacking in a fundamental, informing, cosmogonic myth? Whatever the history and provenance of such a mythic awareness might be, it is clear that neo-Confucianism of the Sung was founded squarely on such a myth. We refer of course to the *t'ai-chi t'u* (Diagram of the Supreme Ultimate), the basic idea of which is already adumbrated in the *Tao-te ching*: "Tao produced One, One produced Two, Two produced Three, and Three produced the Ten Thousand Things." [7] The mythic symbol of the division of a primordial mass, *hun-tun*, the cosmic egg motif, seems most appropriate to this language.

There has been sufficient work done on the *t'ai-chi t'u* to obviate extended comment here. This cosmogram is, of course, a highly developed synthetic construct. Fung Yu-lan (b. 1890) [8] observes that Chou Tun-yi's (1017-1073) diagram is an adaptation of a prior Taoist one. Chou in fact reversed the sequence of movement in the diagram from bottom (phenomena) to top (absolute) so as to read from top (absolute) to bottom (phenomena), thus making a usable Confucian statement out of Taoist material. What had been a "soteriogram" indicating the pathway to individual salvation became a cosmogram articulating

[5] Thus Derk Bodde, "Myths of Ancient China," *Mythologies of the Ancient World*, ed. S. N. Kramer, New York, 1961, 367-408.

[6] Eric Voegelin, *The Ecumenic Age*, Baton Rouge, 1974, 73.

[7] *Tao-te ching*, ch. 42.

[8] Fung Yu-lan, *A History of Chinese Philosophy*, Princeton, 1952-53, ch. 11.

the process for realizing socio-political order. The Taoist alchemical "soteriogram" was predicated upon the idea of "opposition" (*ni*) or "reversion" (*fan*). That is, by manipulating the inner dynamics of natural processes one could reverse the tendency to decay and rise on the pathway to immortality. But even this "soteriogram" presupposed the logical priority of its inverse, the cosmogonic order, which was to be adopted and adapted by Chou.

Whatever the actual history of this cosmogram, it clearly gives expression to a basic mythic mode of experiencing and perceiving reality—phenomena appear as the end product of a process initiated by the division of a single primordial mass into two. Monism yields a duality, which fructifies into multiplicity—one, two, three.

This mode of experiencing reality, or at least interpreting it, seems evident enough in the thought of Mao Tse-tung (1893-1976). Mao's doctrine of contradictions, ostensibly inherited from Marx, is his cosmogonic myth. Echoing Lenin he states that "In any given phenomenon or thing, the unity of opposites is conditional, temporary and transitory, and hence relative, whereas the struggle of opposites is absolute." [9] Drawing a distinction between external (i.e., secondary) and internal (i.e., primary) causality, he yields to what seems almost a "Jungian slip,"

> External causes are the condition of change and internal causes are the basis of change, and ... external causes become operative through internal causes. In a suitable temperature (external cause) *an egg changes* (internal cause) *into a chicken*, but no temperature can change a stone into a chicken. (italics added). [10]

It is perhaps obvious why the cosmic egg motif is so universal, and why it is most appropriate here.

This idea of a yeasting monad takes on the character of a chartering myth that serves as a paradigm for events in nature, in society and in thought itself, for "the world is nothing else but the material world in a process of unlimited development." [11] This myth (whether Marxist or Maoist) supports Mao's doctrine of class struggle, his view of history, his theory of revolution, his theory of knowledge and of political process.

---

[9] Mao Tse-tung, "On the Correct Handling of Contradictions Among the People (February 27, 1957)," *Selected Works of Mao Tse-tung*, Peking, 1977, V, 392.

[10] Mao, "On Contradiction," *ibid.*, I, 314.

[11] Mao Tse-tung, "Dialectical Materialism: Notes of Lectures," quoted in Stuart Schram, *The Political Thought of Mao Tse-tung*, New York, 1969, 188; also 180, n. 1.

Historiogenesis

There is the convergence of a second mythic type as well. In his work, *The Ecumenic Age*, Eric Voegelin distinguishes four basic mythic modes: theogony, cosmogony, anthropogony and historiogenesis. [12] This last is just as prominent in Confucian and Maoist sensibilities as is cosmogony.

Associated with Confucian historiography is a lively sense of origins and beginnings of an historical and socio-biologic kind. Voegelin's term historiogenesis, developed originally to incorporate a particular kind of Mesopotamian, Egyptian and Israelite speculation on origins, seems admirably suited to cover these Confucian orientations. Historiogenesis is a speculation upon the order of society, its origin, and its course in time that links pragmatic history (*res gestae*) through a legendary and mythological continuum back to an absolute point of beginning. The Pentateuchal narrative is a model of this symbolic form. In its mature development the Confucian myth, though substituting the cosmogonic P'an-ku form of creation for the Biblical idea of direct creation, presents a strikingly similar construct. Diagrammed it would appear thus: [13]

```
B.C.                         ↑

  206              ┃         Han dynasty
  221       historical      Ch'in dynasty—First Empire
 1122             ┃         Chou dynasty        Wu
 1766             ┃         Shang dynasty       T'ang
 2205             ┃         Hsia dynasty        Yü
                            The Five Ti
                  ┃           Shun
             legendary        Yao
                  ┃           also Shao Hao
                              Huang Ti
                              Shen Nung
                              Fu Hsi
                  ┃         The Three Huang
             mythical         Human
                  ┃           Earthly
                              Celestial
Creation          ↓         P'an-ku
```

---

[12] See Voegelin, *op. cit.*, 60, on the four mythic modes; on Chinese historiogenesis see ch. 6, sec. 1.

[13] For a narrative summary of this model see John Fairbank and Edwin Reischauer, eds., *Asia: The Great Tradition*, Boston, 1958, I, 37f.

Notable in this construction as it developed is the smudging of the lines between history, legend and myth, the leitmotif of praise-blame whereby the purpose of history as mirror is to display virtue and criticize misbehavior, and the successful imposition of dynastic cycle upon the forward movement of the sequence.

It is not necessary here to go into a study of the Marxist periodization of history. Suffice it to say that the typical sequence of primitive communism, slave society, feudal society, capitalism, socialism and final communism has been accepted by the Chinese Communists without serious question. It has only raised vexatious questions as to where to fit Chinese history into the procrustean bed, and certain accommodations have been formalized in the process. Perhaps the two most important are placing Confucius as the final gasp of the decaying slave society, and modifying the scheme to treat feudal China as also semi-colonial, harboring therein the early shoots of capitalism.

But these unnatural reconstructions are of less interest than the vivid sense of beginnings and symbolic ordering that attaches to certain events of the Chinese revolution itself. Within the larger Marxist historical framework events such as the Long March achieve a symbolic autonomy of their own. This event is unique. Mao Tse-tung states:

> Speaking of the Long March, one may ask, "What is its significance?" We answer that the Long March is the first of its kind in the annals of history, that it is a manifesto, a propaganda force, a seeding-machine.

And, linking this to the mythical times of the traditional construct, he avers:

> Since Pan Ku divided the heavens from the earth and the Three Sovereigns and Five Emperors reigned, has history ever witnessed a long march such as ours? ... Let us ask, has history ever known a long march equal to ours? No, never.

The Long March is a "missionary campaign" bearing witness to the miracles of the birth and formation of Chinese communism, a paradigm for the subsequent success of the Chinese revolution, for, he says, "there will be many more Long Marches." So also Chou En-lai confided to Edgar Snow that "China has started on a second Long March. We have just taken the first step. Yes, this is only the first step." In an attempt to recreate afresh in a new generation the experience of the Long March the Great Proletarian Revolution swept China. Not surprisingly, the striking affinity of this with the Israelite form of exodus myth has been noted on a number of occasions. [14]

We have, thus, the convergence of two common mythic types in the Chinese experience, whether traditional or transformational—cosmogony and historiogenesis. This convergence would seem to be an important consideration in understanding the nature of continuity and discontinuity in the Chinese Confucian-Maoist transformation. However, the convergence of mythic forms conceals a substantive difference. The dualities of the neo-Confucian *t'ai-chi t'u* metaphysics of primal complementarity and neo-Marxist (i.e., Maoist) metaphysics of primal contradiction have different operations and yield divergent results.

DIVERGING PRINCIPLES

Reciprocity yields harmony as the most fitting mode of activity, whereas contradiction yields struggle. We shall display elements of these two ways by commenting on three representatives: two represent the principle of reciprocity, with the second of these, K'ang Yu'wei, displaying a transitional form; the third, namely Mao, represents the principle of contradiction. In K'ang we see many differences from more usual Confucian sentiments, but significant continuities mark K'ang's view as merely transitional (in the Wachian sense), not transformational. Mao is clearly transformational, but without, as we have said, leaving the basic mythic forms.

Hsi-ming (Western Inscription)

Something of the essential Confucian spirit appears, for instance, in the classic *hsi-ming* passage of Chang Tsai (1020-1077), [15] an important precedessor of the systematizing Chu Hsi (1130-1200). It begins by elaborating a Confucian form of *analogia entis* by treating the whole cosmos on the analogy of the family (*analogia familiae*). Heaven and Earth are my father and mother. In their commingling I am brought forth. All creatures are my companions, all persons my relations. The sage epitomizes virtue by conjoining (*ho*) all things in himself. Out of this relation flows all proper virtue. Committed to this vision, one finds it efficacious both for life (service) and in death (peace).

---

[14] For the above quotes and reference see Kazuhiko Sumiya, "The Long March and the Exodus: 'The Thought of Mao Tse-tung' and the Contemporary Significance of 'Emissary Prophecy,'" *China and Ourselves*, ed. Bruce Douglass and Ross Terrill, Boston, 1970, 189-223.

[15] See Fung Yu-lan, *op. cit.*, II, 493ff.

The irreducible element in this model is the basic Confucian notion of receiving and returning: life has been given by others, gratitude is the return of the filial. Assuming reality as a "singular entity yet with dual embodiment" (*yi-wu erh liang-t'i*), reciprocal action then expands to embrace all meaningful activity within this cosmos. Two never become simply the one, but perpetually remain distinct amidst inter-activity. Relationships in the family most directly concretize this truth of reciprocal activity.

Without Boundaries

K'ang Yu-wei (1858-1927) represents a late but striking transition within the neo-Confucian family of thinkers. [16] Impressed early in life by the vigor of Western and Japanese encroachments upon China, he devoted his life to constructive reform that would make the dynasty a continuing and viable entity. His moment of glory came in the one-hundred days reform of 1898, but with its sudden failure, his efforts for change were shunted to the sidetrack of history.

K'ang was in the line of scholars who argued the priority of the New Texts. In his theoretical construction K'ang welded together two ancient views of history. The one (from the *Kung-Yang* commentary on the *Spring and Autumn Annals*), almost totally ignored in Chinese speculations on history, spoke enigmatically of three progressive ages: *ju-luan* (Entering Chaos), *sheng-p'ing* (Rising Peace), *t'ai-p'ing* (Great Peace); the other, a utopian vision of an ideal past age called *ta-t'ung* (Great Unity, in this case to be succeeded by a period of Lesser Tranquility, *shao-k'ang*), was described in an equally enigmatic passage in the *Li-yün* chapter of Li-chi (Book of Rites). Thus the visionary era of *ta-t'ung* was equated with the third stage of *t'ai-ping*, and all fixed into a progressive historical framework, introducing a new form of historiogenesis into the Chinese thought world. On the basis of this synthesis K'ang then proceeded to let his imagination run free and constructed a view of world civilization in which, for one thing, all national, family and sexual boundaries would be eliminated. Human society would consist of small discreet communities organized under a beneficent and non-meddling world government; property would be held communally; there would be sexual freedom (even including a place for homosexuals); children would be raised in public nurseries

---

16 On K'ang see Arthur Hummel, ed., *Eminent Chinese of the Ch'ing Period*, 2 vols., Washington, 1943; L. G. Thompson, *The One World Philosophy of K'ang Yu-wei*, London, 1958.

and schools, and the need for the family would simply disappear.

Despite the elimination of social distinctions and the reckless treatment of the family, this vision remains transitional, animated by a Confucian ordering norm. His thinking works out something like this: human destiny is to live a universal, harmonious and egalitarian existence, but because of boundaries set up amongst and betwixt groupings (family, clan, tribe, nation) selfish aspirations are reinforced and we live amidst suffering. The biological family, with its notion of parental nurture and filial obligation, is the most notorious erector of boundaries. Eliminate the family, and with it traditional notions of parental nurture, and the decks will be clear for substituting public nurture (that is, replace one set of reciprocity relations for another). Realizing that Heaven nourishes us all, obligation will be towards Heaven alone, and all boundaries of separation will be eliminated and the desires of all will find full gratification.

The notion of reciprocity remains in a universalized form, while the particularized and partial notion of reciprocity latent in the idea of filiality is discarded. Combining the ancient ideal of *ta-t'ung* together with the vision of the three stages of progress made it possible to relativize the institution of the family (relegating it to the first two stages), turn Confucius into a prophet, and universalize something of the Confucian ethic.

On the Breaking of the Egg

We have already set forth the shape of the Maoist cosmogonic myth. His understanding of the relative quality of unity and the absolute quality of contradiction give to his thinking a particularly dynamic and forceful movement. Not only metaphysical reality but "social development" itself "is chiefly due... to the development of the internal contradictions in society... [which] propels society and starts the process of the supersession of the old society by a new one." [17] This principle applies to his theory of revolution, as we shall see, as well as to his theories of knowledge and social praxis.

While Mao accepts a very stereotyped and seemingly determinist Marxist view of history, he nevertheless gives primary attention to the dynamic notion of "actively changing the world by applying the knowledge of objective laws," [18] vis., utilizing contradictions to bring about

---

[17] Mao Tse-tung, "On Contradiction," *op. cit.*, I, 314.
[18] Mao Tse-tung, "On Practice," *ibid.*, 304.

violent revolution. But change and revolution, violent or otherwise, is not a once-for-all event. It becomes a permanent element of the human experience, for contradiction is eternal. Thus Mao's eschatology incorporates the ideas of (a) the eternity of struggle and (b) the possibility of retrogression.

First, the eternity of struggle. In an editorial of the Peoples Daily (*Jen-min jih-pao*) of April 5, 1956, he is noted as saying, "Some naive ideas seem to suggest that contradictions no longer exist in a socialist society." Not only is that notion rejected but the opposite rigorously affirmed, that "society at all times develops through contradictions." This includes even communist society, the utopia. "It is obviously incorrect to maintain, as some people do," he says, "that the contradiction between idealism and materialism can be eliminated in a socialist or communist society." Instead contradictions will persist, new ones following old ones in endless succession. "Not everybody will be perfect," we learn, "even when a communist society is established." [19]

As to the possibility for retrogression, if it is the case that struggle is eternal, it opens up the possibility that the wrong pole in this contradiction might at some point gain the upper hand. Everything is certain, it seems (e.g., the inevitable direction of history), yet nothing is certain, at least for the Chinese revolution. "The proletariat seeks to transform the world according to its own world outlook, and so does the bourgeoisie." "In this respect, the question of which will win out, socialism or capitalism, is still not really settled." [20] This was stated in 1957. In 1963 an even stronger statement was made. "The guarantee that communists will be free... and will for ever remain invincible," depends upon the generative force of revolution continuing in class struggle (society), in the production struggle (nature), and in the struggle of scientific experiment (knowledge-action). Without these, "bad elements and ogres of all kinds" will "crawl out" and it is possible that "the whole of China would change its color." [21] Apparently this indeterminacy will forever remain, even as do struggle and revolution.

We earlier described the Maoist vision as a dynamic view in which history is a linear process urged onward by lively contradictions. But now we see struggle and contradiction as permanent realities while the

---

[19] See Schram, *op. cit.*, 303f.

[20] Mao Tse-tung, "On the Correct Handling of Contradictions," 409.

[21] Mao Tse-tung, "The Seven Well-written Documents on Chekiang Province Concerning Cadres' Participation in Physical Labor," *Quotations from Chairman Mao Tse-tung*, Peking, 1966, 41.

outcome remains elusive. Apparently this is one of several signs that
cyclical content is increasingly superimposed upon linear process or
form. Perhaps this does seriously compromise a progress view of history.
Nonetheless, whether linear or cylical, the processes of contradiction
stand in sharp relief against the background of the Confucian tradition
of reciprocating harmony.

THE ETHIC-RITUAL CONNECTION

Ritual may be defined as a regularized activity that acts out a myth
or inculcates the norms of a religious community. The religious community constitutes the social matrix within which ritual and myth find
meaning. A religious social grouping—in Wach's terms whether natural
or specific—is a grouping in which resides the authority (explicit or
implicit) for establishing final norms that govern the beliefs and
behavior of individuals, and which has a transcendent referent (explicit
or implicit). A political grouping also establishes norms, but these are
not necessarily final (no truth beyond itself) or bearing a transcendent
referent (actualizes a greater reality). To the degree that political group
norms do claim finality or transcendence, to that degree we consider
them religious. Often in society religious norms, whether defined by
church, ancestral grouping or monastic community, are distinct from
or in conflict with political norms. This has been sufficiently demonstrated by others in the case of China and need not claim our attention
here. In Marxist society finality is claimed (e.g., it claims final insight
into and interpretation of reality as it is) while transcendence (i.e., a
reference to a beyond which would dissolve the *nothing but* of this
worldly reality into a *something other* as well) is rejected. Ritual enables
these norms (whether or not final and transcendent) to enter into the
traditioning process.

Ethics may be defined as largely the practical handling of the problem
of evil. There would be no Confucian ethical system were there no
perceived ethical problem. Confucius lived in an age that was anything
but a paradigm of virtue, unless the political struggle for hegemony
with all the dislocations this assumes and engenders is considered virtuous. For Confucius it was a problem—therefore his ethics. The
problem of evil, however, was not asked or answered in soteriological
terms as in Christianity or Buddhism. The former made evil a theological problem, the latter an ontological; one tradition produced the
divine-savior figure, the other the primal-enlightener; the Confucian,

in contrast to both, translated the question of evil into ethical and behavioral terms.

It is striking that an essentially ethical system also proved to be as much, if not more, ritual oriented than the savior-enlightener systems. The whole of life itself, in fact, was often conceived as ritual. This may suggest that the usual myth-ritual association, so effectively elaborated by Eliade and others, is an overrated connection. One might, in fact, speak of at least three general functions of ritual. On the one hand it lives the myth. On the other hand, just as the religious community provides the matrix for ritual, so also ritual provides the matrix for the theorizing of the religious community, giving rise in its turn to a deepening of myth. Both of these functions can be assumed in our discussion below. At the same time, however, it may relate in a direct way to its partner in religious action, ethics. If in Christianity the ritual (e.g., baptism or sacrifice of the mass) enacts the myth, in the Confucian setting it is much better to say that rites enable the ethic. It is the ethics-ritual connection that is to the fore rather than the myth-ritual, and this ritual is conceived not primarily in soteriological but in axiological terms.

Confucian Evil

Chou Tun-yi, standing at the fountainhead of neo-Confucian thought and practice, may help us identify something of the issue of evil in Confucianism. Chou posits humanity as essentially good. Indeed, man is the epitome of the generative cosmic processes. Things (*wu*) are fixed, discreet, particular, without ability to interpenetrate. Humanity, besides being thus discreet and possessed of the principle (*li*) of the *t'ai-chi* and its dynamic forces (*ch'i*), is also spiritual (*shen*) and thereby penetrating and interacting with all things. Integrity (*ch'eng*) in this activity denotes the highest quality of goodness. Whence then evil?

Here Chou introduces the concept of *chi* (incipient action). Chou himself defines this as "movement as yet without form, in between being and non-being," and goes on further to say that "integrity (*ch'eng*) lies in the state of nonactivity; with the *chi* come (both) goodness and evil." [22] Somehow in the liminal passage from potential (*wu*) to actual (*yu*) the possibility for evil exists, though not as inherent in the thing itself, but only as an outcome of the individual's

---

[22] On Chou Tun-yi see Fung Yu-lan, *op. cit.*, ch. 11; on *chi* see Thomas Metzger, *Escape from Predicament*, New York, 1977, 86f., 110, 265, n. 243.

response to environmental stimuli (*kan-tung*). At this moment of incipient activity lurks the possibility of evil. The passage from potential to actual constitutes at least three stages in a continuum: the prior state of primal equilibrium, the transition state of arousal, the fully expressed activity itself ideally realized in harmony. If at the moment of environmental stimulation there is no space or temporal gap between being and action, but action is instantaneous, unreflective and direct, then the behavior will accord with the antecedent and interior good (the prior state of equilibrium), and action will be harmonious with public (*kung*) or universal values. If, however, even a split second of reconsideration or calculation (all of which open flood gates to desire) is permitted to intervene between stimulus and action, then particularized, selfish and partial (*ssu*) values ensue, and behavior is deflected from the norm. The question as to the metaphysical basis for evil within the individual that might account for the arising of a calculating and selfish mind in the first place is not asked. In Chu Hsi's more dualistic structure the answer is found in human desire, which by definition is something requiring restriction and regulation, though not evil in itself. In either case the causal role of environment is primary. This understanding of the rise of evil action, moreover, places a premium upon a prior and interior equilibrium as the basis for direct action and an external harmony as the proper outcome of such action. Self-cultivation realized in social activity bridges the two.

Self-Cultivation as Ritual Enablement

Perhaps two things need to be said about neo-Confucian self-cultivation as regards its form and its function. A major advance in the practice of Confucian self-cultivation is introduced in Sung neo-Confucianism, which incorporates certain Buddhist and Taoist concepts and techniques. One of the more important innovations is simply the amount of time spent in contemplation. Chu Hsi practiced and advocated devoting one-half of the day to quiet-sitting (*ching-tso*), with the other half devoted to the study of texts. [23]

Such quiet-sitting (*ching-tso*) was a key but not the only element in the neo-Confucian development of self-cultivation. It had obvious links to Buddhist *tso-ch'an* (*zazen*, sitting in meditation) which is a specific Chinese development of the Buddhist *dhyana* (Ch'an, Zen)

---

[23] The following discussion is based in part on Wm. Theodore de Bary, "Neo-Confucian Cultivation and the Seventeenth-Century 'Enlightenment,' " *The Unfolding of Neo-Confucianism*, New York, 1975.

tradition. Both practices had sitting (*tso*), breath control and many other practices in common. There was sufficient preoccupation with quiet sitting in neo-Confucianism that an extensive genre of literature providing guides to contemplative practice developed.

More important than mere similarities and differences in outward practice is the different function of quiet-sitting in each system of self-cultivation. In Ch'an the practice in itself was the very essence of the meditation and, most dramatically in the case of the *lin-chi* school, tied closely to a discreet experience of "awakening" (*satori, wu*). In the neo-Confucian setting the relation between experience and practice was much more diffuse, enlightenment being less an aim than a pre-supposed commitment to seriousness (or as otherwise stated, to learning —*wei-hsueh*); when a discreet unitive experience was involved it was less "ontological," "intellectual" or "intuitive" than moral. The sense of being one body with the universe never became a case of totally undifferentiated unity but retained the element of mastery, moral direction, or reverence. Liu Tsung-chou (1578-1645), for instance, compared the self in Ch'an meditation to a gourd floating in water, but in the Confucian experience to riding a boat with one hand on the tiller, an image derived from Wang. [24] The moral tone of the unitive experience is particularly evident by its frequent association with commiseration, which entails commitment to remedial action. The *locus classicus* for definition of this experience is of course Mencius. [25] The sense of freedom implied in it recalls Confucius' attainment in which absolute freedom and absolute moral rectitude are correlative. [26] Self-cultivation and the unitive experience also quickly translated into a socio-political force for, as Yen Yüan (1635-1704) maintained, the design of self-cultivation is "to change the world" (*chuan-shih*) and not alternatively be "changed by the world" (*shih-chuan*). Wang Fu-chih, in interpreting Chang Tsai's Western Inscription (*hsi-ming*) writes that "achievement is man's part in the transformation of the universe; he certainly does not just leave it to Heaven." [27] In this way self-cultivation leads to affirming universal (*kung*) values rather than particular (*ssu*) and partial ones; this endeavor, moreover, occurs within

---

[24] See Frederic Wakeman, *History and Will*, Berkeley, 1973, 253.
[25] *Mencius*, 2:44.
[26] *The Analects*, 2:4.
[27] See Ian McMorran, "Wang Fu-chih and the Neo-Confucian Tradition," *The Unfolding of Neo-Confucianism*, 453. On the importance of human agency see Metzger, *op. cit.*, ch. 3.

the sense of a deep underlying harmony, of a unitary reality which bids for a profound sense of human commiseration.

An Ethical Dilemma

But of course actual realization of the public good did not always issue that easily from the ritual of self-cultivation. This becomes especially clear as we turn to the social sphere. [28] Of particular interest for our concerns is the Confucian ethical dilemma evident throughout the history of the Confucian tradition. This dilemma lies at the heart of the ritual enactment of the Confucian ethic, especially in its social form. One might say that Fan Chung-yen represents one pole of this dilemma and K'ang Yu-wei the other. It is the dilemma of the concrete particular or private (*ssu*) and the universal or public (*kung*). How can one both maximize the importance of ancestor, family and clan through social ritual, yet at one and the same time maximize public virtue? Mo Ti's proposal of *chien-ai* (universal love), the legalist proposal for impartial law (*fa*), and the Taoist proposal for naturalism (*tzu-jan*) were early alternatives to the Confucian proposal for social ritual. These were all pre-Ch'in.

After centuries of relative weakening of the Confucian commitment, Fan, as an early neo-Confucian, revived the proposal for social ritual and gave an unprecedented significance to family and clan loyalty, [29] accepting of course the *Ta-hsüeh* (Great Learning) paradigm in which a natural order beginning with self-cultivation led through completion of the family and establishment of the state to the eventual ecumenic peace (*t'ien-hsia p'ing*). Anthropologists have abundantly documented that, at least in south China, the vision was illusory, and the strength of clan and strength of empire were in exactly inverse relation. K'ang, whose ecumenic vision never left the drawing boards, sought a completely public (*kung*) morality, and in doing so called for the abolition of every particularizing boundary including, or perhaps especially including, those of the family. Despite this ritual heresy his ethical commitment was still thoroughly Confucian as we have shown. This aberration aside, the weight of the Confucian tradition was with the family, and when the moral seriousness of self-cultivation ritual met

---

[28] On the neo-Confucian sense of dilemma because of the lack of fit between metaphysical (ideal) and experiential (real) realms see Metzger, *op. cit.*, ch. 3.

[29] On Fan Chung-yen see Hummel, *op. cit.*; James Lin, "An Early Sung Reformer: Fan Chung-yen," *Chinese Thought and Institutions*, 105-31; Denis Twitchett, "The Fan Clan's Charitable Estate, 1050-1760," *Confucianism in Action*, ed. David Nivison, Stanford, 1959, 97-133.

with the inherently limiting communal commitments of ancestral ritual the tension between universal (*kung*) and particular (*ssu*) commitments could not help but be present. This dilemma ultimately broke the Confucian tradition as a viable socio-political force, for commitment to the partial blocked the doorway leading to the ecumenic age. This door was to be flung open, or so it seemed, by a new force, Communism, whose very name *Kung-ch'an tang* celebrates the virtue of the public or common (*kung*). Where Confucius faltered, Mao stepped the more surely.

The Maoist Ethic-Political Connection

It is in the ritual sphere that the Maoist commitment to contradiction finds its most disruptive (and constructive?) expression. We have spoken of the ethic-ritual connection. With Mao we must change somewhat the terms of our discourse, for the ethical commitment has to be differently understood. With Chou Tun-yi, for instance, we found the self as the highest expression of the Absolute in the realm of phenomena, and in his being man shared the dual modality of quiescence and movement. Unity had a logical priority over duality, and quiescence over activity. Abiding in reverence, quiescence or unity was the basis from which universally valid ethical (*kung*) activity would issue. Presupposed in all of this was a stable, universal human nature.

With Mao the self is the highest expression of the Absolute law of contradiction. Human freedom is presumably the destined goal as humanity moves away from the realm of necessity (to use a Marxist formulation). Contradiction reaches its most refined and highest expression in the human mind and in human society. Public virtue (*kung*) as a value to be implemented is not predicated upon the positing of a universal human nature, that is upon what *is*, but upon the utopian view of what *ought* to be and what contradiction means to bring about. In the shift from a Confucian to a Maoist world we experience a shift, we might say, from an ethic of responsibility founded upon the understanding of reality as it is given, and accepting into itself all the ambiguities that this involves, to an ethic of ultimate ends founded upon an idea of what ought to be, and rejecting as evil any item that does not lead to that end. Though the latter can lead to a quietist option, in the Maoist case it is unambiguously revolutionary.

As a consequence, the ethical commitment does not have quite the same status in Mao as in Confucius. For Confucius the ethical commitment in one's everyday activity was primal, underivative, complete.

Politics was to be ethicized, that is, the *means* were to be transformed for they constituted living. For Mao the commitment to the end is primal. Moreover, this end must be gained. In fact, because human society and human nature are changeable and malleable, they should be changed. Therefore ethics is to be politicized, that is, the *end* is to be realized by means of, not merely in, the present. Facilitating attainment of the final goal—public good (*kung*) or service to the people (*wei jen-min fu-wu*)—becomes the monovalent yardstick for judging all activity. Since, moreover, the universal public good is a political entity itself, ethics must become a function of politics. With this the political commitment becomes a primal datum, and human experience and reality are reordered in its terms. It is now the political-ritual connection that is foremost. To be sure ethics is invoked in politics, but politics determines what ethic to invoke, and the ritual is in service of that political invocation.

Maoist Evil

The politicizing of ethics redefines the problem of evil and its solution. Furthermore, because of the unrelieved Maoist emphasis upon human reality as social reality, evil must also be conceived primarily in socially significant categories. As good a place as any, therefore, to commence a discussion of Maoist evil is Mao's classic formulation of the "four thick ropes":

> A man in China is usually subjected to the domination of three systems of authority: (1) the state system (political authority), ranging from the national, provincial and county government down to that of the township; (2) the clan system (clan authority), ranging from the central ancestral temple and its branch temples down to the head of the household; and (3) the supernatural system (religious authority), ranging from the King of Hell down to the town and village gods belonging to the nether world, and from the Emperor of Heaven down to all the various gods and spirits belonging to the celestial world. As for women, in addition to being dominated by these three systems of authority, they are also dominated by the man (the authority of the husband). These four authorities—political, clan, religious and masculine—are the embodiment of the whole feudal-patriarchal system and ideology, and are the four thick ropes binding the Chinese people, particularly the peasants. [30]

---

[30] Mao Tse-tung, "Report on an Investigation of the Peasant Movement in Hunan," *op. cit.*, 44.

These four authorities delineate one of the networks of evil that constitute the human problem. Specifically, they designate the feudal-patriarchal system. A second network comes under the designation of capitalism-imperialism, which in the case of China was an evil that largely impinged from without. A third network of evil, belonging properly to the post-revolutionary period, comes under the designation of "revisionism." These three instances define the contemporary problem of evil for which the Chinese revolution—political and cultural—is the preferred solution.

The concept of evil implied in the Maoist construction is obviously quite different from that of the neo-Confucian. Although the origins of evil are not given a direct ontological status in either Maoist or Confucian terms, in Mao's thought evil is much more radically analyzed. Perhaps more correctly, evil in Mao is a radical temporal category: that which lags behind the onward process displays itself as evil. This presupposes Mao's commitment to a Marxist teleology or philosophy of history. This process does have ontological status (dialectical materialism) and, that which lags behind the process and threatens to reverse it is so to speak, "anti-matter" and thus evil, and consequently is to be relegated to the dustbin of history. The technical Maoist term for absolute evil is the lesser pole in an "antagonistic contradiction." Thus, evil emerges amidst the class struggle within the historical process; persons, ideas and groups allied with the passing phase become evil, those allied with advancement good. In time, however, these also may become evil. Slave society, for example, was in advance over primitive communism, but Confucius as representative of the dying phases of slave society was retrogressive; similarly, although Ch'in Shih-huang, representing the emerging forces of feudal society, was at one time good, any feudal identity in the present is evil. Thus evil becomes a function of time, and good becomes those political forces that "seize the day, seize the hour" and urge forward the motive powers of history. This yields a radical qualitative distinction between good and evil as a matter of "before and after," with the evil person sometimes, but not always, salvageable in Mao, whereas in neo-Confucian thought the evil person was distinguished quantitatively from the good person as a matter of "more or less," and in theory always remediable. Relative distinctions resisted becoming absolute.

It would be simplistic to assume that this exhausts the subtleties in a Maoist doctrine of evil, but it is sufficient to indicate one fundamental direction of his thinking. Nevertheless, one could also develop a definition of evil in Mao that does not require this processual, historico-genetic construction. We earlier suggested that the Maoist ethic was an ethic of ultimate ends. Here goal, not process, provides the context for defining evil. The Maoist commitment is to a totally egalitarian society as the chief end of humanity. Indeed, it is not at all unlike K'ang Yu-wei's vision of ends. In his *On Peoples Democratic Dictatorship*, Mao describes the communist world order in K'ang's terms—*ta-t'ung ching-yü* (realm of great harmony)—and comments upon it. Anything that obstructs this realization is *ipso facto* evil. Since *kung* (community) is the chief good, the principal evil is *ssu* (partiality, selfishness)—a definition that walks in rhythm with neo-Confucian sensibilities, though more dogmatic and extreme in its formulation. Thus, in Mao evil can be defined either in terms of process (evil is backwardness), or goal (evil is contra-public community). Actually, both are necessary, and it is in the integral relations of these two definitions—the latter visionary, the former revolutionary—welded together by his doctrine of contradiction that Mao's social ritual is to be understood.

Commenting on K'ang's vision Mao writes: "K'ang Yu-wei wrote the book 'Universal Harmony' but he did not and could not, find the path to it... The only path to universal harmony lies through the people's republic led by the working class." [31] Here the two are wedded—goal and process. Defining evil in terms of ends (moral contradictions) discloses its real character and content as selfishness; defining evil in terms of process (social contradictions) discloses the obstacles to its elimination. To remove the obstacles one acts politically, and to inculcate the new norms one also acts politically. Ethics "dissolves" in the political "solution," and ethics (as knowledge of the good) becomes coterminous with political actions. If, as we said earlier, ethics is the practical handling of the problem of evil, politics can then be said to be a particular kind of ethical action that handles particular evils. But with Mao a visionary ethic of ultimate ends translates into a revolutionary politics of historical process. This process is the social ritual, whether it operates on the level of super-structure (re-education) or infrastructure (social grouping), and ideally the two, knowledge and action, blend into one.

The Political Way

To complete a violent revolution (whether military conquest or

---

[31] Mao Tse-tung, "On the People's Democratic Dictatorship," *ibid.*, IV, 414.

expropriation of landlords) by a peaceful revolution the elites must change the motivations and behavior of individuals. Presumably that should be relatively easy if the masses are "poor and blank;" in fact it is exceedingly difficult. As early as 1943 Mao in his important statement "Concerning Methods of Leadership" said:

> When there are masses, there are in all probability three groups; those who are comparatively active, those who are average, and those who are backward. In comparing the three groups, the two extremes are in all probability small, while the middle group is large. As a result, leaders must be skillful at consolidating the minority activists to act as a leading nucleus, and must rely on this nucleus to elevate the middle group and capture the backward elements. [32]

Clearly Mao is aware of the difficulty involved. But with the will a way must be provided. And since, as Mao apparently realized, the primary group(s) to which one belongs largely shapes and guides the values one professes, in order to get at attitude change within the individual it is incumbent that the primary group associations that shape individual behavior be altered so as to support the policies, practices and values of the revolution.

If change was to come about, then, it had to include change at the primary group level, not merely at the level of state and party. A principal means for achieving this was the *hsiao-tsu* (small group). As Whyte states it: "The Chinese Communist strategy involves encapsulating people in groups and then insuring that these groups do not compete for individual loyalties by mobilizing them as entire units." [33] In contrast to most pre-existing primary groups that characterized the "familism" (to use Kitagawa's term) of traditional China, it was synthetic (inspired by outside political leadership), not natural, and utilitarian (oriented toward attitude change in support of state policies and measures) rather than self-fulfilling. This no doubt, together with the formidable obstacle to change presented by the pre-existing social substructure, accounts for the only limited success of this continuing effort.

The *hsiao-tsu* was instituted at virtually every level of society, being a cell or building block for larger socio-political groupings. It was used amongst party members, cadres, students, workers, peasants, candidates for thought reform. Whyte demonstrates its direct antecedent in the Russian revolution, while Wakeman demonstrates its indirect (at least)

---

[32] Martin Whyte, *Small Groups and Political Rituals in China*, Berkeley, 1974, 11.
[33] *Ibid.*

antecedent in the neo-Confucian instinction of the *hsiang-yüeh*. [34] No doubt other patterns in Chinese society provided further conscious or unconscious models. The peculiar conditions of mid-20th century also influenced its development.

A comparison of a traditional model (*hsiang-yüeh*) and the Communist *hsiao-tsu* strategy for changing social attitudes and behavior can illustrate the contrasting ritual aspects of the two processes—one primarily ethical, the other political. In 1518 Wang Yang-ming devised a strategy to rehabilitate rebels into civil society in southern Kiangsi. Actually, the concept of *hsiang-yüeh* (Community Compact), as it was called, goes back to the neo-Confucian Lü Ta-lin (1044-1090) and his brothers of the Sung.

In Wang's hands the *hsiang-yüeh* became a striking instrument for moral and social rectification. The text of the compact begins with a typical neo-Confucian appeal to degenerate "customs" and "accumulated behavior" as the source of evil. That some individuals should become anti-social was not mere happenstance or individual guilt but a shared responsibility of the community. It followed that in moral reform the whole community was therefore also to be involved. The specific strategy was to form the villagers into a Community Compact to ensure that the *li* (rites or codes of behavior) would be upheld and mutual assistance would be available in all areas of need. A compact chief, with assistant chiefs and associates, was to be selected. Records were to be kept of compact members and their daily activities, including one record book displaying good and evil deeds of the members for praise or blame. Once a month on the 15th, usually in a temple grounds, meetings were held.

The meeting itself commenced by three ceremonial beats on the drum. First the compact was publicly renewed, then good and evil deeds were displayed, a community meal held, and, after a concluding three-fold ceremonial beat of the drum, a final warning and dispersal. During the renewal of vows all members, prostrating northwards before the censors, pronounced together: "From now on, all of us compact members will reverently obey warnings and instructions. We will unite as one mind and join together in virtue, and will arrive at goodness together. If anyone should have any double-mindedness, outwardly doing good but secretly doing evil, let the gods and spirits destroy him."

---

[34] Wakeman, *op. cit.*, 8-12. For a translation of the compact see Wing-tsit Chan, *Instructions for Practical Living and Other Neo-Confucian Writings*, New York, 1963, 298ff.

In the course of displaying evil deeds the sense of community responsibility, mutuality and reciprocal obligation received dramatic demonstration. After announcement of these deeds, which were amplified by the assembly members, the guilty party was caused to kneel before the assembly and plead guilty, promising reform. A mutual drinking of the wine of "expiation" followed. The compact leaders drank saying: "We have not been able to advise and instruct you in time so that you have fallen into this trouble. How can we be free from guilt?" In turn the guilty one drank to his punishment, and with that, all having borne the guilt, this part of the ceremony was ended. After the meal, as the final act of the drama, all members lined up on the east and the west, and bowing, withdrew. The whole ceremony, through numerous actions, the lay-out itself, and the wording reinforced the sense of mutuality and reciprocal obligation.

As for the *hsiao-tsu* the ideal model for its implementation was demonstrated by the land reform campaign of the early fifties. At least three, and sometimes four stages, constituted this process. First a land reform work team, which was itself a *hsiao-tsu* of trained personnel, was sent into a village. This was Mao's "leading nucleus." It intruded upon the network of preexisting social groupings by immediately establishing contact with the poorest and most disgruntled of the local populace. These persons were guided to connect their specific grievances with the given ideology of class struggle. A highly ritualized "confessional" service, the *su-k'u wa-ken* ("speak bitterness and dig up the roots") session was introduced to implement this connection. [35] These persons were then encouraged to contact friends (i.e., utilize already existing natural or primary relations) and thus establish a village network of support. The conclusion of this phase was the formation of a new organization devoted to village social reform. The third stage forcused on action. The emerging group of new village "elite" (now in conflict with prior village elites) summoned the villagers to meetings of which the highly structured and ritualized struggle meetings served as the climax. The desired practical issue of all this, aside from physical elimination of the landlord, was land redistribution. A fourth stage of follow-up involving reexamination and consolidation would sometimes occur later. This model was repeatedly utilized in the successive campaigns that swept China.

---

[35] See Lowell Dittmer, *Lin Shao-ch'i and the Chinese Cultural Revolution*, Berkeley, 1974, 301.

To illustrate the workings of the *hsiao-tsu* one case, typical of many, can be cited. In his book *Fanshen* (literally, "turning the body over"), William Hinton [36] follows in great detail the process from the early Anti-Traitor Campaign, through Land Reform, to the establishment of Peasant Associations in a small village of northern China in pre-revolution days (1945-1948). The sequence of campaign upon campaign which he witnessed during his six-months' stay (March-August 1948) as a participant observer is almost unbelievable and abundantly demonstrates the primarily political rather than moral character of the process. After the revolution (1949) the successive wave of campaigns was to continue unabated, including collectivization, communization, rural socialist education, cultural revolution, the anti-Confucius anti-Lin Piao campaign, and finally anti-bourgeois-right campaign, bringing us up to the death of Mao.

The case under comment is a self-examination and mutual criticism meeting on the village level. In the village of Chang-chuang, Hopei (Hinton calls it Long Bow) struggle against the landlords with the consequent expropriation and re-distribution to the poorer elements (a process termed *fan-shen*), had recently been completed. Re-distribution had involved the traditional format of work teams going in to organize the peasants. In the distribution there had developed strong sentiments that Party members of the local branch had aggrandized themselves and in a variety of ways had abused the local populace. In part to clear the air, a campaign for the purification of the local Party branch took place in a fascinating open and public process—a special case of the process of mediated and regulated conflict traditional with the Party.

The criticism sessions themselves were prepared for weeks in advance. The Party members subjected themselves to long hours recollecting misdeeds and preparing confessions. As for the delegates, they were coached in ideology and in forthright participation so that they could draw out the Party members and make the encounter a serious one.

The criticism sessions lasted eight successive days. Presumably, after confession and criticism the members would be punished according to peasant wishes and restored to their active Party role. As such the process was redemptive in purpose. The work team participated in the proceedings as upholder of the norms. The presence of interested

---

[36] William Hinton, *Fanshen*, New York, 1966.

peasants as observers indicated the educative (as distinct from re-educative) purpose of the process.

The participants filed into the room—in this case an abandoned Catholic church—after which followed the ceremony of the three-fold bow (*chü-kung*) before a portrait of Mao. The local branch Party members then broke out in a seemingly unrehearsed (certainly discordant) rendition of the Internationale. When the last cacophonic strains died out the work team leader briefly reviewed the purpose of the meeting. The local branch secretary was called upon for a few remarks. A spokesman for the peasant delegates next rose to express the wish that the Party members be frank and honest in their self-examination. The work team leader, acting as moderator, then called for the first self-criticism. The twenty-six members one after another criticized themselves before the thirty-three delegates. The comrades all used a similar format: a review of personal history, a recital of wrongs, an expression of regret and occasionally a suggestion of possible means of restitution. Sometimes the confessor would be interrupted if the audience felt he or she was not sufficiently forthright. After the self-examination the audience—primarily delegates, but the others as well—cross-examined the would-be penitent so as to extract as fully as possible details about motives, circumstances and degree of penitence. The range of wrongs exposed in this eight-day hearing was considerable, including everything from laziness to rape. But worst of all was forgetting of class. Twenty-two party members, appropriately repentant, passed the peasant muster.

This incident has much in common with the *hsiang-yüeh* procedure developed by Wang Yang-ming. This is not to deny, of course, that the "criticism" element is a direct descendent of intra-Party techniques of rectification developed in the Soviet Union. The differences include the three-cornered structure of this form of criticism in which a third and outside party—the work team—monitored the process, whereas in the *hsiang-yüeh* the norm defining authority was the leadership within the village. The revolutionary vs. maintenance functions of the two operations with respect to local authority is obvious. The Communist version, furthermore, involved far greater intensity, particularly in the ruthless searching out of faults. In the *hsiang-yüeh* setting, faults were not to be overplayed to the excessive loss of esteem (face) by the guilty party. The abstract stress upon class consciousness as the prime norm, rather than upon conventional behavior, likewise differentiates. Nonetheless, in both cases the character of the process as a redemptive and redintegrative *rite de passage* (i.e., van Gennep's preliminal rite of separation, liminal rite of transition [confessional and accusation], postliminal rite of incorporation) is obvious.

We have been looking at this ritual process as one of bringing about attitudinal change. Through isolation from the group and criticism the guilty were prepared for a return to wholeness. The example we have considered is a paradigm of small scale social transformation sought through *hsiao-tsu* activity. But the Chinese revolution is virtually unique in its attempt to apply the paradigm to society on a mass scale. The paramount instance and the climax of a Maoist development of the *hsiao-tsu* model is, of course, the Great Proletarian Cultural Revolution (GPCR).

A few words will help to bring this major event into the framework of the analysis here set forth. In a detailed study of the GPCR and its principal demon, Liu Shao-ch'i, Dittmer [37] demonstrates that it was neither purely a political power struggle played out in the Machievellian mode by Mao (the "conspiracy" theory), nor purely a massive education enterprise by Mao the "experimenter" (the "spontaneity" theory), though of course it was both. Through a cumulative series of defeats and frustrations that exposed ideological commitments differing from those he himself held, Mao slowly felt his way to inciting popular criticism of Party leaders by the mass "democratizing" of the *hsiao-tsu* model. These Party leaders were not responsive to Mao through the normal channels of power nor did they share Mao's primal commitment to mass participation as a norm for effecting change. It is not without interest that an implied Confucian critique of Mao became the occasion for the outburst of the campaign. In any case, in this process the person and thought of Mao and his representatives played the functional equivalent of the "work team" (controlling the norm), displacing meanwhile the work teams actually deployed in the early stage by Liu.

This macro-social extension of the criticism meeting provides an ideal example of the politicization of ethics and political-ritual. In the run-of-the-mill criticism movements of the Communist revolution the primary function is rectification of the gap between ought (norm) and is (object of criticism) by criticism and is a redemptive and redintegrative process; the secondary function is mobilizational—a pedagogic and participatory process. In either case the goal is change. When Mao introduced the concept of the mass line in the GPCR the reverse

---

[37] Our discussion of the Cultural Revolution depends heavily on Dittmer, *op. cit*

priorities obtained—participation of the latent energy of the masses usurps all other values. Thus, as the mass line became increasingly emphasized in the GPCR—even to the point of extreme fragmentation—the participatory dimension became paramount, and the self-criticism that Liu was repeatedly forced to make served an increasingly condemnatory rather than redemptive function. The hiatus between norm and object was artificially polarized until it became an antagonistic contradiction, indefinitely sustaining thereby the is-ought contradiction and perpetuating its value for pedagogy. To save the nation (masses) it were better that one man perish (Liu). The GPCR maximized the value of popular participation and thereby achieved redemption on a higher level—not for the lone object criticized, but for the subject masses criticising.

An interesting analogue to this concerns Liu Shao-ch'i's perspective on cultivation. He had consciously attemped a synthesis of Communist and Confucian concepts, most notably in his best known work in his very large corpus, "On How to Be a Good Communist." For him cultivation was still primarily an ethical and individual endeavor. He laid great stress upon individual virtue as a good in itself (e.g., the "steeling" of one's will) and upon conforming the continuing means of revolution to these values. For Mao cultivation was pre-eminently a social and political process. End values continually intruded upon the process to make their sudden, if transitory, demands and bend contingent means to their sometimes unpredictable purposes. The characteristic difference between the revolutionary style of Liu and Mao can perhaps be thematized by contrasting catch-phrases: for Liu the primary task was "uniting two into one," which has clear reciprocity implications; for Mao it was "dividing one into two," which clearly spotlights contradiction. To this end the GPCR intensified contradiction, joining ritual in service of this political invocation. That the military was eventually called in to avert total chaos was merely the final indication that the process must remain sufficiently cohesive so as to be recognizably political.

Mirror Paradigms for Society

In commenting upon the meaning of the Mao phenomenon Joseph Kitagawa writes: "In a real sense, Maoism is more akin to a quasi-religious, if not a religious, movement, here using these terms in a Chinese sense of their meaning. What we are witnessing is the emergence of a Marxist-inspired, new form of 'immanental theocracy,' dedicated to the creation of a new culture, a new society, and a new man." [38] The key term is "immanental theocracy." This rightly describes the ontology (already discussed) imbedded in both the Maoist and neo-Confucian world-views. Both ontologies seek a social enfleshment. In both morality is eminently social. And in both systems a ritual, by traditioning a myth and an ethic, enabled the embodiment in individual and community.

There are both different types of community and different kinds of individual embodiment. To use Wach's typology for the former, we can discern three degrees of ecclesial organization. Such organization may be viewed on a continuum leading from hierarchically organized community to extreme egalitarian organization. The middle form has tendencies that move in both directions and is thus "transitional" in Wach's technical use of the term. Clearly the Confucian paradigm for community (save for the transitional case of K'ang Yu-wei) fits the former and the paradigm defined by the thought of Mao the latter. In Mao's case, however, it is readily, indeed forcefully, admitted in his political writing that the present actual form of community is a middle or transitional form—it is the Dictatorship of the Proletariat under the form of "democratic-centralism." Be that as it may, it appears interesting, to say the least, that the principle of reciprocity yields heirarchy, and the principle of contradiction egalitarianism. This is not without reason, however, for reciprocity heightens concrete obligation (e.g., to parent) and role definition (*cheng-ming*), whereas contradiction intensifies abstract obligation (e.g., to masses) and disrupts too readily routinized roles or balanced relationships. The neo-Confucian "clan" and the Maoist "commune," as well as neo-Confucian *hsiang-yüeh* and Maoist *hsiao-tsu* illustrate the differing mechanisms for actualizing social embodiment.

Individual embodiment occurs in at least two modes: in the highest and normative mode it occurs in the form of the sage (*sheng-jen*), and as lesser refractions of this norm it occurs amongst the people in the mode of the man of virtue (*chün-tzu*) or the hero (*feng-liu jen-wu*). Both traditions, the Confucian and the Maoist, yield considerable data for interpreting those embodiments.

Historically perceived, Confucius was a reformer and Mao a revolutionary, to use Wach's suggestive though not completely adequate categories again. Sociologically perceived, though Confucius shares in

---

[38] Joseph Kitagawa, "The Many Faces of China," unpub. mss., 1971, 15.

the reformer type, he is also in transition to the sage, prophet and founder types. Mao best embodies what might be designated the reformer-revolutionary type, with transition in the same directions. Psychologically speaking, the sage (cf. Wach's category of "seer") self-consciousness comes to dominate in both. Eventually both understand themselves as peculiarly representative of the inner meaning of history; for Confucius a deep inner sense of timely (*shih*) correspondence with divine will (*t'ien-ming*); for Mao an abiding sense of encapsulating the aspirations of the people at a particular stage in history. This defines the deepest content of their respective charismas. As for the lesser refractions that occur in daily life, the literature of both Confucian and Communist provenance unendingly displays models for emulation—from the popular illustrations of filial piety and virtue as told from parent to child, to figures enshrined in the numerous ethico-political cults of traditional China; [39] and from the tales of local work heroes to those selected heroes and model communities (Tachai) given a national press and accorded national idealization (if not idolization as in the old) in the PRC. But this is a study in itself, not possible to launch out upon here.

It should be abundantly clear by now that whatever the difference, the interrelationship of the Maoist world-view with the prior Confucian one is both certain and complex. We have hardly begun to isolate the processes and mechanisms of this historical transformation. Nonetheless it is clear that the social paradigms yielded by the two views are both very different, and so much alike. In fact, they almost appear as mirror images, the one of the other.

Indeed, one might at the great risk of over-simplification say that the image of the Chinese socio-political paradigm is stamped equally upon both, the one being the egalitarian obverse of the other (hierarchical). What we might term the Chinese socio-political paradim may be depicted as follows:

Heaven

Sage

State or Political

Realm

Son   _____   Father

Filiality, as the relation of the son towards the father, ties both time and space together. It goes on *in perpetual regression* (the father

---

[39] See C. K. Yang, *Religion in Chinese Society*, Berkeley, 1967.

maintains the ancestral cult in which situation he is son to the ancestors), as well as *in perpetual succession* (every son becomes a father who in turn has a son). This same unilateral character shows itself also *vertically* in terms of the social hierarchy. The son is filial to his father, who is subservient to the official, who is loyal to the emperor, who is designated Son of Heaven. This sonship is bestowed by heavenly mandate (*t'ien-ming*), which is known in no other way than by the sign of peace immanent within the social order ("immanental theocracy"). The summation of all specific virtues is generally designated humanness (*jen*). In this order, the Sage, who ought to be Emperor, most perfectly embodies this virtue. This paradigm may be depicted as in Diagram A.

In the modern historical transformation, what transpires is the collapse of the integrity of this traditional "immanental theocracy" with its social paradigm based on reciprocity and moral obligation. By transforming commitments through the ritual of revolution a new "immanental ontocracy" is established erecting an alternative paradigm built on contradiction. This paradigm may be depicted as in Diagram B.

Points A and A' are functionally equivalent as already demonstrated in our discussion of mythic congruence. Points B and B' are also equivalent. It is certainly not by chance that Mao has asserted that "the People has taken the place of the ancestors. The People, not the victorious Communist party." [40] Or again in Mao's famous recast tale of the "Foolish Old Man," "Our God is none other than the masses of the Chinese people." This last statement simply collapses the B'-A' line into a single point, just as in traditional society the Confucian tendency was to embrace both father and heaven within the ancestor-origin concept. C' corresponds to C. As the relation of the son towards the father in filial obedience is the basis of all virtuous action, so also the selfless (*wu-ssu*) subordination of the individual to the masses is the prime requisite for all action to be truly "for the people" (*wei jen-min*) and therefore valid. E and E' designate the authority that defines the norm in both systems. This norm is discerned by the representative figure, whether the primal sage (Confucius) or primal hero (Mao), as an empiric datum of social reality (family-ancestor nexus, people-class nexus) expressing the truth of prior reality (A and A'). The circumference of the triangles describes the norm in both its social and ontic modes.

---

[40] Andre Malroux, *Anti-Memoirs*, New York, 1970, 465f.

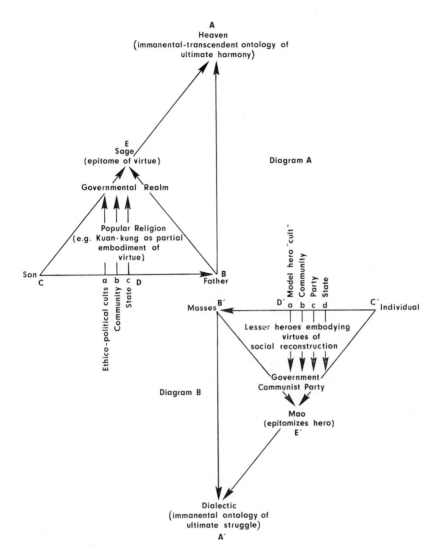

Finally, D-E and D'-E' enclose the communal embodiment of the two systems in its various models. The concept of "ethico-political cults" (Da), derived from Yang, is meant to include in its broader definition both the worship of heaven as an imperial service as well as the more specific ethico-political popular system of deities and venerated heroes. The ethico-political significance of the first is clear. The best Confucian rationale for the last is probably the judgment made in the Confucian Commentary to the *Book of Changes*: "The sages devised guidance by the way of the gods, and the (people in the) empire became obedient." [41] To the degree that the Confucian ethos could legitimate the vast welter of gods, goddesses, deified heroes and the like, to that degree this system (Da) became a socio-religious embodiment of the Confucian ethic. This was paralleled by the specifically Confucian mode of community, namely family-ancestor-lineage-clan (Db), as well as by the specifically political mode (Dc) which always existed in tension with the Confucian ethos even while legitimated by it. In the case of D′, to the institution of revolutionary hero adulation (D′a), commune-brigade-production team (D′b) and the political state itself (D′d), we add the Party (D′c) as a specifically Communist supplement to the communal modes. To be sure there were Confucian factions and schools that wielded considerable political clout in earlier times (esp. during Ming times), but none rationalized in a way comparable to the modern institution of Party (*tang*), and certainly not to the Communist Party. Rising above all forms of community, including empire and Party, looms the authority symbol of sage and hero—a position of lonely eminence. Just as Confucius bemoaned his isolated estate, so Mao described himself as a "lone monk walking the world with a leaky umbrella." [42] But in their loneliness the two sages persisted to define the norm for shaping human community, transforming human commitments in the process.

WHITHER TRADITION?

Tradition, transition and transformation. We have compared a traditional actuality with a transformed actuality, perhaps partly forgetting that what is called tradition was once a transformation, and that what is now called transformation strives to become tradition. Our discussion, dealing as it has with large-scale comparison, has made only passing reference to transitional stages (one thinks of the interregnum from 1911-1949) and forms (one thinks of K'ang Yu-wei, transitional to Mao; Liu Shao-ch'i, transitional to Confucius). A refined study would have to take transitions much more seriously.

Awaiting that refinement, we can nonetheless draw out from the foregoing study some broad implications for history of religions. Certainly our subject matter has something to say about the scope of the history of religions. We would not follow one such as Baird at this

---

[41] See Yang, *op. cit.*, 145.
[42] See Sumiya, *op. cit.*

point, for whom the scope of the history of religions is limited only by the scope of each scholar's definition. [43] We prefer to walk within the Wachian tradition which is concerned with viewing humanity in the light of its being *homo-religiosus*. [44] There is a limit to the usefulness of definitions of religion which set aside this intentional dimension. Rather than narrowing the scope, this gives it focus. Thus, even such an overtly secular phenomenon as the "Maoist transformation of China" harbors inherently religious intention (in the sense of finality, if not transcendence).

We earlier proposed a distinction between finality and transcendence in our discussion of religious community. In the neo-Confucian articulation it is much easier to discern a transcendent dimension, exemplified by the *t'ai-chi-t'u*. To be sure it is nevertheless eminently immanent. But there are more secularist tendencies as well, such as in K'ang Yu-wei, where the sense of that which is beyond or greater than the merely human-historical is greatly diminished. The Maoist proposal is secular by confession. Reality is a "nothing but"—matter in motion. It is without question that final norms are present—but they are defined politically, not religiously. Authority for defining the norm does not pass beyond the immanent process of revolution and the eminent thought of admissably contingent humans—Marx, Lenin and Mao. No transcendence is claimed. Is it implicit? Perhaps, but not necessarily so. In any case, demonstration of that point is not essential to establishing the significance of the comparisons here put forward. If Maoist thought and society is not religious (claiming both finality *and* transcendence), it nevertheless by assuming the stance of the final arbiter of truth functions as a religious equivalent without in fact being religious. To claim a *homo-religiosus* at the ontological level does not everywhere require a *homo-religiosus* at the epistemological level. What is more important for the history of religions is to perceive that the epistemologically "non-religious" might in certain instances indeed function in ways that can be best illuminated by beginning from epistemologically (and ontologically?) "religious" man—i.e., *homo religiosus*. Without this direction in analysis certain elements in Mao remain unilluminated.

Our study has hinted that it is a comparison of the respective traditioning processes, not a contrasting of tradition with transformation, that is the most fruitful engagement. Transformation is really a

---

[43] Robert Baird, *Category Formation and the History of Religions*, The Hague, 1971.
[44] Joachim Wach, *The Comparative Study of Religions*, New York, 1961.

fancy term to designate the onset of a new traditioning process. As such, to compare transformation (early Confucian or neo-Confucian) with transformation (Maoist) is merely to compare the first step in one traditioning process with the first step in another, and each traditioning process in turn builds selectively upon those that precede. The study of "the Maoist transformation" confirms, we believe, the value of this way of proceeding.

The question still remains as to whether anything really "new" has emerged in "the Maoist transformation." To be sure new mechanisms for implementing social order, new combinations of ideas and a new breadth in scale have taken place. But to what degree this is accompanied by a genuinely new insight into the human condition, as it is and as it ought to be, and as to how it may be so, is not so certain. Here history will have to aid in the religious and philosophical quest. How enduring the new symbols become, and what transpires in the new traditioning process, will have much to say here. Will the Maoist transformation endure as a revelatory moment in history to be compared with the moment of Buddha, Confucius, Jesus, Mohammed, or Marx? Perhaps, as history moves on, Mao will appear more like a transition than a transformation. Who knows? Let the new tradition tell.

IV

TRANSITIONS AND TRANSFORMATIONS
IN JAPANESE RELIGION

BUDDHISM AND THE NATIONAL COMMUNITY
IN EARLY JAPAN

MANABU WAIDA

University of Alberta

Historians of religion often claim that there exists a dialectical relationship between tradition and new conditions in all historical religions. As Joseph Kitagawa wrote:

> In every situation, the meaning of a new condition is to a greater or lesser degree colored and conditioned by the weight of the given tradition, whereas tradition is inevitably modified and reinterpreted by new conditions. In many cases, the adaptation of a tradition to new conditions is rationalized and authenticated by appeal to certain features of the tradition itself, and thus the new attitudes, new experiences, and new interpretations become incorporated into the body of the tradition. [1]

This is an important dictum that we should keep in mind when delineating the structure of the changes and transformations that Buddhism has undergone in its historic encounter with the Japanese national community in the course of the sixth through the tenth centuries A.D. To be sure, Buddhism has never lost its cosmopolitan or international dimension characteristic of the universal religion and yet, in its contact with Japanese experience, it has been considerably modified in accordance with the great emphasis the Japanese people placed upon the more immediate, particular and concrete world of human existence.

Japanese Religion and Buddhism: Preliminary Considerations

Japanese religion, as I observe it, seems to have kept intact certain themes, trends, and principles from prehistoric and protohistoric times down to the present. Despite the tremendous changes and transformations they have undergone, the basic religious experience of the Japanese people has remained substantially unchanged. It is important to remember that the foreign religions were accepted by the Japanese either because they carried some doctrinal and liturgical elements congenial to the people, or because they could be modified in accordance with

---

[1] J. M. Kitagawa, "The Buddhist Transformation in Japan," *HR* 4 (1965), 319.

a certain outlook on life and the universe peculiar to the Japanese. True, we have to take into consideration the fact that Buddhism, Taoism, Confucianism and Christianity were transplanted to Japan one after another in different periods of her history. However, for all the novelties that these religions have brought with them, I would presume that their contribution has been primarily to refine, enrich and amplify the "ground tones" of the Japanese religious outlook, or *Weltanschauung*, rather than to revolutionize it.

Japanese religion in this sense might be understood in terms of *cosmic religion*. I am inclined to hold that Japanese religion has remained essentially cosmic in nature and orientation regardless of changes and transformations throughout the centuries. Accordingly, the history of Japanese religion may be properly studied, in my view, as a dynamic process of reinterpretation and revalorization of the cosmic religion that is constituted by myths, symbols, rituals, and social order, all integrated into a unified whole by certain themes, trends, and principles.

In cosmic religion gods, men and objects of nature are conceived as members together of a single ordered and homogeneous cosmos. "The cosmic rhythms manifest order, harmony, permanence, fecundity. The cosmos as a whole is an organism at once *real, living*, and *sacred*." [2] Accordingly, not only are its many deities located within the common world of nature and society, but the universe or world itself is also perceived as something sacred, holding soteriological values within itself. Nature and society are recognized as distinct from each other and yet, at the same time, the world of nature and the social world are seen as closely interdependent entities, without substantial cleavage between them. As in the case of many peoples in the ancient world, the Japanese have long cherished a strong need for, and a special perception of, the creation and renovation of the cosmos through the seasonal rituals, especially the spring festival for praying for good crops and the harvest festival in the fall.

In view of its remarkable significance, the place of the phenomenal world of nature in the context of Japanese cosmic religion may be elaborated in more detail. In nature, in natural objects, and especially in the natural rhythm of the seasons the ontophanic or kratophanic quality of life is experienced. "Central to this cosmic religion is certainly

---

[2] M. Eliade, *The Sacred and the Profane*, New York, 1961, 117.

the notion of kami," [3] a term which is usually translated as gods or spirits, but which also means the numinous quality of nature. In such a religion man does not consider himself in any way separated from cosmic existence and the rhythm of nature; whenever he feels exhausted under the social pressures of urban life, he feels he can return to the rural mode of existence (*furusato, yamazato*), embraced and enlivened by the bosom of nature. In contrast to many cosmic religions which emerged with the rise of urban and cosmopolitan society during the third millennium B.C. and afterwards, which usually showed remarkable indifference to the world of nature as a locus of personal salvation and which tried to locate the soteriological goal in other-worldly reality, [4] Japanese religion has always tended to accept the phenomenal world of nature as authentic, real and sacred. [5]

While the world of nature is unquestionably essential in cosmic religions, the importance of the social world should not be overlooked. Significantly, in cosmic religion the rhythm of social life— from family life through the village community to the state—is coordinated with, and articulated by, the natural cycle of the year, for nature and society are seen to be interdependent and interrelated. It is widely known that, among peoples committed to cosmic religion, the king's celebration of the New Year's festival was considered essential not only for ensuring good harvest but also for the renewal and proper maintenance of the given social order. This is certainly true with Japanese religion, as recent studies have demonstrated. [6] The early Japanese seem to have been fully aware of the cosmos as "a community of living beings, all sharing the kami (sacred) nature." [7] This outlook on the world may perhaps be associated with the distinctive tendency among the Japanese to "emphasize a limited social nexus," [8] the supreme expression of which may be found in the

[3] J. M. Kitagawa, *Religion in Japanese History*, New York, 1966, 12; see Sōkichi Tsuda, "The Idea of *Kami* in Ancient Japanese Classics," *T'oung Pao* 52 (1965-66), 293-304.

[4] For a general perspective see J. M. Kitagawa, "Primitive, Classical, and Modern Religions," *The History of Religions: Essays in the Problem of Understanding*, Chicago, 1967, 19-65; Robert Bellah, "Religious Evolution," *Am. Soc. Review* 29 (1964), 358-74.

[5] Hajime Nakamura, *Ways of Thinking of Eastern Peoples*, Honolulu, 1964, 350ff. Cf. William R. LaFleur, "Saigyō and the Buddhist Value of Nature," *HR* 13 (1973-74), 93-126, 227-46.

[6] Robert Ellwood, *The Feast of Kingship*, Tokyo, 1973; Manabu Waida, "Sacred Kingship in Early Japan: A Historical Introduction," *HR* 15 (1976), 319-42; Manabu Waida, "Conceptions of State and Kingship in Early Japan," *ZRG* 28 (1976), 97-112.

[7] Kitagawa, *Religion in Japanese History*, 12.

[8] Nakamura, *op. cit.*, 407ff.

institution of sacred kingship or in what Kitagawa calls the principle
of "immanental theocracy." [9]

It is true that Japanese cosmic religion was destined to undergo a
process of remarkable change when Buddhism was introduced, but
Buddhism was also modified and accepted in accordance with these
two major features of Japanese cosmic religion: the *Weltanschauung*
characterized by the notion of kami and its cosmic orientation; and the
ethos of the national community characterized by the sacred kingship
ideology.

Contrary to oft-repeated opinions, I am inclined to a view that the
impact of Buddhism on Japanese history in its formative period has
been somewhat overemphasized. Certainly, by the sixth century A.D.
when Buddhism reached Japan, it had already undergone a long history
in India, Central Asia, China, and Korea; it had developed and
articulated its doctrines, scriptures, systems of meditation, monastic
orders, and liturgical systems. It is also true that the Japanese, culturally
somewhat backward as they were, became fascinated by the intricacies
of Buddhist art, architecture and rituals. However, all this should
not lead us to assume that Buddhism came into a religious and ideological vacuum. From the beginning of the fifth century on, the
imperial court, i.e., the central focus of the Japanese national community, had been tirelessly producing and elaborating the ideological
structure of sacred kingship, which was to be brought to completion
early in the eighth century. [10] The indigenous tradition was not
spiritually dead and waiting to be revitalized by a foreign religion;
rather, it was a powerful living force in an ongoing process of self-
realization. As far as I can observe, Buddhism failed, at least in its
initial encounter with the Japanese, in leaving its mark on the sacred
kingship ideology of the national community centered around the
imperial household.

My study is based, therefore, on the assumption that, in order to
properly assess the historical dynamics of Buddhism in ancient Japan,
one ought to take seriously the depth, strength, and vitality of the
indigenous tradition into which Buddhism, as a universal religion, was
introduced. Given this way of viewing the historical context of early
Japan, one cannot say that culturally-advanced Buddhism was poured
into "primitive" Japan like water flows from high to low places.

---

[9] J. M. Kitagawa, "The Japanese *Kokutai* (National Community): History and
Myth," *HR* 13 (1974), 219.

[10] See Waida, "Sacred Kingship," 319-42; and "State and Kingship," 104ff.

Rather, it is much nearer the truth to say that the Japanese people kept a firm hand on Buddhism, using the doctrines, liturgies, and monastic orders of the newcomer for their own soteriological purposes. In short, it seems that the national community of Japan contained Buddhism within its sacred kingship ideology. [11] I would presume that until the middle of the eighth century the religious life of the Japanese was still primarily cosmic and communal in orientation, revolving around the notion of kami and the principle of sacred kingship.

The Ritsuryō State and its Sacred Kingship Ideology

It is very important to keep in mind that during the sixth and seventh centuries East Asia was undergoing one of the most crucial changes in its political history. These kingdoms in Korea (Koguryŏ, Silla and Paekche) were rapidly growing as independent states, sometimes cooperating and sometimes vying with each other. After three centuries of political disintegration and cultural provincialism, China was reunited in 589 by the Sui dynasty and, with its collapse in 618, was regenerated as the T'ang, which was to usher in the golden age of Chinese history and civilization. The balance of power which had been maintained between China (T'ang), Korea and Japan was destroyed when the combined forces of Silla and T'ang defeated Paekche (allied with Japan) in 663 and Koguryŏ in 668. Thus, with T'ang in China and Silla in Korea, the contemporary political situation of East Asia pressed Japan to build up a centralized state strong enough to resist any possible attacks from abroad. The inevitable consequence was the formation, in the latter half of the seventh century, of a state armed with an administrative apparatus borrowed from the Chinese along with the indigenous sacred kingship ideology. This administrative apparatus was patterned on the T'ang legal codes called ritsuryō; hence, historians have come to designate this political structure as the ritsuryō state. However, the creation of the ritsuryō state was also accompanied by the completion of the sacred kingship ideology which had been developing since the beginning of the fifth century.

The creation of the bureaucratic hierarchy of the state was made possible by a grand synthesis of the court rank system based on Con-

---

11 Nakamura, op. cit., 528, says the Japanese "were inclined to utilize it [Buddhism] as a means and an instrument to realize a certain sociopolitical end. They were not converted to Buddhism. They converted Buddhism to their own tradition."

fucian-oriented principles and the system of titles (*kabane*) derived
from indigenous social ideals. The central government consisted of
two major parts: the *Jingi-kan*, which was concerned with the traditional Japanese cosmic religion or kami affairs; and the *Dajō-kan*,
which dealt with all "secular" aspects of government. In addition, there
were certain organs which, though strictly speaking did not form part
of the government, existed to supplement it and symbolize its continuity
with the emperor's personal household. These included the head-
quarters of bodyguards and palace guards.

The state was generally conceived as a liturgical community, in
which each of the noble families was given its proper and meaningful
place. This liturgical community was believed to have its exemplary
model in the mythical sacred history. Moreover, it was believed that
the state, as a liturgical community, could be renewed whenever the
Enthronement Festival was celebrated. The Enthronement Festival
was indeed the supremely important occasion when the ideal national
community on the level of the mythical history could be translated
into reality and re-presented on the plane of profane history. Among
the families taking part in the celebration of the festival were those
who had long served the ruler's personal household in the performance of their magico-religious, economic, and military functions.
When the structure of the *ritsuryō* state was completed in the eighth
century, the families charged with magico-religious functions were
integrated into the *Jingi-kan*, while those with economic functions
were mostly systematized into the Ministry of the Imperial Household
of the *Dajō-kan*. In addition, the military families and groupings, who
had served as imperial guards, were incorporated into a special system
of bodyguards and palace guards. In short, the state at the beginning
of the eighth century constituted a perfect cosmos as liturgical community.

The state had at its head the emperor who was recognized as sacred
and divine. It is remarkable that, after the war of succession in 672,
the emperor's status was so highly elevated that he come to be clearly
understood to be the kami incarnate. The emperor was now regarded as
akitsu.mi.kami, i.e., the kami who has manifested himself in the
phenomenal world as a human being. [12] Further, the sacred kingship

---

[12] The emperor was explicitly referred to as kami in the second half of the seventh
century; cf. *Manyōshū*, iii.235; xix.4260, 4261; *Nihonshoki*, ed. Taro Sakamoto et al.,
Nihon Koten Bungaku Taikei, Tokyo, 1965-67, II, 456; *Nihongi*, trans. W. G. Aston,
London, 1956, II, 359.

ideology of this period held that the emperor was a lineal descendant from Amaterasu, from Ninigi, and from Jimmu, the first mythical emperor. The kingship ideology, as it was established in the *Kojiki* (comp. 712) and the *Nihongi* (720), was unfolded in terms of the sacred history which involved the divine beings and their words and deeds in primordial mythical time. The following four themes make up the central scenario of the sacred history:

First comes the cosmogony of Japan's eight islands, resulting from the activity of Izanagi and Izanami. [13] I maintain that, from the point of view of sacred kingship, this is the most important of the various cosmogonic myths because it is precisely this which brings into being the sovereign's cosmos, the land of the great eight islands, as it was understood in the second half of the seventh century. Here is established the locus for the sacred history in which such divine beings as Amaterasu, Ninigi and Jimmu take actions to provide exemplary models for the emperor and his state.

Secondly, Amaterasu, the Sun Goddess, comes into being when Izanagi washes his left eye, and she is entrusted by him to rule the *Takama-no-hara* ("Plain of High Heaven"). It is in this heavenly domain that Amaterasu hides in the so-called rock cave, from which she is lured out by the mythical ancestors of the families charged with magico-religious functions. This sacred action in heaven certainly provides the exemplary model for the *chinkon-sai*, the ceremony of calling back the lost soul of the emperor, [14] performed by the priestly families during the Enthronement Festival on the day of the winter solstice (i.e., the day before the harvest festival). [15] I would hold that the meaning of the mythico-ritual complex of the *chinkon-sai* lies in the emperor's repetition or reenactment of the rebirth of the Sun Goddess Amaterasu at the critical time of the winter solstice. The sovereign is homologized with Amaterasu who, of the divine beings playing important parts in the sacred history, seems to be most closely associated with the magico-religious functions of kingship, though we cannot ignore her natural connection with economic functions.

Thirdly, Ninigi enters into the sacred history, representing the economic functions of kingship. He is genealogically connected with

---

[13] Franz Numazawa, *Die Weltanfänge in der japanischen Mythologie*, Paris, 1946, 201ff.

[14] N. Matsumoto, *Essai sur la mythologie japonaise*, Paris, 1928, 82ff.; M. C. Haguenauer, "La Danse rituelle dans la cérémonie du Chinkonsai," *J. Asiatique* 216 (1930), 299-350.

[15] Cf. *Nihonshoki*, II, 473; *Nihongi*, ed. Aston, II, 373.

Amaterasu through her son; cosmologically, he is born in the heavenly domain named *Takama-no-hara* and, at Amaterasu's command, descends vertically from this heavenly zone onto the summit of Mount Takachiho, located in the earthly domain called *Ashihara-no-nakatsu-kuni* ("Central Land of Reed Plains"). [16] He is entrusted with an important mission: to transform this desolate and infertile land into the *Mizuho-no-kuni*, the land blessed with rich rice-grains. This is probably his only *raison-d'être*, as his name Ninigi ("grain spirit") would suggest. Especially noteworthy are the following three themes connected with his descent: (1) When he descends, Ninigi is given by Amaterasu the rice grain harvested in her celestial rice fields; (2) he descends from heaven to earth in the form of a new-born baby covered by the *ma.toko.o.fusuma* (a piece of cloth which covers the bed); and (3) Ninigi, himself representing the economic functions, is accompanied by the mythical ancestors of the families in charge of magico-religious and military functions. In other words, the imperial court on earth has its exemplary model in this heavenly court charged with magico-religious, economic, and military functions. Significantly, Ninigi's descent from heaven is symbolically reenacted during the Enthronement Festival on the day of the harvest festival. Now homologized with Ninigi, the future emperor joins with Amaterasu in tasting the newly harvested rice grain and undergoes the initiatory sleeping on the *fusuma* (a piece of ceremonial cloth on the sacred bed). We are of the opinion that the meaning of the mythico-ritual complex of the heavenly descent lies in the emperor's repetition or reenactment of the birth of Ninigi on the day of the harvest festival, which really marks the beginning of the New Year in the agrarian cycle of ancient Japan.

Fourthly, the stage on which the sacred history is unfolded shifts from heaven to earth with the emergence of Jimmu, the great-grandson of Ninigi. His role in the context of the sacred history is military in nature, rather than priestly or economic. His concern is exclusively directed towards the subjugation of the forces of evil (i.e., the "earth spiders," "unruly kami," etc.) dominating the land, as well as towards the establishment of a new order centering around the imperial household. In the course of the "eastward migration," Jimmu searches for the center of the world, defeats the evil forces and, guided by a giant crow and a golden kite, enters Yamato. Here he establishes the

---

[16] On this theme, see M. Waida, "Symbolism of 'Descent' in Tibean Sacred Kingship and Some East Asian Parallels," *Numen* 20 (1973), 60-78.

imperial palace, which symbolizes at once the *center of the world* and the *cosmic axis*. I am inclined to the view that the *historicized* account of the Emperor Jimmu's actions is a mythic representation of some very important rites pertaining to the Enthronement Festival. [17] These included (1) the ceremonial searching for the center of the universe; (2) the nocturnal procession, on the day of the harvest festival, from one ritual building (the *Kairyū-den*) to another (the *Daijō-gū*); and (3) the *Kume-mai* dance. Especially noteworthy is the last-mentioned dance, accompanied by the *Kume-uta* song: it is essentially a ritual combat, reenacting the mythical battle between Jimmu and the evil forces. I would maintain that the meaning of the mythico-ritual complex of the *Kume-uta* song and *Kume-mai* dance lies in the emperor's repetition of the symbolic birth of Jimmu as ruler of Japan on the first day of the New Year; the sovereign is now homologized with Jimmu.

From what we have been observing, we are led to a conviction that sacred kingship in early Japan is manifested and proclaimed in the context of two different, though interwoven, conceptions of the world: the "genealogical" and the "cosmo-magical," to use Heine-Geldern's terms. [18] On the one hand, the sacrality and divinity of the emperor is deeply rooted in the belief that he is a genealogical descendant from Amaterasu, Ninigi, and Jimmu. The emperor is especially linked with these divine beings in the course of the Enthronement Festival; by repeating or reenacting what they did *in illo tempore*, the sovereign comes to assume the magico-religious, economic, and military functions of kingship represented by each of them. The notion of the Japanese emperor as *Tenshi* ("Son of Heaven") could be rightly located in the context of this genealogical conception of the world; basic to the sacred kingship ideology in ancient Japan is certainly the belief in the lineal descent of the emperor from Amaterasu, Ninigi and Jimmu.

On the other hand, the sacred and divine nature of the emperor is expressed also by the belief in the parallelism between macrocosmos and microcosmos. During the Enthronement Festival, the emperor is believed to obtain sacrality and divinity by repeating or reenacting what was done by Amaterasu, Ninigi and Jimmu on the two cosmic zones of heaven and earth in the beginning of mythical time. The mythico-ritual complexes of the calling back of the lost soul of Amaterasu,

---

[17] See also Kitagawa, "The Japanese *Kokutai*," 214ff.

[18] R. von Heine-Geldern, "Zwei alte Weltanschauungen und ihre kulturgeschichtliche Bedeutung," *Anzeiger der Österreichischen Akad. der Wissenschaften, Phil.-hist. Klasse* 94 (1957), 251-62.

the heavenly descent of Ninigi, and the ritual combat of Jimmu with the evil forces presuppose the perfect correspondence of the terrestrial imperial court with the celestial court. It is clear that during the Enthronement Festival the emperor is mystically identified with Amaterasu, Ninigi and Jimmu in turn; the sovereign is now the kami himself, i.e., god and man simultaneously. The conception of the emperor as *akitsu.mi.kami* is located in this cosmo-magical conception of the world. The emperor's repetition of what the divine beings did in the beginning is the sacred action which renews or renovates the imperial court on earth after the model of the heavenly court.

The sacred history now comes to an end, but Jimmu is skillfully linked with Ōjin, the fifteenth emperor, in such a way that the thirteen emperors in between are fabricated. [19] Thus the fiction of the genealogical continuity of the imperial line from Amaterasu and Ninigi to Jimmu and Ōjin came to be established. It is also very important to note that the Ōjin dynasty of the fifth century was connected genealogically with the sixth-century dynasty of different origin by an ambiguous assertion that the Emperor Keitai, founder of the sixth-century dynasty, was "a descendant in the fifth generation" of the Emperor Ōjin. The kingship ideology concerning the lineal descent of the imperial household from the Sun Goddess Amaterasu was thus firmly established at the beginning of the eighth century. [20]

There is no doubt that the several decades after the war of 672 were truly of great significance in the history of ancient Japan; this was the era when the highly centralized bureaucratic structure known as the *ritsuryō* state came to be created for the first time. From the perspective of the sacred kingship ideology, it was the most decisive period throughout Japan's history; not only was the state conceived as a liturgical community with its paradigm in heaven, but also the sovereign who ruled the state was explicitly called *akitsu.mi.kami*, whose divinity and sacredness was ultimately derived from the sacred history. The Enthronement Festival was of pivotal importance. The sense of belonging to this liturgical community was constantly enlivened and strengthened at the time of the spring festival (*toshigoi*) when the emperor granted the rice seeds to be sown in the paddy

---

[19] The number of fabricated emperors was determined in accordance with the Chinese notion of sacred numbers; and their long Japanese names were invented and elaborated between the mid-sixth century and the beginning of the eighth.

[20] Cf. M. Inouye, *Nihon kodai kokka no kenkyū*, Tokyo, 1965, 181-82, 189; and his *Shinwa kara rekishi e*, Tokyo, 1965, 268-72, 275-80.

fields of his estates according to the heavenly model presented in the myths. When the ceremony of granting the rice seeds was stopped in the latter half of the seventh century, the practice was simply replaced by another form, i.e., the distribution of the symbolic offerings (*nusa*). From the eighth century on, the symbolic offerings were distributed every spring by the emperor through the *Jingi-kan* to as many as 3,132 kami who resided at 2,861 different shrines throughout the country. This had to be done precisely because the offerings from the throne were symbolic of the *ritsuryō* state as a holy national community under the rule of the manifest kami. The sacred kingship ideology which sustained this sort of practice was of course not created overnight; its embryonic form was first produced in writing during the reigns of the Emperors Keitai (507-31) and Kimmei (540-72), then modified to some extent during the reign of the Empress Suiko (593-628), and finally brought to completion at the beginning of the eighth century in the *Kojiki* and the *Nihongi*. [21]

Buddhism within the Ritsuryō State

It is within this larger context of the national community with its conception of kami and sacred kingship ideology that we have to view the changes and transformations of Japanese Buddhism. Buddhism seems to have left no distinctive marks on Japanese mythology, nor did it constitute a central core of the sacred kingship ideology. As Max Weber aptly remarked, "the state functioned not as a patron (*Schutzpatronat*) but as the religious police (*Religionspolizei*) of Buddhism." [22]

Buddhism was introduced to Japan during the first half of the sixth century. The *Nihongi* has handed down the tradition that in 552 the king of Paekche presented an image of Buddha Sakyamuni and some copies of scriptures to the Japanese court; the event as such probably occurred not in 552, but in 538. [23] The date is, of course, significant only to the extent that it pinpoints the official introduction of Buddhism to the Japanese court; however, many naturalized Chinese and Koreans had undoubtedly been Buddhists prior to this date. [24] More important

---

[21] See Waida, "Sacred Kingship," 323ff.

[22] Quoted in Nakamura, *op. cit.*, 526.

[23] See *Nihongi*, trans. Aston, II, 65; cf. Inouye, *Shinwa kara*, 474-76, 503, and his *Nihon kodai no kokka to Bukkyō*, Tokyo, 1971, 9.

[24] M. Anesaki, *History of Japanese Religion*, London, 1930, 52; Inouye, *Shinwa*, 503-05.

questions for us concern the aspects of Buddhism that were adopted
and the way in which they were understood by the Japanese.

There is good indication that Buddhism was received initially in
terms of foreign kami, whose presence was interpreted sometimes as
beneficial, and sometimes harmful, depending on the circumstances.
When the Buddhist gifts from Paekche were officially presented, the
court circles were divided into two parties, the one favoring acceptance
by the court and the other opposing it. The anti-Buddhist party
argued successfully that the emperor in Japan had been serving the
kami in accordance with the seasonal cycle of the year and that,
should he worship the foreign kami, he would probably incur the
wrath of the native kami. [25] We may, of course, suspect that the new
teaching was not fully understood by those engaged in the debate, but
the episode indicates clearly that Buddha was recognized by the
Japanese only in terms of the kami of foreign countries, as distinct
from those of their own land. There is, moreover, concrete evidence
that Buddha was referred to by the two Chinese characters meaning
buddha and kami, [26] implying that the notion of Buddha was understood as a divine form of the kami. People in those days believed
sincerely in a *marebito* (a kami who visits them from far across the
sea at certain appointed times of the year), and as such Buddha was
also received. The early Japanese, at least up to the eighth century,
were not concerned with the different attributes and functions of the
Buddhas and Bodhisattvas introduced to them; what they were interested in was the blessing and practical benefits they could expect of
these foreign kami.

Another equally distinctive feature of Japanese Buddhism in its
initial stage is that it was accepted as a religion of certain clans (*uji*).
Buddhist temples were accordingly built and maintained as *uji-dera*
(temples of the clan) somewhat analogous to the particular liturgical
communities that had special rapport with certain kami. One of the
earliest temples ever built on this basis was the Hōkō-ji (later called
the Asuka-dera), erected by the Soga clan at the end of the sixth
century. The Soga was followed in this by many other more or less
influential noble families until the number of the temples built had
grown to over forty by the year 645 [27] when the way was opened to

[25] *Nihongi*, trans. Aston, II, 66-67; see also "Gangōji engi," *Jisha engi*, in *Nihon
Shisō Taikei*, XX, Tokyo, 1975, 8-9.

[26] *Ibid.*, 9-10; *Nihongi*, trans. Aston, II, 102.

[27] *Nihonshoki*, II, 563, n. 22:9.

the so-called Taika reforms. These temples were built primarily for the devotional cult, in the hope of increasing the merits of the deceased relatives. [28] It may also be noted that not only the building of the temples but the making of images and the copying and reading of scriptures as well were undertaken for similar reasons. [29]

As the clan-sponsored temples increased in number, they came to be put under control of the national community as a whole. The state control of Buddhism took three different but interrelated forms of expression: (1) the organization of the supervisory system for monks and nuns (*sōgōsei*); (2) the creation of the regulations for monks and nuns (*sōniryō*); and (3) the transformation of clan-sponsored temples to state-sponsored temples. Through these efforts, the state tried to protect and promote Buddhism insofar as the latter did its best to serve the well-being of the national community.

First, the supervisory system [30] was initiated by the Empress Suiko in 624 when she made appointments of the three ecclesiastical positions of *sōjō*, *sōzu*, and *hōzu* for the control of monks and nuns. [31] The first two of these positions were in charge of the discipline and punishment of the priesthood, while the last one was charged with financial matters. Although this system was abolished in 645, it was revived in 683 by the Emperor Temmu with the replacement of *hōzu* by *risshi*, or preceptors. [32] What is particularly noteworthy is the fact that when the structure of the *ritsuryō* state was completed early in the eighth century, the clerical officials were placed under the administrative supervision of the *Genbaryō*, an office dealing with "foreign guests," which was in turn in the hands of the Ministry of Civil Administration (*Jibushō*) of the *Dajō-kan*. [33] Thus, in the capital monks and nuns were subordinate to the *Genbaryō* through the three clerical officers, while in the rest of the country they were controlled jointly by a provincial governor and a specially-appointed provincial preceptor

---

[28] Kōyū Sonoda, "Kokka Bukkyō to shakai seikatsu," *Nihon rekishi* 4, Tokyo, 1976, 355-56; M. Inouye, *Nihon jōdokyō seiritsushi no kenkyū*, Tokyo, 1975 (new ed.), 27-40.

[29] *Ibid.*, 7-29.

[30] On the supervisory system in general, see Inouye, *Nihon kodai kokka*, 323-47; Kyoko Nakamura, trans., *Miraculous Stories from the Japanese Buddhist Tradition*, Cambridge, Mass., 1973, 18-20.

[31] *Nihongi*, trans. Aston, II, 152-54.

[32] *Ibid.*, II, 203 ;359.

[33] On the administrative structure of the *ritsuryō* state, see George Sansom, "Early Japanese Law and Administration," *Trans. Asiatic Society of Japan*, 2nd ser. 9 (1932), 67-109, and 11 (1934), 117-49.

(*kokushi*). The way in which Buddhism was administered by the
ritsuryō state is striking; it shows a sharp contrast to the way in which
the Japanese cosmic religion was treated, for the latter was under the
supervision of the *Jingi-kan*, which was at least theoretically on equal
status with the *Dajō-kan* itself.

Second, the regulations for monks and nuns, [34] which were a part of
the eighth-century *ritsuryō*, were similar in spirit to the supervisory
system mentioned above. The government made it a rule to issue
certificates to qualified monks and nuns to authorize their ordination
so that they could be distinguished from non-ordained or self-ordained
monks and nuns. Ordained persons were ordered to settle within the
temple enclosure except when they were allowed, by a special permit,
to go out for meditation in the mountains. They were allowed, also
with permission, to go out for begging, and this only in the morning.
Thus, the regulations strike us generally for the number of restrictive
measures they set on what monks and nuns could do in pursuit of the
path, as well as for the number of punishments prescribed for them.
In this respect, the regulations for monks and nuns were tremendously
different in form and substance from the *Jingiryō* (the regulations
for the worship of the kami), [35] in which no restrictive measures as
we find applied to monks and nuns were employed for priests serving
the kami; instead, what we find in the *Jingiryō* is mostly a list of the
prescribed observance of the seasonal festivals and the Enthronement
Festival which were considered essential to maintaining the well-being
of the national community.

Third, the government policy of transforming clan-sponsored temples to state-sponsored ones [36] was made public in 645, but it was not
until the reigns of the Emperor Temmu (672-86) and his wife,
Empress Jito (686-97), that the policy was translated into reality.
In the meantime, temples had increased in number; they numbered
forty-odd in 645, but they increased to 545 by the year 692. [37] These
temples came to be financially supported by the state itself. As Nakamura stated, "the government not only furnished emergency building

---

[34] *Ibid.*, 11 (1934), 127-34; J. M. Kitagawa, "Religions of Japan," *The Great Asian
Religions: An Anthology*, New York, 1969, 258-59; Nakamura, *Miraculous Stories*,
20-23; see also Inouye, *Nihon kodai no kokka to Bukkyō*, 44-51.

[35] Sansom, "Early Japanese Law," 11 (1934), 122-29.

[36] J. M. Kitagawa, *Religions of the East*, Philadelphia, 1968, 287-88.

[37] G. B. Sansom, *A History of Japan to 1334*, Stanford, 1958, 66; *Nihonshoki*, II,
563, n. 22:9.

funds, but did not hesitate even to provide vast sums for running expenses." [38]

Clearly, "the aim of the government in sponsoring Buddhism was not the salvation of the people but the protection of the state." [39] This is evident, for example, in the orders that the Emperor Temmu sent in 685 to all the provinces: "In every house a Buddhist shrine should be provided and an image of Buddha with Buddhist scriptures placed there. Worship was to be paid and offerings of food made at these shrines." [40] "Every house" in the edict cannot refer to every house of the common people, but probably means every official house in the provincial capital. [41] About ten years later, in 694, orders were issued from the Empress Jito to the effect that one hundred copies of the *Konkōmyōkyō* (*Sutra of the Golden Light*) should be sent and deposited in the various provinces, that they should be read annually at the beginning of the New Year, and that the fees to the monks were to be defrayed from the public revenues of the province. [42] The prestige and high reputation of the *Konkōmyōkyō*, as well as of the *Hokekyō* (*Lotus Sutra*) and the *Ninnōkyō* (*Benevolent King's Sutra*), had been well-established by this time. Called generally the "three scriptures protecting the state," they were enthusiastically received and recited at the beginning of the New Year and on some other occasions. Especially interesting is the fact that ten persons were ordained annually at the end of the year so that they might recite the *Konkō-myōkyō* at the beginning of the New Year in the imperial court. [43] As Hori noted, this practice was started in 696 [44] and from that time on the government continued to issue ordination certificates to ten persons every year until the early ninth century when the number was expanded from ten to twelve. The *Konkōmyōkyō* was recited primarily for ensuring good harvest and securing the well-being of the national community, so in many respects the recitation of the sutra during the New Year's days may be called a Buddhist version of the communal festival of *toshigoi* (praying for good harvest) essential for Japanese cosmic religion. [45]

---

[38] Nakamura, *Ways of Thinking*, 439.

[39] Kitagawa, *Religion in Japanese History*, 35.

[40] *Nihongi*, trans. Aston, II, 369.

[41] Charles Eliot, *Japanese Buddhism*, London, 1935, 208; see also Inouye, *Nihon kodai no kokka to Bukkyō*, 51-52.

[42] *Nihongi*, trans. Aston, II, 416.

[43] *Ibid.*, II, 421.

[44] Ichiro Hori, *Nihon jōdai Bukkyō bunkashi*, Tokyo, 1943, II, 200.

[45] Kōyū Sonoda, *op. cit.*, 370-71.

A series of these measures taken by Temmu and Jito to put Buddhism under the state's control was consummated in 741 when the Emperor Shōmu (724-49) proclaimed that in each province there was one state-sponsored official temple. The state-sponsored temple in each province, though generally known as *Kokubunji*, was called more formally by the name of *Konkōmyō-shitennō-gokokuji*, which means the temple for the protection of the nation by the four Deva kings. Shōmu seems to have cherished two basic objectives: (1) to ensure good harvest by the belief in the four Deva kings as preached in the *Konkōmyōkyō*, and (2) with support of the merits accumulated thus by the Buddhist piety, to pray to the kami of heaven and earth for the protection of the national community. [46] About ten years later, Tōdaiji was built in Nara as the national cathedral administering to all the state-sponsored temples in Japan.

In many respects, the construction of Tōdaiji with its colossal image of the Cosmic Buddha was the most memorable event in the early history of Japanese Buddhism. In the course of over two hundred years since its introduction from Korea, Buddhism made a number of significant contributions to raise the standard of Japanese culture not only in religious doctrines and liturgies, but also in fine arts, architecture, and aesthetics in general. After all, the Buddhism that reached Japan was not a simple religion but the "bearer of civilization" on the continent. It must be emphasized, however, that Buddhism up to the middle of the eighth century was generally accepted by the Japanese in the context of their cosmic religion characterized by the notion of kami and the sacred kingship ideology and that it was strongly expected to serve the interests of the national community, that is, the *ritsuryō* state.

The Decline of the Ritsuryō State and Its Consequences

At the beginning of the eighth century, the state constituted a perfect cosmos as liturgical community with the emperor (manifest kami) at its head. This liturgical community was sustained by the sacred kingship ideology which was, in turn, grounded in what the pantheon of the native kami did *in illo tempore* in the sacred history as described by the myths.

However, the *ritsuryō* state did not function as well as the architects of the system had intended. Visible signs of its fading vitality began to show by the middle of the eighth century, and from that time on

---

46 Inouye, *Nihon kodai no kokka to Bukkyō*, 54-55.

the *ritsuryō* regime disintegrated slowly but steadily until the middle of the tenth century when its recovery was deemed hopeless. The compilation of the *Engishiki* (*Procedures of the Engi Era*) in 927 was perhaps the last effort made by the central government to "restore and reinforce the ideal of the seventh-century *ritsuryō* state" [47] as a liturgical community.

There seem to be several reasons, external and internal, for the decline and fall of the *ritsuryō* regime. First is the change in the East Asian political situation; it became clear, as time went on, that Japan was under no military threat from overseas, a fear which had motivated the creation of the regime. Second, the imperial control of the government came virtually to an end in the mid-eighth century as the Fujiwara family rose to power. Third, the fiscal basis of the state was severely weakened as the landholdings of noble families, shrines, and temples developed into private estates or manors (*shōen*). [48] Thus, as the existence of the *ritsuryō* state itself became increasingly jeopardized, the entire system of the native kami associated with the state inevitably came to be called into question and forced to adjust itself to a new situation.

A change in the religious situation is symbolized partly by the fact that the Emperor Shōmu (r. 724-49), who built the national cathedral of Tōdaiji in Nara, claimed to be a "servant of the Three Treasures." [49] Although the kami nature of the emperor was never questioned outright, it must be admitted that his claim to be a servant of Buddhism marks "an astonishing departure from the previously held ideas of kingship in Japan." [50] It was during the reign of this emperor that there developed among the nobles in the capital a new idea, which aimed at rationalizing the rapprochement between Buddhism and the cult of the kami, the idea being that the kami of good nature revere and protect the teaching of the Buddha. This idea of the kami as the guardians of the Buddhist teaching was certainly behind an incident that occurred when the huge image of the Lochana Buddha was erected at the Tōdaiji. The kami Usa Hachiman of Kyushu (western Japan),

---

[47] J. M. Kitagawa's review of F. G. Bock, trans., *Engi-Shiki: Procedures of the Engi Era, Books I-V*, in *JAAR* 39 (1971), 573.

[48] Sansom, *A History of Japan to 1334*, 83-89; Kozo Yamamura, "The Decline of the Ritsuryō System: Hypotheses in Economic and Institutional Change," *Journal of Japanese Studies* 1 (1974), 3-39.

[49] *Shoku Nihongi*, ed. K. Kuroita, Tokyo, 1935, 197; G. B. Sansom, "The Imperial Edicts in the Shoku-Nihongi," *TASJ*, 2nd ser. 1 (1924), 26.

[50] R. Tsunoda et al., comps., *Sources of Japanese Tradition*, New York, 1958, 99.

so we are told, delivered an oracle promising that he would assist in the construction of the Cosmic Buddha and would urge the kami of heaven and earth to do the same. The oracle also declared that this kami desired to pay respect to the newly-founded cathedral, and accordingly, the divine cart of the kami was brought from the west to the capital, and finally a shrine was built for the kami beside the cathedral so that he might remain a guardian of the temple and its teaching. [51] Thus, a way was opened for the formation of a theory (*honji suijaku*) upholding the coexistence of Buddhism and Shinto, which was to characterize the ideological structure of the national community in medieval Japan.

However, an equally important idea regarding the relations of the two religious systems developed along a somewhat different line in the rest of the country, and it appeared under the leadership of *ubasoku*, or charismatic, "self-ordained" monks. This idea, too, was to promote the formation of the theory mentioned above, regarding the coexistence of Shinto and Buddhism. The basis of this idea was that the kami found himself in anguish and suffering simply because of his being a kami, and yearned, accordingly, for deliverance from the phenomenal world. In order to be released from the world, the kami usually asked a monk to read a certain Buddhist scripture, and the kami's request of this was communicated in the form of oracles. It may be noted that from the eighth century on it became fashionable to read Buddhist scriptures before the altar at which a kami was enshrined. [52] In 741, for example, the Emperor Shōmu sent copies of those scriptures which served the national interest to the kami Usa Hachiman mentioned above, and built a pagoda attached to the shrine. [53] About forty years later, in 783, the same kami was even awarded the title of *bosatsu* (bodhisattva), presumably on the grounds that he had been released from the phenomenal world. [54] The most exemplary of several instances testifying to the kami in search of salvation in the Buddhist sense is found in the *Nihon Ryōiki*, compiled by the monk Kyōkai early in the ninth century. [55] The earliest of a long series of Buddhist hagiographical literature in early and medieval

---

[51] *Shoku Nihongi*, 206.

[52] Enchō Tamura, *Asuka Bukkyōshi kenkyū*, Tokyo, 1969, 190-216.

[53] *Shoku Nihongi*, 165.

[54] Yoshiyasu Kawane, "Ōdo shisō to shinbutsu shūgō," *Nihon rekishi* 4, Tokyo, 1976, 277f.

[55] Nakamura, *Miraculous Stories*; W. R. LaFleur, "Kyōkai and the 'Easternization' of Japan: A Review Essay," *JAAR* 43 (1975), 266-74.

Japan, the *Nihon Ryōiki* is invaluable in presenting to us a vivid picture of the world of meaning for the eighth-century people as viewed by a Buddhist monk. The story in question concerns the great kami of Taga, Shiga Prefecture (central Japan). This kami, in the form of a monkey, asks a monk to recite the *Lotus Sutra* for him:

> The monk asked the monkey, "Who are you?" Whereupon the monkey replied, "I was the king of a state in the eastern part of India. In my state about one thousand men... became followers of monks, neglecting agricultural matters. Therefore, I suppressed them, saying, 'There should not be so many followers.' At that time I limited the number of followers, but not the acts carried out in pursuit of the path. Even if I did not suppress the practice of the teaching, however, to prevent men from following monks was a sin. This is why I was reborn as a monkey and the kami of this shrine. Please stay here and recite the *Hoke-kyō* so that I may be released from this life." [56]

This important story as well as many other stories in the *Nihon Ryōiki* were probably utilized for evangelical purposes by the *ubasoku*, or "self-ordained" Buddhist monks who worked among the common people, wandering from village to village. [57] Certainly, what these "self-ordained" monks were doing was against the spirit and substance of the government's regulations for monks and nuns (*sōniryō*), for the regulations prohibited them from setting up unauthorized training centers and preaching Buddha's message to congregations of the people. [58] In this sense, it may be said that a wide variety of their activities were carried out outside the *ritsuryō* regime and against its ideology. Particularly noteworthy is the fact that whether they were aware of it or not, "self-ordained" monks challenged the ideological structure of the *ritsuryō* state by refusing to grant the kami the supreme authority that had been acknowledged them, and by subordinating them to the status of sentient beings in need of release from this life through Buddhist teaching. We may recall that the *ritsuryō* state constituted a liturgical community with a comprehensive pantheon, which integrated not only the major kami of the imperial household and noble families in the capital city, but also the minor kami in the rest of the country.

The religious and ideological structure of the *ritsuryō* state was visibly undermined by the increasing emergence of the Buddhist

---

[56] Nakamura, *Miraculous Stories*, 254; cf. Kawane, *op. cit.*, 274-75.

[57] See Kitagawa, *Religion in Japanese History*, 38-45.

[58] Sansom, "Early Japanese Law," 11 (1934), 128.

temples, called *jingū-ji*, in the latter half of the eighth century and through the ninth. Literally meaning "shrine-temple," *jingū-ji* were built on the compounds of those shrines which had been usually given the symbolic offerings (*nusa*) by the emperor in accordance with the principle of the *ritsuryō* state. In many instances, wealthy landlords of the local community took initiative in building them, usually under the leadership of the self-ordained monks who had received a message from the kami in search of release from the world. [59] Once the *jingū-ji* were completed, the image of the Buddha or Bodhisattva was dedicated, while Buddhist scriptures were deposited and recited for the kami. Significantly, but unfortunately for the *ritsuryō* state, as Buddhist temples of this kind increased on the shrine compounds, many shrines lost interest in receiving the symbolic offerings from the state. This became an historic fact during the last quarter of the ninth century, [60] and by the middle of the tenth century the symbolic offerings had been distributed only to the twenty-two prominent shrines designated later as "specially privileged." [61] This almost total collapse of the cultic system inherent in the *ritsuryō* regime may be interpreted as a bankruptcy of the *ritsuryō* state as a liturgical community that existed in an ideal form at the beginning of the eighth century.

It may be noted in this connection that the *Kokubunji*, those state-sponsored temples in the various provinces whose building plans were initiated by the Emperor Shōmu for the protection of the state, ceased functioning properly by the beginning of the tenth century. According to the "Opinion on Twelve Matters" (*Iken Jūnikajō*), which was presented to the throne by the Confucian scholar Miyoshi Kiyotsura in 914, a number of provincial governors were no longer concerned with the administration of these temples, specially-appointed preceptors (*kōdokushi*) declined in quality, and residing monks were mostly married and involved in agriculture and commerce. [62] Moreover, many of the Buddhist images, halls, and additional structures had fallen into decay and disuse by 939. [63]

The fatal blow to the ideological structure of the *ritsuryō* state came

---

[59] Kawane, *op. cit.*, 273-75.

[60] Yoshiro Sakurai, "Chūsei ni okeru hyōhaku to yugei," *Nihon rekishi* 5 (1975), 308.

[61] Seishi Okada, "Ritsuryō-teki saishi keitai no seiritsu," *Kodai ōken no saishi to shinwa*, Tokyo, 1970, 161.

[62] *Honchō Monzui*, ed. K. Kuroita, Tokyo, 1941, 52.

[63] Inouye, *Nihon kodai no kokka to Bukkyō*, 58.

with the phenomenal rise of the belief in what is called *goryō-shin*. [64] Though often, and rightly, rendered the malevolent spirits of the dead, *goryō-shin* refers, more strictly speaking, to the malevolent spirits of those nobles who killed themselves or were executed under the suspicion that they had attempted the overthrow of the state. As Hori remarked, "by 863 there had already come into existence five major *goryō-shin* deities: the spirits of two disenthroned crown princes, the real mother of one of these princes, and two ministers who had suffered martyrdom." [65] When the general well-being of the national community was threatened, for example, by famine, epidemic, drought, flood, the falling of a thunderbolt, and so on, the common people as well as the nobles attributed this to the anger of the *goryō-shin*. The appearance of the *goryō* of Sugawara no Michizane (845-903), one of the highest ministers of the time who died in exile, marked the climax of this belief, and ushered in the so-called *goryō-shin* age (Hori), which was to continue up to the twelfth century. It may be noted that the *goryō-shin* made their appearance in anger, protesting against the total regime of the *ritsuryō* state with the emperor (manifest kami) at its head, and that against this onslaught of the *goryō-shin* the traditional liturgical system inherent in the *ritsuryō* state was totally powerless, impotent, and irrelevant. [66] It was the monks and semi-professional practitioners of the Mantrayana Buddhism of Tendai and Shingon who played the major roles in soothing these angry, malevolent spirits.

Certainly, by the middle of the tenth century the *Zeitgeist* had completely changed. True, the sacred and divine nature of the emperor was never called into question openly, and he continued to reign as *akitsu.mi.kami*, but the *ritsuryō* state as a liturgical community had lost its meaning and relevance, its cultic system had been functioning very poorly, and its sacred kingship ideology was no longer taken at face value. The syncretism between Shinto and Buddhism was making constant progress on the various levels of doctrine, liturgy, and religious community not only in the capital city, but especially in the rest of the country. Under these circumstances, the classical form of the sacred kingship ideology, which had sustained the *ritsuryō* state, was destined to give way gradually to the new kind of syntheses which were achieved by the esotericized or mantrayanized Mahayana Buddhists.

---

[64] Ichiro Hori, *Folk Religion in Japan: Continuity and Change*, ed. J. M. Kitagawa and A. L. Miller, Chicago, 1968, 71-73, 112-17.

[65] *Ibid.*, 112.

[66] Kawane, *op. cit.*, 280-83; Sakurai, *op. cit.*, 308-11.

THE POET AS SEER: BASHŌ LOOKS BACK

William R. LaFleur

University of California at Los Angeles

Until very recently it was an unchallenged assumption in the Western university that the various intellectual disciplines were separated from one another into spheres of scrutiny according to lines that were natural, necessary, and even "rational." Thus, sociology was or, at least, ought to be separate from the natural sciences, psychology from philosophy, religion from the arts, and so forth. Although it was granted that nodal points of merged interests existed, the so called "inter-disciplinary" studies that focussed upon such hyphens in the academy were usually considered to be no more than *ad hoc* arrangements, things which in no way would disturb the inevitability of the basic separation of spheres.

Recently, Stephen Toulmin has challenged this. By looking at their historical evolution, he sees the various disciplines as changing "conceptual populations." [1] There is nothing necessary and inherently rational in the divisions which exist; fission and hybridization go on all the time. Social reasons—that is, the influential members of existing professions, rather than intellectual reasons often prevent the creation of new sub-disciplines. [2]

The implications of this for the study of non-Western civilizations are quite profound. Toulmin himself suggests how this approach, for instance, can clarify the specificity of scientific concerns in China's past. [3] "Understanding" need not proceed according to the intellectual distinctions currently accepted in our own acadamy. Other paradigms are possible and may, in fact, be weighty with tradition in an other culture. The study of Japanese civilization provides an interesting case in point. Fortunately, the point at issue here has already been nicely clarified by the studies of Joseph M. Kitagawa. For one of the most valuable insights into Japanese culture is, I think, Kitagawa's insistence that within Japanese history there is *a tradition of refusal* to bifurcate

---

[1] Stephen Toulmin, *Human Understanding*: *The Collective Use and Evolution of Concepts*, Princeton, 1972, 360; the influence of the thought of Wittgenstein is clear.
[2] *Ibid.*, 299.
[3] *Ibid.*, 218.

things elsewhere thought naturally divisible. Thus, for instance, already in early times the Japanese

> ...did not draw a line of demarcation between the sacred and profane dimensions of life, or between *matsuri* (religious rituals) and *matsuri-goto* (political administration), both of which were ultimately under the authority of the emperor who himself was directed by the divine will. 4

In his studies of *kokutai* or the national community, Kitagawa has richly documented the weight of this tradition. 5

Likewise, aesthetic and religious experience merged easily in Japan from early times. Quite expectably, Kūkai (774-835) made this a central aspect of Buddhism there. Kitagawa writes:

> Kūkai in presenting religion as art represented the central core of Japanese piety, and in this he may be rightly regarded as a paradigmatic figure of Japanese religious history. 6

Here too the weight of tradition is on the side of the assimilation and merger of the two spheres. And Japan is a civilization in which the "new" is usually added to the "old" without displacing it. Watsuji Tetsurō termed this the "stadiality" of Japanese culture, the addition of new levels while retaining the earlier. 7 Kitagawa's *Religion in Japanese History* is a rich and systematic demonstration of this: somehow all of the past's religious experience is valued in some way and is not jettisoned merely because something new appears on the scene.

This refusal to bifurcate certain spheres is, I think, very important, heuristically valuable for understanding the specificity of Japanese intellectual history. For the point is that "refusal" does not imply inability. On the contrary, the possibility of making a separation is understood, envisioned, and *then* rejected. For instance the complex intellectual tools devised in the medieval period to articulate why Buddhism and Shinto are the Janus-faces of one phenomenon—for instance *honji-suijaku* and *ryōbu-shintō*—presuppose a recognition that,

---

4 Joseph M. Kitagawa, *Religion in Japanese History*, New York, 1966, 19.

5 Joseph M. Kitagawa, "The Japanese *Kokutai* (National Community): History and Myth,"*HR* 13 (1974), 209-26.

6 Joseph M. Kitagawa, "Master and Saviour," *Studies of Esoteric Buddhism and Tantrism*, ed. Koyasan University, 1965, 1-26 (quote p. 23).

7 "Stadiality" or "multi-leveledness" is a translation of *jūsōsei*, a concept set forth by Watsuji in "Nihon Seishin," *Watsuji Tetsurō Zenshū*, Tokyo, 1962, IV, 314ff.

potentially at least, the two "religions" were really divisible. More than likely the type of dialectics developed especially in Shingon and Tendai Buddhism, according to which *full* understanding is that position at which underlying relatedness was grasped, shaped the contour of this intellectual development. [8] Within Buddhism the notion of "*sui generis*" would be a conceptual error, something which implies some notion of "self-existent being" and clearly conflicts with the teaching both of *anatman* and *pratītya-samutpāda*. Perhaps the weighty side of the Japanese tradition, one which refuses categorical bifurcations, is evidence that the Buddhist style of thinking here was imbibed deeply into the national experience. The interesting thing is that, according to the logic of this, the coexistence with Shintō is not a conceptual compromise or tactical ploy but a conceptual necessity.

But in the present paper I wish to look very closely at a specific instance of this, a case where it can be clearly seen that the Japanese tradition is one of a refusal to make an understood distinction. In this case I wish to look at the nexus of religion and art, that which Kitagawa called "the central core of Japanese piety." My focus will be textual and historical, the analysis of a somewhat less than opaque passage of prose and one haiku verse by the great poet Bashō (1644-1694). I borrow some of the techniques of structural analysis in order to understand and comment upon the specificity of the work under scrutiny, especially the way in which Bashō in this passage is consciously reflecting upon his own received tradition.

The passage is short but dense. It is in Bashō's most celebrated work, the *Oku no hosomichi*, often translated as "The Narrow Road to the Far North". Bashō as a poet on pilgrimage has portrayed himself as having just passed the barrier at Shirakawa. He has gone through the town of Sukagawa and stands at its edge. I translate the crucial section as follows: [9]

> On the edge of this post-town was a great chestnut tree, in the shade of which a world-despising monk had taken his refuge.
> I mused that this might be the very mountain where once was written a poem about "picking up horse-chestnuts." With something in hand to write on, I jotted down the following:

---

[8] The most important notion here is that of *jita funi*, "self and other: not two," a position clearly different from that of monistic systems. The Buddhist position refuses to sacrifice either the harmony or the tension here.

[9] *Bashō bunshū*, in *Nihon koten bungaku taikei*, Tokyo, 1959, XLVI, 76-77.

"The Chinese written character for 'chestnut' is comprised of
'west' and 'tree' and is, therefore, linked up with Amida's Paradise
in the West. This is why Gyōgi Bosatsu all throughout his lifetime
used the wood of this tree both for his walking stick and for the
pillar supports of his house.

Men of the world
Fail to see its blossoms:
Chestnut of the eaves."

The density holds, in fact, a rather rich lode of images and ideas—
all related through Bashō's literary genius.

In explicating this, an initial recognition of Makoto Ueda's warning
is apropos. Ueda summarized contemporary Japanese scholarship on
Bashō by pointing out that this poet's craft was such that he often
omitted certain materials and changed the facts of his experience in
order to "present his theme more effectively." [10] Therefore, everything
counts in a passage by Bashō. There are no "throw-aways" or gratuitous
bits of unassimilated information. With this in mind, I would open
the text as follows.

Bashō hints at his theme immediately even if implicitly. The setting
is not "background" but the introduction of his subject. Therefore,
his statement at the beginning that he is standing at the edge or
outskirts (*katawara*) of the town is not without significance; it
announces that the forthcoming passage will be about putting distance
between one thing and another. This is followed by the introduction
of the "world-despising monk" and the "chestnut tree." I suggest that
at this point all of what will follow is already present in embryo:
chestnuts and world-rejection will pervade. Also important is the
mention of the monk as having "taken his refuge" under the tree;
dependency and reliance (*tanomu*) will also be important in the rest
of the paragraphs. The fact that the Buddhist monk is taking shelter
under a tree is thick with associations in that religious tradition. The
classical portrayal of Śakyamuni's enlightenment is one under a pro-
tective tree, the so-called "bodhi tree" or *ficus religiosus*. No Buddhist
familiar with the tradition would miss the allusion. Furthermore, there
quite likely is also an association between the implied "coolness" sought
under the tree and the Buddhist nirvana which was classically described

10 Makoto Ueda, *Matsuo Bashō*, New York, 1970, 24ff. The great change in Bashō
scholarship came with the publication in 1943 of the journal of Bashō's companion
Sora which, in the words of Donald Keene, "came as a bombshell to Bashō worship-
pers." See Keene, *World Within Walls: Japanese Literature of the Pre-modern Era,
1600-1867*, New York, 1976, 99ff.

in terms of coolness. So, in view of these implications, it is clear that the place of refreshment is also one of practice; it is a multiple "refuge."

At this point, at least as Bashō tells it, a snippet of verse enters his mind. And "snippet" is precisely what it is; Bashō provides his reader with only two words: *tochi hirou*, "picking up [horse] chestnuts." Critical scholarship on this is generally agreed that the obscure allusion is, in fact, to a poem by Saigyō. The two words are lifts from a verse which Bashō's readers steeped in the literary tradition would have recognized. The original poem by Saigyō and my translation is as follows: [11]

yama fukami	Deep wooded mountain—
iwa ni shitataru	Water dripping off the rocks
mizu tomemu	Gets to be a puddle
katsukatsu otsuru	While I pick up now-and-then
tochi hirou hodo	Falling horse chestnuts.

Fascinating is the way in which Bashō lets his prose flow on, in no way bothered by the fact that Saigyō had, in fact, written about horse-chestnuts (*tochi* 橡) whereas his own discussion will be about a different variety, the ordinary chestnut (*kuri* 栗). The two species merge into one because the poet has the license; but perhaps it also reinforces on one other level the envisioned assimilation of Bashō's location and experience with that of Saigyō, the poet of the twelfth-century he most admired and sought to emulate. The identification with Saigyō was especially important to Bashō, a point deserving further attention below.

The identification with Saigyō will be, as we shall see, much more than sentiment; it will be the kingpin of the verbal structure of this passage. For Bashō characteristically views Saigyō as a monk-poet of an earlier epoch who had more or less mastered the art of world-rejection. This point, interestingly, is present in the mere mention of *tochi* or horse chestnuts. Concerning them Makoto Ueda writes: [12]

> These [horse] chestnuts are not of an ordinary variety; they are only found deep in the mountains.... Unlike ordinary chestnuts they are not very tasty; in fact, to be edible they have to be cooked. It is obvious, then, that they symbolize wild, untouched nature seldom glimpsed by those who are busy pursuing their pleasures in the "floating world."

---

[12] Ueda, *op. cit.*, 137.
[11] *Nihon koten zensho* edition of the *Sanka-shū*, verse no. 1290.

Saigyō's original poem, therefore, was one in which he portrayed himself in quite straightened circumstances. Literally very distant from urban society or the "world," deep in the mountains, he was picking up a less than savory nut. Moreover, these were falling from the tree only infrequently (*katsukatsu*) and the poet in the meanwhile was likely getting wet from the dripping water. Obviously, the world-despiser knows hardships—cumulative ones. But the motif of world-rejection, the note of "distance" implicit from the very first words of the passage, is here greatly reinforced. The theme exfoliates.

Having by this point moved the imagined location far beyond the outskirts of Sukagawa to someplace "deep in the mountains," Bashō says he felt moved to respond to the situation by writing something down. The remainder of the passage is this bit of prose and one haiku, all internal within the larger piece. What he writes is quite remarkable although once again fairly dense. It consists basically of a sustained reverie on the orthography of the Chinese written character for "chestnut," *kuri* in Japanese. It strikes Bashō as terribly significant that "chestnut" is an ideograph comprised of two basic radicals. That is, *kuri* written as 栗 is made up of 西, the radical meaning "west" and 木, meaning "tree." For Bashō or, at least, for his literary invention, this is marvelous good fortune. It suits him well, therefore—as, later, it did Ezra Pound and Ernest Fenollosa—to take the written Chinese character as a medium for poetry, something of a pictogram. [13] He reasons, at least for literary purposes, as follows: if "chestnut" is comprised of "west" and "tree," it can legitimately be called the "tree of the west" and, thus—as Bashō states it—this tree is "linked up with Amida's Paradise in the West (*Saihō Jōdo*, 西方淨土)." This flagrant non sequitur is a literary find for Bashō. His prose holds that the ideograph contains a hidden etiology of the item it represents. Thus, the writing conceals the origins of the tree; it tells that it originally derived from the Paradise of Amida. It, of course, is then really a sacred tree in some sense even when it grows in this, the profane, world. With this suggested, the reason why Bashō found a

---

[13] Modern scholarship holds, in contrast to Pound and Fenollosa, that although the written character presents itself visually, it is by no means a pictogram. For an interesting and recent discussion of this in the context of poetic theory, see Andrew Welsh, *Roots of the Lyric: Primitive Poetry and Modern Poetics*, Princeton, 1978, 100-32. Bashō's own view is, of course, impossible to ascertain; his view here may be purely a literary construct.

Buddhist monk taking refuge under such a tree becomes increasingly clear. Characteristic and traditional phrases about "taking refuge in Amida's grace" are what is redolent in all of this.

But before either suggesting the structural elements in this passage or moving on with the exegesis, it is important to amplify the matter of Saigyō as what was called above "the kingpin of the verbal structure of this passage." The point here is important and easily overlooked. The anomaly is that, in fact, the *name* of "Saigyō" never explicitly appears. Yet that name becomes critically important. This is simply because this name is written with two characters, *sai* 西 referring to "west" and *gyō* 行 indicating "go" or "going." It is for obvious reasons a name with which Bashō can do verbal magic. The fascinating thing here is that although the word "Saigyō" never surfaces explicitly in the text, it is the fulcrum. Moreover, precisely by *not making it overt* Bashō has crafted an extraordinary device for recapitulating and reinforcing his motif of "hidden" ones, away from the "world" where they would be easily seen. Bashō has literally "hidden" Saigyō away in his text. A combination of literary skills is required for finding him there. But once discovered, he is seen as all-important for the very text in which he only surreptitiously "appears."

The architectonics are so subtle that it becomes necessary to move forward and backward in the text—and repeatedly at that. But before going on with the exegesis a brief look at the underlying structure of theme and composition is in place. On the hypothesis that "everything counts" and there are no "throw-aways" in Bashō's writing, we can sketch the basic structure in terms of a progressive elaboration of the theme of placing *distance* between a position called "A" and one called "B." "Placing distance" might also be referred to as a "going." Thus the poet's literal movement from the post-town to the chestnut tree on the edge of that town is already an anticipation of the monk discovered there who is described as a rejector of the world, that is, one who put distance between himself and society. Chestnuts remind the poet of horse-chestnuts and that, in turn, of Saigyō, a world-renouncing monk. His name means "going west," that is, putting distance between here and there and, in explicitly religious vocabulary, between the secular world and Amida's Western Paradise.

Schematically the progression of ideas would be as follows; the conceptual affinities run both horizontally and vertically:

"A" or "here"	*distancing/going*	*"B" or "there"*
1. post-town	[a going]	edge [of town]; chestnut tree
2. world/society	rejecting	[monk under the tree]
3.	[away in mountains]	horse-chestnuts
4. [the world]	going	west = Saigyō
5.		west's tree = chestnut
6. world/society	distance	West Paradise of Amida

Not only, then, is the "movement" in the text a many-layered one between poles "A" and "B" but under each of these two rubrics—when considered vertically—there are direct links with the others in the set.

But the text goes on. We return to it at that point where the poet has suggested that the "chestnut" is rightly written as it is since it derives from Amida's Paradise in the West. Next the text states:

> This is why Gyōgi Bosatsu all throughout his lifetime used the wood of this tree both for his walking stick and for the pillar supports of his house.

But the rationale implied in "this is why" is not exactly limpid. In order to grasp it some background concerning the man called "Gyōgi Bosatsu" is essential. Gyōgi—sometimes pronounced Gyōki—lived from 670 to 749 and is one of the most fascinating and enigmatic figures in early Japanese written history. This is not the place to detail what is known about him through modern Japanese scholarship; [14] focus here will be on things relevant to Bashō's concerns. Gyōgi was, first of all, a holy man who lived at a time when Buddhism was still a rather new arrival in Japan from the continent and was still something much confined to the elite and literate classes. Early in his career Gyōgi was, apparently, just as much a shaman as a Buddhist (in the classical sense). He was a preacher among the masses rather than a monastic and scholar. In fact, he was viewed with considerable apprehension and alarm by both the government and the Buddhist hierarchy. In 717, that is, when he was 47 years old, he was arrested for his activities.

But old age brought a sudden change in his fortune. In 745 he was adopted by the government and made an archbishop (*daisōjō*). Of course, in this the support of the masses was also marshalled

14 See Inoue Kaoru, *Gyōki*, Tokyo, 1959; and esp. Hori Ichiro, *Hori Ichiro chosakushū*, Tokyo, 1977, I, 423-63.

behind imperial and ecclesiastical projects to a new degree. Kitagawa notes: [15]

> The fact that Gyōgi, who had neither training abroad nor ecclesiastical standing in the Buddhist hierarchy, was suddenly elevated to the position of archbishop, bypassing all ecclesiastical dignitaries, indicates how eager the court was to secure the cooperation and support of the masses for the project of erecting the image of the Lochana Buddha.

Gyōgi assisted greatly in the promotion of this project but died three years before the great image was dedicated at an "eye-opening" ceremony in the great temple Tōdaiji, in the capital at Nara.

What exactly Bashō knew in detail of Gyōgi is, of course, impossible to determine. But from this brief mention of him in the present context, we can, I think, single out three things of importance. The first of these is that Bashō knew of Gyōgi's reputation as a *devotee of Amida*. Although there may be some historical question about exactly to what degree Gyōgi, in fact, was such, there is no doubt that latter traditions recognized him as such. The phenomenal growth of Amidist pietism in later centuries may have exaggerated, due to his fame by that point, Gyōgi's role in this. But in the time of Bashō there was no doubt: Gyōgi was the ancient Amidst par excellence. In Bashō's prose under consideration here the link then is evident; Amida has been mentioned and Gyōgi as the archaic Amidist fits in naturally.

The second detectable item is Bashō's awareness of Gyōgi's reputation as a saint who *walked* extensively. Materials at our disposal suggest that Gyōgi walked among the common people, to whom he preached and for whom he constructed bridges, canals and the like. But the important thing for Bashō was that the great sage had led an ambulatory life. He capitalizes upon a legend of Gyōgi's use of chestnut wood for a walkingstick in order to see a natural "fit": the Amidist sage walks about with the help of a stick, the wood of which means "tree of the Western [Paradise]" when analyzed as a written character. [16] Implicit in this motif of Gyōgi as walker is, of course, the whole going/distancing structure of the entire passage. The link with Saigyō, one of the great peregrinating poets of the past, is also evident. And, undoubtedly, Bashō's presentation of himself as writing this while

---

[15] Kitagawa, *Religion in Japanese History*, 43.

[16] The walking-stick (*tsue*) is symbolic as well as functional. For another instance of this see Joseph M. Kitagawa, "Three Types of Pilgrimage in Japan," *Studies in Mysticism and Religion*, ed. E. E. Urbach *et al.*, Jerusalem, 1967, 155-64.

on a poetic journey is something which completes the sequence of identifications.

A minor recapitulation and expansion of theme occurs in the reference to Gyōgi's use of chestnut wood as support pillars in his house. There is a neat parallel between the walking stick (*tsue*) and pillars (*hashira*), both of which are used for support by Gyōgi; he stays close to Amida's wood whether indoors or out, whether at home or on the road. But at the same time the very motif of support and reliance carries the imagery back again to the opening sentence and its reference to the world-despising monk discovered as one seeking refuge under the chestnut tree. Between that opening line and the mention of Gyōgi there had also been the indirect glimpse—via the terse scrap from Saigyō's poem about horse-chestnuts—of that poet standing in the mountains and depending there upon the nuts of that tree for basic sustenance. These were all, I would suggest, interwoven and reinforcing strands. Each in its own way but then also the group collectively emphasizes reliance, dependence, and being sustained.

The correspondence here between Bashō's selection of images and what had come to be *the* central principle of Amidist piety is remarkable. It is true, as Kitagawa points out, that this piety had undergone a long development and had developed in various directions. [17] But in spite of various doctrinal and socio-religious forms, there was always in Amidism a basic and easily symbolized motif, namely, that of reliance and *dependence upon Amida.* This was translated into Amida's utter and total reliability. Bashō would not have had to explain the point to his readers: walking-sticks and pillars made of Amida's wood were eminently dependable.

But there is one other, a third, thing which Bashō seems to have known about Gyōgi, namely, that he had a reputation of being a "seer", in fact, an extraordinary one. In the *Nihon ryōiki*, a critically important text for the spread of Buddhism in early Japan and one composed at the end of the eighth century and beginning of the ninth, Gyōgi is presented as the most important religious personality. And his most distinguishing characteristic is his possession of what is called his "heavenly eye" or "penetrating eye" (*tengen* 天眼). In the *Nihon ryōiki* this capacity of Gyōgi for sight beyond that of ordinary people plays an important role. Because of it he can see behind immediate events the whole karmic chain of causality which brought them into

---

[17] Kitagawa, *Religion in Japanese History*, 117.

being. He is the "seer" who verifies and validates the way in which the system of karmic reaction takes effect; his capacity for sight transcends that of ordinary mortals and is, in fact, that of a "heavenly" being, the highest in the six-staged taxonomy of medieval Buddhism. It is a shamanic skill wed to the Buddhist scheme of reincarnation. With his heavenly eye Gyōgi can see the karmic chain of rebirths or incidents antecedent to any event or phenomenon witnessed by others in the present.

The stories about Gyōgi in this early text are roughly-hewn gems; they make their point directly and with minimal finesse. For instance, the following episode is given in the *Nihon ryōiki* to demonstrate the supernatural skill Gyōgi possessed: [18]

> In the village of Gangō-ji in the old capital, there was once held a service at which the Most Venerable Gyōgi was invited to preach Buddhist teachings for seven days. Accordingly, both clergymen and laymen gathered to listen. In the congregation a woman whose hair was smeared with animal oil, listened to the preaching. He saw and accused her, saying: "That smell is offensive to me. Take the woman whose hair is smeared with blood far away." Greatly ashamed, she left the place.
>
> Although our mediocre eyes see only the hue of oil, the sage's penetrating eye sees real animal blood. He is an incarnation of the Buddha, the sage in disguise.

Gyōgi's attitude is equally imperious in another episode, one in which his penetrating eye enables him to see the reasons why a certain woman's child frets and cries incessantly during Gyōgi's sermons. He tells the woman to throw the child into a stream of water. The following ensued: [19]

> Though troubled by doubts, the mother could not stand the loud cries and threw him into the deep stream. The child rose to the surface and, treading water and rubbing his hands together, he stared at her with big shining eyes and said with bitterness, "What a pity! I planned to exploit you by eating for three more years." Bewildered, the mother came back to her seat to hear the preaching. The venerable master asked her, "Did you throw away your child?" Whereupon she told him the whole sequence in detail. Then he explained, "In your previous existence you borrowed his things and did not return them, so he became your child and got back what you owed him by eating. That child was your creditor in your past life."

18 Kyoko Motomochi Nakamura, trans., *Miraculous Stories from the Japanese Buddhist Tradition: the* Nihon ryōiki *of the Monk Kyōkai*, Cambridge, Mass., 1973, 201, 160f., 167-71.
19 *Ibid.*, 201-02.

From these episodes it is not *immediately* evident how Gyōgi gained his wide following among the common people. Perhaps there was an attractive charisma even in his otherwise forbidding characteristics; moreover, it cannot be doubted that his explanations of things made certain aspects of life and the world suddenly intelligible and even "just"—the theodicy of karma.

Almost nine centuries and an obvious difference in literary finesse separate the *Nihon ryōiki* from Bashō's *Oku no hosomichi*. But the interesting thing is that, in spite of these profound differences, in both cases Gyōgi is presented as a *seer* extraordinary. I suspect that the seventeenth century poet relied upon his reader's knowledge of Gyōgi as seer to make his allusion to him more meaningful. Even in Bashō's text Gyōgi is one who sees the true origins of the chestnut, its derivation in Amida's Western Paradise. In some sense he still sees around the corners of the ordinary, diurnal world and grasps things other men miss. By Bashō's time and through Bashō's craft all the rusticity in the earlier account has been rubbed off; Gyōgi has become a gentle sage and seer.

But the fact that he remains a seer is important. It is emphasized in Bashō's text by the sudden and telling comparison made between Gyōgi and the "men of the world" mentioned in the concluding haiku. The juxtaposition is swift and sharp: his extraordinary *sightedness* is contrasted with their abysmal *sightlessness*:

yo no hito no	Men of the world
mitsukenu hana ya	Fail to see its blossoms:
noki no kuri	Chestnut of the eaves.

The point is in the vivid contrast. Gyōgi, the holy man with an extraordinary capacity for sight, sees even the paradisal origin of the chestnut—and acts accordingly—whereas men of the world (*yo no hito*) even fail to see (*mitsukenu*) something as obvious as the blossoms of the chestnut by the eaves. The paradox is patent: he who belongs really to Amida's world sees also this one clearly, whereas those who belong to this world see neither very well.

But, although the principle can be stated in such a way, its specific application is far from clear. What does Bashō mean by being a "person of the world"? Would he include or exclude himself? Is it really a religious notion or one quite strictly artistic in the modern sense? Moreover, is Bashō himself not surprisingly "modern" in spite of his citation of exemplary figures out of the past and his reveries on religious symbols? The answers to these and other related questions deserve some attention here even if they must, finally, be left open, an invitation to further studies.

Bashō is so well known through his travel diaries that it is easy to overlook the fact that it was not until 1684 that he made his first important journey and that only during the last decade of his life was there a close connection between his pilgrimage and his poetry. Perhaps a good deal of the motivation for this came, in fact, from his growing fame, the sheer pressure upon him of people wanting to learn the way of haiku from the age's acknowledged master. Undoubtedly the journeys were, in part, to escape these pressures and the fact that "society" had in some sense begun to asphixiate his art.

But something more was involved. Concerning the first journey, that of 1684, Makoto Ueda writes: [20]

> He had made journeys before, but not for the sake of spiritual and poetic discipline. Through the journey he wanted, among other things, to face death and thereby to help temper his mind and his poetry. He called it "the journey of a weather-beaten skeleton," meaning that he was prepared to perish alone and leave his corpse to the mercies of the wilderness if that was his destiny. If this seems to us a bit extreme, we should remember that Bashō was of a delicate constitution and suffered from several chronic diseases, and that travel in seventeenth-century Japan was immensely more hazardous than it is today.

We know from other sources—especially the journal of his companion, Sora—that Bashō was widely recognized wherever he went. Therefore, there may have been some poetic hyperbole in the image of himself as dying alone and unseen. But the prospect of dying—even if surrounded by admirers at the time—was clearly part of the possible consequences of the rigorous journeys.

It would be wrong, then, to picture Bashō as having merely moved into a romantic persona, a ploy through which he could capture the sympathy and credulity of later generations. On the contrary, he left adequate evidence that he was during these years suffering from a certain anxiety about his own creativity. [21] And this took focus in what he took to be the necessity of escaping from social pressures,

[20] Ueda, *op. cit.*, 25-26.

[21] James Foard, "The Loneliness of Matsu Bashō," *The Biographical Process: Studies in the History and Psychology of Religion*, ed. Frank Reynolds and Donald Capps, The Hague, 1976, 363-91.

the suffocation of his art by its own success. In such circumstances, therefore, the exemplary role of what in Japanese is called the *inja* (隠者 —literally, "hidden one") or recluse had great appeal. In classical times figures such as Nōin (能因) and Saigyō (1118-1190) comprised the model, poets who were also Buddhist monks leading a comparatively ambulatory life.

For Bashō, as we have seen, Saigyō was of prime importance. What it meant for Saigyō to have been an *inja* or recluse can be seen in some of the following materials. [22] Having served as a guard in the retinue of Retired Emperor Toba, Saigyō at age twenty-three decided to "throw the world away" (*yo o suteru*). He wrote: [23]

> During the time I was coming to a decision about leaving secular life, I was on Higashiyama with a number of people and we were composing verses expressing what we felt about the gathering mists there:

> sora ni naru   A man whose mind is
> kokoro wa haru no   At one with the sky-void steps
> kasumi nite   Inside a spring mist
> yo ni araji tomo   And begins to wonder if, perhaps,
> omoitatsu kana   He might step out of the world.

It is quite clear from what he wrote at the time that this matter of "rejecting the world" was a matter both of losses and of gains. It was not strictly a matter of jettisoning all things of concrete value in the hope of gaining some strictly spiritual benefit. In Saigyō's case too the desire to make of world-rejection something which would be a fillip for the poetic vision was clearly a part of things. He traded off the involvement in society in order to enrich his relationship with the natural world and create conditions for the poetry which would come out of this.

This was present already when he made his initial decision; already then there was a sense of the paradox: [24]

---

[22] Bashō would have known of Saigyō through the latter's poetry and quite probably also through the hagiography called the *Saigyō monogatari*; see my "The 'Death' and the 'Lives' of Saigyō: the Genesis of a Buddhist Sacred Biography," *The Biographical Process*, 343-61. On the extensive literature in Japanese on the *inja*, see "Inns and Hermitages: the Structure of Impermanence," in my *The Karma of Words: Buddhism and the Literary Arts in Medieval Japan* (forthcoming).

[23] *Sanka-shū*, no. 786; translation from my *Mirror for the Moon: Selected Poems by Saigyō*, New York, 1978, 34.

[24] *Sanka-shū*, no. 2083; trans. from *Mirror for the Moon*, 84.

Written when I was petitioning Retired Emperor Toba to grant me his
permission to leave secular life:

oshimu tote	So loath to lose
oshimarenubeki	What really should be loathed:
kono yo kawa	One's vain place in life;
mi o sutete koso	We maybe rescue best the self
mi o mo tasukeme	Just by throwing it away.

The important feature, I think, is that running throughout the corpus
of Saigyō's poetry is the supposition that a world-rejecting posture is
a *sine qua non* for a capacity for some kind of special clairvoyance,
one which is both religious and aesthetic. Saigyō repeatedly insists upon
the fact that he has through his reclusive life come to see the world
and society in a new way: [25]

haruka naru	Boulder-encircled
iwa no hazama ni	Empty space, so far away that
hitori ite	Here I'm all alone:
hitometsutsu made	A place where man can't view me
monoomowabaya	But I can review all things.

The implication seems to be that in Saigyō's set of values it is only
by conscious positioning of one's self within the depths of the forest
—in spite of the loneliness and suffering this entails—that focus
and perspective can be gained. Distance from society seems necessary
to understand even it; proximity to the "world" by contrast is a
position which leads to certain blindness.

It is, I think, this notion that it is the "worldly" man who is blind
that impressed Bashō. It was something which made increasing sense
to him as he grew older; its paradoxes seemed verified by his own
personal experience. As he literally moved in the ambit of the religious
pilgrim he discovered that his poetic vision was newly stimulated.
The linkage between movement and vision is the important one. The
danger in "worldliness" lies—at least from within the Buddhist perspective—in its false fixity, its refusal to live in accordance with the
underlying movement and mutability (*anicca*) of all things. The
advantage in world-rejection lies precisely in the mobility it provides
and the clairvoyance which comes from this. It seems congruent with a
point made by Han Jonas, namely, that in the case of sight the cognitive

---

25 *Sanka-shū*, no. 2079; trans. from *Mirror for the Moon*, 83.

feat depends upon movement; "we should not be able to 'see' if we had not previously moved." [26]

Given the fact that so much of the most important imagery in classical Buddhism is that of sight and vision, it is easy to see how in the structure of things there was a close nexus between "enlightenment"—however defined—and the practice of pilgrimage. The mundane is not so much evil as it is spiritually dangerous because *easily routinized*, a world of settled but seriously impaired sight. Precisely because pilgrimage breaks the charm of the ordinary it serves the purposes of religious vision.

But, of course, in such a context aesthetic vision is virtually the same thing. Or, at least, in the cultural context of Japan the weight of tradition is one which would invite these two into synthesis. It is, as mentioned above, not a matter of the religious and artistic being conceptually indivisibile for the medieval Japanese mind but a situation in which the two are *consciously* and *deliberately* joined. And it is this tradition into which Bashō fits as well. In the passage we have considered his selection of both Saigyō and Gyōgi must be more than merely fortuitous. Concerning Gyōgi I have argued that he stands within the tradition as the paradigmatic "seer," the one who looks with ease into the land of the dead, moves with his "penetrating eye" into the complex former lives of people who stand before him, and—at least in Bashō's prose—sees the paradisal origins of natural phenomena. Gyōgi's capacity as clairvoyant is shamanic in nature. But it is wed to the cosmology of Buddhism. Kitagawa rightly takes him as a very important figure and then astutely observes the following: [27]

> It was from this tradition, the Buddhist fusion with primitive shamanism and divination, that the creative impulse was elicited in the Heian period as well as in the subsequent history of Japanese religion.

Bashō too tapped into and gave renewed life to that creative impulse.

And the juxtaposition and merger with Saigyō in the same passage reinforces the same points from within the tradition of the Buddhist *inja*, the monk who is not only "seer" but poetic visionary. The crucial thing is that in Bashō's prose the two stand *together* to form one paradigm, that of a visionary who is simultaneously religious and aesthetic.

---

[26] Han Jonas, "The Nobility of Sight: a Study in the Phenomenology of the Senses," in *The Philosophy of the Body: Rejections of Cartesian Dualism*, ed. Stuart Spicker, New York, 1970, 312-33 (quotation from 330).

[27] Kitagawa, *Religion in Japanese History*, 45.

But it still is necessary to ask: to what extent is Bashō's very self-consciousness about all of this really, perhaps, an indication that he is more modern than medieval? Within Japanese scholarship there is considerable discussion about whether Bashō—in spite of his seventeenth century dates—is the quintessential medieval figure or, on the contrary, one in whom something distinctively modern can be seen. [28] My approach would be to ask whether the *distinction* between medieval and modern might not be less sharp in Japanese history than it is in the West. I would suggest that the materials considered above permit the following observations about this particular problem.

First, when Gyōgi of the eighth century, Saigyō of the twelfth and Bashō of the seventeenth are compared and contrasted, there are some senses in which there is more affinity in world-view between the latter two than between the former two. Whereas Gyōgi's vision is literally supernatural and "miraculous" in the way he possesses shamanic ability assimilated to the *siddhi* of classical Buddhism, Saigyō and Bashō both live in a world of somewhat reduced and "naturalized" epistemic possibilities. This is to say that some of the features we ordinarily in the West associate with the naturalistic perspective of modernity are already present—at least implicitly—in the world of the twelfth-century Saigyō. Karma, rebirth, etc. are, of course, there in Saigyō's world as they are in that of Bashō; but no claims are made for a kind of clairvoyance enabling one to see into the *details* of other lives and into the Paradise of Amida. "Modernity" comes as a more gradual and gentle change of perspective and much less a crisis necessitating a radical critique of the religious episteme per se. [29]

This agrees with my second observation, namely, that the tradition of artist/poet as religious seer is the one which bears the weight of the medieval tradition and is not, like its counterpart in the West, a distinctively "modern" phenomenon. [30] For in the West the emphasis upon

[28] See Tomiyama Susumu, "Bashō ni okeru chūsei no keishō to danzetsu," in *Bukkyō bungaku kenkyū*, Kyoto, 1961, X, 157-80; Tomiyama argues for increasing distance between Bashō's posture and the medieval synthesis of poetry and Buddhism although his argument is primarily from silence.

[29] On a somewhat related point Robert Bellah has written that in China and Japan "... the reversal in primacy of contemplation and action was also taking place, even if pianissimo, so to speak, compared to the West"; in his "To Kill and Survive or to Die and Become: The Active Life and the Contemplative Life as Ways of Being Adult," *Daedalus*, 1976, 57-76 (quotation from 71). The fact that it was "pianissimo" is important and accurate here.

[30] This point emerged in a discussion with Japanese scholars; see my "Seiyō ni okeru Nihon no Chūsei bungaku kenkyū no mondai to tenbō," and subsequent discussion publ. in *Gakujutsu kokusai kōryū sankō shiryōshū*, Tokyo, 1976, 1-24.

the poet as *vates* or "seer" is largely an aspect of developing Romanticism. It is a synthesis which comes into being after the Renaissance and the growth of science had already radically changed the episteme of the West. For, as M. H. Abrams has so clearly demonstrated in his *Natural Supernaturalism*, Romanticism "took shape during the age of revolutions," [31] something expressed well within a year of the fall of the Bastille by the philosopher C. L. Reinhold as follows: [32]

> ...the most striking and distinctive characteristic of the spirit of our age is a convulsion of all hitherto known systems, theories, and modes of conception, of an inclusiveness and depth unexampled in the history of the human spirit.

It is in such a context of revolution and change that, according to Abrams, the poet is seen by the Romantics as a "seer." He writes: [33]

> ...to the Romantic poet, all depends upon his mind as it engages with the world in the act of perceiving. Hence the extraordinary stress throughout this era on the eye and the object and the relation between them.

It is clear that in some important sense the poet is to receive and revivify religious functions from an archaic past. So Carlyle in discussing "The Hero as Poet" expands on the significance of the Latin term *vates* which he takes to mean poet, prophet, and seer. And Ruskin states something very close to what we have observed in the medieval Japanese tradition when he writes: [34]

> The greatest thing a human soul ever does in this world is to *see* something, and tell what it *saw* in a plain way.... To see clearly is poetry, prophecy, and religion—all in one...; [it is to be] a Seer.

Examples could easily be multiplied.

The parallel with the Japanese material is interesting. But there is also a striking difference inasmuch as the "seeing" function in the

---

[31] M. A. Abrams, *Natural Supernaturalism: Tradition and Revolution in Romantic Literature*, New York, 1971, 334.

[32] Trans. in *ibid.*, 348.

[33] *Ibid.*, 375.

[34] John Ruskin, *Modern Painters*, New York, 1856, III, 268; quoted in Abrams, *op. cit.*, 375f. See also M. A. Abrams, *The Mirror and the Lamp: Romantic Theory and the Critical Tradition*, New York, 1953.

case of the Romantic poets takes into itself the *prophetic* role as well, something which on the one hand makes it the inheritor of a weighty Western tradition and, on the other, links it historically to the *revolutionary* events of modern Western experience. For as Abrams points out,

> ...at the formative period of their lives, major Romantic poets—including Wordsworth, Blake, Southey, Coleridge, and later, after his own fashion, Shelley—shared the hope in the French Revolution as the portent of universal felicity, as did Hölderlin and other young radicals in Germany.

Therefore, even when these millenarian expectations were disappointed, "Romantic thinking and imagination remained apocalyptic thinking and imagination, though with varied changes in explicit content." [35] So strong is this interest in historical events of the future that in Wordsworth even the figure of the hermit is made meaningful as the survivor of some future deluge and catastrophe—and as such becomes "the prophetic figure *par excellence*." [36]

The role of the Buddhist seer, by comparison, is less related to the events of a specific epoch. In the case of Gyōgi clairvoyance was thought to extend into the past so as to see the shape of karmic patterns. But much more typical is the insistence of poets such as Bashō that our greatest loss lies in failing to see the natural things near at hand and before our own eyes. Being attached to "the world" leads to such occlusion of the eye and mind.

Whatever modernization has meant in Japan it seems not to have been accompanied by the same motif of a revolutionary sweeping away of the past. The language used to describe the changes of modernity has not been so pervaded by notions of radicality and intensity. And this difference, is, perhaps, not a minor one, a slight variation from the pattern known in the West: on the contrary, it might be one which has made the *whole process* of becoming "modern" significantly and interestingly different from our own. Shaped by its own specific tradition, the Japanese experience deserves continuous attention and study.

---

[35] M. A. Adams, *Natural Supernaturalism*, 64-65.

[36] Geoffrey Hartman, *The Unmediated Vision: an Interpretation of Wordsworth, Hopkins, Rilke, and Valéry*, New York, 1954, 33. Saigyō is something of an exception here within the ambit of Japanese culture; he commented directly on events in his day and often wrote verse on such things; see the "Introduction" to *Mirror for the Moon*.

THE SECULARIZATION OF JAPANESE RELIGION *

Measuring the Myth and the Reality

WINSTON DAVIS

Kwansei Gakuin University

For historians and sociologists of religion one of the most important spinoffs of modernization theory has been a subset of problems concerning secularization. While definitions of the phenomenon differ, [1] the concepts of secularization which have grown out of theoretical studies of modernization fall between two extremes. The first sort declares that the decline of religion is *inevitable*. The original statement of this position pictured religion as the unhappy victim of the advance of science and reason. As Continental scholars liked to put it, Mythos was dethroned by Logos. This idea was conventional wisdom for many of the thinkers of the 18th and 19th centuries. A corollary of the Doctrine of Social Progress, this notion has yet to be exorcized from the catalogue of academic obsessions. The decline of religion for Auguste Comte was part of the general law of the evolution of society and corresponded to the development of individuals from infantile theologians to mature natural philosophers or scientists. [2] Max Weber's discussions of *die Entgötterung* and *Entzauberung der Welt* link the decline of religion and magic to the overall process of the rationalization of society and ultimately to the destiny of modern civilization itself. More recent versions of the inevitable decline theory treat religion as part of a syndrome of social, economic, political and psychological changes which, collectively, make up "the modernization process."

The other extreme makes the decline of religion ultimately *impossible*. Scholars working in the *Religionswissenschaft* tradition are the first to come to mind. G. Van der Leeuw, for example, declares that

* This study was made possible in part by grants from the National Endowment for the Humanities and the Center for Research in International Studies of Stanford University.

[1] See Larry Shiner, "The Meanings of Secularization," in *Secularization and the Protestant Prospect*, ed. James Childress and David Harned, Philadelphia, 1970, 30-42.

[2] "The Progressive Course of the Human Mind," in *Sociology and Religion: A Book of Readings*, ed. Norman Birnbaum and Gertrud Lenzer, Englewood Cliffs, N.J., 1969, 28.

"religion exists always and universally." [3] Rudolf Otto's stress on "divination" as an *a priori* category of the human mind and Mircea Eliade's emphasis on the essential religiousness of man (*homo religiosus*) [4] both seem to imply that secularization just cannot take place. This position seems to rest upon the historical generalization that religion has existed *de facto* in all cultures up to the present and concludes, falsely I think, that it therefore will continue to do so in the future *de iure*. In its more philosophical versions, this theory seems to stand upon an analysis of the "essence" of human nature. Otto, for example, believed that the experience of the numinous is a "fact of our nature." The history of religions therefore presupposes man's eternal capacity for apprehending the Holy. Implied in this argument seems to be the intimation that man achieves maturity only when he develops these religious sensibilities. [5]

Some sociologists have also stressed the ultimate impossibility of secularization. Emile Durkheim, while believing that religion continually embraces a smaller part of social life, saw in what he called "the cult of the individual" a quasi-religious integration of modern society. The structural-functionalist school which took its inspiration from him has been deeply imbued by a piety which, as Nisbet puts it, "represents a conviction that full understanding of social phenomena is impossible save in terms of a recognition of the unalterable, irreducible role of the religious impulse." [6] This tendency is quite apparent in the works of Talcott Parsons who, elaborating Durkheim's fundamental postulate that collective representations are symbols for the integration of society, has consistently sought to ground both ethical norms and culture *per se* in the templates of religion. What others took to be the enervation of religious institutions, Parsons has regarded as instances of "value-generalization." [7] His seminal essay, "Christianity and Modern Industrial Society," was therefore cast as an alternative

---

[3] G. van der Leeuw, *Religion in Essence and Manifestation*, New York, 1963, II, 600.

[4] Rudolf Otto, *The Idea of the Holy*, New York, 1958; Mircea Eliade, *The Sacred and the Profane*, New York, 1959, 23, writes: "To whatever degree he may have desacralized the world, the man who has made his choice in favor of a profane life never succeeds in completely doing away with religious behavior."

[5] Otto, *op. cit.*, 15, 176. Otto, of course, did not argue that all men actualize this potential; see p. 149.

[6] Robert Nisbet, *The Sociological Tradition*, New York, 1966, 261.

[7] Talcott Parsons, "Christianity and Modern Industrial Society," in *Sociological Theory, Values, and Sociocultural Change: Essays in Honor of Pitirim A. Sorokin*, ed. Edward Tiryakian, New York, 1967, 33-70; "Religion in a Modern Pluralistic Society," *Review of Religious Research* 7 (1966), 125-46.

to Pitirim Sorokin's view of secularization as an inevitable consequence of the transition from an "ideational logico-meaningful sociocultural supersystem" (*sic*) to a "sensate pattern" of culture in which "the World takes flesh." Following Parsons, Robert Bellah in his development of a neo-evolutionary analysis of religious history adopts a modified Eliadean position and insists that "neither religious man nor the structure of man's ultimate religious situation evolves, then, but rather religion as a symbol system." [8] Thus he seems to imply that *homo sapiens* is essentially *homo religiosus*. While the notion that secularization is ultimately impossible is more sophisticated than the inevitable decline theory, it too has a built in theoretical bias. It tends to transform instances of religious decline (however defined) into simple cases of religious change.

The two general theories I have mentioned stand at the antipodes of the study of secularization. Both rely heavily upon specific modernization theories for their underpinnings. There is a tendency in both theories to presuppose that cultural change, and religious change in particular, is synchronic with the overall transformations of society. This bias is especially strong in traditional functionalism, which saw in religion a symbolic means for effecting social solidarity. [9] Proponents of both types of theory have tended to analyze modernization by drawing up two lists of predicates, one under the heading "tradition," the other under "modernity." Modernization, therefore, means simply moving from the first to the second list. Such dichotomous configuration theories of modernization have the tendency to smother the historical specificity of religious change under the soft pillow of sociological abstraction. Like functionalism in general such theories assume that religious change is eurhythmic, i.e. changing in step with the other changes of society. [10] One of the dangers in this double list approach is that tradition and modernity easily become falsely reified and artificially contrasted. As Joseph Kitagawa points out, "we are often presented with a stereotyped dichotomy between a supposedly irrational worldview in which tradition-equals-religion-equals-pre-modern-think-

---

[8] Robert Bellah, *Beyond Belief*: *Essays on Religion in a Post-Traditional World*, New York, 1970, 21.

[9] For a critique of the functionalist's tendency to assume that cultural and social change are always synchronic see Clifford Geertz, *The Interpretation of Cultures*, New York, 1973, 142-69.

[10] Reinhard Bendix, *Embattled Reason: Essays on Social Knowledge*, New York, 1970, 250-314.

ing, on the one hand, over against a modern-equals-secular-equals-rational scientific mode of thinking on the other." [11]

I offer no new alternatives to these theories. Instead, I would simply like to point out the importance of the kind of analyses careful historians of religion have been doing, perhaps intuitively, all along. Rather than assuming that the decline of religion, however defined, is either inevitable or impossible, I shall assume that it is possible, not necessarily unilinear, and therefore reversible. Such is my hypothesis. I shall try to demonstrate by statistical and historical examples that there is no universal measure for "the secularization process"—whatever that means!—and that even within a single religious system "the general decline of religion" is a meaningless jumble of words. It is my position that the concept of secularization can be rehabilitated only if we take a more nominalistic approach to the subject. This would entail 1) breaking religious systems into their component parts, e.g. belief, emotion, and modes of expression and behavior, 2) determining which of these parts is dominant, which recessive, 3) defining and operationalizing the concept of decline within each part, and 4) investigating specific cases in the history of religions in this way. Since lack of space prevents a more thoroughgoing methodological statement of the problem, in this essay I shall concentrate on the first two points and their application to the alleged decline of religion in modern Japan. Following Larry Shiner, I shall assume that the meaning of secularization includes the complementary notions of desacralization, differentiation, and the transposition of religious beliefs and behavior to the "secular" sphere. [12]

Flying to Japan in the summer of 1971, I had a conversation with a Japanese banker on his way home from a seminar in the United States. When he learned that I was studying Japanese religion he shook his head and sadly assured me that there no longer was such a thing. I was later to hear the same thing from many other Japanese. While I suspect that this opinion is, in part, a reflection of the this-worldly work ethic of upper-middle-class white collar workers (the so-called "economic animals"), statistics seem to bear this position out. A recent Gallup survey of religious beliefs around the globe produced the following results. [13]

[11] Joseph M. Kitagawa, "Some Reflections of a Historian of Religions," unpublished manuscript, 10.

[12] Shiner, *op. cit.*, 41.

[13] *Gallup Opinion Index Reports, No. 130: Religion in America*, Princeton, 1976, 1-17.

QUESTION: "How important to you are your religious beliefs?"
RESULTS (abbreviated):

	very important	fairly important	not too important	not at all important	don't know
India	81%	14%	3%	2%	—
United States	56	30	8	5	1
United Kingdom	23	26	26	20	5
Scandinavia	17	28	39	13	3
Western Europe (av.)	27	32	26	13	2
Japan	12	34	44	10	—

QUESTION: "Do you believe in God or a universal spirit?" (Those who said "yes" were also asked the following questions: "Do you believe that this God or universal spirit observes your actions and rewards or punishes you for them?")
RESULTS (abbreviated):

	believe in God	don't believe	don't know	God observes	doesn't observe	don't know
India	98%	2%	—	90%	6%	2%
United States	94	3	3	68	19	7
United Kingdom	76	14	10	34	28	14
Scandinavia	65	25	10	28	27	10
Western Europe (av.)	78	16	6	43	22	13
Japan	38	34	28	18	7	13

QUESTION: "Do you believe in life after death?"
RESULTS (abbreviated):

	yes	no	undecided
India	72%	18%	10%
United States	69	20	11
United Kingdom	43	35	22
Scandinavia	35	44	21
Western Europe (av.)	44	39	17
Japan	18	43	39

The survey concludes that "the United States stands at the top of the industrial societies in the importance religion plays in the lives of its citizens. Japan, which also has a high level of education, stands at the opposite extreme." [14]

I present this information not because I find it significant, but because it brings out the difficulty, or rather the impossibility, of measuring overall, cross-cultural religiousness or secularity by such simple sociometric techniques. Beneath the superficially simple questions asked in the survey are such unquantifiable problems as the

---

[14] *Ibid.*, 2.

relative importance of belief *per se* in each religious system and the relationship between religion and the national identity. The poor showing of the Japanese in this survey is not, of course, explained by the figures themselves. The fact that religious beliefs are "fairly important" to more Japanese than to any other group, while they score lowest among those holding these beliefs to be "very important" could very well be attributed to the notorious capacity of the Japanese for self-effacement. Furthermore the Japanese, who have a deep appreciation for ambiguity both in literature and in daily conversation, dislike committing themselves in a public way to any political, ideological or religious opinion. The low incidence of belief in God can be attributed in part to the fact that Japanese religions do not school their adherents in the abstractions of theology. Finally, the poor showing of the Japanese in the last question has to be counterbalanced by the importance Japanese place on ancestor worship.

Turning to Japanese surveys, there does seem to be evidence of a decline of religious belief since the War. During the War itself, when religion was one of the tools of national ideology and thought-control, 72% responded positively to the Nishitani survey which asked "do you believe in the *kami* and Buddha?" In 1946, 56% of the respondents in the Jiji Tsūshinsha survey said that they were "inclined to believe in religion." While the same survey uncovered a wide range of negative feelings towards religion, only 1.5% said they thought religious teachings are a "lie." The Nagamatsu survey of the same year showed 77% replying that they had a "religious attitude" (*shinkō-shin*). Since this was a broader question than the one asked by Jiji Tsūshinsha, a larger number of positive responses might have been expected. Nevertheless, the Jiji Tsūshinsha survey of 1947 using its original question likewise showed an increase of believers, rising from 56% to 77%. Believers in Buddhism went up from 33.2% to 54.3% and Christians increased from 1.3% to 6.0%. Shintō, discredited by the surrender, decreased from 8.7% to 6.8%. The dramatic shifts indicated by these surveys in the immediate post-war period are difficult to interpret. What is clear is that much of the hyper-ventilated overbelief of the war years continued to exist during the immediate post-war period and was sustained through the early 1950's. A Yomiuri newspaper survey of 1952, for example, found that 65% of the Japanese believed in a religion. [15]

15 *Shūkyō Benran* (Nihon Shūkyō Renmei), Tokyo, 1948, 350-61; Suzuki Norihisa, "Nihonjin no shūkyō ishiki kenkyū ni tsuite," *Shūkyō Kenkyū* 38 (1965), 119-30.

Our data thus far is "soft," based as it is on different survey techniques and questions. Evidence becomes much better after the beginning of the government's *Survey of the National Character of the Japanese* conducted every five years beginning in 1953. By using the same questions and sampling methods over an extended period of time, the findings of this research project can be regarded as comparatively "hard" evidence. One of the questions posed by this survey is: "Do you have some kind of religious faith or attitudes?" (*nani ka shinkō to ka shinshin*). The percent of positive replies made every fifth year are as follows (a dash indicates the question was not asked in that year): —/35/31/31/25. Over a fifteen year span, religious beliefs and attitudes seem to have declined about 10%. Of the believers, those who said they did something religious regularly or daily were: —/—/ 30/36/32. This means that at the time of the most recent survey (1973), about 8% of the population could claim to believe in and practice religion on some regular basis. [16]

The *Survey of the National Character of the Japanese* therefore is no more flattering than the international Gallup poll itself. In fact, it seems to indicate still weaker commitments to religion among the Japanese. Before we draw our conclusions, however, we should look at evidence from the same survey which makes the picture even more complicated. The number of Japanese who believe that a religious attitude (*shūkyōshin*) is important has remained about the same: —/72/77/76/69. In the 1973 survey, 63% said "revering one's ancestors" is "*extremely* important," while 76% held "filial piety" in similar esteem. These feelings—which one naturally associates with "ancestor worship"—seem to be divorced from "religion" (*shūkyō*) by the Japanese. At least, only 28% indicated that religious feelings (*shūkyōteki na kokoro*) were "*very* important." [17] These figures seem to show that while individuals are hesitant to commit themselves to any specific religious belief, they believe that in principle religion is important for people. The unbelief revealed in this study therefore cannot be equated with a principled disbelief.

The findings of this government survey incline one to wonder

---

[16] *Nihonjin no Kokuminsei*, ed. Hayashi Chikio *et al.*, Tokyo, 1975, No. 3, 448.

[17] One reason for the low scores on religious commitment in all of these surveys is that the word religion (*shūkyō*) seems to imply 1) doctrines and 2) specific public commitments to them—neither of which are part of the genius of Japanese religion. Many people usually forget to include their Shintō affiliations when asked to name their *shūkyō*. Notice that in this survey's principle question regarding belief, the words *shinkō* (faith) and *shinshin* (religious attitude) were used and not *shūkyō*.

whether belief should be the measure of Japanese religiousness and
secularity at all. This suspicion is underscored by Basabe's study (1967)
of the religious attitudes of Japanese men aged 20 through 40 living
in metropolitan areas. [18] In this study, 14% said they believed in some
religion; 22.1% said they did not believe; 59% were indifferent.
The lines between these groups were by no means clear. For example,
the traditional Buddhists (who constituted 35% of the believers)
displayed what a Westerner might call a high level of theological
nonchalance. Eighty-three percent believed that "as religion is something depending on man's moods and feelings, it is perfectly right
for him to accept or reject it." Forty-four percent believed that "God
is nothing more than a yearning existing in man's heart." Forty-two
percent thought that "there is no such thing as an afterlife, but because
people want an afterlife, they believe in it." In spite of the fact that
customs like *Obon* (All Souls Day) are important for these traditional
believers, only 34.6% agreed that "at *Obon* time, the spirits of the
ancestors return to their homes." Still more revealing was the finding
that of those styling themselves unbelievers, 32.5% have Buddhist
and Shintō altars in their homes, 57.6% participate in festivals and
pilgrimages, and 27% carry an amulet on their person. Of those indifferent to religion 59.3% have Buddhist and Shintō altars, and
34.5% offer prayers before these altars. Six percent do so daily,
while 28.4% do so occasionally. Sixty-one percent now and then participate in pilgrimages to shrines or temples and 43.1% carry amulets.
In short, Basabe found that even among believers there is a low level of
commitment to specific beliefs. On the other hand, he found that those
calling themselves unbelievers or indifferent to religion continue to do
religious things. The *Shūkyō chōsa* study (reported in the *National
Character of the Japanese*, No. 2) which investigated feelings of
reverence likewise found that the number of Japanese having religious
feelings far exceeds the number willing to call themselves believers.
While believers in this survey stood at 28%, those who claimed to have
"experienced feelings of reverence before a Shintō shrine" were 71%.
Sixty-nine percent said that they had "experienced feelings of reverence
before a statue of the Buddha or while listening to a sutra." Only
25% clearly deny ever having such feelings. [19]

   What these findings indicate is that "in Japan, the criterion of

---

[18] Fernando Basabe, *Religious Attitudes of Japanese Men: A Sociological Survey*,
Tokyo and Rutland, 1968.
[19] *Nihonjin no Kokuminsei*, 1970, No. 2, 50.

'believer' and 'non-believer' does not suffice to make an adequate distinction between those souls that are truly religious and those which are irreligious or indifferent." [20] While belief naturally seems to be an appropriate index of religiousness to the Westerner (and the Japanese sociologist trained in Western sociology), by itself it tells us only part of the story. The reason for this is that religious praxis (*shugyō*) and feelings (*kimochi*) and not belief *per se* form the core of Japanese religion. The best way to understand the real genius of this religion (and its putative decline) is to turn from what the Japanese believe or think about religion to what they feel and do. This, of course, takes us from statistics to a more humanistic examination of religious behavior.

Without a doubt, the greatest secularizing influence on Japanese religion was the growth of a money economy. A process at work in Japanese history since even before the Tokugawa period, the growth of market relationships disrupted both class relationships and family ties. [21] During this period of economic development a group of writers whom Smith calls "technologists" appeared with the express purpose of showing the farmer how to increase the prosperity of his own family. Not only did the opinions of these technologists run counter to the ascriptive hierarchy and Confucian principles of Tokugawa society; their utilitarian, functional rationality also inspired a vehement attack on religion. Farmers should rely upon themselves and not just on the gods. The following passage is taken from a contemporary book on sericulture:

> Let two men be equally lucky, one will succeed and the other fail by reason of differences in skill. Even in good growing years when everyone prospers, yields nevertheless vary with skill. Although everyone is the same distance from heaven, it is plain that there are differences in ability [*jinriki*]. People who do not recognize this fact stupidly pray to the Buddha and *kami*, or they blame the eggs for their bad results and envy the success of others. The Buddha and *kami* may help ever so much, but if one's sericultural methods are slipshod [*orosoka*], one is not going to get good results. But if one's methods are made sound by inquiring tirelessly about methods from experts, one will get good results even in bad years. [22]

---

[20] Basabe, *op. cit.*, 121.

[21] See Winston Davis, "Toward Modernity: A Developmental Typology of Popular Religious Affiliations in Japan," Ithaca, East Asia Papers, No. 12 (1977); Morioka Kiyomi, *Religion in Changing Japanese Society*, Tokyo, 1975, 39-72, 155-67.

[22] Thomas Smith, "Ōkura Nagatsune and the Technologists," in *Personality in Japanese History*, ed. Albert Craig and Donald Shively, Berkeley, 1970, 140f. During

These changes in the economy also weakened groups which traditionally had been in charge of local festivals. The result was often the
formation of rival festival factions within the villages. [23] As time went
on "sacred time and space" within many of these villages began to
shrink. For example, in pre-modern Japan, *sakaki* branches, sacred
festoons and *yin-yang* symbols (actually images of male and female
genitalia) often bedecked the gates of a village, marking off the village
as, in some sense, sacred space. All adult males in the village were
regarded as "children of the clan" (*ujiko*) and were collectively
responsible for the abstinences and taboos imposed by the local clan
god (*ujigami*). Because the village was in a state of perpetual ritual
purity, its residents often could dispense with special purification rites
before the spring and autumn festivals. When special abstinences were
performed by the Shintō priests of the village they were considered
rituals carried out on behalf of the entire community, and not as
means of raising the level of purity of the individual celebrants themselves. Gradually all of this began to change. The symbols which once
had been hung from the village gates were withdrawn to places inside
the village and were fixed to the entrance to the shrine precincts, or
above the altars of individual houses. (The spread of these domestic
altars was a reflection of the growing sense of independence among
smaller scale families.) As sacred space was constricted, sacred time
was curtailed. Throughout Japan the demands of more "rational" work
schedules made it increasingly difficult to spend as much time on
festival celebrations or in mourning. Originally, festivals were not
conceptually distinguished from their preparations or postludes. Later
on, however, the preparatory abstinences and the ceremonies held on
the eve of the festival (*yoimatsuri*) and the night after (*uramatsuri*)
were separated from the festival itself. [24] This degraded both. Sacred
time was often reduced to some fraction of the festival day itself,
often to the parade to and from the shrine. These changes naturally
destroyed the continuity and unity of traditional festivals. Taboos which
interfered with people's work were gradually eliminated. The number
of "sacred people" connected with festivals also declined. First, lay
celebrants and oblationers took over from the community the respon-

---

this period there were others, like Ninomiya Sontoku, who tried to combine traditional
religious piety with a this-worldly work ethic.

[23] See Winston Davis, "Parish Guilds and Political Culture in Village Japan,"
JAS 36 (1976), 25-36.

[24] Yanagita Kunio, *Nihon no matsuri*, Tokyo, 1942, 49.

sibility for the preparations and abstinences of festivals. Later on, their roles were often taken over by hereditary or professional priesthoods. With the decline of a purely lay priesthood the interest and involvement of many people began to wane. [25]

The folklorist Yanagita Kunio points out many other subtle changes which took place in the festival faith of the common folk. [26] In the Meiji period the government itself, in its frantic efforts to modernize the country, played a major role in the secularization of folk practices. Local customs such as ritual transvestism and orgies, dressing up as ghosts at *Obon*, and cutting down trees for making New Year's decorations were prohibited in the name of decorum and frugality. After the Tokyo dialect was declared the standard language, country folk suddenly realized that the words of traditional religious chants and songs they were used to were now considered "dialectical" and crude. Those who moved to the cities usually forgot them. Another secularizing item introduced by the government was the Occidental solar calendar which was first used in 1873. On January 4th of that year five traditional religious holidays based on the lunar calendar were abolished, and on October 14th various imperial festivals were promulgated. Even the equinoxes were decreed sacred to the memory of the imperial ancestors. These changes worked havoc with local custom. Even when festivals were not abolished outright, the new calendar made them come at the wrong time. The association of religious celebrations with specific seasons had aesthetic connotations which were extremely significant to the people. Special kinds of food offerings were no longer available when festivals were celebrated according to the new calendar. After the introduction of the solar calendar many villages simply gave up their festivals without further intervention by the government. On March 22, 1876 Sunday was made the national day of rest at the suggestion of foreign teachers. In 1877 Christmas, which has virtually no religious meaning in Japan, was introduced in Tokyo by the Maruzen Department Store. In that year the store began to sell *Kurisumasu purezento* as they do even now. In 1888 Christmas cards were introduced. The new postal service made it possible for people to send cards to one another at New Year's instead of visiting each other in person. This tended to break down the high level of social interaction which

---

[25] Chiba Masaji, *Matsuri no hōshakaigaku*, Tokyo, 1970, 70-71; Edward Norbeck, "Pollution and Taboo in Contemporary Japan," *SW Jour. Anthr.* 8 (1952), 269-85.
[26] Yanagita Kunio, *Japanese Manners and Customs in the Meiji Era*, Tokyo, 1957, *passim*.

is an important aspect of genuine religious festivals. Japanese industry
was also influenced by the new calendar. Unlike the traditional guilds
which had celebrated holidays as holy days dedicated to the worship
of patron saints, the new industries established in the Meiji period were
comparatively secular enterprises.

In the days before the introduction of the solar calendar there had
been a saying "when whores are faithful and eggs are square, the moon
will come up on the last day of the month." After the imposition of
the new calendar there were times when the moon *did* come up on the
last day of the month, apparently without the help of whores or eggs. [27]
Naturally, not all Japanese were willing to accept this state of affairs.
Most farmers continued to follow the lunar calendar for all practical
purposes. An article in a periodical published in 1915 complained:

> Ask any child and he will tell you that the 8th day of the 4th month
> is the Buddha's birthday, and that during the Obon festival the boiling
> caldrons of hell are opened for the condemned souls to escape. But
> even an old fellow like myself will not be able to tell you why the
> (new fangled) Foundation Day and the Emperor's birthday need to be
> commemorated. To exalt these days that the people care nothing about,
> the government makes everybody put up lanterns, and a flag that looks
> like an advertisement for red pills. The old holidays were celebrated
> because the people felt them to be festive occasions. It is asking too
> much to make the people celebrate days they do not feel to be festive. [28]

While the word *hare* today is generally thought of in connection with
the weather (meaning "clear," or "bright"), it has broader connotations. It also refers to something which is public, open, common, or to
society itself. It is associated with formal occasions, but also with
refreshment and novelty. Festivals themselves were therefore associated
with *hare* conditions. They were traditionally regarded as extraordinary
days when people could eat special food, wear special clothing and
enjoy special activities and events. The opposite of *hare* is *ke*, a term
referring to what, instead of clear and bright, is dark and gloomy.
Rather than something public, *ke* is private. Accordingly, *ke* is associated with informal things, such as an old kimono one might put
on when at home. *Ke* therefore can be thought of as "the grind," or
to use H. G. Wells' word, "everydayishness." Thus the cheap millet

---

[27] The saying is the epigraph of Hakuin's sermon, "The Plain Looking Courtesan's
Ballad of Bravado," *The Embossed Tea Kettle*, London, 1963, 157. See Yanagita,
Japanese Manners, 257.

[28] *Ibid.*, 261.

that farmers used to eat as everyday fare was called *ke-shine*. Festivals, on the other hand, were an opportunity to indulge the palate in "something different" (*kawarimono*) or what sometimes was called "occasional food" (*tokidoki*). Before the Meiji period peasants thought of rice, fish, tea and *sake* (which one thinks of today as the "typical" Japanese diet) as festival fare. The custom of eating rice every day was spread through the countryside by young conscripts returning from urban camps where they had grown accustomed to a better diet. Before this, rice had been grown primarily to pay taxes. Drinking customs also changed during this period. In 1872 the government prohibited the private brewing of *sake*. This brought to an end the tradition of making sacred rice wine (*miki*) which was drunk in the presence of the local *kami*. After this, wine for festivals had to be purchased. Drinking alone, instead of from a common jug, also became more common in the Meiji period—although even nowadays it is sometimes regarded as a sign of alcoholism. Only in the past few years have small bottles of beer become common in Japan. Eating alone on separate trays also became widespread in the Meiji period. Before this, such a way of eating was seen only at funerals. The Japanese also used to make a clear-cut distinction between work and festival dress. Although, after the end of the sumptuary legislation that had been in force during the Tokugawa period, commoners were free to wear whatever colors they chose, traditional dark blues and greys continued to be favored for everyday use. Gradually, however, people began to wear throughout the week the brighter colors which formerly had been worn only during festivals. Rouge and other cosmetics which also had been used only at festival times became part of a woman's daily makeup. What we see in these changing customs seems to be indicative of a leveling of the traditional distinctions between *hare* and *ke*, or between festival time and ordinary time. This growing indifference to the uniqueness of festival customs might well be regarded as a symptom of secularization.

The Japanese festival was originally a ritual performed within the local community by local people. To worship the *kami* therefore meant serving and waiting upon them in a specific place. Demographic mobility and travel (including pilgrimage itself) therefore tended to disrupt the age-old festivals of the local community. In ancient Japan, festivals had been held in the dark. Conducted by the local inhabitants, the rituals and festivities centered around a bonfire built in a family courtyard. So far removed were these *matsuri* from the spectacles we nowadays call festivals that in some parts of Japan it was believed that

if a stranger watched them he would die. [29] Today, many of these
fire festivals have been transformed into daytime festivities in order to
attract larger crowds. This is especially obvious in events like the
Kumano Fire Festival which these days features the burning of enormous pine torches in broad daylight. Since Yanagita seemed to equate
the authenticity of a festival with its indigenous or locative nature, he
naturally had a rather critical attitude towards pilgrimage. He felt that
the mass pilgrimages which spread throughout Japan during the Tokugawa period played an important part in the degeneration of traditional
festivals. So numerous did pilgrims become that temple inns *(shukubō)*
could no longer hold them. Putting up in secular *ryōkan*, the pilgrims
could go on pilgrimages without coming into direct contact with priests
and could even avoid the maigre fare of the *shukubō*. Pilgrimage finally
became the kind of recreation it is to this day. Yanagita was especially
critical of the custom called *sensharei* which literally meant pasting
pieces of paper bearing one's name to a thousand shrines. Some people
spent so much time and money indulging in "pilgrimages" of this
sort that they were criticized by contemporaries for pestering the
kami. [30] Still another symptom of the degeneration of festival traditions was the development of the collection boxes *(saisenbako)* placed
in front of shrines. In many out-of-the-way places such boxes still do
not exist. He notes, with delightful humor, that where a *saisenbako* is
placed before the shrine in a small village, the scattered offerings of
rice are quickly devoured by sparrows and neighborhood urchins see
to it that nothing glitters in the offering box too long. Originally,
if gifts were made to the shrine they were usually presentations of
land, cloth, sake or rice. As travel and pilgrimage increased, strangers
began to visit festivals in which, because they *were* strangers, they were
not allowed to participate. Not knowing how to worship the local *kami*
properly, they would offer a few coins before the shrine. Money
offerings thereby became substitutes for real participation in the worship of the *kami*. In ancient times it had been an insult even to mention
the word "money" in the presence of a nobleman, let alone a god.
Yanagita concluded that throwing coins into the *saisenbako* was not
much different from the Westerner's demeaning custom of tipping
servants and underlings. [31]

Yanagita also believed that the decline of religious custom could be

---

[29] Yanagita, *Nihon no matsuri*, 53, 48.
[30] "Ujigami to ujiko," *Teihon Yanagita Kunio shū*, Tokyo, 430.
[31] *Nihon no matsuri*, 229-43.

measured in terms of the roles of and attitudes towards children. Since infant mortality was as high in Japan as it is in all premodern societies, there were many magical spells used to ensure the health and safety of children. After the spread of modern medicine in the Meiji period, these spells began to be rejected by many people as superstitious. [32] Childbirth itself had been surrounded by numerous taboos. In some parts of Japan parturition huts were used to sequester new mothers and women who were having their menstrual periods. To avoid contaminating others with their "red pollution" these women were expected to eat food which had been prepared in a separate place. In modern times, it became simply too expensive for women to spend long periods of time in ritual seclusion and the custom died out.

As adults became less involved in local religious customs they often turned their own festival roles over to children. Today children's festivals abound in Japan: the festivals of the road-god, *Tanabata*, *Jizōbon*, the Chrysanthemum festival, and rites to drive away birds (*orioi*), moles (*mogurauchi*) and other pests. In one city in Western Honshū I watched a children's festival which features a parade of *omikoshi* [33] in which had been "enshrined" such juvenile deities as Snoopy, a longtime favorite of Japanese children, and Taiyaki-kun, a fish (actually a fish-shaped, bean-filled cookie) who figured as the tragic hero of a popular children's song. The streets resounded with the same *"wasshoi, wasshoi!"* that welcomes the *kami* in more solemn processions. Even the celebrations of New Year's Eve are entrusted to children, something Yanagita considered a sure sign of secularization. Only in more conservative villages where religious traditions persist do elders continue to dominate festivals. In some places, however, children have always played an important festival role. Divine children (*ochigosan*), who were sometimes the children of Shintō priests, were often treated as gods and were expected to deliver oracles. Nowadays these children merely distribute amulets and dance, their oracular powers having vanished. Only in one remote fishing village in Wakayama prefecture have I seen people actually worshiping divine children. [34]

As in contemporary America, the handling of death is still another

---

[32] In one village which I visited in Shiga Prefecture cattle used to be taken to the shrine once a year to drink sacred rice wine and be blessed. After the introduction of vaccinations this custom disappeared, though amulets for the protection of cattle are still sold.

[33] God-carts or palanquins used to transport symbols of *kami* during processions.

[34] Winston Davis, "The *Miyaza* and the Fishermen: Ritual Status in Coastal Villages of Wakayama Prefecture," *Asian Folklore Studies* 36 (1977), 1-29.

index of secularization. Since it was one of the greatest pollutions, death was traditionally surrounded by taboos. It even contaminated the fire in the family hearth. A bereaved family was cut off from all neighbors lest its pollution contaminate them too. Only the members of the family could carry the coffin. Special huts were set up for mourners in some parts of the country where they had to live for 49 days after the funeral. It was taboo to eat with members of a family in which there had been a death. Families often divested themselves, at least temporarily, of their herds, crops, and crop seed when a death occurred. Because such customs were financially disadvantageous they have disappeared in modern times. The period of mourning decreased from the maximum of 49 days to 21 days, and then to 7 days. Nowadays very little time is spent in official mourning.

Contrary to the fears of the pious, secularization is often a necessary condition for the development of a more humanistic culture. What happened to the Japanese way of handling death during the Meiji period is, in some ways, a case in point. While there had always been taboos against coming into direct contact with the bereaved, cooperative groups had long existed which dug the grave and helped the family in whatever way they could. But as death taboos grew less important, more humane attitudes developed. Members of cooperative funeral associations began to assume the duty of carrying the coffin. We even find people willing to put taboos aside and eat with the bereaved family.

There was still another side to the treatment of death. In the 1870's professional undertakers began to appear in Tokyo. This was about the time when this profession became widespread in the West. Needless to say, the undertaker seriously altered traditional ways of dealing with death. According to Yanagita, even total strangers would come to the large funeral processions staged by an undertaker. Funerals became not only professionalized but commercialized. In the end, like religious festivals themselves, they threatened to become spectacle. [35] After the Russo-Japanese War, individual grave markers became quite popular. Families began to compete among themselves to see which could raise the largest monument.

In view of the central place of feeling and emotion in Japanese religion the slightest change in the aesthetic nuances of a festival can affect its total impact and religious significance. No one who has

---

[35] Cf. the automated mausoleums in which a push of a button produces a recorded recitation of Buddhist sutras; and the fact that it is often the undertaker who finds a Buddhist priest to perform the funeral just as the manager of a wedding hotel often contacts a Shintō priest for a wedding.

visited Kyoto's famed Zen gardens, originally designed as landscaped catalysts for the awakening of the mind, can fail to notice the disturbing effect of the "explanations" which periodically blare forth from loud-speakers around the grounds. The temple is instantly transformed into a museum. One's pilgrimage degenerates into a superficial, and often silly history lesson. Some of these changes, I suspect, may be more apparent to the foreigner than to the Japanese themselves. This is especially true in cases of cultural incongruity. I once attended the revival of the Buddha's Birthday Celebration *(hana matsuri)* in Gobō, a town in the middle of Wakayama Prefecture. I was especially appalled to see a statue of the infant Buddha carried through the streets of the town while a brass band played "Anchors Aweigh My Boys." [36]

The Lantern Festival which takes place at *Obon* at the Kōkokuji temple near the same town provides us with another example of this kind of aesthetic secularization of religion. Soon after sunset crowds of people begin the long walk up the steps of the temple. Along the way brightly lighted shops selling goldfish, soft drinks and cakes distract the visitor from paying his respects to the graves of the unworshiped ancestors *(muenbotoke)* which lie just off the path in a grove sur-rounded by candles. The religious rites begin in the temple at the top of the hill. After a recitation of the Heart Sutra, a well known band of *shakuhachi* (Japanese flute) players wearing basket-like hats circum-ambulates the temple three times and begins to march slowly down the hill. Behind them comes a procession of lovely paper lanterns held aloft on long bamboo poles, each illuminated by a small candle. Long paper streamers are attached to the bottom of each lantern. In the paper walls of each the words *namu-Amida Butsu* have been cut out with exquisite care. Families which have lost loved ones during the past year carry pure white lanterns. The other lanterns are brightly colored. After the procession reaches the clearing halfway down the hill, the lantern bearers take their places on the sloping hillside.

The action which followed had the essential ingredients of all Japanese festivals, mixing sport and ritual. Four strong young men came into the arena one by one, staggering under enormous, smoulder-ing torches. Each torch, measuring about a yard and a half in diameter and seven feet in length, was said to weigh over 800 pounds. Made of half dry branches, the ends of these torches were set ablaze before

---

[36] After being discontinued after the war, this festival was revived as part of a commercial and industrial festival *(shōkō matsuri)* which is why it is celebrated one month late. (The word *matsuri* is often used in a purely commercial context).

they came into the arena. Each man was expected to circle the arena three times, hopefully without incinerating himself, before putting his burden down. All of the details of the performance—the measurements of the torches, the names of the participants and so on—were announced over the loudspeakers, which as usual in Japan were set too loud. In the meantime, the *shakuhachi* players had taken their positions at the end of the arena behind other microphones which—as though in competition with the clamor of the announcer's loudspeaker—magnified the ancient plainsong of the instruments into deafening shrieks throughout the evening. The climax came when the four torches brightly burning beneath the full August moon were leaned against each other to form a large bonfire. The large white paper lantern representing the temple itself was then carried down the hillside and lowered into the fire. As its streamers and delicate frame caught on fire, the whole area was suddenly illuminated. The contest had become a sacred drama. After this the rest of the lanterns began to move towards the fire. One needed no official "explanation" to sense what was going on. The ancestors who had come back to be with their families for the *Obon* festival were now returning to the Great Majority. The torches with their enormous weight and all-consuming fire had become a pyre waiting to consume the frail lantern-bodies of the ancestors. As they moved down the hillside, each lantern seemed as delicate and finely wrought as the soul of the ancestor it symbolized. The idea of destroying such fragile beauty in this way suddenly became totally repugnant. As I watched, the somber words of Dylan Thomas came to mind: "do not go gentle into that good night...." Yet down the hill they came, one after another, the ancestors themselves walking gently to their own recreation. I should think, though I do not know, that many in the crowd perceived these things as I did, as an acted-out parable not merely about the frailty of life and the crushing inevitability of death—these themes were only too evident—but about the still deeper Buddhist truths of extinction and detachment.

After all of the lanterns had been cast into the fire the crowd began to melt away into the night. Only a handful of us stayed to watch the fire die down and change into embers. As the field became quiet we suddenly became aware of something remarkable that had been going on in front of us for some time. A group of six elderly men were standing together at the end of the field chanting the *rokusai nembutsu*. Throughout the evening they had been standing there chanting the name of Amida Buddha, imploring his mercy on behalf of the returning souls. Yet, in the din of the loudspeakers and the excitement over the lighting of the bonfire, they had been completely obscured. Only after the microphones had been disconnected and the crowd had gone home did we even notice *this very religious event.* The unnatural electronic amplification of the events of the evening had effectively silenced this small choir which in an earlier day had probably been the chorus for the drama which had been unfolding before our eyes.

None of the examples I have given of the secularization of feelings and customs is sufficient by itself to prove that Japanese religion as a whole has "declined." Each example is open to question and further interpretation. The critical reader will have noticed that the concept of secularization running through them is by no means univocal. Hopefully, however, these meanings complement and do not contradict each other. At best, these examples can be taken as the *kind* of material one needs to investigate before pronouncing upon the health of Japanese religion. Even this kind of approach is bedeviled by the problem which until now we have set aside: how to conceptualize secularization in a culture in which the sacred and the profane are not understood as categorical opposites. Throughout Japanese religious history the radical disjunction of the sacred and profane found in some cultures has been replaced by a continuum of experience and feeling which is sacred and profane *à la fois.* In traditional Japanese shamanism, the shaman was often identified with the god he served. Japanese ancestor worship itself breaks down the distinctions between the earthly and the heavenly realms. The Japanese are probably one of the few peoples who maintain that man becomes a *kami* automatically when he dies. Thus "to become a Buddha" (*hotoke ni naru*) has become a euphemism for the verb "to die." The Shintō tradition is filled with hierophanies taking place *in hoc mundo.* The great Shintō scholar Motoori Norinaga wrote that the concept of *kami* included human beings. "It also includes such objects as birds, beasts, trees, plants, seas, mountains and so forth. In ancient usage, anything whatsoever which was outside of the ordinary, which possessed superior power, or which was awe-inspiring was called *kami.* Eminence here does not refer merely to superiority or nobility, goodness or meritous deeds. Evil and mysterious things, if they were extraordinary and dreadful, were called *kami.*" [37] Likewise, throughout Japanese Buddhism, the Mahayana teaching of the Original Enlightenment (*hongaku*), derived initially from the *Awak-*

---

[37] D. C. Holtom, *The National Faith of Japan*, London, 1938, 23-24.

ening of Faith, identifies the essence of this *samsaric* world with Buddhahood itself. [38] As Dōgen put it, "impermanence is the Buddhahood. The impermanence of grass, trees, and forests is verily the Buddhahood. The impermanence of the person's body and mind is verily the Buddhahood. The impermanence of the country and scenery is verily the Buddhahood." [39] The entire world thus became a "predisposition" for a Buddha. The ontology (or me-ontology) established by these teachings quite naturally coalesced with the indigenous religious sensibilities expressed by Motoori. The effect was to locate the sacred within the profane. What we commonly call the sacred is therefore "dehypostatized" by the Japanese and made an adjective qualifying even the most mundane activity. One could say that in Japan perhaps more than elsewhere, "technique and ritual, profane and sacred, do not denote types of action but aspects of almost any kind of action." [40]

Itō Mikiharu concludes from this collapse of the sacred and profane that secularization is ultimately impossible in Japan. Unlike Durkheim's Australians, from whom this dichotomy was originally taken, the Japanese do not divide their year between sacred and profane time. Categories like *hare* and *ke* intermingle throughout both the busy agricultural season and the months when the farmer is idle. The relationship between *hare* and *ke* is therefore complementary. Space which is *hare* may soon be treated as *ke,* and vice versa. Unlike the absolute either/or dichotomies of western logic, Japanese culture—at the *implicit or structural level*—is based on a "logic of relative contrasts." Even when religious customs change—at the *explicit level of culture*—there is always a tendency for the original implicit categories to reassert themselves in a new guise. Thus, even if many Japanese no longer visit Shintō shrines at New Year's, the old festival spirit (*hare*) can still be felt in the "secularized" parties held at that time of year. [41]

The difficulty with this position (based on the distinction between implicit and explicit culture in the works of Boas, Wissler and Mur-

---

[38] Yoshito Hakeda, trans., *The Awakening of Faith Attributed to Asvaghosha,* New York, 1967, 37.

[39] Cited in Nakamura Hajime, *Ways of Thinking of Eastern Peoples,* Honolulu, 1964, 352.

[40] Edmund Leach, "A Definition of Religion and its Uses," *J. Royal Anth. Inst.* 90 (1960), 202.

[41] Itō Mikiharu, "Nihon bunka no kōzōteki rikai o mezashite," *Kikan jinruigaku* 4 (1973), 3-30. See Durkheim's distinction in *The Elementary Forms of the Religious Life,* New York, 1965, 53.

dock) is that it encourages a schizophrenic break between the history and structure of culture. If Itō is right, we have wasted our time in seeking evidence for secularization in diachronical statistics, economic history, folk customs and the aesthetics of rituals. The issue is to be settled by theory and definition. Historical changes in religious ideas, institutions and behavior have no effect at all upon the basic "structures" of religion. But can the problem of secularization be solved so easily? The criteria Itō uses to distinguish between the explicit and the implicit elements of a culture are something of a mystery. He seems to have two alternatives. Either implicit culture (structure) is to be identified with a society's archaic mazeways and behavioral patterns, or it is discovered through an act of ("phenomenological"?) intuition. Both of these solutions have obvious drawbacks. History changes even the oldest of customs and intuition is notoriously fallible. While I therefore cannot agree either with Itō's definition of the problem or his solution, his emphasis on the "logic of relative contrasts" is important to bear in mind. This way of thinking—and feeling—may even help to account for the unexpected overlap between religious behavior and unbelief pointed out by Basabe. [42]

Itō's research serves to underscore the importance of the persistence of religious and quasi-religious activities in contemporary Japan. The period when our "hardest" statistical evidence indicates religious belief declined in Japan paradoxically coincides with the phenomenal growth of the so-called New Religions. Most of these movements can be regarded as atavistic revitalization movements based on religious and magical practices such as shamanism, ancestor worship, purification rituals and exorcism which can be traced back to prehistoric times. [43] In addition to the New Religions, new magazines such as Matsushita Konosuke's *P.H.P., The Light of the House, Women's Friend*, and *Inner Trip*, all deeply imbued with practical, religious idealism, sell hundreds of thousands of copies each month. Biographies of the founders of the Kamakura sects of Buddhism have become enormously successful. A large proportion of the population continues to visit shrines and temples at New Year's. Many people still observe religious (or magical) taboos even though they no longer explicitly believe in the retributive powers of ghosts and *kami*. Many Japanese firms provide weekend retreats for the "spiritual education" of their employees, a function performed by the public schools in prewar Japan. One could,

---

[42] See above 268.

[43] Joseph M. Kitagawa, *Religion in Japanese History*, New York, 1966, 333.

of course, argue that this persistence of religious behavior is merely
the "implicit structure" of Japanese culture reasserting itself. If all that
were meant by this was the recrudescence of *historic* religious tendencies, Itō's formulation would be perfectly acceptable. In any case,
there is no doubt that the paradoxical coincidence of the decline of
religious belief measured by the opinion polls on the one hand, and the
rise of the New Religions on the other can only be understood by
supposing that this statistical unbelief is largely *situational*. It is symp-
tomatic of that existential drift for which the Japanese have such
talent, rather than any disciplined, philosophical commitment to
atheism.

The statistics themselves seem to bear this out. In addition to the
evidence we have already seen, in an admittedly small survey of the
religious opinions of 270 people, 43% said that they were "too busy,"
to believe, "didn't have the opportunity," were "too young," or simply
were not believers at the present moment. Another 14% thought that
religion was necessary for others but not for themselves. [44] These
figures, together with the evidence from Basabe and the *Survey of the
National Character of the Japanese*, seem to indicate that much unbelief grows out of social situations in which there is little or no social
opportunity or incentive to believe. On the other hand, Japanese
continue to respond quite readily to formal situations which call for
"religious" behavior, e.g. weddings, funerals, and ground breaking
ceremonies. Well educated people from higher income families who
generally score lowest in religious belief are generally the most scru-
pulous in their performance of these public rituals. [45] Religious activity
of this sort, carried out as a matter of social principle (*tatemae*),
contrasts strongly with the kind of zealous devotion and commitment
demanded by the New Religions. Religious affiliations of the latter
sort are often disruptive and, in many cases, are actually considered
"antisocial." [46]

Another area of Japanese culture where the "logic of relative con-

---

[44] *Nihonjin no Kokuminsei*, No. 2, 47.

[45] Whether these occasions can be called instances of faith or mere empty custom
has become a legal as well as an academic conundrum. In 1965, for example, the town
officials of Tsu in Mie Prefecture hired four Shintō priests to conduct a traditional
groundbreaking ceremony; the litigation that ensued went from court to court until
July, 1977, when the Supreme Court found that the ceremony did not violate the
constitutional statement which prohibits the state and its organs from engaging in
"religious activity."

[46] James Dator, *Sōka Gakkai, Builders of the Third Civilization: American and
Japanese Members*, Seattle, 1969, 141.

trasts" is clearly in evidence is the relationship between magical attitudes and the goal-rationality (Weber: *Zweckrationalität*) one commonly associates with modern industrial societies. While I believe the "overall secularization" of different cultures cannot be compared, here we do have an example of a striking contrast between Japan and the West. Contemporary research on 16th and 17th century England, for example, has gone far beyond Weber in demonstrating the rationalizing effect Puritanism had upon society. Keith Thomas in his monumental study *Religion and the Decline of Magic* shows that:

> ...in England magic lost its appeal before the appropriate technical solutions had been devised to take its place. It was the abandonment of magic [under the influence of Puritanism] which made possible the upsurge of technology, not the other way around. Indeed, as Max Weber stressed, magic was potentially "one of the most serious obstructions to the rationalization of economic life." The technological primacy of Western civilization, it can be argued, owes a sizable debt to the fact that in Europe recourse to magic was to prove less ineradicable than in other parts of the world. [47]

Although the examples of Ishida Baigan, Suzuki Shōsan and various Confucian thinkers of the Tokugawa period could be cited to the contrary effect, *in general*, popular Japanese religion had no comparable disenchanting effects upon society or nature. The voice of the "technologist" was seldom heard in religious circles. Popular religion in Japan continues to be deeply colored by the magic of charms, amulets, omens and taboos. Even today statistical studies have shown that while religious faith which is low in utilitarian content (what I call magic) declines as individuals advance from junior high school (20.5%) to college (10.9%), a more utilitarian (magical) faith actually increases (from 7.6% to 14.3%). [48] That Japan could industrialize more rapidly than any other country in Asia was due to the exploitation of very traditional values such as discipline, frugality, and loyalty. Religion *per se* probably did as much to hinder as to

---

[47] New York, 1971, 656f. See also Christopher Hill, *Society and Puritanism in Pre-Revolutionary England*, New York, 1967, 124-44; Robert Merton, *Social Theory and Social Structure*, New York, 1968, 628-60; E. P. Thompson, "Time, Work-Discipline, and Industrial Capitalism," *Past and Present* 38 (1967), 56-97.

[48] Sugiyama Meiko, "Religious Behavior of the Japanese," *Seminar on Theory, Methods and Applications of Multidimensional Scaling and Related Techniques* (August 20-24, 1974, University of Calif. at San Diego), 159. My thanks to Hayashi Chikio for drawing this research to my attention.

encourage this process. [49] Magic like Japanese religion itself was highly situational and quickly learned to adjust to new conditions. Neither in the village nor in the new cities were there synods or bishops to enforce the mores and taboos of the local *ujigami*. The "disenchantment of the world" which is said to be both the prerequisite and the byproduct of industrialization therefore did not take place in Japan as the result of a head-on confrontation between a secularizing religious ideology and gross superstition or magic as it did among the "hot Protestants" in England. The greatest contribution of Japanese religion to the "modernization" of the country was negative: the barriers it put in the way of industrialization were negligible. Its contextual "logic of relative contrasts" enabled religious taboos to make a graceful and judicious retreat. On the positive side, popular religion also provided the modernizing elite with some of its most powerful ideological tools, e.g. the *ujigami*. Absorbed and revalorized by the "imperial system," these symbols became a means for extending the particularistic social nexus of the village to the nation itself. The sacred space which disappeared in the local community as a result of the development of a market economy thus reappeared in the national-istic mythology of Japan, the Divine Land. While amulets may have been discarded by many Japanese, the political slogans of the prewar regime had, themselves, a hypnotizing, amuletic effect. [50]

In this paper I have suggested that while it is possible to study secularization it is not productive to treat the problem as the overall decline of religion *per se*. Instead, depending upon the culture one is dealing with, it is wiser to use a less ambitious, and more cautious approach, e.g., a "multiple scoring" of beliefs, feelings, morals, and customary behavior. In other words, while it is virtually meaningless to talk about the general secularization of religion in a society, and even more obscure to discuss the comparative levels of secularization in various societies, it may be possible to take the measure of the well-being and/or decline of the various *aspects* of religion in a specific society. Even then, not all of these aspects will carry equal weight. I have tried to show that in Japan, where *praxis* and feeling are the core of religion, the problem of secularization can be more fruitfully studied by examining changing religious customs rather than the

---

[49] Maruyama Masao, "Bera 'Tokugawa Jidai no Shūkyō' ni tsuite," *Nihon kindaika to shūkyō rinri* (Japanese trans. of Robert Bellah's *Tokugawa Religion*), trans. Hori Ichirō and Ikeda Akira, Tokyo, 1962, 321-54.

[50] Tsurumi Shunsuke, *Nichijōteki shisō no kanōsei*, Tokyo, 1967, 34-55.

decline of religious beliefs. Finally, I have suggested that the lack of clear-cut distinctions between the sacred and the profane in Japan does not make the concept of secularization (in my limited sense of the word) impossible. It merely reminds us that even after we have discarded the idea that secularization is a logical impossibility or part of some inevitable *Weltplan* of history, we are still left with a set of complex problems of interpretation and proof.